The Cambridge

Second Language Assessment

Edited by

Christine Coombe
Peter Davidson
Barry O'Sullivan
Stephen Stoynoff

CAMBRIDGE
UNIVERSITY PRESS

CAMBRIDGE UNIVERSITY PRESS
Cambridge, New York, Melbourne, Madrid, Cape Town,
Singapore, São Paulo, Delhi, Tokyo, Mexico City

Cambridge University Press
32 Avenue of the Americas, New York, NY 10013-2473, USA

www.cambridge.org
Information on this title: www.cambridge.org/9781107677074

© Cambridge University Press 2012

This publication is in copyright. Subject to statutory exception
and to the provisions of relevant collective licensing agreements,
no reproduction of any part may take place without the written
permission of Cambridge University Press.

First published 2012

Printed in the United States of America

A catalog record for this publication is available from the British Library.

Library of Congress Cataloging in Publication data

The Cambridge guide to second language assessment / Christine Coombe . . . [et al.].
     p.   cm.
Includes bibliographical references and index.
ISBN 978-1-107-01714-6 – ISBN 978-1-107-67707-4 (pbk.)
1. English language – Study and teaching – Foreign speakers.   2. Second language acquisition – Study and
teaching.   I. Coombe, Christine A. (Christine Anne), 1962–   II. Title: Guide to second language assessment.
PE1128.A2C319   2012
428.2′4–dc23   2011036567

ISBN 978-1-107-01714-6 Hardback
ISBN 978-1-107-67707-4 Paperback

Cambridge University Press has no responsibility for the persistence or
accuracy of URLs for external or third-party Internet Web sites referred to in
this publication and does not guarantee that any content on such Web sites is,
or will remain, accurate or appropriate.

CONTENTS

ACKNOWLEDGMENTS

THE CO-EDITORS

The Cambridge Guide to Second Language Assessment has been a truly collaborative endeavor that has benefited from the contributions of many dedicated professionals. The editors would particularly like to thank the chapter authors: Ramin Akbari, Mashael Al-Hamly, Neil Anderson, Brock Brady, Annie Brown, J. D. Brown, Liying Cheng, Andrew Cohen, Andy Curtis, Fred Davidson, Zohreh Eslami, Hossein Farady, John Flowerdew, Glenn Fulcher, Margo Gottlieb, Tony Green, Ingrid Greenberg, Angela Hasselgreen, Roger Hawkey, Nancy Hubley, Wayne Jones, Elif Kantarcıoğlu, Anne Katz, Young-Ju Lee, Azizullah Mirzaei, Lindsay Miller, Keith Morrow, Kerry Purmensky, John Read, Ali Shehadeh, Sun-Young Shin, Spiros Papageorgiou, Lynda Taylor, Salah Troudi, and Sara Cushing Weigle.

We would also like to recognize the four anonymous reviewers who provided invaluable comments on a draft of the manuscript, the editors at Cambridge University Press (Jane Walsh and Karen Brock), our copy editor, Sylvia Goulding, and Quin Paseka who helped us chase down several permissions. All of these individuals demonstrated extraordinary commitment, patience, and attention to detail throughout the project, and numerous colleagues and students from around the world who expressed interest in and support for the project at crucial stages in the development of the book.

There are numerous individuals who we express our gratitude to from a personal perspective.

Christine wishes to acknowledge family members, Carl Coombe, Cindy Coombe, and Marion and Howard Mathewson for their continued support of her professional endeavors and her students and colleagues at Dubai Men's College.

Peter would like to recognize his wife Cigdem for all her patience, and his two daughters, Ceyda and Emily, who continue to provide him with inspiration, and his colleagues and students at Zayed University.

Stephen wishes to thank his wife, Toshiko, for her patience and support while he worked on the volume.

Barry would like to pay tribute to Don Porter and Cyril Weir, who have supported him from the beginning and continue to inspire and encourage his work. He would also like to thank the many teachers he has worked with over the years from whom he has learnt so much.

Christine Coombe
Peter Davidson
Barry O'Sullivan
Stephen Stoynoff

THE CO-EDITORS AND THE PUBLISHERS

We wish to thank the following publishers for permission to reprint material from their books:

Davidson, F. (2003, April). Crafting a test of academic language proficiency: Some comments on reverse engineering and certain philosophical tensions in large-scale testing. Presented at the American Educational Research Association, Chicago, United States. Reprinted with permission by author.

Davidson, F., & Lynch, B. K. (2002). *Testcraft. A teacher's guide to writing and using language test specifications.* New Haven and London: Yale University Press. Reprinted with permission of Yale University Press.

Li, J. (2006). *Introducing audit trails to the world of language testing.* Unpublished Master's Thesis, University of Illinois at Urbana-Champaign, United States. Reprinted with permission by author.

Teachers of English to Speakers of Other Languages. (2006). *PreK-12 English language proficiency standards.* Alexandria, VA: Author. Reprinted with permission from TESOL Publications.

Council of Europe. (2001). *Common European Framework of Reference for Languages: Learning, teaching, assessment.* Cambridge: Cambridge University Press. Reprinted with permission from Cambridge University Press.

Alderson, J. C., & Wall, D. (1993). Does washback exist? *Applied Linguistics* 14, 115–129. Reprinted with permission from Oxford University Press.

Long, M. H., & Norris, J. M. (2000). Task-based teaching and assessment. In M. Byram (Ed.), *Encyclopedia of language teaching* (pp. 597–603). London: Routledge. Reprinted with permission from Cengage Learning Services.

Ishihara, N., & Cohen, A. D. (2010). *Teaching and learning pragmatics: Where language and culture meet.* Harlow, Essex, England: Longman/Pearson. Reprinted with permission by Pearson Education.

Carroll, B. 1980. *Testing communicative performance.* Oxford: Pergamon.

Turnitin Instructor User Manual. (2008). Retrieved January 19, 2008, from www.submit.ac.uk/static_jisc/documentation/Instructor_Manual.pdf. Reprinted with permission from iParadigms, LLC.

Extract from FCE (Level B2) Speaking Scale.

Cambridge ESOL Common scale for writing assessment.

Every effort has been made to trace the owners of copyright material in this book. We would be grateful to hear from anyone who recognizes their copyright material and who is unacknowledged. We will be pleased to make the necessary corrections in future editions of the book.

ABBREVIATIONS

ACT	American College Testing
ACTFL	American Council of Teachers of Foreign Languages
AFT	American Federation of Teachers
AILA	International Association for Applied Linguistics (or Association Internationale de Linguistique Appliquée)
ALTE	Association of Language Testers in Europe
AMEP	Adult Migrant Education Program
AYLLIT	Assessment of Young Learner Literacy
BEC	Business English Certificates
CAL	Center for Applied Linguistics
CASAS	Comprehensive Adult Student Assessment System
CAT	Computer Adaptive Test
CBI	Content-Based Instruction
CBT	Computer-Based Test
CCSE	Certificates in Communicative Skills in English
CCSSO	Council of Chief State School Officers
CEFR	Common European Framework of Reference
CLT	Communicative Language Teaching
CPE	Cambridge Proficiency Examination
CREDE	Center for Research on Education, Diversity and Excellence
CRESST	Center for Research on Evaluation, Standards, and Student Testing
CRT	Criterion-Referenced Tests
CTELT	Current Trends in English Language Testing
CTT	Classical Test Theory
CUEFL	Communicative Use of English as a Foreign Language
DCT	Discourse Completion Test
DIF	Differential Item Functioning
DRPT	Discourse Role-Play Tasks
EALTA	European Association for Language Testing and Assessment
ECML	European Centre for Modern Languages
EFL	English as a Foreign Language
ELL	English Language Learner
ELP	European Language Portfolio
ELTS	English Language Testing Service
ESL	English as a Second Language
ESOL	English to Speakers of Other Languages
ETS	Educational Testing Service
FCE	First Certificate in English
GRE	Graduate Record Exam
HTML	Hypertext Markup Language
IATEFL	International Association of Teachers of English as a Foreign Language
IELTS	International English Language Testing System
ILTA	International Language Testing Association
KET	Key English Test

L1	First Language
LTRC	Language Testing Research Colloquium
MCQ	Multiple-Choice Question
MDCT	Multiple-Choice Discourse Completion Task
MFRM	Multi-Faceted Rasch Measurement
NBPTS	National Board of Professional Teacher Standards
NCATE	National Council for the Accreditation of Teacher Education
NCELTR	National Centre for English Language Teaching and Research
NCLB	No Child Left Behind
NEA	National Education Association
NLP	Natural Language Processing
NS	Native Speaker
NNS	Nonnative Speaker
OPI	Oral Proficiency Interview
OSHA	Occupational Safety & Health Administration
PBT	Paper-based TOEFL
PET	Preliminary English Test
PRT	Picture Response Test
RELC	Regional English Language Centre
SAI	Self-Assessment Instrument
SD	Student with Disability
SEAMEO	Southeast Asian Ministers of Education Organization
SEM	Scottish Examination Materials
SL	Second Language
SLA	Second Language Acquisition
SSI	Subject Specialist Informant
TBLA	Task-Based Language Assessment
TBLT	Task-Based Language Teaching
TESOL	Teachers of English to Speakers of Other Languages
TOEFL	Test of English as a Foreign Language
TOEFL iBT	Internet-based TOEFL
TOEIC	Test of English for International Communication
UCLA WebLAS	University of California Los Angeles Web-based Language Assessment System
UCLES	University of Cambridge Local Examinations Syndicate
VESL	Vocational English as a Second Language
VLT	Vocabulary Levels Test
VST	Vocabulary Size Test
WBLT	Web-Based Language Testing
WDCT	Written DCT
WIB	Workforce Investment Board
WIDA	World-Class Instructional Design and Assessment
YLL	Young Language Learner

INTRODUCTION

Second Language Assessment

Christine Coombe

The Cambridge Guide to Second Language Assessment aims to present in one volume an up-to-date guide to the central areas of assessing the second language performance of English by speakers of other languages. The Guide provides snapshots of significant issues and trends that have shaped language assessment in the past and highlights the current state of our understanding of these issues. Co-edited by four leading figures in TESOL, this volume contains 35 chapters written by internationally recognized language-testing professionals and applied linguists.

More specifically, this book seeks to provide an overview of current approaches, issues, and practices in the assessment of foreign / second language performance. It has the following goals:

- To provide a comprehensive overview of the field of second language assessment
- To help teachers of all levels further develop their assessment literacy skills
- To provide language teachers with a theoretical background of key issues associated with language testing, and some practical advice on how to improve the effectiveness of the tests they develop and implement
- To provide an in-depth yet comprehensible and easy-to-understand view of the various issues and approaches inherent in the field of second language assessment, with a particular emphasis on the language skill areas and the use of technology in assessment
- To provide a source of suggested readings or resources for further study in key areas
- To serve as a springboard for discussion on topics related to second language assessment

The chapters in this volume offer a comprehensive picture of the approaches to the assessment of second language performance as well as the complexities underlying much of the second language assessment literature.

A major motivation for this volume stems from a quote by Mertler (2004:1) who stated that assessing student performance is one of the most critical elements of a teacher's job, but many teachers simply do not feel adequately prepared to assess their students' performance. The lack of teacher assessment literacy is well documented in the literature (Cheng, 2001; Stiggins, 2007; Stiggins and Conklin, 1992) and it is this lack that we hope to address with this volume.

What is "Assessment Literacy"?

Definitions of the term "assessment literacy" abound in the literature. For the purposes of this volume we will use the definition put forth by Popham (2004) and Stiggins (2002). They define assessment literacy as an understanding of the principles of sound assessment.

Stiggins (2007: 2) goes on to elaborate on the skills required for teachers and administrators to be considered assessment literate. Teachers and administrators who are assessment literate understand the difference between sound and unsound assessment, evaluation, and communication practices. Those who are assessment literate:

- understand what assessment methods to use in order to gather dependable information about student achievement;
- communicate assessment results effectively, whether using report card grades, test scores, portfolios, or conferences; and
- understand how to use assessment to maximize student motivation and learning by involving students as full partners in assessment, record keeping, and communication.

Why is Assessment Literacy Important for Teachers?

There are a number of compelling reasons why being assessment literate is crucial for language educators, both from a practical and an empirical perspective.

First, and perhaps most importantly, English language teachers with a solid background in this area are well positioned to integrate assessment with instruction, which is a crucial element to effective English / second language teaching. In fact, a common vision among testing specialists is that teachers must be able to recognize different purposes and types of assessment and use them accordingly.

Another important reason is that assessment is a widespread feature of most educational systems in the world today. It has been estimated that teachers spend as much as 50 percent of their time engaged in assessment or assessment-related activities (Stiggins, 1995). Because teachers spend so much of their time involved with testing and assessment, it makes sense that they know as much as they can about this important activity.

An increased knowledge about assessment in general, and second language assessment in particular, will result in increased test validity and the promotion of transparency as teachers will be able to understand better their assessment results and communicate them more effectively to all stakeholders involved in the process. Learning more about assessment and the issues that surround this important topic will also serve as a valuable professional development activity for teachers.

From an empirical perspective, Rogier (2009: 2) points out that every teacher is involved with assessment and testing in some form or another and studies have shown that assessment in the classroom is important to the instructional process (Mertler, 2003; Stiggins and Chappuis, 2005), is pivotal to student education (Popham, 2006), and that when assessment is implemented effectively, student achievement is improved (Campbell and Collins, 2007).

This volume is organized into five sections that reflect the following topics:

- Key issues
- Assessment purposes and approaches
- Assessing second language skills
- Technology in assessment
- Administrative issues

Individual chapters are set out to include some background of the language assessment area under discussion, as well as give a synopsis of relevant research. Authors then relate this research to practice by providing readers with recommendations for classroom practice. Indeed, most of the chapter contents are dedicated to practical applications for the classroom teacher. A list and / or description of further key readings or suggested resources along with discussion questions which can be used in class or in a self-access environment round out each chapter.

The first section of the volume is centered around "Key Issues" in second language assessment. **Barry O'Sullivan** and **Christine Coombe** (with **Salah Troudi** and **Mashael Al-Hamly**) set the book in context with their introductory chapters on the history of language testing (O'Sullivan) and the importance of developing assessment literacy and the challenges associated with it (Coombe, Troudi, and Al-Hamly). The remaining twelve chapters in this section deal with a number of important issues relating to second language assessment. **Ramin Akbari** and **Hossein Farhady** offer a comprehensive view about some of the principles underlying sound assessment, namely validity and reliability. **Barry O'Sullivan** describes his perspective on an effective process for the development of an assessment instrument. **Fred Davidson** and **Glenn Fulcher** provide invaluable information on the importance of test specifications for language assessment and how to develop them. The linkage between assessment and instructional aims and learning is the topic of **Anne Katz's** chapter, which provides an excellent lead-in to **Margo Gottlieb's** chapter on language standards. From Gottlieb's chapter, which focuses on standards from a North American context, we move to Europe with **Elif Kantarcıoğlu** and **Spiros Papageorgiou's** chapter on the Council of Europe's Common European Framework of Reference, which is a tool for setting clear standards to be attained at successive stages of learning and for evaluating outcomes in an internationally comparable manner. **Liying Cheng** and **Andy Curtis** then present us with crucial information about the key concepts of test impact and washback and the implications that these have for teaching and learning. In his chapter on the importance of test-taking strategies, **Andrew D. Cohen** reminds us that it is our responsibility as teachers to insure that our students have the requisite strategies to perform well on tests and that this knowledge will further serve to reduce student test anxiety. The last three chapters of this section take us back to the teacher perspective. **James Dean Brown** provides information on what teachers need to know about assessment; **Annie Brown** offers her insights on various ethical considerations on language testing and assessment; and **Stephen Stoynoff** and **Christine Coombe** give their views on how best to provide professional development to teachers in the area of language assessment.

The second section of this book focuses on assessment purposes and approaches. The nine chapters in this section bring together authors and their views on how to effectively assess certain stakeholders in the educational process as well as which approach to utilize in order to achieve maximum benefit. **James Dean Brown's** article on choosing the right type of assessment serves to set this section in context. Brown reminds us that the assessment purpose should match the decisions that are being made, and that the assessment type should match the curriculum objectives or learning points being taught in the context of the decision making. **Keith Morrow** takes us back in time to the advent of communicative language teaching and the complexities of transferring these concepts to communicative language testing. He takes the view that CLT is now largely history but its impact can still be felt in present-day language testing. Alternative forms of language assessment constitute the basis for **Christine Coombe, Kerry Purmensky,** and **Peter Davidson's** chapter where they effectively describe the major differences between traditional and alternative assessment and focus on two of the major types of classroom alternative assessment, namely projects and reflective written portfolios. This chapter provides a context for **Ali Shehadeh's** chapter on task-based language assessment. Here, Shehadeh describes task-based language assessment and its characterizing features, main components, development, and classroom implementation and utilization. Self- and peer assessment are the main focus of **Neil J Anderson's** chapter on how to involve students in their own assessment. Indeed the author believes that if we want to gather the best possible assessment data to improve language teaching and learning, we must include students in that process. The remaining chapters in this section center around different types of testing and assessment and how best to assess certain language groups. **Anthony Green** offers his insights into the development of effective placement tests in order to ensure that students are placed appropriately in their respective language programs. **Zohreh R. Eslami** and **Azizullah Mirzaei** provide information on the assessment of second language pragmatics and how it relates to language assessment. **Angela Hasselgreen** suggests ways that young learners can be assessed effectively, and **Ingrid Greenberg** provides information on the assessment of workplace ESL needs analysis and assessment.

Section 3 of this volume is dedicated to the assessment of language skills and subskills. In each of these chapters, authors provide brief reviews of the literature and practical applications of assessing these skill areas. **Nancy J. Hubley** gives an overview of the issues related to assessing the reading skill; **Sara Cushing Weigle** shares her expertise on the assessment of F/SL writing; **John Flowerdew** and **Lindsay Miller** provide us with information on how best to assess the listening skills of our students; and **Barry O'Sullivan** shares his knowledge on speaking assessment. **Wayne Jones** and **John Read** offer their recommendations on the assessment of language subskills, grammar, and vocabulary.

The fourth section of this volume centers around the usage of technology in language assessment. **Peter Davidson** and **Christine Coombe** provide an overview of the current state of computerized language assessment. **Sun-Young Shin** shares her views on the benefits and challenges of utilizing Web-based assessment with second language learners and **Young-Ju Lee** provides us with important information on popular software to facilitate language assessment.

The final section of the Guide focuses on various administrative issues surrounding second language assessment. **Brock Brady** deals with the issue of how to manage assessment in large EFL classes and offers recommendations on how this would best be accomplished. **Anthony Green** and **Roger Hawkey** provide expertise on how to manage the process of marking subjective assessments through the use of rubrics and rating scales. Finally, **Lynda Taylor** shares her expertise on "accommodations" in language testing, the term used to describe the principle and process of modifying test content, format, or administration in order to meet the specific needs of an individual test taker, or group of test takers, in the interests of fairness and equity.

References

Campbell, C., & Collins, V. L. (2007). Identifying essential topics in general and special educational introductory assessment textbooks. *Educational Measurement: Issues and Practice*, 26(1): 9–18.

Cheng, L. (2001). An investigation of ESL / EFL teachers' classroom assessment practices. *Language Testing Update*, 29: 53–83.

Mertler, C. A. (2003). Preservice versus inservice teachers' assessment literacy: Does classroom experience make a difference? Paper presented at the annual meeting of the Mid-Western Educational Research Association, Columbus, OH, October 2003.

Mertler, C. A. (2004). Secondary teachers' assessment literacy: Does classroom experience make a difference? *American Secondary Education*, 33(2): 49–64.

Popham, W. J. (2004). All about accountability: Why assessment illiteracy is professional suicide. *Educational Leadership*, 62(1): 82–3.

Popham, W. J. (2006). Needed: A dose of assessment literacy, *Educational Leadership*, 63(6): 84–5.

Rogier, D. (2009). English-language teachers' perspectives on assessment. In partial fulfillment of EdD in TESOL, Exeter, UK: University of Exeter.

Stiggins, R. J. (1995). Assessment literacy for the 21st century. *Phi Delta Kappan*, 77(3), 238–45.

Stiggins, R. J. (2002). Assessment crisis: The absence of assessment for learning. *Phi Delta Kappan*, 83(10): 758–65.

Stiggins, R. (2007). Conquering the formative assessment frontier. In J. McMillan (Ed.), *Formative classroom assessment*. New York: Colombia University Teachers College Press.

Stiggins, R. J., & Chappuis, J. (2005). Using student involved classroom assessment to close achievement gaps. *Theory Into Practice*, 44(1): 11–18.

Stiggins, R. J., & Conklin, N. (1992). *In teachers' hands: Investigating the practice of classroom assessment*. Albany, NY: SUNY Press.

SECTION I

KEY ISSUES

The chapters in this section provide an introductory overview of some of the "Key Issues" in second language assessment. We set the book in context with introductory chapters on the history of language testing by volume co-editor Barry O'Sullivan, and the importance of developing assessment literacy and the challenges associated with this endeavor by volume co-editor Christine Coombe with Troudi and Al-Hamly.

In Chapter 1, O'Sullivan provides us with a historical perspective on second language tests and assessment, starting from the earliest tests in China some 1500 years ago to trends and developments in modern-day second language assessment.

Following on from the historical developments in the field, Coombe, Troudi and Al-Hamly define what they mean by assessment literacy and briefly review the research in the area of F/SL assessment literacy. They then list a number of barriers that prevent teachers from becoming assessment literate. Ways to overcome these barriers and recommendations on how teachers can develop their assessment literacy skills round out this chapter.

The remaining twelve chapters in this section deal with a number of important issues relating to second language assessment and its implementation. Chapters 3 by Akbari and 4 by Farhady offer a comprehensive view of some of the important principles underlying sound assessment, namely validity and reliability.

Next, in Chapter 5, O'Sullivan shares his views and provides examples on what constitutes an effective process for the development of an assessment instrument. Although the focus of his chapter is on developing larger-scale tests, he makes it clear that classroom tests can be constructed from these processes.

The focus of Chapter 6 is on the importance of test specifications and on how to effectively develop them. In this chapter, Davidson and Fulcher provide crucial information on why the use of test specifications is important for language assessment and share with us a process of how to develop them.

Chapter 7 examines the connection between assessment and instruction in language classrooms. Rather than viewing assessment as external to instruction, Katz focuses on how assessment can be linked to learning in order to answer such questions as *What are students learning? How well are they learning it?* and *How can instruction support learning?*

Because the linkage between assessment and instructional aims and learning is the topic of Katz's chapter, her work provides an excellent introduction to Gottlieb's chapter on language standards. In Chapter 8 the author focuses on standards from a North American context. In addition to providing a definition of a standard, Gottlieb shares with us the major characteristics of high-quality language standards.

In Chapter 9, the focus of Kantarcıoğlu and Papageorgiou is on standards originating from Europe, in the Council of Europe's Common European Framework of Reference. The CEFR is a tool for setting clear standards to be attained at successive stages of learning and for evaluating outcomes in an internationally comparable manner.

Cheng and Curtis, in Chapter 10, then present us with invaluable information about the key concepts of test impact and washback and the implications that these concepts have for the teaching and learning process.

In his chapter, Cohen reminds us that it is our responsibility as teachers to insure that our students have the necessary test-taking strategies to perform well on tests and that this knowledge will further serve to decrease their anxiety about tests.

The last three chapters of this section take us back to teacher concerns and assessment literacy. JD Brown shares his views on what information teachers need to have about why and how to analyze their assessments; Annie Brown provides her insights and raises issues on various ethical considerations on language testing and assessment; and finally, Stoynoff and Coombe examine the state of how best to provide professional development to teachers in the area of language assessment.

CHAPTER 1

A Brief History of Language Testing

Barry O'Sullivan

THE EARLIEST OF TESTS

Formal testing began about 1,500 years ago in China, with the introduction of the Kējǔ, or Imperial Examination, during the Sui Dynasty (581–618). Following this period, the so-called nine-rank system classified imperial officials and military officers into a complex series of ranks. Over the centuries that followed the test gradually became more and more standardized in its approach, so that by the last quarter of the 19th century the examination had developed a complex administrative and operational mechanism with a significant impact on Chinese society, in particular its education system.

The examinations, which were based on the ancient Confucian texts, had, for many years, some important benefits. The basis of the whole system was that it was designed (at least in theory) to identify the most suitable people within the empire for positions of rank within the bureaucracy regardless of their social class and could be taken by any imperial subject on any number of occasions. Because the system was built on a pyramid model, with many people attempting the local (lower) levels in order to progress through to the highest possible level, the practice of standardization and specification was quickly adopted. Therefore, the different local versions of the examination tended to be very similar in content and emphasis – as well as in terms of the tasks performed by the test takers. This standardization of content and approach had obvious assessment as well as social and political benefits to the empire, in that it encouraged a cultural uniformity in people's thinking on the importance of education to the empire rather than to purely local considerations.

As mentioned above, the idea was that the Kējǔ offered all members of Chinese society an equal opportunity to enter the Mandarin class if they merited it. In practice this was not so as the education that was needed to pass the nine levels was not supported by the administration. In addition, the education system came to focus solely on preparing people to pass the test. The test itself had led to its own education industry that competed with the official education system and, by the time the Empire collapsed in the early 20th century, the education system had been completely destroyed by the test. This is possibly the best example there is of negative washback.

However, in its time the Kējǔ served a purpose that was unheard of in the rest of the world. Indeed, Burton (1631: 630), in his famous philosophical treatise, entitled *Anatomy of Melancholy*, pleaded for "rectors of benefices to be chosen out of the Universities, examined and approved, as the literati in China," though this plea was ignored (at least in Europe) for another century and a half.

THE TEST GOES WEST

Testing came to Europe in the 16th and 17th centuries in the newly founded universities and began to spread into the wider community in the late 18th century, particularly in France and Prussia. However, the following anecdote gives us some indication of the attitude to testing among the governing elite in Britain at that time. When recalling his final examination at the University of Oxford some years earlier, the Earl of Eldon recalled:

> I was examined in Hebrew and History.
>
> 'What is the Hebrew for the place of a skull?'
>
> I replied: 'Golgotha'.
>
> 'Who founded University College?' [this was Eldon's and his examiner's college]
>
> I stated . . . that King Alfred founded it.
>
> 'Very well' said the examiner, 'You are competent for the degree.' (Earl of Eldon, 1775, cited by Morris, 1961: 28)

THE FORMALIZATION OF TESTING

Testing became a bigger issue in Britain in the 19th century when the establishment realized they needed to select people according to capability and end the practice of patronage (the French and Germans had already come to that conclusion almost half a century earlier). The introduction of competitive examinations to the civil service in the UK was preceded by the Oxford University Commission, which led to the introduction of examinations within the education system in 1850, and the Northcote–Trevelyan Report (1853) to Parliament which reminded members that:

> [I]t may be repeated that no other means can be devised of avoiding the evils of patronage, which, if, in this case, less objectionable because of the comparatively small number of superior appointments, is more objection- able in its effects on the public business of the country . . . (Northcote and Trevelyan, 1853: 12)

By the end of the century, both Britain and the United States had introduced the concepts of mass education and with it the notion of mass assessment.

THE BIRTH AND GROWTH OF THE LANGUAGE TESTING INDUSTRY

The story of modern English language testing really begins in the early part of the 20th century with important innovations on both sides of the Atlantic.

EARLY DEVELOPMENTS IN THE UNITED KINGDOM

In the UK, 1913 saw the introduction of the Cambridge Proficiency Examination (CPE) by the University of Cambridge Local Examinations Syndicate (UCLES). The examination was used to test the language performance of people from the colonies who wished to enter the British education system. Although just twelve people sat the examination in its first year, it was important as it was firmly based on a coherent philosophy of language learning developed by Henry Sweet (1899; see Figure 1.1 for an overview). Sweet can be seen if not as the founder of applied linguistics then as its inspiration, because of his emphasis on language use (rather than on language knowledge) and his systematic approach to understanding how this use is manifested.

Part 1

Phonetics (teaching of & practical application) – "start with the spoken language"

Part 2

Grammar; Vocabulary; Study of Texts; Translation; Conversation

Part 3

Essays on language & languages

Figure 1.1   Overview of Sweet's Rationally Progressive Method

When we compare Figures 1.1 and 1.2 (the contents of the first CPE), we can see the influence the method had on the developers of the CPE, with sections designed to gain an insight into the candidate's ability in the same aspects of language as described by Sweet. (For a fuller description of the development of the original CPE and a copy of that examination, see Weir, 2003.)

The examination is also important as it set a precedent for the approach to assessment that still dominates Britain and much of Europe, the assessment of language through performance, where the test content was central and validity was key.

Writing

Translation (English to French or German) – 2 hours

Translation (from French or German to English) + English grammar – $2\frac{1}{2}$ hours

Essay – 2 hours

English Literature – 3 hours

English Phonetics – $1\frac{1}{2}$ hours

Oral

Dictation – $1\frac{1}{2}$ hours

Reading & conversation – $1\frac{1}{2}$ hours

Figure 1.2   Contents of the first CPE (1913)

EARLY DEVELOPMENTS IN THE UNITED STATES OF AMERICA

In the United States, people such as Thorndike (1911, 1912), Hillegas (1912), and Courtis (1914) were exploring assessment from a totally different perspective. They were all interested in standardizing the way we looked at student written performance, with Thorndike developing the first standardized test in 1908. This test was of handwriting, and the whole process through which he developed it tells us much about why testing in the United States in the century that followed (and to a large extent to this day) went in the direction it did. Instead of estimating a scale based on his own experience, or on the experience of his colleagues (the method used by his contemporaries in Europe), Thorndike took a large sample of student handwriting and asked a group of almost 200 teachers to rank these scripts in order of legibility. He then took their data and created a scale upon which he placed each script. Selecting a set of exemplar scripts as the basis of his scale, Thorndike then asked teachers to simply compare their students' handwriting with those samples on the scale. The closest match gave the level.

Using the same basic methodology, Hillegas (1912) developed the first standardized scale for written composition and Courtis (1914) compiled the first standardized test of English, in which he combined a number of these scales with additional measures to come up with a profile of each candidate. Figure 1.3 shows an example of this profile taken from Courtis' paper describing the procedure (1914: 391).

Courtis explains that:

> On the basis of these tests and the requirements of the school it is possible to say that an eighth-grade child of standard ability should be able to write an original story at the rate of 18 words per minute and that legibility of the writing should be 60 on the Ayres scale [an alternative to Thorndike's handwriting scale], and the quality of the story "Good"; that in the story there should not be more than five mistakes in punctuation per hundred

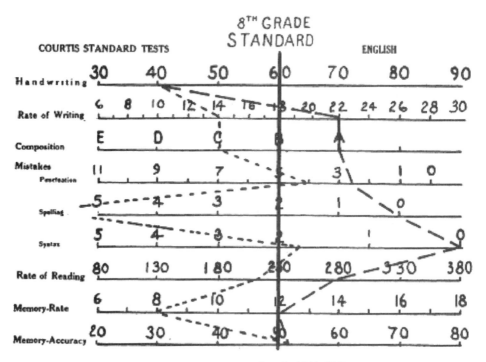

Figure 1.3   Example of standard and actual scores (Courtis, 1914: 391)

words, two in spelling, and two in syntax; that in careful reading of the given material under standard conditions, the rate should be 230 words per minute, and that in the reproduction of the material read, 12 of the original words should be used per minute and that these words should constitute 50 per cent of the words used in the reproduction. The graph shows the actual scores made by two members of the same class. (Courtis, 1914: 391)

Handschin (1920) discusses the earliest foreign language tests to use this "new" approach, which Carroll (1954: 2) describes as representing "a revolt from the subjectivity, unreliability, lack of comprehensiveness, and general cumbersomeness of the old-style examinations."

The work described here, when coupled with the multiple-choice question (MCQ) format developed by Kelly (1915) in his *Kansas Test of Silent Reading* and referred to by Samelson (1999: 249) as a "piece of educational technology . . . as American as the assembly line and probably as alienating," marked the beginning of large-scale testing in the United States and provided the impetus for the birth of psychometrics, spawning the testing industry we now know. The first MCQ published appears innocuous to us now (see Figure 1.4), but at the time it represented a revolution in the way tests were developed.

Below are the names of four animals. Draw a line around the name of each animal that is useful on the farm:

cow   tiger   rat   wolf

Figure 1.4   The first multiple-choice question (Kelly, 1915)

The key difference between the approach to test development in the United States and that in Britain and Europe was that the U.S. tests looked first to standardization and psychometric excellence, then to content and validity, even though this actually went against much of the thinking of people like Thorndike who started with output and then combined his knowledge of statistical scaling with content specialists to come up with performance level indicators.

At this same time, the Modern Languages Association of Maryland's 1913 Committee declared that the curriculum should drive the learning environment and not tests, though the impact of this declaration was limited by an acceptance of the practical limitations to the direct testing of speaking. The combination of these events marked the beginning of the dominance of *objective* testing in the United States (which still survives today) and the beginning of the business of testing.

THE POST-WWII YEARS

By the 1940s, high-stakes testing in the United States had moved almost entirely to a standardized multiple-choice format. With the single exception of the military-inspired Foreign Services Institute Oral Proficiency Interview (OPI; the first modern test of speaking and the first to use a standardized rating scale), language testing in the United States continued to follow suit. The development of the first major test of English as a foreign language in the United States in the early 1960s marked the heyday of the application of this approach in the English testing domain. The Test of English as a Foreign Language (TOEFL), which remained essentially unchanged for 40 years, was to begin life as a major innovation in the standardization of English language tests, and to end, almost tragically, as a "relic of ould decency"[1] out of date and out of touch with the reality of late-twentieth-century thinking.

The social, academic, and political rationalization for developing the TOEFL is brilliantly described by Spolsky in his book *Measured Words* (1995) so I will not be discussing that aspect of the test here. Instead, I will briefly locate the TOEFL with relation to another movement of the early 1960s: The study of how language is used in different domains of society, work, and study. The study of language for specific purposes emerged, according to Swales (1984: 11), with Barber's *Some measurable characteristics of modern scientific prose* (1962), in which he identified key features of language use specific to the domain of scientific writing. The fact that the developers of the TOEFL were the first to build a major English language test around a definition of the language needs of a specific population by looking to the domain in which they would be expected to study marks it as a particularly important test. We might not agree nowadays with the solution they came up with, but if we look to the tradition from which they came we should see that they developed the most up-to-date test of the time.

THE GROWING INDUSTRY

The development of general proficiency examinations continued in the three decades following the introduction of the TOEFL, particularly with the creation by the University of Cambridge Local Examinations Syndicate (UCLES, now known as Cambridge ESOL) of its main suite of examinations, based on the original (though much revised) CPE and on the later (immediately post-World War II) First Certificate in English (FCE). Specific purpose tests took a little time to get going with the next major attempt coming again from the makers of TOEFL. The Test of English for International Communication (TOEIC) was introduced in 1979, in response to a request from the Japanese Ministry for Trade and Industry for a test of language for business purposes. The test, the core of which remains exactly as it was when the test first emerged, remains popular, though there are grave doubts as to its specificity (it appears to focus entirely on general English) and on its approach to result reporting – it adopts a norm-referenced reporting system in which the performance of each individual is reported in terms of the rest of the candidature. Douglas (2000) seriously questions the validity of norm referencing for specific purpose tests, arguing that since this type of test must tell us if an individual has the ability to survive linguistically in a domain (e.g., has enough English to work as a nurse), we should report performance in terms of a pre-set criterion or pass mark.

By the early 1980s, test developers in the UK began to explore the possibility of creating tests of language for specific purposes and came up with the English Language Testing Service (ELTS), which soon became the International English Language Testing System (IELTS). The approach taken to these examinations highlights the different approaches on both sides of the Atlantic (see Davies, 2008, for an interesting history of early testing of English for academic purposes in the UK). The original ELTS included papers aimed at students who planned to study particular disciplines (there were six modules in total: Life Sciences, Social Studies, Physical Sciences, Technology, Medicine, and General Academic, in addition to a nonacademic module) and the focus was on language use, with equal emphasis on the productive and receptive skills. With the review of the ELTS (Criper and Davies, 1988) came the realization that the complexity of the design made it difficult, if not impossible to replicate, and with no evidence to show that having six distinct modules resulted in meaningful advantages to students in those disciplines, the decision was taken to change the test. At the same time, it was decided to make the new test more *international* in flavor and shorter. The result was that in 1989 the six modules became three (Physical Science & Technology, Life & Medical Sciences, and Business Studies & Social Sciences) each with options in reading and writing, whereas all candidates sat for the same speaking and listening papers. By 1995, the test was to change again. Now there were to be no domain-specific modules, and all candidates took the same papers with just an academic and general training (nonacademic) option for the test.

The reason for looking at how the IELTS changed over a relatively short period was to highlight one interesting phenomenon about the success of tests for specific purposes. As a result of the changes outlined here, the IELTS has become less specific in terms of both content and of its cognitive demands, which no longer reflect the study domain. While this can be seen as negative, it has made results on the test more generalizable, in other words, it is more a general test of proficiency now and thus has more marketability, just like the TOEIC. It is not a surprise that both are used for a range of decisions, such as migration and immigration, as well as for their original purpose.

CHANGE IN THE AIR

During this time of rapid development, a number of things were happening. Bachman (1990) introduced to language testing worldwide many of the elements of the U.S. assessment philosophy. In many ways, his seminal work sparked a renewed interest in language testing and encouraged a new professionalism in the field. Testing was also becoming big business, with first the TOEFL and TOEIC attracting millions of candidates annually, and the IELTS growing from a few thousand to well over a million candidates per year. The Cambridge ESOL Main Suite began to decline as other players such as Michigan, City & Guilds, and Trinity entered the field and the emphasis began to change from general to specific purpose testing in the early years of the 21st century.

Even the "Atlantic divide" (O'Sullivan, 2006) began to shrink. The TOEFL/FCE comparability study (Bachman et al., 1995), in which the U.S. authors concluded that the technical qualities of the former (U.S.) test far outweighed the validation claims of the latter (UK) test, sparked changes in the attitude of UK examination toward psychometric quality and led to changes in their practices. At this point in time, it seemed that the proponents of the psychometric view of quality were gaining an upper hand. However, it soon became clear that this was not the case. By the final years of the 20th century, the emphasis had clearly begun to shift, with TOEFL's developers looking toward more European-type formats for inspiration for their latest versions. By the time the TOEFL iBT (Internet-based TOEFL) appeared in the early years of the new century, it looked far more like a European test than any test developed in the United States since 1930.

Of course psychometrics still has a place in language testing; the most important impact of the TOEFL/FCE study was that it changed the perceptions of the European examination boards toward the need to establish the psychometric quality of their tests. This situation was helped by the emergence of new statistical processes, such as those based on Rasch (1960/1980; 1961), which are more acceptable for performance and criterion-referenced test analysis than the traditional "classical" test statistics. In fact, the recent publication of the manual for linking examinations to the CEFR (Common European Framework of Reference, Council of Europe, 2009) suggests that psychometrics are alive and well in Europe, with the very narrow view of test validity contained in the manual reflecting thinking in the United States from the 1950s or earlier!

LANGUAGE TESTING TODAY

Things are changing in language testing. Ever since Bachman (1990) presented his model of language ability, and demonstrated how this could be used to support a language test which was designed to reflect the then current thinking in educational measurement, a new level of professionalism has emerged, with a growing worldwide cadre of scholars and practitioners with levels of expertise that far exceed those of their predecessors. As testing knowledge spreads, people are beginning to realize that for *good* testing to happen, the domain to which it applies must be taken into consideration when interpreting the validation argument that accompanies it.

Most testing is done at the classroom, school, regional, or national level. If we are to take seriously the argument (made by Weir, myself, and others) that the test taker in particular and validation in general should be at the heart of development, then tests simply *must* be built around the test taker. So, for example, when developing a series of affordable English examinations for use in Mexico (Abad Florescano et al., 2011), the team looked carefully at the potential test takers and came to the conclusion – among others – that existing word lists would not be suitable as the proximity of Spanish to English meant that only a custom-built word list would do.

The implication here is that international examinations are only of value if they are designed to be used in a specific domain. Having worked on test development and validation projects across the world over the past decade, I have come across many instances of this type of misuse of language tests. Until now, administrators and policymakers have argued, with a lot of success and some justification, that no local test could match the international examinations for quality. No longer. Nowadays, there are many examples of excellent local examinations in which the knowledge of the local domain (culture, language, society, etc.) contributes significantly to the format and contents of the test.

The process of *professionalization* has led, over time, to one of test *localization*. The latter process is the most significant current development in language testing as it is based on the assumption (correct, in my view) that in almost all circumstances local tests are more likely to allow us to make more valid assumptions about test takers than non-test-taker specific competitors. While this has always been the case, the level of professionalism among local testers has begun to change dramatically (just look at the country of origin of most doctoral candidates in the United States and the UK over the past decade – you will find that they are almost all from places other than those two countries).

All this has led to *fragmentation* in the language-testing industry. There are still a number of big players, but these are competing for a limited (though large) market, which is defined by a small number of very specific domains – international business and country-specific higher education. As local expertise matures and confidence in localized solutions grows, this market will become ever more focused and local tests will begin to dominate specific markets.

FINAL THOUGHTS

I had thought of finishing this chapter with a sort of *Tomorrow's World*[2] view of the future of language testing. Sadly, many of the authors in this book (including myself) are children of a less technology-rich time. As such, we are probably not the best people to ask about the future. It is more likely that you, the readers, know more about the subject than I do, so instead I will ask you to think about how language testing will change over the coming years and decades. How big (or small) a part will technology play in these changes? Will we finally devise a level of artificial intelligence that will allow us to crack the voice-recognition problem and allow humans to interact with (not simply talk to) a machine? Will our machines also be creative, allowing them to interpret what we are saying and more accurately evaluate it? Is this even what we want of the future?

While we depend more and more on technology in our daily lives, we must consider the impact of any over-reliance on something we don't always fully understand. Technology can go wrong and unless it delivers on artificial intelligence, its contribution to testing (consistency of scoring) is always going to be limited. This is because, while consistency (i.e., reliability) is an important aspect of validity, it cannot guarantee validity – a test can be consistently telling us something that is either just wrong, or is not what we think it is.

So, until we reach a time when we can fully rely on the advances that technology brings to our daily lives (and tests) we should be cautious of its benefits. With that in mind, I'll leave you with a quote from the film *2001: A Space Odyssey* by Stanley Kubrick (1968) in which the sole survivor of a spaceship crew (Dave) pleads with the ship's computer (HAL) to open the pod doors to allow him into the part of the ship where HAL is housed (HAL has begun to malfunction, taking over the ship and killing the other crew members, and *knows* that Dave intends to shut him down).

> **Dave**: All right, HAL. I'll go in through the emergency airlock.
>
> **HAL**: Without your space helmet, Dave, you're going to find that rather difficult.
>
> **Dave**: HAL, I won't argue with you anymore! Open the doors!
>
> **HAL**: [almost sadly] Dave, this conversation can serve no purpose any more. Goodbye. (2001: A Space Odyssey)

Suggested resources

Davies, A. (2008). *Assessing Academic English: Testing English proficiency 1950–1989 – The IELTS solution*. Cambridge: Cambridge University Press.

Murdoch, S. (2007). *IQ – A smart history of a failed idea*. New York: John Wiley and Sons.

Spolsky. B. (1995). *Measured words*. Oxford: Oxford University Press.

Discussion questions

1. Think about how testing is normally done in your country or institution. By which of the two main philosophies of language testing (United States or UK) was it likely to have been influenced? Why do you think that happened?

2. How has language testing changed in your context (country, institution, etc.) since you became a teacher or since you were a young learner?

3. Will computers replace humans as assessors of language performance (speaking and writing)? When? Why or why not? How?

References

Abad Florescano, A., O'Sullivan, B., Sanchez Chavez, C., Ryan, D. E., Zamora Lara, E., Santana Martinez, L. A., Gonzalez Macias, M. I., Maxwell Hart, M., Grounds, P. E., Reidy Ryan, P., Dunne, R. A. & Romero Barradas, T. de E. (2011). Developing affordable 'local' tests: The EXAVER project. In B. O'Sullivan (Ed.), *Language testing: Theories & practice*. Oxford: Palgrave.

Bachman, L. (1990). *Fundamental considerations of language testing*. Oxford: OUP.

Bachman, L., Davidson, F., Ryan, K., & Choi, I.-C. (1995). *An investigation into the comparability of two tests of English as a foreign language: The Cambridge TOEFL Comparability Study*. Cambridge: CUP.

Barber, C. (1962). Some measurable characteristics of modern scientific prose. Reprinted in J. Swales (Ed.) (1988), *Episodes in ESP* (pp. 1–16). New York: Prentice Hall.

Burton, R. (1631). *Anatomy of melancholy*. Project Gutenberg e-book. Retrieved December 8, 2005, from www.gutenberg.org/etext/10800.

Carroll, J. B. (1954). *Notes on the measurement of achievement in foreign languages*. Unpublished manuscript.

Council of Europe. (2009). *Relating language examinations to the Common European Framework of Reference for Languages: Learning, Teaching, Assessment (CEFR): A manual*. Strasbourg: The Language Policy Division. Retrieved May 18, 2009, from www.coe.int/T/DG4/Portfolio/documents/Manual%20Revision%20-%20proof read%20-%20FINAL.pdf.

Courtis, S. A. (1914). Standard tests in English. *The Elementary School Teacher*, 14 (8): 374–392.

Criper, C., & Davies, A. (1988). *ELTS validation report*. London: The British Council/ Cambridge: University of Cambridge Local Examinations Syndicate.

Davies, A. (2008). *Assessing Academic English: Testing English proficiency 1950–1989: The IELTS solution*. Cambridge: Cambridge University Press.

Douglas, D. (2000). *Assessing languages for specific purposes*. Cambridge: Cambridge University Press.

Handschin, C. H. (1920). Tests and measurements in modern language work. *Modern Language Teacher*, 4: 217–225.

Hillegas, M. B. (1912). *A scale for the measurement of quality in English composition by young people*. New York: Teachers College.

Kelly, F. J. (1915). *Kansas silent reading test*. Topeka, KS: Kansas State Printing Plant, 1915.

Kubrick, S. (1968). *2001: A Space Odyssey*. Metro-Goldwyn-Meyer.

Morris, N. (1961). An historian's view of examinations. In S. Wiseman (Ed.), *Examinations and English education* (pp. 1–43). Manchester: Manchester University Press.

Northcote, S. H. & Trevelyan, C. E. (1853). *Report on the organisation of the Permanent Civil Service*. Presented to both Houses of Parliament in February 1854. Retrieved April 27, 2006, from www.civilservant.org.uk/northcotetrevelyan.pdf.

O'Sullivan, B. (2006). *Testing times: Daring to lead or failing to follow?* Plenary address at the TESOL international conference, Tampa, FL, March 2006.

Rasch, G. (1960/1980). Probabilistic models for some intelligence and attainment tests. (Copenhagen, Danish Institute for Educational Research), expanded edition (1980) with foreword and afterword by B. D. Wright. Chicago: The University of Chicago Press.

Rasch, G. (1961). On general laws and the meaning of measurement in psychology. In Proceedings of the Fourth Berkeley Symposium on Mathematical Statistics and Probability, IV (pp. 321–334). Berkeley, California: University of California Press.

Samelson, F. (1999). Assessing research in the history of psychology: Past, present, and future. *Journal of the History of the Behavioural Sciences*, 35, 247–255.

Spolsky, B. (1995). *Measured words*. Oxford: Oxford University Press.

Swales, J. (1984). ESP comes of age? – 21 years after 'Some measurable characteristics of modern scientific prose'. *UNESCO Alsed – LSP Newsletter*, 7, 2 (19): 9–20.

Sweet, H. (1899). *The practical study of languages: A guide for teachers and learners*. London: Dent. (Republished by Oxford University Press in 1964, Ed. R. Mackin).

Thorndike. E. L. (1911). A scale for measuring the merit of English writing. *Science*, 33: 935–938.

Thorndike, E. L. (1912). The measurement of educational products. *The School Review*, Vol. 20, No. 5 (May, 1912), 289–299.

Weir, C. J. (2003). A survey of the history of the Certificate of Proficiency in English (CPE) in the 20th century. In C. J. Weir & M. Milanovic, *Continuity and innovation: Revising the Cambridge Proficiency in English examination 1913–2002* (pp. 1–56). Studies in Language Testing, Vol. 15, Cambridge: UCLES / Cambridge University Press.

Notes

[1] A *relic of ould decency* is an Irish expression, which refers to the memory of a time gone by, usually meant in a negative way. Used by James Joyce in *Ulysses* (1922) to describe O'Callaghan, a former solicitor now stricken off the rolls: "Has that silk hat ever since. Relics of ould decency. Mourning too. Terrible comedown, poor wretch! Kicked about like snuff at a wake."

[2] *Tomorrow's World* was a TV program that ran for almost 40 years on BBC in the UK. The program highlighted developments in science and technology and often was the place where these were first seen. However, it also included many objects that, when we look back at them now, appear to verge on the lunatic!

CHAPTER 2

Foreign and Second Language Teacher Assessment Literacy: Issues, Challenges, and Recommendations

Christine Coombe, Salah Troudi, and Mashael Al-Hamly

INTRODUCTION

It has long been acknowledged that assessment is an integral part of the teaching–learning process (James, McInnis, and Devlin, 2002). In fact, Cowan (1998) calls assessment the engine that drives learning. One of the effective ways of enhancing learning within higher education is through the improvement of assessment procedures.

Research shows that the typical teacher can spend as much as a third to one half of his / her professional time involved in assessment or assessment-related activities (Herman and Dorr-Bremme, 1982; Stiggins and Conklin, 1992; Cheng, 2001). Almost all do so without the benefit of having learned the principles of sound assessment (Stiggins, 2007).

Now more than ever our educational systems are under pressure to be accountable for student performance and to produce measurable results. Without a higher level of teacher assessment literacy, we will be unable to help students attain higher levels of academic achievement. Being assessment literate means "knowing appropriate testing practices, acquiring a wide range of assessment techniques and utilizing tests that accurately assess higher order concepts" (Hoyt, 2005, as cited in Rogier, 2009). Assessment literacy is generally divided into two areas: Teacher assessment knowledge and teachers' perspectives on assessment knowledge (Wang, Wang, and Huang, 2008). In this chapter, we look at the first area of assessment literacy, that of teacher assessment knowledge, and address some issues and challenges related to assessment literacy.

CURRENT STAKEHOLDER VIEWS OF LANGUAGE ASSESSMENT

HOW EL STUDENTS VIEW ASSESSMENT

For many students, assessment is not an educational experience in itself, but a process of guessing what the teacher wants (McLaughlin and Simpson, 2004). For the typical EF/SL student, assessment is generally seen as something done to them by their teachers. Many students see tests as threats to their competence and as something to be "got through." The more able students enjoy the experience but most students, no matter what their level, feel anxious and worried about assessments as there is great pressure in today's educational world to succeed. When tests or assessments are high-stakes, students often suffer from high levels of test anxiety.

HOW EL TEACHERS VIEW ASSESSMENT

Teachers often experience similar feelings to those of their students. For those teachers who are not involved in setting tests or assessments for their students, they feel that a gap between teaching and testing is in evidence. Oftentimes they feel that those who write the tests are not in touch with the realities of the classroom. Research by Jacobs and Chase (1992) found that testing and assessment-related activities are the least pleasant aspect of a teacher's job.

HOW EDUCATIONAL BOARDS VIEW ASSESSMENT

Virtually every set of standards of teacher competence developed recently, including those developed by the National Education Association (NEA), the American Federation of Teachers (AFT), the Council of Chief State School Officers (CCSSO), the National Council for Accreditation of Teacher Education (NCATE), and the National Board of Professional Teacher Standards (NBPTS), have identified and endorsed a set of assessment competencies for teachers (Wise, 1996, as cited in Stiggins, 1995).

In the field of English language teaching, TESOL, partnered with the National Council for the accreditation of Teacher Education (NCATE), created the TESOL / NCATE standards for ESOL teacher education. Assessment constitutes one of the five knowledge domains within these standards. In Europe, the Common European Framework of Reference and the European Portfolio for Modern Languages are requiring language teachers to adopt new ways of assessing language ability (Stoynoff and Coombe, Chapter 14).

Clearly, there is widespread global recognition that language assessment literacy represents an important aspect of teachers' professional knowledge.

RESEARCH ON ASSESSMENT LITERACY

Language teachers with a solid background in assessment are well positioned to integrate assessment with instruction so that they utilize appropriate forms of teaching. Despite the importance that is relegated to being assessment literate, our progress toward an assessment-literate educational culture has been slow.

As such, it is surprising to find that preservice and in-service teachers often don't have the necessary skills to effectively administer sound assessments in the classroom (Brookhart, 2001; Campbell and Collins, 2007; Mertler, 2005). According to Rogier (2009), both teacher education programs and certification policies are at fault for not making sure teachers are adequately trained before entering the classroom (Mertler, 2005; Stiggins, 1991, 1995). Research shows that only half of teacher education programs include a course on assessment skills and the 50 percent that do include any assessment don't cover the skills completely (Schafer, 1993).

Research continues to characterize teachers' assessment and evaluation practices as largely incongruent with recommended best practice (Galluzzo, 2005; Mertler, 2003; Zhang and Burry-Stock, 1997, as cited in Volante and Fazio, 2007: 750).

In North America, there continues to be relatively little emphasis on assessment in the professional development of teachers. For example, out of ten Canadian provinces and 50 U.S. states, only Hawaii and Nebraska currently invest significant funds which are specifically targeted to improve assessment and evaluation practices within schools (Volante and Fazio, 2007).

Research on teaching in mainstream classrooms has revealed that the day-to-day assessment of student learning is unquestionably one of the teachers' most demanding, complex, and important tasks (Calderhead, 1996, as cited in Cheng, 2001: 54; Shulman, 1986). Teachers view student evaluation as a central teaching function in their classrooms. This is evidenced by the time spent on assessment-related activities.

In the SL education literature, Bachman (2000) reported that a survey of the TESOL organization membership conducted in the 1990s found about half of the respondents had completed a course in language testing, and Stoynoff (2009) determined that about half of the graduate programs in the *Directory of Teacher Preparation Programs in TESOL* (Christopher, 2005) required graduates to complete coursework in language assessment. These results are similar to a recent study completed by Brown and Bailey (2008) in which 60 percent of the respondents were from outside the United States. Based on these data, it appears that half of all ESOL teachers may not have completed coursework in language assessment (Stoynoff and Coombe, Chapter 14).

While there is rich literature and a plethora of research studies on ESL/EFL teachers' assessment practices (e.g., Cheng, Rogers, and Wang, 2008), there continues to be a gap in the area of assessment literacy and what constitutes teachers' knowledge. In fact, as far as teacher preparation in assessment is concerned in EFL contexts, teachers in Hong Kong report that they received little or no training in assessment (Falvey and Cheng, 1995). Shohamy (1998) and Ferman (1998) found that EFL teachers in Israel felt they lacked the knowledge and training required to practice assessment procedures. More recently, Troudi, Coombe, and Al-Hamly (2009) found in a study done with tertiary-level English-language teachers in the United Arab Emirates and Kuwait, that teachers often felt marginalized in the area of assessment because of their perceived lack of knowledge about the subject.

DEFINING ASSESSMENT LITERACY

Interestingly, the term "assessment literacy" is not listed in the *Dictionary of Language Testing* (1999), ALTE's *Multilingual Glossary of Language Testing Terms* (1998), or Mousavi's *Encyclopedic Dictionary of Language Testing* (2002). While each of these volumes devotes ample space to the concept of assessment, the issue of how educators become assessment literate is not mentioned. Despite the lack of definitions in these important assessment volumes, the term "assessment literacy" has been defined by a number of well-known assessment experts.

According to Popham (2004) and Stiggins (2002) assessment literacy is simply an understanding of the principles of sound assessment. Implicit in this definition is that assessment-literate teachers have the know-how and understanding needed to assess their students effectively and maximize learning.

Those educators who are deemed to be assessment literate are familiar with the principles of sound assessment and how to meet specific standards of quality. The characteristics of sound assessment according to Stiggins (2007: 8–28) are that they:

1. arise from and serve clear purposes;

2. arise from and reflect clear and appropriate achievement targets;

3. rely on a proper assessment method (given the purpose and the target);

4. sample student achievement appropriately; and

5. control for all relevant sources of bias and distortion.

Assessment-literate educators come to any assessment knowing what they are assessing, why they are doing so, how best to assess the achievement of interest, how to generate sound samples of performance, what can go wrong, and how to prevent these problems before they occur (Stiggins, 1995: 240). Language teachers and administrators need the necessary tools for analyzing and reflecting upon test and assessment data in order to make informed decisions about instructional practice and program design.

By developing assessment literacy, language educators will not only be able to identify appropriate assessments for specific purposes, such as student placement, but will also be able to analyze empirical data to improve their instruction.

BARRIERS TO ASSESSMENT LITERACY

As well as a lack of coursework in the area of assessment, there are a number of additional impediments or what Stiggins (1995) calls "barriers" to assessment literacy.

The first and perhaps most important reason is "fear." According to Stiggins (1995), educators often carry with them an accumulation of layers of negative emotions associated with assessment. This fear of assessment has often been cultivated over many years of unpleasant assessment experiences. The foundations of this fear are often rooted in the assessments that we have undergone as young people. Fear represents a prominent barrier to assessment literacy because it closes many educators off from even reviewing their own assessment competence.

Another reason why teachers do not want to become involved in or increase their knowledge of assessment is put forth by Alderson (2001). He states that the field of assessment is often viewed by teachers as an arcane "Ivory Tower" where many of the journals are not accessible to the average classroom teacher.

Concerns close to the teachers' daily lives constitute another important reason for the lag in the development of assessment literacy. With the increasing demands of the workplace, some teachers feel that it is simply easier not to worry about assessment. These teachers are content to let others write the assessments for them.

Another significant barrier to assessment literacy is that there are insufficient resources allocated to assessment. It has been stated time and time again that although administrators pay lip service to the importance of assessment, very few actually back it up with the resources needed to make assessment programs more successful. Administrators view assessment and assessment-related activities as being part of a teacher's job and often do not provide reduced teaching loads or extra remuneration for those who get actively involved in such activities.

All of the factors mentioned above conspire against teacher involvement in assessment and increased levels of assessment literacy in our teachers.

PRACTICAL APPLICATIONS

WHAT ASSESSMENT SKILLS ARE NEEDED TO BE ASSESSMENT LITERATE

A number of well-known assessment scholars and organizations have put forth lists of characteristics of what it takes to be assessment literate. Several of the ones we find most relevant will be highlighted in this section.

According to the *Seven Standards for Teacher Development in Assessment* developed by the American Federation of Teachers, the National Council on Measurement in Education and the National Education Association (1990), teachers should be skilled in:

1. choosing assessment methods appropriate for instructional decisions
2. developing appropriate assessment methods
3. administering, scoring, and interpreting the results of both externally produced and teacher-produced assessment methods
4. using assessment results when making decisions about individual students, planning teaching, developing curriculum, and involving students
5. developing valid grading procedures which use student assessment
6. communicating assessment results to students, parents, and other stakeholders
7. recognizing unethical, illegal and inappropriate assessment methods and uses of assessment information

In a useful online publication from SERVE at the University of North Carolina, they recommend that assessment-literate teachers know:

- How to define clear learning goals, which are the basis of developing or choosing ways to assess student learning
- How to make use of a variety of assessment methods to gather evidence of student learning
- How to analyze achievement data (both qualitative and quantitative) and make good inferences from the data gathered
- How to provide appropriate feedback to students
- How to make appropriate instructional modifications to help students improve
- How to involve students in assessment process (e.g., self and peer assessment) and effectively communicate results
- How to engineer an effective classroom assessment environment that boosts student motivation to learn (SERVE Center, University of North Carolina, 2004)

Sadler (1998, as cited in White, 2009: 6) shares these characteristics of an assessment literate educator:

- Superior knowledge about content and substance of what is to be learned
- Knowledge about learners and learning and a desire to help students develop, improve, and do better
- Skills in selecting and creating assessment tasks
- Knowledge of criteria and standards appropriate to assessment tasks
- Evaluative skills and expertise in the analysis and use of assessment information
- Expertise in giving appropriate and targeted feedback

In the TESOL/NCATE standards for ESOL teacher education, in the assessment domain, teachers are expected to understand:

- issues of assessment for ESL
- language proficiency assessment for ESL (including how to develop assessments and use them to inform instruction)

The preceding lists have detailed some of the more important aspects of what it means to be assessment literate. Language departments and institutions will need to reflect on their own assessment needs and compile lists of skills and abilities that they would like to see in their respective teachers. A commonality in all of the lists is that those who are assessment literate understand what assessment methods to use in order to gather dependable information about student achievement, communicate assessment results effectively, and understand how to use assessment to maximize student motivation and learning.

RECOMMENDATIONS FOR ACHIEVING ASSESSMENT LITERACY

First, it is crucial that we develop a universal understanding of what constitutes a good assessment and to build a common, articulated set of criteria for exemplary language assessment. This certainly does not negate the recognition of different views about the nature of education which might lead to dissimilar approaches to assessment. There remains an urgent need to encourage and organize professional development through both online training of teachers and face-to-face assessment workshops at all levels.

If we are to achieve assessment literacy, we need to provide teachers with the requisite professional development and time to implement those practices learned. A few workshops are insufficient. Successful professional development in assessment will require significant change in our educational practices and a time commitment on the part of teachers.

Successful professional development in the area of assessment literacy needs to take into account the learning styles and workload of today's language teachers. In order for teachers to achieve assessment literacy the availability of assessment resources, especially online, is critical.

CONCLUSION

Teachers will be expected to be far more assessment literate in the future than they are today or have been in the past (Stiggins, 2007).

Assessment-literate educators come to any assessment knowing what they are assessing, why they are doing so, how best to assess the achievement of interest, how to generate sound samples of performance, what can go wrong, and how to prevent these problems before they occur (Stiggins, 1995: 240).

It was best stated by Bracey (2000) – there might come a time when tests and test scores recede from prominence, but that time is not now. In view of the importance of assessment in today's educational institutions around the world, "assessment literacy" is a necessity for all language educators.

Suggested resources

Alderson, J. C., Clapham, C., & Wall, D. (1995). *Test construction and evaluation*. Cambridge: Cambridge University Press.
This volume describes and illustrates the principles of test design, construction, and evaluation. Each chapter deals with one stage of the test construction process. The final chapter examines current practice in EFL assessment.

Bachman, L. F., & Palmer, A. S. (1996). *Language testing in practice: Designing and developing useful language tests*. Oxford: Oxford University Press.
This book relates language-testing practice to current views of communicative language teaching and testing. It builds on the theoretical background set forth in Bachman (1990). The authors discuss the design, planning, and organization of tests.

Bailey, K. (1998). *Learning about language assessment: Dilemmas, decisions, and directions*. TeacherSource Series, D. Freeman (Ed.). Boston: Heinle.
This text provides a practical analysis of language assessment theory and accessible explanations of the statistics involved.

Brown, H. D. (2003). *Language assessment: Principles and classroom practice*. Hertfordshire, UK: Prentice Hall.
An accessible book on assessment by an experienced teacher and teacher trainer.

Cambridge Language Assessment series, by J. C. Alderson & L. Bachman (series editors). Cambridge: Cambridge University Press.
This excellent series of professional volumes includes:

- *Assessing languages for specific purposes*, Dan Douglas
- *Assessing vocabulary*, John Read
- *Assessing reading*, Charles Alderson
- *Assessing listening*, Gary Buck
- *Assessing writing*, Sara Cushing Weigle
- *Assessing speaking*, Sari Luoma
- *Assessing grammar*, Jim Purpura
- *Assessing young learners*, Penny McKay
- *Assessing languages through computer technology*, Carol Chapelle & Dan Douglas

Coombe, C., Folse, K., & Hubley, N. (2007). *A practical guide to assessing English language learners*. Ann Arbor, MI: University of Michigan Press.
This co-authored volume includes chapters on the basics of language assessment. The content revolves around two fictitious language teachers; one who has very good instincts about how students should be assessed and the other who is just starting out and makes mistakes along the way.

Hughes, A. (2003). *Testing for language teachers* (2nd ed.). Cambridge: Cambridge University Press.
This practical guide is designed for teachers who want to have a better understanding of the role of testing in language teaching. The principles and practice of testing are presented in a logical, accessible way and guidance is given for teachers who devise their own tests.

Studies in Language Testing Series, by M. Milanovic & C. Weir (series editors). Cambridge: Cambridge University Press.
This series focusing on important developments in language testing has been produced by UCLES/Cambridge ESOL in conjunction with Cambridge University Press. Titles in the series are of considerable interest to test users, language test developers, and researchers.

Discussion questions

1. Why is it important for a teacher to be assessment literate?

2. In this chapter the authors discuss how different stakeholders view the assessment process. Do you agree or disagree with their views? Can you add anything to these views?

3. The authors cite several barriers to assessment literacy. Can you personally relate to any of these barriers? Can you think of any other barriers that are not currently on the list?

4. Several well-known lists of assessment-literacy content are presented in this chapter. Based on your particular educational and cultural context, can you think of any content that needs to be added to these lists?

5. Think about your own knowledge in the area of F/SL assessment. What areas are you strong in and what areas do you think you need to improve?

References

Alderson, J. C. (2001). Testing is too important to be left to testers. In C. Coombe (Ed.), *Selected papers from the 1999 & 2000 CTELT conferences* (pp. 1–14). Dubai: TESOL Arabia Publications.

ALTE. (1998). Multilingual glossary of language testing terms. *Studies in Language Testing* 6. Cambridge: Cambridge University Press.

American Federation of Teachers, National Council on Measurement in Education, National Education Association (1990). Standards for teacher competence in educational assessment of students. *Educational Measurement: Issues and Practice*, 9/4: 30–32.

Bachman, L. F. (2000). Modern language testing at the turn of the century: Assuming that what we count counts. *Language Testing*, 1/1:1–42.

Bracey, G. (2000). Thinking about tests and testing: A short primer in assessment literacy. Paper presented at the American Youth Policy Forum, Washington, DC. ED 445 096.

Brookhart, S. M. (2001). The standards and classroom assessment research. Paper presented at the Annual Meeting of the American Association of Colleges for Teacher Education.

Brown, J. D., & Bailey, K. M. (2008). Language testing courses: What are they in 2007? *Language Testing*, 25(3), 349–383.

Calderhead, J. (1996). Teachers: Beliefs and knowledge. In D. C. Berliner & R. C. Calfee (Eds.), *Handbook of educational psychology* (pp. 709–725). New York: MacMillan Library Reference.

Campbell, C., & Collins, V. L. (2007). Identifying essential topics in general and special education introductory assessment textbooks. *Educational Measurement: Issues and Practice*, 26(1), 9–18.

Cheng, L. (2001). An investigation of ESL/EFL teachers' classroom assessment practices. *Language Testing Update*, 29: 53–83.

Cheng, L., Rogers, T., & Wang, X. (2008). Assessment purposes and procedures in ESL/EFL classroom. *Assessment & Evaluation in Higher Education*, 33: 9–32.

Christopher, V. (2005). *Directory of teacher education programs in TESOL in the United States and Canada*. Alexandria, VA.: TESOL.

Cowan, J. (1998). *On becoming an innovative university teacher*, Buckingham: RHE & Open University Press.

Falvey, P., & Cheng, L. (1995). A comparative study of teachers' beliefs about assessment principles and practices. *Language Testing Update*, 18: 38–39.

Ferman, I. (1998). *The impact of a new English foreign language oral matriculation test on the educational system*. Unpublished MA thesis, Tel Aviv University.

Galluzzo, G. R. (2005). Performance assessment and renewing teacher education. *Clearing House*, 78/4:142–145.

Herman, J., & Dorr-Bremme, D. (1982). *Assessing students: Teachers' routine practices and reasoning*. Paper presented at the annual meeting of the American Educational Research Association, New York.

Hoyt, K. (2005). Assessment impact on instruction. New Visions in Action. National Assessment Summit. Meeting conducted in Alexandria, VA, April 2005.

Jacobs, L. C., & Chase, C. I. (1992). *Developing and using tests effectively: A guide for faculty*. San Francisco, CA: Jossey-Bass.

James, R., McInnis, C., & Devlin, M. (2002). *Assessing learning at Australian Universities*. Center for the Study of Higher Education, the University of Melbourne, Australia. Retrieved May 17, 2008, from www.cshe.unimelb.edu.au/assessinglearning/

McLaughlin, P., & Simpson, N. (2004). Peer assessment in first year university: How the students feel. *Studies in Educational Evaluation*, 30/2: 135–149.

Mertler, C. (2003). Preservice versus inservice teachers' assessment literacy: Does classroom experience make a difference? Paper presented at the annual meeting of the Mid-Western Educational Research Association, Columbus, OH, October 2003.

Mertler, C. A. (2005). Secondary teachers' assessment literacy: Does classroom experience make a difference? *American Secondary Education*, 33(2), 49–64.

Mousavi, S. A. (2002). *Encyclopedia dictionary of language testing* (3rd ed.). Taipei: Tung Hua Book Company.

Popham, W. J. (2004). All about accountability: Why assessment illiteracy is professional suicide. *Educational Leadership*, 62/1: 82–83.

Rogier, D. (2009). English language teachers' perspectives on assessment. In partial fulfilment of EED 2009 Language Teacher Education module, Exeter, UK: The University of Exeter.

Sadler, D. R. (1998). Formative assessment: Revisiting the territory. *Assessment in Education*, 5: 77–84.

Schafer, W. D. (1993). Assessment literacy for teachers. *Theory into Practice*, 32(2), 118–126.

SERVE Center (2004). Classroom assessment: Assessment literacy. University of North Carolina. Retrieved May 1, 2008, from www.serve.org/Assessment/Classroom/Literacy.php.

Shohamy, E. (1998). Inside the 'black box' of classroom language tests. *Studia Anglica Posnaniensia*, XXXIII: 343–352.

Shulman, L. S. (1986). Paradigms and research programs in the study of teaching: A contemporary perspective. In M. C. Wittrock (Ed.), *Handbook of research on teaching* (3rd ed.). New York: Macmillan.

Stiggins, R. J. (1991). Relevant classroom assessment training for teachers. *Educational Measurement: Issues and Practice*, 10(1), 7–12.

Stiggins, R. J. (1995). Assessment literacy for the 21st century. *Phi Delta Kappa*, 77(3), 238–245.

Stiggins, R. J. (2002). Assessment crisis: The absence of assessment for learning. *Phi Delta Kappa*, 83/10: 758–765.

Stiggins, R. (2007). Conquering the formative assessment frontier. In J. McMillan (Ed.), *Formative Classroom Assessment*. New York, NY: Columbia University Teachers College Press.

Stiggins, R. J., & Conklin, N. (1992). *In teachers' hands: Investigating the practice of classroom assessment*. Albany, NY: SUNY Press.

Stoynoff, S. (2009). A survey of developments in ESOL testing. In C. Coombe, P. Davidson & D. Lloyd (Eds.), *Fundamentals of language assessment: A practical guide for teachers*. Dubai: TESOL Arabia Publications.

TESOL/NCATE Standards. (2003). Retrieved on August 24, 2009, from http://clas.uncc.edu/linguistics/Internal%20documents/NCATEP12Standards.pdf. Alexandria, VA: TESOL.

Troudi, S., Coombe, C., & Al-Hamly, M. (2009). EFL teachers' views of English language assessment in higher education in the United Arab Emirates and Kuwait. *TESOL Quarterly*, 43/3: 546–555.

Volante, L., & Fazio, X. (2007). Exploring teacher candidates' assessment literacy: Implications for teacher education reform and professional development. *Canadian Journal of Education*, 30/3: 749–770.

Wang, T. H., Wang, K. H., & Huang, S. C. (2008). Designing a web-based assessment environment for improving pre-service teacher assessment literacy. *Computers & Education*, 51, 448–462.

White, E. (2009). Are you assessment literate? Some fundamental questions regarding effective classroom-based assessment. *OnCue Journal*, 3/1: 3–25.

Wise, A. E. (Ed.) (1996). Quality teaching for the 21st century (special issue). *Phi Delta Kappa*, 78: 190–224.

Zhang, Z., & Burry-Stock, J. (1997). *Assessment practices inventory: A multivariate analysis of teachers' perceived assessment competence*. Paper presented at the Annual Meeting of the National Council on Measurement in Education, March 1997, Chicago, IL.

CHAPTER 3

Validity in Language Testing

Ramin Akbari

INTRODUCTION

Any instrument designed for the measurement of psychological traits should have a number of features, as a minimum, for it to form a sound basis for educational decisions. A test should produce consistent, error-free results (or to have the minimum possible amount of measurement error), should have enough evidence and theoretical support for the interpretation of its results, and at the same time must be convenient to use in terms of the resources it needs (time, equipment, training for test administrators, ease of scoring etc.).

Consistency of results and being error free are the concerns of reliability, a topic discussed in Chapter 4 of this book. Relevance and theoretical evidence for the interpretations fall within the domain of validity (the present chapter's topic), while ease of administrations and the required logistics are dealt with in discussions of test practicality.

The consensus in language testing is that among the three features of any good test, validity is the most important one since, if there is no validity, there is no test (Oller, 1979). The rest of the chapter provides a brief account of the basics of validity; it first looks at different aspects of validity from a traditional (or classical) perspective, and then moves on to a more recent definition of the concept, which emphasizes the social and interpretive aspects of the term.

WHAT IS VALIDITY? THE TRADITIONAL PERSPECTIVE

The term "validity" became part of the psychological testing literature during the 1950s, as a measure of test quality. Validity in the traditional approaches to psychological measurement is a characteristic of a test, and this is in sharp contrast to what is the dominant perspective nowadays, where validity is no longer the property of the test but of the interpretations that are made of test results.

In the traditional view, validity is defined as the simple question of whether a test measures what it is supposed to measure. For example, a test that is designed to measure vocabulary through analogies, but turns out to measure general intelligence instead, is no longer a valid test since it is not measuring an aspect of language proficiency. In other words, a test should measure the intended skill, ability, or components, and should provide enough proof for its claims to relevance.

This general, and somewhat vague, conceptualization of validity is further elaborated on through breaking the concept into different types of validity: face validity, content validity, criterion-related (or empirical) validity, and construct validity (Harrison, 1983).

Face validity refers to the physical appearance of the test (its print, layout, legibility) and whether the test strikes the test takers, as well as test designers, as relevant to the skill or component it is trying to measure. For example, whether the test takers regard a grammar test as really testing grammar (not vocabulary or first language knowledge) is an aspect of a test's face validity. It should be pointed out here that face validity, however, is viewed as one of the least important members of the validity family and can easily be dispensed with if there are theoretical / practical justifications for using a form that does not strike the test takers as being directly relevant. For example, cloze tests might seem confusing and as a result not a suitable proficiency measure from a test taker's perspective, but the theory behind the test provides ample justification for its use and consequently, face validity can be overruled here. In addition, face validity is the most subjective member of the validity family in the traditional perspective, while other types of validity are more evidence-based and empirical and as a result, relatively less controversial.

Content validity, another member of the validity family, deals with the adequacy of a test in terms of its content or the sample of behavior it sets out to measure. Every test, by definition, includes or elicits a sample of behavior from the test takers, and one of the threats to the soundness of a test stems from the way the sampling is done. Content validity, therefore, checks the representativeness of a test content to make sure content sampling has been carried out in a theoretically justifiable manner.

Content selection is not a difficult challenge for achievement tests since what the test is supposed to measure comes from a predefined domain of a curriculum and / or a textbook. In such cases, test designers first prepare a detailed map of the curricular or textbook content and then start the sampling process by means of a table of specifications. Content selection becomes specifically more challenging when one attempts to design a proficiency test since proficiency is a very difficult concept to define, with no predetermined content domain to select items from. As a result, there is always the risk of construct underrepresentation, or the condition in which less of what should be tested is included in the instrument (Messick, 1996). In addition, the existence of different theories of language proficiency makes content specification a controversial issue since, if proficiency is defined in terms of performance or task completion, the content would be totally different from when the construct is viewed as knowledge and skills.

Having appropriate content is one of the basic requirements of having a good test. However, there is always the risk that our content is not adequate enough (in terms of coverage and relevance), and the scores of our test takers on our test might be different from their scores on similar tests of the same ability or domain. To make sure that our test is a good one and measures what it is supposed to measure, test designers resort to criterion-related validity, which checks the extent to which the results of two tests correspond, or correlate.

Criterion-related validity is a statistical concept whereby a newly designed test's results are correlated with already established tests of the same skill or domain to see the degree of correlation between test takers' scores. The logic here is that if a test accurately measures a certain component or skill of the L2, it should closely correlate with other tests that measure the same component or skill. For example, the results of a vocabulary test designed by a teacher can be correlated with the results of a reputable proficiency test given to the same group of test takers to see the degree of correspondence. If the analyses show that the teacher-made vocabulary test correlates more with the grammar component than the vocabulary part of the criterion test, then the new test is more likely a test of grammar, not of vocabulary (of course, having the same test format for both, since if the formats are different, the correlation results will be affected by test formats too).

Criterion-related validity is usually established in either a concurrent (concurrent validity) or predictive (predictive validity) manner. In concurrent validity, both the newly developed test and the criterion test are administered at the same time to a group of test takers and the scores obtained on both tests are correlated. If the new test shows a strong, positive correlation with the criterion test, then it enjoys concurrent validity. In predictive validity, there is a time gap between the administration of the newly developed test and the criterion test, and sometimes the criterion is not necessarily a test. For instance, a test designed to measure learners' academic aptitude might be administered to a group of students at the beginning of the semester, and then the test designer might wait until the end of the semester to collect data on students' grade point average; a strong, positive correlation here indicates a high degree of predictive validity for the new test. It is not uncommon, of course, for a test to be empirically validated by both concurrent and predictive methods. The most important type of validity, however, is known as construct validity. In other words, a test will not be a test if its construct validity is not established, or if it is compromised.

Construct validity is concerned with the psychological reality of a test, that is, it asks the question of what it means to know a language and what the nature of that knowledge is. Bachman (1990) and Bachman and Palmer (2010), for example, regard knowledge of language, or communicative competence, as comprising of two general types of knowledge: Organizational knowledge, and Pragmatic knowledge. Each of these knowledge types is further divided into smaller knowledge categories of Grammatical and Textual (for Organizational knowledge) and Functional and Sociolinguistic (for Pragmatic knowledge).

Construct validity is both abstract and empirical; abstract in the sense that it must be based on a theory of proficiency or the skill it aims at measuring, and empirical since it must be checked statistically against that theory through highly sophisticated statistical techniques (factor analysis, for instance). Whether a test is a composite of a set of skills or components, or measures each individually and discretely, is related to the question of construct validity. In other words, it is the construct validity that at the end of the day provides the general guidelines as to what goes into a test and what format the test should take.

The ideas discussed so far are mostly part of classical views of validity; these ideas are still relevant and part of any sound test design process. Language testing, however, has become sociopolitically more sophisticated and issues that were not regarded as relevant a few decades ago are now important since the view today is that a test cannot be impervious to the social settings and reality of the lives of test takers for whom the instrument is designed. Since tests have socioeconomic implications and can change people's lives, an acknowledgement and awareness of the social dimension of language testing has become part of the new approaches to test validation.

A New Approach to Validity

Earlier in this chapter, reference was made to the fact that traditional views of measurement regard validity to be a property of the test, while more recent approaches view validity to be concerned with the inferences that are made of test scores. There are still people, however, who regard validity as being test-based and the dispute as to where validity is to be located is far from over (see, for example, Borsboom, Mellenberg, and van Herdeen,

2003, 2004). It is not in the scope of this brief introductory paper to engage in this debate; what is important is being aware of the complexity of interpretations of the term "validity" itself.

The traditional view of validity was psychometric and cognitive, in the sense that it tried to justify the use of a test by making references to the theories behind the ability being measured (for example, theories of language proficiency) and the way individuals possessed or manifested this ability. In spite of the fact that language was, in addition to being cognitive, a social phenomenon, language testing avoided engaging in discussions of the social dimensions and consequences of test use since a reconceptualization of validity was needed for such debates to become academically viable.

It was Messick (1989a, 1989b, 1995, 1998) who proposed a new approach to validity, regarding it as a unified concept that is more concerned with judgment rather than statistics. Messick stated that every test is designed to be used for a purpose, and as a result, the applications to which a test is put should form the foundation for a test's validity. Validity, then, is the process by means of which test designers try to gather evidence for a specific interpretation of test results. In other words, validity is an attempt to know what a test score *means* rather than merely focusing on what a test is trying to measure.

The core of validity, in this conceptualization, is construct validity, and other types of validity would be pieces of *evidence* in support of the construct, which is the final interpretation of test scores; if reference is made to content or structure of tests, it is within this grand scheme of justifying a certain test interpretation. In the words of Messick:

> Validity is an integrated evaluative judgment of the degree to which empirical evidence and theoretical rationales support the *adequacy* and *appropriateness* of *inferences* and *actions* based on test scores and other modes of assessment. . . . Broadly speaking, then, validity is an inductive summary of both the existing evidence for and the potential consequences of score interpretation and use. Hence, what is to be validated *is not the test or observation device as such but the inferences derived from test scores or other indicators* [italics added] – inferences about score meaning or interpretation and about the implications for action that the interpretation entails. (Messick, 1989b: 13)

Messick further deconstructs construct validity into six aspects that provide the required scaffold or framework for establishing the validity of a test. For a test to enjoy construct validity, the following aspects or characteristics must be present: content, substantive, structural, generalizability, external, and consequential.

The content aspect deals with the adequacy of a test's content, its relevance, and appropriacy in terms of difficulty and item design; the substantive aspect is concerned with the theory behind test takers' performance on the items and the way items or tasks relate to the theory. The structural aspect addresses the question of whether the scoring rubric of the test is in accordance with the theory behind the test and has enough rational justification. Generalizability investigates the extent to which test scores and their interpretations can be applied or generalized across samples and contexts, while the external aspect deals with the extent to which a test correlates with other measures of the same component, skill, or ability using the same or different methods of testing. Finally, the consequential aspect focuses on issues of fairness, bias, distributive justice, as well as washback (Messick, 1996).

Messick's theory has added a new dimension to the validity debate, one that brings into the picture the question of social consequences of test use and fairness. Social responsibility, in fact, becomes an extension of validity, requiring test score interpretation to take place in a fair manner: "Validity . . . implies considerations of social responsibility, both to the candidate (protecting him or her against unfair expulsion) and to the receiving institutions" (McNamara and Roever, 2006: 19). The key to this social responsibility, or fairness, is the concept of consistency. Interpretation of test scores should be consistent and rational so that it would be fair across candidates.

To have consistency of interpretation, two threats to validity should be addressed: construct underrepresentation, and construct-irrelevant variance. Construct underrepresentation is concerned with the adequacy of the sample (both in terms of content and task) that a test includes, and the risk that this sample is less than what is the required for real-life performance. If the test content or its sampling prove inadequate and less than what it takes to perform the action in real life, candidates would be erroneously viewed as qualified in the test in spite of the fact that they do not have the ability to function adequately in real communicative situations.

In the case of construct-irrelevant variance, the risk is related to the inclusion of some unwanted, irrelevant factors that can affect the test takers' scores and as a result, lead to incorrect interpretations. For instance, if a test systematically results in better scores for males than for females, then it is contaminated by gender as an illegitimate factor affecting test takers' performance. Test validity, in Messick's view, is the struggle to minimize these two sources of risk.

Messick's model of validity is not without criticism; there are some language testers who find the framework limited, especially when it comes to its social dimension. Critical theorists in education regard any instance of measurement and testing as an act of discrimination in which people in control can exercise power in terms of candidates' gender, social class, and gender. In addition, they argue that any measurement is motivated by a set of values that are chosen and defined by those who are in power and have the means to impose those values on educational systems.

The Relationship between Reliability and Validity

Reliability and validity are closely related in the new approach to second language test development and design. In the traditional approach, however, the relationship is indirect and not completely transparent.

Reliability deals with consistency of measurement and the amount of error that exists in the measurement of a skill, component, or ability. To come up with consistent and rational judgments, it is essential to make sure that construct-irrelevant variance, which is a source of unreliability itself, is minimized. However, construct-irrelevant factors, since they are systematic and as a result consistent for a group of test takers, can result in reliability figures to be over-estimated. A somewhat similar relationship exists between reliability and validity in classical models, but it is not in the scope of this brief paper to delve into this topic.

Conclusion

Language testing is about making decisions, and a test is a tool that provides a relatively reliable, objective means for decision making. A language test as an instrument should meet a number of standards for it to provide a sound basis for measurement and evaluation. Validity is one of the most (if not the most) important features that is concerned with the main purpose for which a test is designed: making correct, justifiable interpretations of the scores and being fair to test takers in measuring their abilities. This process of interpretation requires attention being paid to different aspects of test design and structure, making language testing a discipline aimed at precision, as well as social accountability.

Suggested resources

Bachman, L. & Palmer, A. (2010). *Language assessment in practice*. Oxford: Oxford University Press.

Chapelle, C. (1999). Validity in language assessment. *Annual Review of Applied Linguistics*, 19, 254–272.

Davies, A., & Elder, C. (2005). Validity and validation in language testing. In E. Hinkel (Ed.), *Handbook of research in second language teaching and learning* (pp. 795–813). Mahwah, NJ: Erlbaum.

Fulcher, G., & Davidson, F. (2007). *Language testing and assessment: An advanced resource book*. London: Routledge.

Messick, S. (1996). Validity and washback in language testing. Language Testing, 13, 241–256; *American Psychologist*, 50, 741–749.

Messick, S. (1998). Test validity: A matter of consequence. *Social Indicators Research*, 45, 35–44.

Discussion questions

1. Look at a test you have designed for your class; is it an adequate sample of the course book or domain you have been teaching? What features of your teaching are not included in your test?

2. Have you ever taken a test that you later on thought was not fair? In what respects did the test strike you as lacking enough justification in terms of content and scores?

3. What are the points that you will consider in your test development that have a bearing on your test validity? What precautions would you take to make sure the test will lead to fair interpretations?

4. Do you think validity is a concept that is fixed for a test, or does it change from one sample to the next?

References

Bachman, L., (1990). *Fundamental considerations in language testing*. Oxford: Oxford University Press.

Bachman, L., & Palmer, A. (2010). *Language assessment in practice*. Oxford: Oxford University Press.

Borsboom, D., Mellenbergh, G. J., & van Heerden, J. (2003). Validity and truth. In H. Yanai, A. Okada, K. Shingemasu, Y. Kano, & J. J. Meulman (Eds.), *New developments in psychometrics: Proceedings of the international psychometrics society 2001* (pp. 321–328). Tokyo: Springer.

Borsboom, D., Mellenbergh, G. J., & van Heerden, J. (2004). The concept of validity. *Psychological Review*, 111, 1061–1071.

Harrison, A. (1983). *A language testing handbook*. London: McMillan.

McNamara, T., & Roever, C. (2006). *Language testing: The social dimension*. Oxford: Blackwell Publishing.

Messick, S. (1989a). Meaning and values in test validation: The science and ethics of assessment. *Educational Researcher*, 18, 5–11.

Messick, S. (1989b). Validity. In R. L. Linn (Ed.), *Educational measurement* (pp. 13–103). Washington, DC: American Council on Education and National Council on Measurement in Education.

Messick, S. (1995). Validity of psychological assessment: Validation of inferences from persons' responses and performance as scientific inquiry into score meaning. *American Psychologist*, 50, 741–749.

Messick, S. (1996). Validity of psychological assessment. *American Psychologist*, 50, 741–749.

Messick, S. (1998). Test validity: A matter of consequence. *Social Indicators Research*, 45, 35–44.

Oller, J. W. (1979). *Language tests at schools*. London: Longman.

CHAPTER 4

Principles of Language Assessment

Hossein Farhady

INTRODUCTION

Test development is a long and complex process that requires the implementation of several systematically designed steps. Some of these steps include planning to determine the content of the test, preparing the items, reviewing the items, and piloting the items. This chapter contains a short introduction to the main principles that should be followed by test developers. It briefly introduces the key concepts of validity, reliability, and practicality and provides guidelines for pre-testing or piloting.

The first three steps are described in other chapters of this book (Chapters 5 and 6) and the last step, piloting, will be detailed here. Before piloting the test, we make sure, to the best of our judgment, that the test content is appropriate and that it closely corresponds to the materials upon which it is made, that the items are well written and are in compliance with the rules of item writing, and that necessary modifications are made on the basis of the suggestions made by the reviewers. However, our judgment, no matter how sound it might be, is subjective and needs to be empirically and objectively verified. This is accomplished by piloting which is the administration of the test to a group of examinees who have features similar to those of the target group.

PROPERTIES OF A GOOD TEST

Every assessment should meet three important criteria: validity, reliability, and practicality.

VALIDITY

Validity is certainly the most important single characteristic of a test. If it is not valid, even a reliable test is not worth much. Furthermore, where reliability can be estimated statistically without referring to the content of the test, validity is directly related to the content and form of the test. Validity is defined as "the extent to which a test measures what it is supposed to measure." This means that if a test is designed to measure examinees' language ability, it should measure their language ability and nothing else. Otherwise, it will not be a valid test for the intended purpose.

As an example, suppose a test of reading comprehension is given to a student and on the basis of his test score, it is claimed that the student is very good at listening comprehension. This kind of interpretation may not be valid even if there is a good relationship between reading and listening abilities because that particular score can be a valid indication of the student's reading comprehension ability only. This means that a test can be valid for one purpose but not the other. It also means that validity is not an all-or-none purpose phenomenon, but a relative one.

In order to claim that a test is valid, it should be evaluated from different dimensions. Every dimension constitutes a different kind of validity evidence and contributes to the overall validity of the test. Among many types of validity, three types – face validity, content validity, and criterion-related validity – are considered important. Each will be discussed briefly. For a more comprehensive look at validity, see Chapter 3 of this volume.

I. FACE VALIDITY

Face validity refers to the extent to which the physical appearance of the test corresponds to what it is supposed to measure. For instance, a test of grammar should contain grammatical items and not reading comprehension items. Of course, a test of reading comprehension may very well measure grammatical ability as well; however, that type of test will not show high face validity. It should be mentioned that face validity is perceived of as not a very crucial or a determinant type of validity. In some cases, a test that does not show high face validity has proven to be highly valid by other criteria. For instance, a cloze test is believed to be a valid test of grammar, while it doesn't seem so on appearance. However, appearance of a test may sometimes influence test taker performance and jeopardize the overall validity of a test. As an example, if test takers have the impression that the test will be in multiple-choice form but then they face a fill-in-the-blank form test, even on the same language points, the test will not seem face valid to them and it may influence their performance. Therefore, teachers and administrators should not be overly concerned about the face validity of their tests, but they should not ignore it either.

2. CONTENT VALIDITY

Content validity refers to the correspondence between the content of the test and the content of the materials to be tested. Of course, a test cannot include all the elements of the content that are taught. Nevertheless, the content of the test should be a reasonable and representative sample of the total content to be tested. In order to examine the content validity of a test, a careful examination of the correspondence between the content of the test and the materials to be tested is necessary. This would be possible through scrutinizing the table of specifications designed for the test at the preparation stage of test development (Chapter 6 of this volume). Although content validity, like face validity, is determined subjectively, it is, however, crucial for the overall validity of the test.

3. CRITERION-RELATED VALIDITY

When we are somehow satisfied with face and content validity of the test, we need to compare it to an outside criterion to see whether our test is doing a good job against the criterion. If test takers perform similarly on both tests, then we can claim that the new test is as good as the criterion test. Criterion-related validity, then, refers to the correspondence between the scores on the newly developed test and those of the criterion test. The outside criterion is usually a well-known test whose reliability and validity are already established.

As an example, suppose that a new test of language proficiency is developed by a group of teachers. Since the new test is a proficiency test, TOEFL can be selected as the outside criterion measure of language proficiency. In order to determine the criterion-related validity of the new test, these two tests are administered to a group of students and the two sets of scores are correlated. The degree of correlation is the criterion-related validity index of the new test validated against TOEFL. It means that to the extent that the two tests correlate, they provide similar information on examinees' language proficiency.

Criterion-related validity is of two major types. If the newly developed test is administered along with the criterion test concurrently, the validity index is called concurrent validity. However, when the two tests are given within a time interval, the correlation between the two sets of scores is called predictive validity.

A few points need to be mentioned here. First, in contrast to face and content validity, which are determined subjectively or logically, criterion-related validity is established objectively or empirically. That is why it is often referred to as empirical validity and frequently reported in the literature. Second, in selecting the criterion measure, we should make sure that it is a valid and reliable test itself. That is why standard and international tests such as TOEFL, IELTS, and so on are often selected as outside criteria. Third, when we use criterion-related validity, we should be careful with the interpretation of the validity of our test. That is, we should explain that our test is valid to the extent that the criterion measure itself is valid. Therefore, validity is a relative concept and the question about how the criterion measure itself is validated is a legitimate one. Finally, the criterion should have the same purpose as that of the new test. For instance, it is not appropriate to validate an achievement test against a proficiency test.

No matter how difficult validation procedures might be, it is an inevitable part of the test construction process. Test developers must go through the validation process in order to make sure that the test is measuring what it is designed to measure.

RELIABILITY

Reliability is one of the most important characteristics of a test. In order to understand the concept of reliability, an example may be helpful. Suppose a student takes a test of grammar comprising one hundred items and receives a score of 40. Suppose further that upon the student's quest to improve his or her score, s/he takes the same test two days later and gets a score of 90. Finally, suppose that the teacher doubts his / her second performance and asks the same student to take the same test for a third time. This time s/he gets a score of 70. What would you think of these scores? What would you think of the test? What would you think of the student?

Assuming that the student's knowledge of English cannot change within this short period of time, the best explanation would be that there must be something mysterious about the test. How would you rely on a test that does not produce consistent scores? How can you make sound decisions on the basis of such test scores? This is the essence of the concept of reliability, that is, producing consistent scores. Although the example may demonstrate a very extreme case, it is not, however, impossible. Reliability is technically defined as "the extent to which a test produces consistent scores at different administrations to the same or similar group of examinees." If a test produced exactly the same scores at different administrations to the same group, that test would be perfectly reliable. This perfect reliability, nevertheless, does not practically exist in reality. There are many factors influencing test score reliability. These factors range from examinees' differing mental and physical conditions to the precision of the test items, to the administration, to the number of items in the test, the number of test takers, and scoring procedures. Therefore, reliability is "the extent to which a test produces consistent scores."

Statistically, reliability is represented by the letter "r". Its magnitude fluctuates between zero and 1 as the minimum and maximum degrees of test score reliability. It should be mentioned that "r" is calculated independently without reference to the content or the form of the test. It solely deals with the scores produced by a test. In fact, one can estimate "r" without having much information about the content of the test. Thus, when we talk about the reliability of a test, we refer to the scores and not to the content or the form of the test. This does not mean that the content, the function, or the form of the test influences test reliability. It simply means that we can calculate reliability without referring to the test itself because we only need the scores.

Calculating reliability requires some statistical knowledge which is explained in Chapter 12. In the following section, an attempt is made to explain the procedures in as non-technical terms as possible. Four common methods of estimating reliability will be briefly explained: (1) test–retest, (2) parallel forms, (3) split–half, and (4) KR-21.

I. THE TEST–RETEST METHOD

If we want to see whether a test produces consistent results, the simplest way is to administer it to a group of test takers twice. The first administration is called "test" and the second administration is referred to as "retest". The correlation between the two sets of scores obtained from testing and retesting would determine the reliability. Since there is a time interval (usually more than two weeks) between the two administrations, this kind of reliability estimate is also known as "stability of scores over time."

Although obtaining reliability estimates through the test–retest method seems very simple, it has some practical disadvantages. First, it is not very easy to have the same group of examinees available in two different administrations. Second, if the time interval between the two administrations is short, there might be practice and memorization effects carried over from the first administration. On the other hand, if the interval is too long, there might be a learning effect, that is, the examinees' state of knowledge will not be the same as it was in the first administration. To avoid these problems, other methods of estimating reliability have been developed.

2. PARALLEL FORMS METHOD

In order to remove some of the difficulties with the test–retest method, scholars have developed the parallel forms method. In this method, two parallel forms of a single test are given to one group of examinees. The correlation between the scores obtained from the two tests is computed to be the reliability of the scores. This method has an advantage over the test–retest method in that there is no need to administer the test twice. Thus, the problem related to the length of interval between two administrations is solved. Nevertheless, this method has a shortcoming in that constructing two parallel forms of a test is not an easy task. There are certain logical and statistical criteria that a pair of parallel forms of a test must meet. Therefore, most teachers and test developers avoid this method and prefer to use other methods of estimating reliability.

3. SPLIT-HALF METHOD

In the test–retest method, one group of examinees is needed for two administrations and in the parallel forms method two forms of a single test are needed for a single administration. Each of these methods has its own disadvantages as mentioned in this chapter. To avoid these shortcomings, the split-half method was developed. With this method, a single form of a test is given to a single group of examinees in a single administration. Then each examinee's test is split (divided) into two halves. The correlation between the scores of the examinees in the first half and the second half is calculated to be the reliability of the test scores. Since this method of estimating reliability stems from inside the test assuming that the two halves are equal, it is sometimes referred to as "rational equivalence" or "internal consistency reliability."

Two points should be taken into account in using the split-half method. The first is the concern about dividing the test into two halves that are as equal as possible. The best way to do so is to use odd and even numbered items to form each half, that is, items numbered 1, 3, 5, 7, and so on will constitute the first half, and items numbered 2, 4, 6, 8, and so on will form the second half. The second point is that since the test is divided into two halves, the reliability estimate also relates to one half of the test. To calculate the reliability of the total test, Spearman-Brown's prophecy formula (Brown, 1910; Spearman, 1910) is used to adjust the reliability for the whole test.

$$\text{reliability of the total test} = \frac{2(\text{reliability of one half of the test})}{1 + \text{reliability of one half of the test}}$$

For instance, if the split-half reliability of a test is calculated to be .80, the reliability of the full-length test will be as follows:

$$\text{reliability of the total test} = \frac{2(.80)}{1 + .80} = \frac{1.60}{1.80} = .89$$

As you may notice, the reliability estimate of the whole test is higher than that of one half of the test. This is always the case since the longer the test, the more reliable it tends to be.

4. THE KR-21 METHOD

The previously mentioned methods to estimate test score reliability require a statistical procedure called "correlation." Despite the fact that the majority of teachers and nonprofessional test developers are often familiar with the concept of correlation, to avoid potential complications in calculating correlation, two statisticians – Kuder and Richardson (Kuder and Richardson, 1937) – developed a series of formulae to be used in testing. One of these is used to estimate test score reliability through simple mathematical operations. The formula is called KR-21, with K and R standing for the initials of the two statisticians, respectively, and 21 referring to the number of the formula in the series. This formula is used to estimate the reliability of a single test given to one group of examinees in a single administration. This method requires only the testers to calculate two simple statistical parameters of the mean and the variance of test scores. The methods of computing the mean and variance are explained in Chapter 12.

The KR-21 formula is as follows:

$$\text{KR} - 21 = \left[\frac{K}{K-1} \right] \left[1 - \frac{(M)(K-M)}{KV} \right]$$

Where:

K refers to the number of items in the test;

M represents the mean of test scores; and

V is the variance of test scores.

A numerical example follows:

Suppose a one-hundred-item test is administered to a group of students. The mean and variance are computed to be 65 and 100, respectively. The reliability of the scores will be computed using the KR-21 formula:

$$KR - 21 = \left[\frac{K}{K - 1} \right] \left[1 - \frac{(M)(K - M)}{KV} \right]$$

$$KR - 21 = \left[\frac{100}{100 - 1} \right] \left[1 - \frac{65(100 - 65)}{(100)(100)} \right] = \left[\frac{100}{99} \right] \left[1 - \frac{52,275}{10,000} \right]$$

$$= \left(\frac{100}{99} \right) (1 - .23) = \left(\frac{100}{99} \right) (.77) = .78$$

The procedure may seem a little complex, but with some practice, it will prove easy and very useful. The KR-21 method is the most practical and most commonly used method of estimating reliability.

After covering the first two characteristics of a good test, that is, validity and reliability, in the next section we will briefly explain the next characteristic, namely, practicality.

PRACTICALITY

Practicality refers to facilities available to test developers regarding the development, administration, and scoring procedures of a test. As far as administration is concerned, test developers should be attentive to the possibilities of giving a test under reasonably acceptable conditions. For example, suppose a team of experts decide on giving a listening comprehension test to large groups of examinees. In this case, test developers should make sure that facilities such as audio equipment and / or rooms with suitable acoustics are available. Otherwise, no matter how reliable and valid the test may be, it will not be practical.

Regarding the scoring procedures of a test, we should pay attention to the problem of ease of scoring as well as ease of score interpretation. For instance, most people would agree that composition is a valid test of writing ability. However, using composition for a large number of test takers will not be practical because it requires a huge amount of time and energy to score them.

It should be mentioned that sometimes there are trade-offs between ease of development, administering, and scoring a test. For instance, developing a multiple-choice test is quite time and energy consuming but it is easy to score. On the other hand, essay-type tests are easy to develop but difficult to score. Therefore, test developers and users should keep a balance between high and low practicality factors. It should also be mentioned that when the decisions that are to be made on the test scores are critical and the number of test takers is manageable, we can ignore the practicality factor and use a test which will not normally be used for large-scale administrations.

ITEM CHARACTERISTICS

The purpose of piloting a test is to determine the characteristics of individual items as well as those of the test as a whole. Item characteristics include item facility, item discrimination, and choice distribution. A detailed technical description of these concepts is beyond the scope of this chapter; however, an attempt will be made to explain them in as nontechnical terms as possible.

Generally, a test consists of some items. An item has two main parts: the stimulus and the response. A "stimulus" or a "stem" is the part of the item that poses a problem to be solved, a task to be completed, or a question to be answered. The solution to the problem, the performance on the task, or the answer to the question is called a "response." Since, more often than not, items are in multiple-choice formats we will focus on the characteristics of multiple-choice items in this chapter. In a multiple-choice item, one of the choices is the "correct response" and the others are wrong responses or "distractors." Characteristics of a multiple-choice item include item facility, item discrimination, and choice distribution.

ITEM FACILITY (IF)

Every item in a test should have a reasonable degree of facility appropriate to the objectives of the test and the expected language ability level of the test takers. An item should not be too easy to be answered by both less able or more able test takers. Nor should it be so difficult that no one can answer. Ideally, items should be designed at the ability level of an average test taker. Objectively speaking, an item is appropriate if 50 percent of the test takers respond to it correctly. In a technical sense, the desirable item facility is .50 indicating that 50 percent of the test takers responded correctly. Item facility, then, can be determined by calculating the proportion of correct responses given to a certain item. For example, if 60 out of 100 examinees give correct responses to a particular item, the item facility will be calculated to be .60. The following formula illustrates the point.

$$IF = \frac{\text{Number of correct responses}}{\text{Total number of responses}} = \frac{60}{100} = .60$$

The higher the value of the item facility, the easier is the test item. For example, an item facility of 1 refers to an extremely easy item because all test takers have provided a correct response, and an item facility of zero means that the item is extremely difficult because nobody has given a correct response to that item. Although the desirable value of item facility is .50, not all items meet the desirable facility level in real practice. Nor do we want them to because there must be items below and above the desirable level to encourage less able students and to challenge more able students, respectively. That is, there should be a range of item facility values for test takers within which test developers would keep the items. The acceptable range for item facility depends on, in addition to the content of the item, the number of choices in the item as well, because the more choices, the more chances the test takers will get the correct response without having the necessary knowledge. For example, for items with 2, 3, 4, and 5 choices, test takers have 50, 33, 25, and 20 percent chance of getting the item right, respectively even without having the required knowledge. Therefore, the acceptable range will be the desirable item facility adjusted for the chance probability (chance probability is divided into two halves, and each half is either added to or subtracted from the expected item facility because the chance can work either positively or negatively). Table 4.1 presents the range of acceptable values of item facility for different multiple-choice items.

Number of choices	Calculation	Acceptable range
2 choices (true / false)	.50 + or − .25	.25 − .75
3 choices	.50 + or − .16.5	.33.5 − .66.5 (rounded up to .33 and .67)
4 choices	.50 + or − .12.5	.37.5 − .62.5 (rounded up to .37 and .63)
5 choices	.50 + or − .10	.40 − .60

Table 4.1 Range of acceptable values of item facility for different multiple-choice items

Items with facility indexes below or above the values mentioned in the table are considered either too easy or too difficult. Therefore, depending on the context of assessment, such items are recommended to be either modified or discarded.

ITEM DISCRIMINATION (ID)

One of the many purposes of testing is to distinguish knowledgeable examinees from less knowledgeable ones. Each item of the test, therefore, should contribute to this process by demonstrating a certain degree of power to discriminate examinees on the basis of their knowledge. This power, called item discrimination (ID), is calculated by first ranking the scores on the whole test from the highest to the lowest and then dividing them into two groups: high and low. The number of examinees who have given correct responses to a particular item in each group is counted and used in the following formula to determine the values of item discrimination:

$$\text{Item Discrimination} = \frac{\text{Number of correct responses in the high group MINUS Number of correct responses in the low group}}{{}^{1}/_{2} \text{ of the total number of responses}}$$

Item discrimination, unlike item difficulty, can range from − 1 to + 1. The higher the positive value of ID, the more powerful the item is in discriminating knowledgeable test takers from less knowledgeable ones. The ideal ID value is + 1 which indicates all knowledgeable test takers responded to the item correctly and all less knowledgeable ones missed it. A low value of ID indicates that it does not discriminate between knowledgeable and less knowledgeable test takers. A negative ID means that more knowledgeable test takers missed the item than less knowledgeable ones. Such items usually have a technical problem such as misspelling, tricky distractors, or are miskeyed and should be examined carefully and either modified or discarded. An agreed convention for an acceptable ID range is .40 and above.

CHOICE DISTRIBUTION (CD)

Acceptable IF and ID values are two important requirements for a single item that are based on the number of correct and incorrect responses given to an item. These values are not related to the way distractors have functioned. There are cases where an item may show acceptable IF and ID, but may not have appropriate distractors. In other words, distractors are not selected by the test takers either because they are so obviously wrong, so obviously irrelevant, or so tricky. Therefore, the last step in piloting a test is to examine the quality of the distractors. The hypothetical data presented in Table 4.2 shows the choice distribution of four sample items administered to 100 subjects. The correct choice for all the items is "a," which is shown in Column 1. Other columns show the hypothetical number of participants selecting the distractors.

Item	a	b	c	d
1	55	25	20	0
2	43	41	10	6
3	40	45	10	5
4	50	25	15	10

Table 4.2   Choice distribution of four sample items

Apparently, all items enjoy reasonable facility indexes. However, in Item 1, choice (d) has not been selected by any respondent. This means that it is not contributing to the quality of the item. In other words, the item is in fact a three-choice item rather than a four-choice one. Therefore, the distractor should be modified.

In Item 2 there is a different problem. Despite the fact that the item has a good facility index, a large number of respondents have selected choice (b), which is an incorrect response. This implies that there is something wrong with this distractor, and thus, it should be modified.

In Item 3, the case is more serious than that of Item 1 or 2. In this item, a larger number of test takers have selected the wrong choice rather than the correct choice. This means that the item will show a negative discrimination value, and thus it should be modified.

Item 4 is an example of a good and balanced choice distribution. The reason is that not only has the correct choice been selected by a reasonable number of subjects, but also the other choices have been selected by a good number of test takers as well.

Based on the results of item analysis, items can be classified into three categories of functioning, nonfunctioning, and malfunctioning. Functioning items are those items that show acceptable IF, ID, and CD patterns. Nonfunctioning items refer to items that violate one or more than one of the criteria set for a good item and should be modified. These modifications may include changing a distractor or revising the stem. Malfunctioning items are items with negative ID and should be discarded. When the items are refined and problematic items modified or removed, our assessment will have a set of good items with desirable characteristics. However, having individually acceptable items does not necessarily mean that their combination as a whole test will function appropriately. That is, the assumption that good items will necessarily produce a good test may not always hold true. Therefore, we should take one more step to determine the characteristics of the whole test.

CONCLUSION

This article dealt with the principles of good tests including reliability, validity, and practicality, and the characteristics of a good item including item facility, item discrimination, and choice distribution at the item level. Despite the fact that developing a test with desirable characteristics is a complex and sometimes difficult task, it is absolutely necessary in order to have an acceptable and defendable test, upon which reasonably sound decisions can be made. Therefore, teachers, administrators, and test users should assume great responsibility regarding the quality of the tests they use. Otherwise, making unjustified decisions on the basis of an invalid and / or unreliable test may have unpredictable and serious consequences on the lives of the test takers.

Suggested resources

Kunnan, A. (Ed.) (1998). *Validation in language assessment*. Mahwah, NJ: Lawrence Erlbaum Associates.

Meyer, J. P. (2010). *Reliability*. Oxford: Oxford University Press.

Osterlind, J. S. (1998). *Constructing test items: Multiple-choice, constructed response, performance, and others*. Dordrecht, Netherlands: Kluwer Academic Publishers.

Spolsky, B. (1995). *The development of objective language*. Oxford: Oxford University Press.

Van Blerkom, M. (2009). *Measurement and statistics for teachers*. New York: Routledge.

Weir, C. J. (2005). *Language testing and validation*. Basingstoke: Palgrave Macmillan.

Discussion questions

1. Discuss some factors that could affect the reliability and validity of students' test scores. How can these be prevented?

2. What does your institution do to ensure that the tests they administer are valid and reliable?

3. Which, in your opinion, is more important: validity, reliability, or practicality?

4. Explain how the number of options may influence test performance.

References

Brown, W. (1910). Some experimental results in the correlation of mental abilities. *British Journal of Psychology*, 3, 296–322.

Kuder, G. F., & Richardson, M. W. (1937). Theory and estimation of test reliability. *Psychometrika*, 2(3), 151–160.

Spearman, C. (1904). The proof and measurement of association between two things. *American Journal of Psychology*, 15, 72–101.

Spearman, C. (1910). Correlation calculated from faulty data. *British Journal of Psychology*, 3, 271–295.

CHAPTER 5

The Assessment Development Process

Barry O'Sullivan

INTRODUCTION

In this chapter, I will present a broad outline of the test development process. In doing this, we will be focusing on larger-scale tests in the first sections of the chapter. However, the model of development we suggest in these early sections will, in the second part of the chapter, be adapted for use in the classroom testing context. I should stress here that test development is a team effort. Whether we are creating a test for a single group of learners or for an international market, it is always best to work as closely as possible with colleagues at all stages of the development process. As a test writer I may feel that the focus of my test is clear, but often I am too close to the test and cannot see its weaknesses.

GETTING STARTED

Before putting pen to paper to actually write a test, there are a number of things you will need to consider. The first of these relates to how you intend to go about the job of identifying all of the things you will need to do to deliver your test. In this section we will review a model of test development which will help you at this early stage.

One model of test development that has been suggested by Cambridge ESOL is shown in Figure 5.1 (overleaf). The most important features of this figure are the identification of the main stages, and the stressing of the need for constant review and monitoring of the process.

PLANNING AND DESIGNING THE TEST

In the planning stage, all of the initial decisions are made. By the end of this stage, we should have a good general idea of what is possible, given the restrictions of the test context (e.g., we may have only a limited number of examiners to deliver a speaking test so we

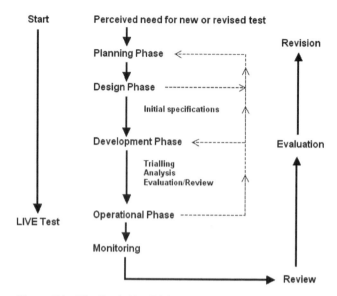

Figure 5.1   The Cambridge ESOL Test Development Model (Saville, 2003)

might either need to expand the testing period or opt for a recording of each performance to be marked later by the examiners).

Of course, before we can get started we must ensure that all participants are very clear about the test takers for whom the test is intended and also of the purpose of the proposed test. The team needs to be explicit when describing exactly what the test will be used for and what inferences we plan to draw from performance on the test. An example of this is where we plan to infer that a person who performs well on a particular test will have demonstrated his / her readiness to move on to the next level of a language preparatory program. If the preparatory program is to work, we really need to be able to define each transition stage (between levels) as accurately as possible to ensure smooth progression through the system for the successful learner.

This part of the process often takes place in a relatively informal setting. We tend to throw out ideas to the team who question them from a number of perspectives, such as:

- Does the proposed test (or task) "fit" with the profile of the test takers (e.g., in terms of their age, culture, gender mix, and language-learning experience)? Will the task motivate or demotivate some test takers? (And how do we know this; there is evidence from oral testing research which shows that when we compare what examiners and test takers say about the topics introduced in these tests there can be a considerable mismatch, even where examiners believe they are familiar with the language and culture of the test takers.)
- How does it "fit" with the inferences we wish to draw? (That is, is this task or item likely to elicit the kind of language that we are planning to assess – e.g., if we are trying to elicit descriptive language in a test of speaking, is the task likely to result in this type of language being used?)
- How will we assess performance? (If we are focusing on grammatical knowledge will we test it by including a "grammar" criterion in a speaking or writing test or will we create a multiple-choice test or a selective deletion cloze in order to test knowledge more explicitly?)

- Is the task replicable? (That is, will it be possible to make more versions of this task that are equivalent in terms of the cognitive processing involved and the likely linguistic output generated?)
- Will it fit into the time-scale we have in mind for the test? (That is, if we plan to have about five or six tasks, and this seems to require 20 minutes of test taker time, it is likely to be impractical to use it – particularly if the amount or range of language elicited is not great.)

So the questions tend to range from the theoretical to the practical. Once we are reasonably happy with the general idea for the design we begin the process of writing up the test specifications and then move to the task design stage in which these specifications will be formalized (though not necessarily finished – the specifications are a living document that may change as we constantly review the different parts of the test during the process). At this point we are drawing a quick sketch of what the test might look like; I say *might* because experience tells us that things change as we try out various ideas.

The Design Statement Table (Table 5.1) is an example of the typical things that will be decided (though not finally – things may still change as the development process continues) during this stage of the process.

Overall design	
Purpose	What is the overall purpose of the test (e.g., university entrance, exit, placement, etc.)?
Intended population	Describe here the test-taking population in as much detail as possible, using the notion of test taker characteristics as a guide (obviously include only potentially relevant parameters).
Intended decisions / stakes	Related to Purpose. Will the test be high or low stakes? (High-stakes tests are seen by the student as being of great importance; low stakes are perceived by students as not being so important.)
Response format	Multiple-choice questions; short-answer format questions; matching questions; essay / composition tasks; "live" or recorded speech
Number of examiners	State total number required (and role: invigilator, marker, etc.).
Number of candidates	State total number and likely group numbers, i.e., for essay type – number per classroom; for speaking – number per test event (e.g., two or three).
Number of tasks / items	State number.
Order of tasks	Where a specific order is required state here.
Weighting of tasks / items	Will all tasks / items be seen as equal in value?
Scoring	MCQ/SAF questions: answer key; rating scale / rubric: holistic or analytic (other?)
Reporting type	Single score or profile (score for individual sub-skills)?

(continued overleaf)

(ctd.)	
Assumptions regarding the test population	
Background knowledge	To what extent do you know this, and how might this level of your knowledge of the population impact on decisions regarding tasks, topics, and format?
Language knowledge	State the level at which the population is expected to be. This can be done in terms of the CEFR or any locally known criteria.
Resources required	
Resources for development	Based on what you have decided to date, what are the resources likely to be required to proceed? This can refer to people, room space, technology, etc.
Resources for delivery	What are the resources that will be needed for the delivery of the test? Can refer to people, space, material production, post / delivery.

Table 5.1   Overall design statement

THE DEVELOPMENT PHASE

In this phase, we begin to think more clearly about the details of the test. We again turn first to the test candidates. We will have considered in the previous stage who they are, why they will take this test, and their experience of this type of assessment. When we are certain that the likely candidates are as clearly defined as possible, we turn to look at the potential tasks, that is, those that are likely to elicit the kind of language we are planning to assess. Once this has been done, we must work on the specifications, which will include examples of the kind of tasks or items we decide to use. To be useful, the specifications should:

- present the purpose of the test (what it will be used for);
- contextualize the test (where it will be used and who will take it);
- describe the test in detail, with examples of test tasks / items (what it will look like);
- list the resources required to administer the test (what we need to deliver the test); and
- describe the test-scoring processes (who will do this and how will it be done).

Obviously, this phase of the process takes some time, as the team will pre-pilot (i.e., try out the task informally with a small number of learners who match the profile of the typical test taker defined earlier) the tasks / items before thinking of including them even at this early stage.

The following two tables suggest, in detail, the things to consider when preparing the tasks (Table 5.2) and when developing the scoring system (Table 5.3). It is not necessary to respond to all of the parameters (rows) in these figures when developing your test, but it would be wise to at least consider them (you might decide, for example, that your writing assessment will have a single task, so a number of decisions will be made for you before you begin). For a more detailed description of the terminology in the tables presented here see Weir (2005).

Task development parameters	
Settings: Task	
Purpose	The requirements of the task; allow candidates to choose the most appropriate strategies and determine what information they are to target in the text in comprehension activities and to activate in productive tasks.
Response format	How candidates are expected to respond to the task (e.g., MCQ as opposed to short answers); different formats can impact on performance.
Known criteria	Letting candidates know how their performance will be assessed; means informing them about rating criteria beforehand (e.g., rating scale available on Web page).
Weighting	Goal setting can be affected if candidates are informed of differential weighting of tasks before test performance begins.
Order of items	Usually in speaking tests this is set, not so in writing tests.
Time constraints	This can relate either to pre-performance (e.g., planning time) or during performance (e.g., response time).
Intended operations	A broad outline of the language operations required in responding to the task. May be seen as redundant as a detailed list is required in the following section.
Demands: Task (note: this relates to the language of the INPUT and of the EXPECTED OUTPUT)	
Channel	In terms of input this can be written, visual (photo, artwork, etc.), graphical (charts, tables, etc.) or aural (input from examiner, recorded medium, etc.). Output depends on the ability being tested.
Discourse mode	Includes the categories of genre, rhetorical task, and patterns of exposition
Text length	Amount of input / output
Writer / speaker relationship	Setting up different relationships can impact on performance (e.g., responding to known superior, such as a boss, will not result in the same language as when responding to a peer).
Nature of information	The degree of abstractness; research suggests that more concrete topics / inputs are less difficult to respond to than more abstract ones.
Topic familiarity	Greater topic familiarity tends to result in superior performance. This is an issue in the testing of all sub-skills.
Linguistic	
Lexical range	These relate to the language of the input (usually expected to be set at a level below that of the expected output) and to the language of the expected output. Described in terms of a curriculum document or a language framework such as the CEFR.
Structural range	
Functional range	

(continued overleaf)

(ctd.)	
Interlocutor	
Speech rate	Output expected to reflect that of L1 norms. Input may be adjusted depending on level of candidature. However, there is a danger of distorting the natural rhythm of the language, and thus introducing a significant source of construct-irrelevant variance.
Variety of accent	Can be dictated by the construct definition (e.g., where a range of accent types is described) and / or by the context (e.g., where a particular variety is dominant in a teaching situation).
Acquaintanceship	There is evidence that performance improves when candidates interact with a friend (though this may be culturally based).
Number	Related to candidate characteristics – evidence that candidates with different personality profiles will perform differently when interacting with different numbers of people.
Gender	Evidence that candidates tend to perform better when interviewed by a woman (again can be culturally based), and that the gender of one's interlocutor in general can impact on performance.

Table 5.2   Considerations for task development

Scoring system parameters	
Scoring plan	How will the scoring be done? Will it be done online or with hard copies (particularly important with recent changes in assessing writing)? How will the scores be recorded? If an answer key is used, who will manage the scoring, how will the scores be recorded?
Criteria (rating scale / rubric)	What type of scale / rubric will be used? Who will develop it? How? How will it be tried out and evaluated?
Answer key	What will be the form of the answer key (photocopied overlay, list of correct responses, etc.)? Who is responsible for making it, who for checking it?
Rater selection	What will the minimum requirements be for prospective raters / markers?
Rater training and standardization	What approach will be taken? Who will do it? Where? When? Will it be monitored? etc.
Accreditation	Will this initial training qualify raters / markers to work on your test for a fixed period (e.g., one or two years), or will there be no limitations after training?
Rating procedures	The rules and regulations for raters / markers – may need to write a formal document
Rating conditions	Where and when will rating / marking take place?
Moderation	How will the rating process be monitored? Who will do it? How will it be reported? etc.
Statistical analysis	Will there be any specific types of analysis used to help generate scores (e.g., multi-faceted Rasch)? What types of analysis will be used to calculate inter- and intra-rater reliability?

Table 5.3   Considerations for scoring system development

TEST ADMINISTRATION AND MONITORING

All aspects of test administration must be controlled as much as possible. Table 5.4 shows the type of things we need to consider with regard to administration, and stresses the need to provide clear, written instructions or guidelines, which must be followed. If this is not done it may not be possible to use the test results for comparative purposes as changing the conditions under which an assessment is done also changes the assessment.

Administration parameters	
Physical conditions	room layout guidelines / procedures (seating of candidates and / or examiners; positioning of invigilators); lighting requirements; background noise limits; pre- and post-assessment considerations (waiting place; entry / exit routes); development of guidelines
Uniformity of administration	setting and monitoring of test structure, timing; monitoring of physical conditions; development of guidelines
Test security	delivery of tests to centers; storage pre- and post-administration at centers; invigilation during administration (who, how many, location in room, monitoring); development of guidelines
Resources required	review actual situation during design and development stages; development of guidelines

Table 5.4   Considerations for test administration

Test development is not static. Even where a test is used only once, the test writer can learn a great deal from the experience. This knowledge can come from an evaluation of the testing process and product (the resulting candidate scores).

The testing process is typically evaluated through: (i) observations ("live" and / or video-taped); (ii) post-test interviews (formal and / or informal with interviewers and / or stakeholders); and (iii) questionnaires (open or closed format with interviewers and / or stakeholders).

Through these procedures, the test writer and user can learn a great deal about the usefulness of a particular test, and can more validly draw inferences from the results given to candidates. In fact, the impact of violation of test administration instructions on the validity of inferences drawn from an administration of a test is a topic that has been rarely discussed in the testing literature. An example of this is where learners are asked to perform a scanning task in a reading test. If the developer has indicated that the task should take five minutes then it is important that this time is given to all test takers. If one examiner allows more (or less) time, then we cannot compare how well his / her test takers performed on the task with those of an examiner who has stuck to the time allowed, so the integrity of the test is called into question.

Of course the test will have to be monitored at all times. The design stage contains many potential pitfalls which the alert test developer must check over. During the administration it is necessary to oversee all aspects of the test and to note any problems, so that they can be addressed either for future administrations or for possible passing criterion re-evaluation.

After the test it is necessary to review all possible aspects of the test, including the items or tasks, all procedures as well as the test administration. The test can be looked at longitudinally, to check that it is still functioning well – changes in society, in language, and in our understanding of language learning and assessment mean that even the best-prepared test will have only a limited shelf life unless it is constantly reviewed.

WRITING CLASSROOM TESTS

I feel that there is almost no difference between the way in which a teacher should develop a classroom test and the way any major test is produced. As we will see in this section, the phases of development are certainly the same, though the content of those phases will, of course, differ to some extent.

PHASE 1: THE PERCEIVED NEED FOR A TEST

While test developers usually act on perceived commercial opportunities or on requests from other commercial or state organizations (e.g., the TOEIC was developed by ETS following a request from the Japanese Ministry for Trade and Industry while the Cambridge BEC suite was developed following a request by the Chinese government), the teacher usually produces tests for specific classes following a strict assessment schedule endorsed by the school (or local education board, or ministry, or all three).

However, the teacher may decide to develop a quiz or diagnostic test to use for formative purposes with his / her class at any time. In this case, all decisions from this point on are in the hands of the teacher.

PHASE 2: DESIGN

While major test developers will tend to focus on identifying the target language of the test (what is to be tested), the profile of the test population, and the suitability of test task or item types, most teachers already know this information and therefore do not feel they need to write the information down in a formal document. While I agree that the teacher does not need to do the research required of a major test developer, it is not such a bad idea to develop a profile of the class, which can then be updated.

In terms of the other design decisions, it might be useful to create a table like the one in Table 5.5. I have completed the table for an imaginary class to give you an idea of the level of detail that would be useful. A table such as this is not totally necessary, of course, as teachers tend to know their students better than anyone, but it nevertheless serves to make you stop to think about the details of what you are testing, how you plan to do it, and why. The rationale supporting the use of a test outline sheet like this (in fact it's a very basic specification) is the same as for writing a lesson plan. Since no self-respecting teacher would consider working without such a plan, why would he / she consider putting a test together without something similar?

At this point in time you are just thinking about the design and you may well change your mind later when you try to write the test; you may, for example, have a great idea for an item or task but then not be able to replicate it in the test.

PHASE 3: DEVELOPMENT

As with any major test, at this point you decide on the number of items or tasks, taking into account your knowledge of the students and the time available. As well as this we consider the nature of the tasks – if we are making a writing test there will be very few (one or two usually); if the items are multiple-choice questions (MCQ), then there may be a lot (likely to be over 20) if the test is to be reliable.

Parameter	Detail
Students	Level 3, all girls (about 15 years old), no repeaters
Type of test	quiz
Purpose of the test	to check that the class has grasped the use of the present perfect to express experience (Unit 3); to identify problem areas for review (class or individual)
The language to be tested	present perfect to express experience
What students should be able to do with the language	demonstrate that they understand what is meant; produce the language in written form
Task / item types	MCQ for recognition, e.g.: I have been to Ireland. A B C A B C SAQ for production, e.g.: I _____ to Ireland. X = exact time ⁝ = sometime
Resources required	space: classroom time: 10 minutes copies: one copy of the test plus answer sheet per student other: none
Reporting	no scores – just verbal feedback to individuals all correct – fine, no problem at all some incorrect – pretty good, just need to work on ____ a lot incorrect – need some additional work (use worksheets) all incorrect – complete review of Unit 3 **Note:** students in last two levels should retake quiz after they do some revision
Test analysis	check if no student could answer an item – there might be a problem with the item

Table 5.5   Example specification for a beginner level reading task

Most teachers have never seen a test specification, and may not really know how it might be used. For classroom tests, the specification is really there to help the teacher remember all of the things that need to be taken into consideration. Some will be completed very easily, while others may present more of a problem. Again, a table such as that shown in Table 5.6 is a good idea to help the teacher to structure his / her specification. You can see that this is almost exactly the same as was suggested for major tests.

Task demands	Description
Format	quiz
Purpose	diagnostic
Response format	MCQ
Time constraints	5 minutes for this part
Intended operations	use of the present perfect to express experience
Test demands	
Input	
Number of items	8
Channel	written
Text length	maximum of 8 words for input text 3 options (visual only based on timeline – like in Unit 3)
Nature of information	concrete statements
Lexical range	based on the official word list for Level 3; no off-list words
Content knowledge	familiar (personal & daily life)
Output	
Channel	MCQ selection
Scoring	
Scoring plan	no scores to be given, just verbal feedback, e.g.: all correct – fine, no problem at all some incorrect – pretty good, just need to work on ____ a lot incorrect – need some additional work (use worksheets) all incorrect – complete review of Unit 3 check all items later to see if any are too easy (all students got it right for example) or too difficult (change for the next time the test is used)

Table 5.6 Example specification for the reception part of the quiz

Whereas an examination board will need to trial the tasks or items extensively, the teacher will generally know what will or will not work with his / her students. However, if a new task or item type is to be introduced to a class, it's not a bad idea to try it out before using it in a test.

PHASE 4: OPERATIONAL

When the test is being taken by the students, it is a good idea to take some notes about the administration. These might focus on:

- The timing – Is it adequate or more / less than adequate?
- The rubric – Are the instructions clear? Do the students need to ask for clarification? If so, note where the problem lies and make a note of what you said to clarify it.

PHASE 5: MONITORING

Some major examination boards put a lot of resources into monitoring and analyzing their tests. Every administration is scrutinized qualitatively (e.g., feedback from examination centers and examiners – and occasionally from candidates) and quantitatively (analysis of items, tasks, etc.). For achievement tests, it is a good idea to perform basic item or task analysis as the sensible teacher will reuse tests over a number of years and needs to know that the test parts are working well. Remember, we should not be surprised if all learners answer a question correctly on an achievement test (after all, we hope they have all learned what we have been teaching), so we focus mostly on questions that have not been answered very well in our analysis (the question might have been unclear; the answer key may have been wrong; the learners may not have studied the aspect of language being tested).

For formative tests, the pressure to perform this type of analysis is far lower. We would still hope that teachers will look at the test performances (i.e., response sheets) to see that no item is either far too easy or far too difficult, as these items may be poor and tell us very little about the students' ability.

Another part of monitoring is a review of the test content and specifications and of the administration. It is definitely worth taking a little time to do this as all information can add to the value of the test, making it better all the time. The test that has been monitored in this way can form the basis of a test bank. This can be a folder in which the teacher stores all tests he / she develops over time, together with the design sheet and specifications. For achievement tests, which will probably be more complex than quizzes having more sections possibly testing slightly different things, it would be a better idea to store by task rather than by test. For teachers who are familiar with computers, this bank would be even better stored (or archived) in a folder created for the purpose.

CONCLUSION

In this chapter we have looked at the test development process. The procedures described here may seem linear, in that we move from one stage systematically to the next. In fact the process is much more iterative – we do something (e.g., make a decision about a task or marking system) and review how this impacts on the rest of the test. This often means revising our thoughts on the content of the test on a regular basis during the development process. And this involves quite a lot of constructive criticism by team members, something teachers are very well accustomed to from their training.

The value of adopting a systematic approach to test development should by now be clear, since the process is quite complex. It should also be clear that while classroom-based assessment may not require the same level of exactitude as a large-scale test, we are essentially looking at the same set of test development procedures for both.

Suggested resources

Alderson, C., Clapham, C., & Wall, D. (1995). *Language test construction and evaluation.* Cambridge: Cambridge University Press.

Brown, J. D. (1996). *Testing in language programs.* Upper Saddle River, NJ: Prentice-Hall. Republished by McGraw-Hill in 2005.

Brown, J. D. (1998). *New ways of classroom assessment.* Alexandria, VA: TESOL.

Coombe, C., Folse, K., & Hubley, N. (2007). *A practical guide to assessing English language learners.* Ann Arbor, MI: University of Michigan Press.

Hughes, A. (2003). *Language testing for teachers.* Cambridge: Cambridge University Press.

Discussion questions

1. What is the main difference between a test developer and an individual classroom teacher at the planning stage of the development phase?

2. "As a teacher, I should create specifications for every test and quiz I use in a class." Think about why you agree or disagree with this statement.

3. Based on what you have read in this chapter you should now be ready to think about what you might include in a test specification for one of your classroom tests. Think about what you would or would not need to include for the specification to be useful for you or a colleague.

References

Saville, N. (2003). The process of test development and revision within UCLES EFL. In W. C. J. & M. Milanovic (Eds.), *Continuity and innovation: Revising the Cambridge Proficiency in English examination 1913–2002* (Vol. 15). Cambridge: Cambridge University Press.

Weir, C. (2005). *Language testing and validation: An evidence-based approach.* Oxford: Palgrave.

CHAPTER 6

Developing Test Specifications for Language Assessment

Fred Davidson and Glenn Fulcher

INTRODUCTION

Educational and psychological testing (in general) and language testing (in particular) are applied intellectual enterprises. Testers develop tests, and doing so compels them to put their beliefs and theories into practical working forms: the actual items or tasks on a test. A key tool for test development has been test specifications, or "specs," also sometimes called "test blueprints."[1]

A test spec is a generative document from which multiple equivalent test items or tasks can be produced. Typically, a spec has two elements: guiding language and at least one sample item. The guiding language sets out the rationale, background, description of resources, and other details to justify and explain the particular items being created. The sample item is an exemplar; and often, specs have more than one sample item.[2] The format of test specs differs based on the rhetorical style of a given test development group. In addition, a spec may have some added elements, as when (for example) the spec sets forth an entire rating system rather than a particular item or task – such a spec would also include a scoring rubric and materials to train raters.

Specs evolve over time and can engender creative dialogue and debate among test developers as we will illustrate with the following example in Figure 6.1. In this example, the "General Description," "Prompt Attributes," and "Response Attributes" are all part of the guiding language, and one sample item is given.[3]

The sample spec in Figure 6.1 produces an item that requires very close and careful reading, and in this case, it focuses on the particular skill of reading statistics that appear in many modern-day texts. We encourage readers to review this spec critically. What are its weaknesses? What can be improved? How are statistics typically rendered in text, such as newspapers? Does the item produced by this spec adequately reflect the real world? Questions such as these cause critical reflection on the theoretical presumptions and rationales behind the test item.

Title: Reading about Statistics in Text: Mathematics word problems

General Description:

The purpose of this item type is to test a student's ability to read and interpret basic descriptive statistics presented in a brief text item stem. The statistical report is from some scientific survey or study and refers to common everyday knowledge. The interpretation is assessed through five multiple-choice responses. One choice is correct. The other four choices -- the distractors -- are wrong because they misinterpret the report in subtle ways. Close reading is required to distinguish between the choices.

Sample Item [Only the material shown in the box is given at the Web site -- the rest of this spec is reverse-engineered]:

Four out of five doctors like Brand X. Which <u>must</u> be true?

   A. Five doctors were surveyed.

   B. Exactly four doctors like Brand X.

   C. More than five doctors had to be surveyed.

   D. Exactly 100 doctors had to be surveyed.

   E. An average of 80% of the doctors surveyed liked Brand X.

[The intended correct choice appears to be ''E'' but is not given in the source.]

Source: IMAGE Mathematics Sample Items Grade 11
www.isbe.net/assessment/PDF/IMAGEGrade11.pdf

Prompt Attributes:

The stem will have two sentences. The first sentence of the stem of the item will present a statistical report or result. Typical forms for such reports include proportions (X out of Y report Z) and averages (the typical X has/does Y). The second sentence of the stem will always read: ''Which <u>must</u> be true?'' The distractors will be wrong because certain mathematical interpretation is **not** possible given the particular language either included (e.g., 'exactly' given in ''B'' above) or not included (e.g., 'at least' **not** given in ''A'' above). The correct choice will be that which is true given a strict and limited reading of the stem.

Response Attributes:

The student will select the intended correct choice in order to get value for the item. In doing that selection, the student will (a) apply mathematical principles of statistical analysis, and (b) by close detailed reading, compare and contrast the various interpretations shown in the five choices.

Figure 6.1   Sample specification[4] (cited in Davidson, 2003)

We encourage readers and their colleagues to enhance this spec so that it (a) does reflect the way that statistical information is rendered in real-world text, and (b), more crucially, so that it might meet the needs of readers' local educational settings.[5]

Traditionally, test specifications have had a purely generative role, as shown in Figure 6.2. The spec in Figure 6.1 is – quite intentionally – problematic. Were it to be trialed, we might not get the results we expected. Even earlier in the process, as item writers try to write equivalent items from this spec, they may (to be quite frank) rebel and claim that it does not really represent the target language skill.

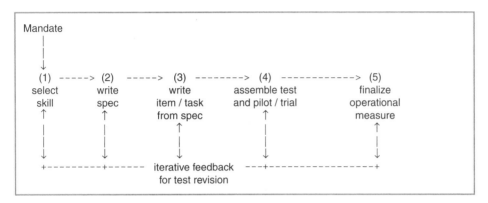

Figure 6.2 The traditional role of test specifications in stages of test development (Davidson and Lynch, 2002: 15)

Tradition would respond to such criticism by compelling the item writers to stifle their discontent and just produce items as required. In such traditional use, the spec would have been written by some core authorities, and once the spec is set (by them), it is not really open to debate. If items generated by this sample spec do not perform well in piloting or trialing, the system would probably jettison the entire spec, or minimally, the spec may be revised – but only by those central authorities, and probably without consultation with the item writers.

However, a spec can assume a much more productive and pro-active role. At a minimum, if item writers are consulted and do indeed have substantive input on revisions to the spec from Stage (3) back to Stage (2) in Figure 6.2, then the item writers are empowered and can affect the design of the entire assessment.

Kim (2006) involved test takers in the development of his test, and he argued forcefully that their input was crucial to the test's overall validity argument. He also involved key stakeholders, such as the coordinator of the language program for whom the test was intended, and he compares the influence of that coordinator with the feedback received from test takers.

A spec like that shown in Figure 6.1 may become operational and – perhaps in a redacted form for test security – it may become part of the test's Web site.[6] In commercial testing, marketing departments often want sample test questions and some language of rationale as they communicate with potential test clients. This wider sphere of communication would, in turn, yield useful feedback to the test developers about their spec, possibly leading to improvement that is responsive to an increasingly wider array of stakeholders and/or revision specs to suit the needs of particular clients.

Figure 6.2 begins with the notion of a "mandate," which is "the combination of forces which help to decide what will be tested and to shape the actual content of the test" (Davidson and Lynch, 2002: 77). Perhaps, in an ideal social climate, increasingly wider circles of feedback can beneficially affect test design, and in turn, increase validity. There is a price to pay, namely, that the mandate becomes a target of debate. Societies deed to testing companies and agencies the responsibility to build tests. In many nations, this authority is written into regulation and even into law, and the crafting of tests is done by an agency of national government (e.g., a ministry of education). If wide democratic debate is fostered about test specs, then such centralized authority is threatened. We encourage our readers to pause a moment and think about a simple question: What is the proper role for the centralized authorities who produce tests – how far out should they cast to receive feedback?

Our example in Figure 6.1 suggests a particular stance about a particular target language skill. The agency that developed this question responded to a number of influences and made some key decisions about that target skill, and this question resulted. The agency responded to a mandate. At a minimum, if this item's developers subsequently seek feedback from many sources (item writers, stakeholders, pilot data, even visitors to its Web site), then the authorities who chose this item type may stop and think and reconsider their response to their mandate. We contend that such minimal authoritative reconsideration is part of good testing practice, from time to time. How can it be fostered? The first step is to ensure that the test developers have specs and that the specs are actually congruent with the items being developed. This is not always the case, as such congruence is a matter of diligent quality control. If no specs are available or if none can be found, then the true first step is reverse engineering.

Reverse engineering is the production of test specs when all that is available is a set of items or tasks (Davidson and Lynch, 2002: 41–44). Fulcher and Davidson (2007: 57–58) suggest several types of reverse engineering, but essentially, the process falls into two broad categories: straight and critical. Straight reverse engineering is when the sample item is thought to be stable and not open to criticism, and so the function of the new spec is to produce equivalent test questions without changing the test rationale. Critical reverse engineering is when the spec seeks to alter or to improve the test item in some way. Our experience has been that it is very hard to do straight reverse engineering, as some improvement seems to creep in, even if very minor. Nevertheless, we have been involved in testing projects where the client said (in unambiguous terms) that all we were to do is produce equivalent test versions.

Returning to the statistics-in-reading item in Figure 6.1, if wider feedback did suggest this item was poorly constructed, and if the core authorities agreed with that criticism – perhaps realizing it for the first time – then even those authorities would have a simple option: to revise the spec before they – again – gave it to item writers for the production of new questions. Critical reverse engineering by the core authorities seems, to us at least, always justifiable. For example, the authorities may realize that the spec does not have any theoretical statement about how statistics are rendered in text.[7] At a minimum, the authorities may review the literature on reading and add some citations to the spec, so as to better justify what they are attempting to do. We have found that such feedback (e.g., from item writers) works even better if the item writers are empowered to actually edit the test spec, but to be quite honest, that is not always necessary.

A far better way to take advantage of critical dialogue about specs is to build a test using specs from the outset, and to seek feedback from as many informed parties as politically feasible. In such spec-driven testing, the entire enterprise is aimed at producing the specs and not at just producing the tests themselves (at least not initially). The specs go through multiple versions, and over time and debate and piloting and quiescence, the specs stabilize and become productive and generative, all before the test booklets are created. The changes in the spec versions can be audited to provide evidence for a validity argument (Davidson and Lynch, 2002: 9).

Li (2006) researched the use of audit trails in spec-driven testing. She presented her audits in a four-part model: (a) how it was – that is to say, how the spec appeared prior to the feedback; (b) the feedback itself; (c) how the spec changed; and (d) reflection notes by the test developer. It is particularly interesting to note that the testing team went beyond the feedback received when the spec was revised:

```
[a] How it was [as excerpted from] Spec version 0.5:
   ''This section is not the overall assessment procedure.
Its purpose is to verify the identity of the test taker.
This section will last approximately one minute.''
   [b] Feedback [received from a rater in the pilot
testing]:
   "I like what is written so far with this, but shouldn't
we have a quick explanation of what will be happening
during the assessment time frame? For example, in
Section One, in addition to Verification, the rater would
state 'for the next 10 to 15 minutes, I will be leading
you through a series of questions. There are no right or
wrong answers; we will simply have a conversation. From
our conversation, I will be able to recommend to your
employer [whether] any English language training courses,
if at all, [are] required.'''
   [c] How it changed [in] Spec version 0.6:
   The spec writers added a section explaining the
purpose of the candidate verification as well as detailed
instructions for test takers.
   [d] Reflection notes:
   Test instructions are the major means by which the
test takers are informed about what they are supposed
to do to accomplish a task. To draw appropriate and
meaningful inferences about the test takers' ability
to use English to perform tasks in a particular domain,
test developers should straightforwardly specify the
instructions for test takers. Otherwise, the inference
drawn from the test performance would be affected.
   To enhance test quality, the spec writers need to
develop instructions that are as explicit as possible.
The feedback received points out this need, so the spec
writers added a detailed explanation of what would happen
during the verification. They also added explanation of
what would happen during other sections.
```

Figure 6.3   Sample audit from Li (2006, 49–51)

Fulcher and Davidson (2007) discuss effect-driven testing. This is a notion that borrows heavily from the philosophical school of pragmatism (see, for example, Menand, 1997), in which the nature of a thing is its effect. Modern educational and psychological testing is intrinsically effect-driven, and test consequence is a viable and valued element in validity arguments. Fulcher and Davidson argue that test effect should be incorporated into test development from the outset, from the very genesis of the earliest versions of test specs. Li's audit (Figure 6.3) should improve the effect of the test's introductory stage.

Suggested resources

Davidson, F., & Lynch, B. K. (2002). *Testcraft. A teacher's guide to writing and using language test specifications*. New Haven and London: Yale University Press.

Fulcher, G., & Davidson, F. (2007). *Language testing and assessment: An advanced resource book*. London: Routledge.

Discussion questions

1. Do you think the developers of the item in Figure 6.1 considered the effect or was their focus elsewhere?

2. If the test is populated with specs like the one in Figure 6.1 and if the test (really) measures close reading skills rather than the ability to read natural text, what signal is the test sending to teachers who are preparing students?

3. If the Figure 6.1 spec were audited (in the manner suggested by Li), what kind of feedback and reflection might ensue?

References

Davidson, F. (2003, April). Crafting a test of academic language proficiency: Some comments on reverse engineering and certain philosophical tensions in large-scale testing. Presented at the American Educational Research Association, Chicago, United States.

Davidson, F., & Lynch, B. K. (2002). *Testcraft. A teacher's guide to writing and using language test specifications*. New Haven and London: Yale University Press.

Fulcher, G., & Davidson, F. (2007). *Language testing and assessment: An advanced resource book*. London: Routledge.

Kim, J. (2006). *The effectiveness of test-takers' participation in development of an innovative Web-based speaking test for international teaching assistants at American colleges*. Unpublished Doctoral Dissertation. University of Illinois at Urbana-Champaign, United States.

Li, J. (2006). *Introducing audit trails to the world of language testing*. Unpublished Master's Thesis, University of Illinois at Urbana-Champaign, United States.

Menand, L. (1997) (Ed.). *Pragmatism*. New York: Vintage.

Popham, W. J. (1978). *Criterion-referenced measurement*. Englewood Cliffs, NJ: Prentice-Hall.

Ruch, G. M. (1924). *The improvement of the written examination*. Chicago: Scott, Foresman and Company.

Notes

[1] The origin of the notion of test specifications is hard to trace, but we have found something very like modern specs in Ruch (1924, e.g., pp. 95–99).

[2] A related term is "table of specifications," which is an organizational tool that helps test builders assemble and craft an entire test. Each generative test spec – such as that in Figure 6.1 – is intended to produce multiple equivalent test items. Higher-order organizational tools are necessary to keep the entire test development under control, and the canonical such tool is a table of specs. In large agencies and companies, this higher-order organizational function is often done through software.

3 Those three elements of guiding language are Davidson and Lynch's (2002) adaptation of a model from Popham (1978).

4 This particular spec is reverse-engineered from an existing sample language test question for which the source is given in the spec. Reverse engineering (a topic to which we will return later) is when the spec author builds the spec from an existing question, for which no guiding language is already available.

5 One way to see how statistics are typically rendered in text is to do a Google search on some topic that often involves statistical information – like "housing starts." The following article discusses new home construction rates in Dayton, Ohio, United States: Retrieved July 7, 2009, from www.bizjournals.com/dayton/stories/2009/06/29/daily33 .html. Clearly, in this example the statistics are given in running text, for instance: "In May, 144 residential building permits were filed, a decrease of 61 percent from the 348 filed in April, but only a 6.3 percent decrease compared to the same month last year." What kinds of test questions are best suited to test the ability to read such material? Is the question in Figure 6.1 really a suitable approach?

6 To be fair, we should acknowledge that the test from which this item was drawn is no longer operational. It has been replaced by another exam.

7 Furthermore, a revised spec could include some screenshots of such in-text use of statistics, like the report about Dayton previously cited.

CHAPTER 7

Linking Assessment with Instructional Aims and Learning

Anne Katz

INTRODUCTION

This chapter examines the connection between assessment and instruction in language classrooms. Rather than viewing assessment as external to instruction, it focuses on how assessment linked to learning is used to answer such questions as, "What are students learning?," "How well are they learning it?," and "How can instruction support learning?," among many others. For teachers, such an approach to assessment provides a window onto classroom learning processes so as to be able to measure and track students' language growth, encourage learner engagement in the learning process, and determine the appropriacy of instruction in meeting students' learning needs. For students, such assessment supports reflection on learning, identifies areas of strengths and weaknesses, and nurtures skills that can lead to life-long learning. Connections between assessment and learning outcomes have also been the basis for determining program accountability – that is, whether programs are delivering intended instructional services to learners.

The term *assessment* refers to a broad array of methods and approaches to collect information so as to make decisions about learning in contrast to the term *testing*, which is used to refer to one form of assessment. In educational contexts, useful assessments serve as an integral component in an integrated framework designed to promote learning known as a *curriculum*. Formats and content of assessments are linked to designated learning targets as well as to instructional approaches, beliefs about learning and teaching, and, in the case of language classrooms, models of language (Shepard, 2000). Figure 7.1 provides a static view of what are actually dynamic relationships among learning, instruction, and assessment as educators determine learning needs, design instruction, and implement assessments. Instruction-linked assessment occurs in curricula designed for language learning at both the system level and the classroom level.

SYSTEM-LEVEL PRACTICE

An educational system is responsible for ensuring that its students benefit from instruction, for example, learn significant and useful content, develop strategies for life-long learning,

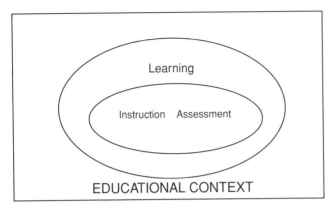

Figure 7.1   Assessment and learning within the educational context

and engage in higher-level learning tasks that will prepare them for future learning or challenging real-life situations. School systems or other administrative bodies use assessment data for accountability purposes, to report learning outcomes and so demonstrate that they are meeting students' learning needs by delivering high-quality instruction.

CLASSROOM-LEVEL PRACTICE

In the learner-centered classroom, teachers use assessment as one of their arsenal of learning tools. They use *summative assessments*, information gathered at the end of a unit of instruction, to measure or "summarize" knowledge and skills learners have acquired from that instruction. Useful summative assessments are framed by learning goals for the unit, goals that teachers share with students along with the criteria that will be used to evaluate students' performances as they engage in learning activities to reach those goals.

Practitioners also employ an array of assessment approaches during instruction and include students as collaborators in the learning process. These assessments are *formative* in nature, designed to monitor and support student learning and to fine-tune instruction so that it meets students' evolving needs. Rather than characterize it as a specific type of assessment – for example, a scoring rubric or portfolio – formative assessment is defined by how various types of assessment are used as part of the learning process. When formative assessment is used to support learning, some practitioners describe such approaches as *assessment as learning* and *assessment for learning*.

BACKGROUND

Classroom teachers vary in their attitudes toward assessment, particularly in terms of its usefulness in teaching language. Let's consider three different scenarios along a continuum of assessment use.

Scenario 1: At one end of the continuum is the language teacher who dutifully administers tests designed for her use by the publisher of her students' textbooks. Additional program, departmental, or district tests may also be incorporated into her plan for assessing her students' learning. She's had little preparation for using alternative approaches to such assessment, much less designing her own assessment tools. She prefers to concentrate her efforts on developing imaginative activities that will engage her students in communicative language use. Her classroom is lively, her students are engaged, she believes a great deal of learning is taking place, but she's just not that sure how or how much.

Scenario 2: Moving along the continuum is the teacher who has developed a few assessments to supplement the program's curriculum. By using classroom-developed rubrics with categories that are relevant to her class's learning goals, she can assess her students' language performances, e.g., role plays, writing samples, debates, and thus she can gather information about their progress in learning specific instructional aims. She feels the information she collects from these performance assessments gives both her and her students a clear picture of their developing skills.

Scenario 3: Near the other end is a teacher who's been reading about and trying out various types of assessment in her classroom for years. In addition to program tests and other assessments shared with fellow teachers, she experiments with new ideas to engage her students in their own learning and assessment. Assessment tasks are seamlessly integrated with instructional ones. Students work together to design scoring rubrics according to clearly articulated criteria and regularly reflect on their learning in learning logs. Through carefully structured feedback – both teacher to student and student to student – she supports students in moving forward with their learning.

This glimpse of varying teacher practice illuminates the somewhat uneven relationship teachers may have with assessment as they plan their lessons. Assessment is often treated as an add-on to the primary focus of instruction and as a source of information about the outcome of carefully planned classroom activities, e.g., summative functions of assessment rather than formative ones. Teachers are familiar with this traditional approach to instruction and assessment given their own experiences as learners in school.

Of course, for many language teachers, the decision as to whether or not to link instruction and assessment has already been made for them. Since the 1980s, primary and secondary schools in the United States, for example, have relied on standards-based learning systems for the design and delivery of instruction and assessment across content areas (see Chapter 8 in this volume for a discussion of standards-based learning systems). Guided by grade-level standards, teachers design lessons using materials aligned with state content-area standards that will help learners in attaining designated learning aims, and then monitor students' progress with standards-referenced assessments. In classrooms serving English learners, English language standards act as a common referent for defining language proficiency and framing the design of instructional aims and assessments. In such systems, assessment focuses on what learners can do in terms of learning objectives derived from standards.

In Australia, communicative language objectives form the basis for designing instruction as well as criterion-referenced techniques and tools to assess English language performances of adult immigrants and refugees served by the Adult Migrant Education Program (AMEP) (Brindley, 1989). Across this large and varied adult education initiative, individual programs developed syllabuses to address local learner needs although they shared a focus on language use via task-based instruction. Indeed, clear objectives based on analyses of learner needs formed the basis for selecting the content of instruction and designing learning tasks; objectives also provided criteria for describing and judging learners' performances. Learners in these programs were encouraged to develop skills in self-assessment by establishing their own language-learning objectives and developing criteria for monitoring their progress over time. Results from criterion-referenced assessments thus provided information about students' achievement of learning targets determined by the teacher as well as by the learners.

The examples of practice from Australia and the United States illustrate how decisions about choosing learning targets, designing instructional activities, selecting materials, and developing assessments are linked within a curriculum geared to an educational delivery system. Standards and frameworks provide a useful structure for organizing learning environments at the system level and, via standardized, traditional forms of assessment, keeping tabs on learner outcomes across learning environments and against a fixed set of criteria. Although such tests can offer a consistent measure of general language ability, teachers may find themselves grappling with the lack of congruence between the results of classroom assessments and those of institutional ones. For many teachers, traditional testing systems do not provide sufficient information to reflect the scope and depth of the learning taking place in individual classrooms (Stoynoff and Chapelle, 2005). Even when standards inform classroom instruction by providing learning targets, well-planned classroom assessments linked to locally relevant instructional aims offer teachers and students a clearer window onto the development of language skills framed by local needs. In a dynamic system of data collection and use, both teachers and students employ assessment to improve and even motivate learning. Such assessments support learning processes as students engage in language activities, such as pair interviews, story retellings, or process writing, and they offer insights into the effectiveness of instructional plans. The remainder of this chapter will focus on these formative uses of classroom-based language assessment.

RESEARCH

Emerging learning theories in education have focused on how students process and make meaning within social contexts, often engaging in reflective practices to help them monitor their learning (Shepard, 2000). This perspective has led to an increasing interest in learner-centered and task-based instructional approaches in language classrooms along with complementary assessment practices that have focused on describing both products as well as the processes students engage in when creating those products. An extensive literature (e.g., Coombe, Folse, and Hubley, 2007; O'Malley and Valdez Pierce, 1996) illustrates how to use a range of assessment types in language classrooms to evaluate and document student progress and growth so as to improve instruction and learning outcomes.

Recent education research has underscored the role of formative assessment in promoting learning in the classroom. From their review of 250 studies of assessment practices across content areas, Black and Wiliam (1998) found that when teachers provided students with feedback on their performances and that information was used, both lower- and higher-achieving students made gains in their scores on conventional tests. Black and Wiliam describe four categories of formative assessment practice: questioning during teacher–student and student–student interaction; feedback through marking; peer- and self-assessment by students; and the formative use of summative tests. These practices provide teachers – and students – with the opportunity to interact around student performances, thus opening the door to improved learning. These practices also reconfigure traditional roles of teacher and student so that the responsibility for learning is shared by all members of the classroom community via feedback provided by teacher to student, student to self, as well as student to student. Central to the effective use of feedback for learning are three components:

- identification of the learning target;
- information about students' current status in achieving that target; and
- explicit guidance on how to reach the target.

This stream of educational inquiry has influenced the work of language-testing researchers who have begun to explore how formative assessment practices are implemented in language classrooms. Acknowledging that assessment consists of a wide array of strategies and products, Rea-Dickins (2001) identified a continuum of formative assessment from "informal" to "formal" to describe the various assessment activities she observed teachers using with their students. At the informal end, assessment is integrated with instruction; teachers and learners interact during instructional time to co-construct knowledge and understanding as the teacher scaffolds student learning through questions and feedback on student responses. At the more formal end of this continuum, assessment activities, such as a writing assignment or dictation, are linked to rather than embedded within instruction, and teachers have fewer opportunities for real-time scaffolding of student performances. In addition to illustrating the variety of formats used in formative assessment, this framework emphasizes its role as an activity in the classroom that is part of the teaching and learning process.

PRACTICAL APPLICATION

Assessment provides teachers with information for decision making at several points during a term of instruction. At the beginning of a course, teachers and students can identify learners' needs, particularly in light of individual students' and course learning targets; during the course, assessment provides information about learners' progress in achieving learning aims; at the end of the course or a unit of instruction, assessment determines the degree of achievement. It is this middle segment – assessment of progress – that this section will focus on by expanding the discussion of formative assessment and the role of feedback at various points of time relative to language performances. These moments in time both during and after a performance provide a window of opportunity to link assessment to instruction and thus support learning. Figure 7.2 shows examples of various kinds of feedback about student language performances that can be provided.

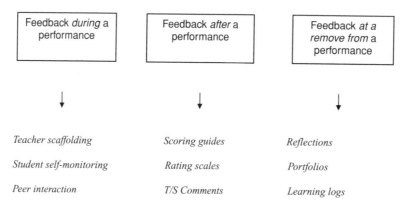

Figure 7.2   Feedback about language performances

Feedback *during* a performance is perhaps the most familiar and common type of formative assessment seen in language classrooms focused on communication and interaction. This feedback occurs orally in real time during question-and-answer segments and tasks embedded into the flow of instruction, and it can be provided by teachers or by students. By co-constructing student participation through interactive sequences that require students to voice their understanding or extend their skills, teachers or student peers can move students forward in the learning process. When teachers plan activities that engage students in interaction – a series of teacher questions to draw out student responses, a group activity that requires collaboration, peer discussion during a task – this is merely the first step in a process of using feedback to support learning. For feedback to be useful, teachers must also exercise skill in observing and interpreting the student talk that is elicited so as to provide appropriate scaffolding, for example, through prompts or paraphrasing or follow-up questions, that will assist learners in developing their language ability.

Much of the literature on classroom assessment has focused on feedback *after* and *at a remove from* student performances. Such feedback is provided in writing via tools such as scoring guides, rubrics, and checklists that record and evaluate student performances using criteria that, ideally, are related to classroom learning targets (see O'Malley and Valdez Pierce, 1996, for an extensive catalogue of performance assessments). This feedback allows students to review their performances more closely, comparing their current skills to specific learning goals. The student role in this assessment / learning process can be nurtured when students articulate the criteria to be used to assess performances and use such tools to assess their own and others' performances. Learner logs, self-assessment surveys, and peer assessment checklists are just some of the tools students can use to guide constructive feedback that will enhance learning.

Careful planning is required to incorporate formative assessments into the classroom:

- Identify learner language needs such as current language proficiency level(s).
- Select language objectives related to learner needs and course learning targets.
- Choose activities that can be used to collect assessment information.
- Modify or select rubrics or other assessment tools that will record performances and provide descriptive feedback.
- Prepare learners for the format of the assessment, its purpose, and their role in it, possibly through self- or peer assessment.
- Develop a timeline for collecting information about student learning.

To help plan a range of assessments linked to designated learning targets, teachers can use an alignment chart like the one in Table 7.1 that shows the relationship across learning objectives, classroom activities, and possible assessments.

Learning objective	Classroom activity	Assessment tool
Students will be able to develop and maintain a "lexical" vocabulary notebook.	Students will create flash cards from their own notebooks using lexical chunks. On one side is the chunk, on the other side is a picture or mnemonic device.	Two parts: A. Students will race against the clock and see how many cards they can name in a minute. Every week they will measure themselves against their previous "score" and against the "scores" of their peers. B. Students will fill in a self-assessment form.

Table 7.1   Alignment chart linking assessment with learning[1]

Note that both students and teachers use assessment to track student progress in attaining learning targets. Such a planning tool can ensure that assessment data related to important learning targets are collected systematically across a period of instruction and used for both formative and summative purposes.

CONCLUSION

Assessment that can both reflect and impact learning is an integral component in the language classroom. In any attempt to implement such an approach, however, there are issues to be considered.

WHAT IS USEFUL FEEDBACK?

Feedback that provides specific and descriptive information to students has been identified as a crucial element in effective formative assessment. However, several studies suggest that determining what constitutes useful feedback, particularly during classroom instructional sequences, is not so simple (Leung and Mohan, 2004; Rea-Dickins, 2001). While taking into account student language proficiency levels and learning needs, teachers must give careful thought to how feedback is structured if it is to support learning and provide beneficial washback. This issue leads to the next one on preparing teachers.

ARE TEACHERS PREPARED TO IMPLEMENT CHANGES IN ASSESSMENT?

Teachers play a pivotal role in turning new ideas for assessment into actual classroom practice. They must interpret suggestions for practice – such as sharing decision making with students – while also adapting them to local instructional contexts and the needs and language levels of their students. Teachers benefit from professional development that will help them reflect on practice, nurture their skills, and extend the scope of their expertise. Program support is crucial in ensuring teachers have sufficient staff meeting time, opportunities to collaborate with one another, and needed resources that will enable them to create learning environments keyed to learner needs.

HOW RECEPTIVE ARE STUDENTS TO NEW FORMS OF ASSESSMENT?

Part of the promise of formative assessment is the active role students play in their own learning: identifying their learning needs, determining language-learning targets, conducting self- and peer assessment, and using criteria to evaluate performances. Students may feel uncomfortable in this new role, perhaps lacking confidence in assessing their own or peers' work. A supportive classroom climate that encourages students to experiment with the added role of assessor to their current one of learner may help students develop confidence in participating more fully in the assessment and learning process.

Suggested resources

Assessment Reform Group. (2002). Assessment for learning: Ten principles. http://arg. educ.cam.ac.uk/CIE3.pdf.

Colby-Kelly, C., & Turner, C. E. (2007). AFL research in the L2 classroom and evidence of usefulness: Taking formative assessment to the next level. *The Canadian Modern Language Review*, 64(1), 9–38.

Coombe, C., Folse, K., & Hubley, N. (2007). *A practical guide to assessing English language learners*. Ann Arbor, MI: The University of Michigan Press.

Leung, C., & Mohan, B. (2004). Teacher formative assessment and talk in classroom contexts: Assessment as discourse and assessment of discourse. *Language Testing* 21(3), 335–359.

O'Malley, J. M., & Valdez Pierce, L. (1996). *Authentic assessment for English language learners*. Reading, MA: Addison-Wesley.

Rea-Dickins, P. (2001). Mirror, mirror on the wall: Identifying processes of classroom assessment. *Language Testing*, 18(4), 429–462.

Discussion questions

1. Based on your experiences as a language learner or language teacher, how would you describe your views on language learning? How would you describe the relationship between learning theory and assessment practices in your context?

2. What types of assessment are you familiar with? Which ones do you use in your classroom? Why?

3. This chapter distinguishes between formative and summative assessment. Do both of these functions of assessment have a place in your classroom? If so, in what ways? If not, why not?

4. What is the role of learners in assessment? In your context, what supports and barriers exist that could affect how learners participate in assessment?

5. Look again at the graphic illustrating feedback *during, after* and *at a remove from* a performance. What kinds of feedback do you provide students in your classroom?

References

Black, P., & Wiliam, D. (1998). Assessment and classroom learning. *Assessment in Education* 5, 7–68.

Brindley, G. (1989). *Assessing achievement in the learner-centered curriculum*. Sydney, Australia: National Centre for English Language Teaching and Research.

Coombe, C., Folse, K., & Hubley, N. (2007). *A practical guide to assessing English language learners*. Ann Arbor, MI: The University of Michigan Press.

Leung, C., & Mohan, B. (2004). Teacher formative assessment and talk in classroom contexts: Assessment as discourse and assessment of discourse. *Language Testing* 21(3), 335–359.

O'Malley, J. M., & Valdez Pierce, L. (1996). *Authentic assessment for English language learners*. Reading, MA: Addison-Wesley.

Rea-Dickins, P. (2001). Mirror, mirror on the wall: Identifying processes of classroom assessment. *Language Testing*, 18(4), 429–462.

Shepard, L. (2000). *The role of classroom assessment in teaching and learning*. Washington, DC: Center for Research on Education, Diversity and Excellence/Center for Applied Linguistics.

Stoynoff, S., & Chapelle, C. (2005). *ESOL tests and testing*. Alexandria, VA: Teachers of English to Speakers of Other Languages.

Note

[1] This alignment chart was created by Jeff Puccini as part of the requirement for the Curriculum Development and Assessment course at SIT Graduate Institute.

CHAPTER 8

An Overview of Language Standards for Elementary and Secondary Education

Margo Gottlieb

INTRODUCTION

Language standards are expressions of the language expectations of language learners on their pathway toward acquiring a new language through listening, speaking, reading, and writing within a school setting. Generally descriptive statements, language standards account for how language learners process or produce language for a given purpose. In large part, language standards within English-speaking societies have been designed for linguistically and culturally diverse students requiring instructional support in developing English as an additional language to achieve academic parity with their English proficient peers.

Language standards have also been crafted for students studying heritage or world languages, including English. Within the United States, standards for foreign language education focus on five goals: communication, culture, connections, comparisons, and communities where "language [is treated as] the heart of the human experience" (ACTFL, 1999). As with other sets of standards, their intent is not to dictate curriculum or a course of study, but to represent student expectations that could be met through teacher use of a wide array of instructional approaches.

A variety of entities worldwide has engaged in the development of language standards. Table 8.1 displays the names of several language standards documents developed for educators of elementary and secondary education students. As is evident by this sampling, there is a range of descriptions for language expectations, as expressed by their titles, from English language proficiency or development standards to bandscales.

Irrespective of how language standards are envisioned, they all represent a developmental continuum that students pass through in the process of language learning. This pathway is marked by levels or stages of language development that indicate benchmarks or milestones toward the attainment of full language proficiency. The range of performance within a level often carries a label descriptive of the stage of development, such as Starting, Emerging, Developing, Expanding, and Bridging (TESOL, 2006).

Entity	Name of language standards	Latest publication date
International organizations		
Teachers of English to Speakers of Other Languages (TESOL)	PreK-12 English Language Proficiency Standards	2006
National organizations		
National Standards in Foreign Language Education Project – American Council of Teachers of Foreign Languages (ACTFL)	Standards for Foreign Language Learning in the 21st Century, 3rd edition	1999
Countries		
Australia	Assessing, Monitoring, and Understanding English as a Second Language in Schools: The NLLIA ESL Bandscales, Version 2	2007
Territories		
Guam	Guam English Language Proficiency Standards	2008; 2011
American Samoa	American Samoa Integrated English Language Proficiency Standards	
Consortia of U.S. States		
World-Class Instructional Design and Assessment (WIDA) Consortium	English Language Proficiency Standards and Resource Guide Prekindergarten through Grade 12, 2nd edition; Spanish Language Arts Standards; Spanish Language Development Standards	2007; 2005; 2011
States		
California	English-Language Development Standards for California Schools, Kindergarten Through Grade Twelve	1999

Table 8.1 Examples of language standards developed by different entities

In a standards-referenced education system, language standards serve as the anchor for curriculum, instruction, and assessment. Language standards provide the cornerstone for the collection, analysis, interpretation, and reporting of data on individual students and student groups across levels of implementation, including language proficiency information from individual classrooms, schools, language education programs, districts, or state levels (Gottlieb and Nguyen, 2007).

In the United States, with its high-stakes accountability for language and content learning, there must be evidence of a direct correspondence between a state's or consortium's English language development standards and its annual English language proficiency test. In essence, the standards themselves are the foundation and source of content and construct validity for the related large-scale test. Language standards also anchor classroom assessment of students' language development. As the identical set of language standards are the grounding for multiple measures for English learners, educators are becoming more attuned to the value of gathering a body of evidence to create defensible data for student performance within a comprehensive assessment system.

BACKGROUND AND KEY ISSUES

Language standards, in large part, are a response by language educators to the K-12 standards-based education movement which has flourished since the late 1980s. Academic content standards for the major subject areas, namely mathematics and science, were the first to emerge for elementary and secondary teachers in the United States. The original bandscales in Australia were designed in 1994 and revised in 2007. In 1997, Teachers of English to Speakers of Other Languages (TESOL), a global association of language-teaching professionals, published English as a second language standards that subsequently were reconceptualized as PreK-12 English language proficiency standards in 2006.

Come 2001, the reauthorization of the federal Elementary and Secondary School Act in the United States, also known as "No Child Left Behind," had a major impact on education reform and language policy. As a result, states or consortia of states were legislated to develop K-12 English language proficiency standards, rich in academic language, and annually administer a language proficiency test. This mandate became a testament of the importance of language education and an awakening for educators of the academic language needs of language learners. Thus, language standards have come to populate the American educational landscape and have, to some extent, steered the direction of language education internationally.

With English learners being the fastest growing segment of the K-12 school population in many countries, language educators needed a way of codifying the process of language development and presenting it in a teacher-friendly document for use in classrooms. Language standards not only have provided a guidepost for educators working with these burgeoning numbers of language learners, they have become the vehicle to concretely describe language learning to other educators and communicate how students progress over time. Thus, language standards have helped teachers collaborate in planning, delivering, and evaluating instruction by differentiating language, according to the levels of language proficiency, in conjunction with content, to meet the needs of their students.

Additionally, language standards have allowed teachers to apply a uniform set of criteria to interpret test results within a standards-referenced system. Thus, language standards have solidified the understanding by educators serving language learners of the developmental progression of language learning and how it can be treated in classrooms on a formative basis in addition to being translated into a high-stakes, summative test for accountability purposes.

The major characteristics of language standards tend to mirror those of language assessment. That is, high-quality language standards must be: (1) reliable, or consistent in their definition, message, and implementation; (2) valid, or designed to represent current linguistic and educational theory and thus reflect construct relevance; (3) limited in bias and sensitivity issues, or developed to promote fairness and equity; and (4) useful, or have ease and practicality for stakeholders (Assessment & Accountability Comprehensive Center, 2009). Thus, the technical qualities of language proficiency tests are directly tied to test specifications that, in turn, reflect the rigor embodied in language standards.

As much as language standards, in general, have benefited the education community serving language learners, there has also been inherent misuse and abuse. On the counter side, language standards have been misinterpreted to negatively impact schools and districts. In some unfortunate instances, they have:

- de-emphasized the critical role of native language in English oral language and literacy development;
- been interpreted as de facto curriculum;
- narrowed the foci of instruction and assessment;
- made teaching and assessment robotic, as in the usage of prescriptive materials, rather than innovative and robust.

The issue at hand is whether the benefits of educational standards offset the potential negative consequences. This view of standards is one of perception – is the glass half-full or half-empty?

RESEARCH

Research on language standards is in its infancy, as the notion of standards-driven education for language learners is a relatively new phenomenon in K-12 settings. In addition, during the last fifteen years, the content of language standards has evolved from an emphasis on social language to one of school-based, academic language development. This paradigmatic shift, reflective of the field of language education, has been motivated by the emergence of theoretical bases on academic languages, multiple literacies, and content-specific discourse (Schleppegrell, 2004, among others). This change has been further felt by the imposition of stringent accountability requirements for student achievement that has resulted in instructional practices gravitating toward teaching language through content rather than in isolation.

A growing alliance between research and practice has been forged around the mutual goal of creating academic pathways to success for English learners through language. This critical role of language in education is echoed by Frances et. al., "Mastery of academic language is arguably the single most important determinant of academic success for individual students. . . . it is not possible to overstate the role that language plays in determining students' success with academic content. Proficient use of . . . and control over . . . academic language is the key to content-area learning" (2006: 7).

To date, research efforts have centered on explaining how the construct of academic language can be represented in specific models or frameworks, couched within language standards, and to some extent, described through observation in content-centered classrooms. With the recent availability of trend data from a new generation of English language proficiency tests, investigators are beginning to examine the washback of language proficiency testing on the use of language standards for instructional purposes and explore the relationship between academic language proficiency and academic achievement for language learners.

For the past several years, an ongoing research initiative of the World-Class Instructional Design and Assessment (WIDA) Consortium (www.wida.us), housed at the University of Wisconsin, Wisconsin Center for Education Research, has centered on the alignment of standards and assessments. It is important work as, although member states – totaling 25 at this juncture – adhere to the same English language proficiency standards and annual language proficiency test, each state has had unique academic content standards and achievement tests. The thrust of the studies has been to determine a correspondence between WIDA's language standards and individual state academic content standards along with the correlation between results from WIDA's English language proficiency test and state achievement tests. Emerging from this research is an aligned assessment system where there is consensus in the underlying construct of academic language proficiency, represented in language standards, that, in turn, is operationalized in the assessment of language proficiency (Cook and Wilmes, 2007).

PRACTICAL APPLICATION

Elementary and secondary educators use language standards as guidance in meeting the academic language needs of their students in their individual classrooms. However, teachers also work within a broader context of schools and districts which means that decisions about language instruction are often embedded within mandated content-based curricula. The major question becomes: How can educators address the language demands of grade-level academic concepts so that language learners, irrespective of their levels of language proficiency, can access the necessary content through language?

If curriculum is viewed as dynamic rather than static, then teachers could be actively involved in its creation and have a voice in its enactment. A multi-step language curriculum framework that has been built around language standards has specifically been designed for this purpose. Its three phases (previewing, planning, and reflecting) provide a systematic, step-by-step process that facilitates the connection between language standards and instructional approaches to meet the needs of language learners in elementary and secondary classrooms (Gottlieb et al., 2009).

Although evidence of language learning occurs throughout the instructional assessment cycle, in the reflecting phase, both teachers and students are afforded opportunities to determine the extent to which language learning has occurred. Data on language are collected, analyzed, and reported so that the information can best be used in a timely fashion. Similarly, one of the primary purposes of the Australian ESL Bandscales is to "promote valid assessment and reporting of ESL progress (and thus lead to improved teaching)" within the context of schooling where language learners are developing both social and academic language (McKay, 2007). As envisioned, language standards are not necessarily targets for instruction and assessment, but are to be viewed as integral to and ingrained into teaching and learning.

An example of the practicality of language standards can be taken from TESOL's 2006 edition, an augmentation of those of the WIDA Consortium. Some features of the language standards include:

- an emphasis on the *language* of the content areas, or academic language, in conjunction with social, intercultural, and instructional language;
- an incremental increase or scaffolding in vocabulary usage, grammatical structures, and discourse as students progress from language proficiency Level 1 to Level 5;
- an independent treatment of the four language domains: listening, speaking, reading, and writing (required by U.S. legislation);
- example topics from academic content standards as the source for contextualizing or embedding language and connecting to the general grade-level curriculum;
- language functions descriptive of what students can do to communicate; and
- the integration of visual, graphic, or interactive supports to assure the availability of multiple modalities and access to meaning for language learners.

These language standards are represented by grade-level clusters (PreK-K, 1–3, 4–5, 6–8, and 9–12), language domains (listening, speaking, reading, and writing) and language proficiency levels (from Level 1, Starting, to Level 5, Bridging). Each language domain forms a continuum across the five incremental levels of language proficiency that is bound by an example content topic (derived from grade-level content standards) referred to as a strand of sample performance indicators. Thus, academic language is integrated into grade-level content appropriate for the students' level of language proficiency to maximize their opportunities to succeed in school.

English Language Proficiency (ELP) Standard 4: The language of science

Language domain: Speaking

Example topic: Solar system

Language Proficiency Level 1	Language Proficiency Level 2	Language Proficiency Level 3	Language Proficiency Level 4	Language Proficiency Level 5
Repeat definitions of key objects in the solar system (e.g., planets, asteroids) with a partner.	Describe appearance and composition of objects in the solar system with a partner.	Compare appearance and composition of objects in the galaxy with a partner.	Present or discuss illustrated processes involving planetary objects (e.g., measuring distances or time spans).	Explain, using technical terms, the structure of the universe using examples of planetary components (e.g., stars and galaxies).

Table 8.2   A strand of sample performance indicators taken from the matrix of TESOL's English language proficiency standards (2006: 84)

Table 8.2 is a strand of sample performance indicators taken from grade-level cluster 6–8 (middle school). In this strand, the content or topic "solar system" is the example backdrop for language development. Thus, language instruction and assessment can be readily differentiated for groups of language learners based on, in this case, their oral language development. In addition, it is suggested that teachers have students work with partners as a means of interactive support. This representation of a language standard offers a tremendous amount of information to aid in building curriculum, instruction, and assessment for teachers of language learners.

Language standards are living documents to be adopted or adapted by educators. Sustained professional development affords teachers and administrators opportunities for ongoing discussion of urgent and relevant issues facing the education of language learners. Through professional learning communities, the orientation for teaching and learning for all students and their teachers can become standards-referenced. As a result, standards can become the universal yardstick and criteria for measuring students' growth in language. By having language standards represent how language learners can process and produce language in meaningful contexts, educators will come to envision the value of these documents for their linguistically and culturally diverse students.

CONCLUSION

The role of language standards in planning, delivering, and evaluating educational services to language learners continues to expand across contexts and stakeholders. The involvement of content and language specialists as members of a collaborative team has gained footing. Having protected time for joint planning of lessons on a daily to weekly basis has spurred creative curricular, instructional, and assessment solutions for language learners. Teams of language and content teachers participating in professional development have helped further the understanding of the important role of language in education. Administrators and school leaders are also beginning to take an advocacy stance on behalf of their linguistically and culturally diverse communities.

Language is central to educating youth around the world. Language standards provide a window for educators of language learners into the systematic progression of language development and the organization of instruction and assessment around language. Through data from language standards, and their derivative language proficiency tests, language education has become aligned with the mission of schools to have students and teachers grow over time and succeed in their goals for learning and teaching.

Suggested resources

Gottlieb, M., Cranley, M. E., & Oliver, A. (2007). *English language proficiency standards and resource guide* (2007 edition), *PreKindergarten through Grade 12*. Madison, WI: Board of Regents of the University of Wisconsin System on behalf of the WIDA Consortium.

McKay, P. (Ed.). (2007). *The NLLIA ESL bandscales version 2: Assessing, monitoring and understanding English as a second language in schools*. Brisbane, Australia: Queensland University of Technology and Independent Schools.

Standards for foreign language learning: Preparing for the 21st century. (1999). Alexandria, VA: American Council on the Teaching of Foreign Languages.

Discussion questions

1. What are the advantages and disadvantages of having language standards as a component of educational accountability?

2. As a language educator, what are the advantages and disadvantages of having language standards for personal or professional accountability?

3. How do language standards help shape the planning of curriculum, instruction, and assessment of language learners?

4. How are stakeholders affected by language standards – are they included in the development process, and what is their impact on educational decision making?

5. Why are language standards an important referent for both formative and summative language testing?

6. Explain how language standards reflect language policy regarding language learners and language education programs.

References

ACTFL. (1999). *Standards for foreign language teaching: Preparing for the 21st century*. Alexandria, VA: American Council on the Teaching of Foreign Languages.

Assessment & Accountability Comprehensive Center. (2009). *Framework for high-quality English language proficiency standards and assessments*. San Francisco, CA: WestEd.

Cook, H. G., & Wilmes, C. (2007). *Alignment between the Kentucky Core Content for Assessment and the WIDA Consortium English Language Proficiency Standards*. Madison, WI: University of Wisconsin, Wisconsin Center for Education Research.

Frances, D. J., Rivera, M., Lesaux, N., Kieffer, M., & Rivera, H. (2006). *Practical guidelines for the education of English language learners: Research-based recommendations for instruction and academic interventions*. Houston, TX: Texas Institute for Measurement, Evaluation, and Statistics at the University of Houston for the Center on Instruction.

Gottlieb, M., Katz, A., & Ernst-Slavit, G. (2009). *Paper to practice: Using the English language proficiency standards in PreK-12 classrooms*. Alexandria, VA: Teachers of English to Speakers of Other Languages.

Gottlieb, M., & Nguyen, D. (2007). *Assessment & accountability in language education programs: A guide for administrators and teachers*. Philadelphia, PA: Caslon Publishing.

McKay, P. (Ed.). (2007). *Assessing, monitoring and understanding English as a second language in schools: The NLLIA ESL bandscales Version 2*. Brisbane, Queensland University of Technology and Independent Schools Queensland.

Schleppegrell, M. J. (2004). *The language of school: A functional linguistics perspective*. Mahwah, NJ: Erlbaum.

Teachers of English to Speakers of Other Languages. (2006). *PreK-12 English language proficiency standards*. Alexandria, VA: TESOL.

CHAPTER 9

The Common European Framework of Reference

Elif Kantarcıoğlu and Spiros Papageorgiou

INTRODUCTION

The Council of Europe (not to be confused with the European Union) is the continent's oldest political organization, founded in 1949. As part of its general aim to foster common democratic principles among its 47 members, the Council of Europe has been active in the area of languages for more than forty years with two complementary bodies: the Language Policy Division in Strasbourg, France, and the European Centre for Modern Languages in Graz, Austria.

Within the general frame of promoting plurilingualism and pluriculturalism among European citizens, the Council of Europe published a number of documents in the 1970s that have been influential to language teaching. Perhaps the most influential of the early documents they published are the notional–functional syllabus by Wilkins (Wilkins, 1976) – that focuses on describing what a learner communicates through language – and three ascending levels describing language achievement (Waystage, Threshold, and Vantage) by Van Ek and Trim (1991; 1998; 2001). More recently, the *Common European Framework of Reference for Languages: Learning, teaching, assessment* (CEFR, 2001) was published. This work, emerging from the ongoing work on communicative objectives (such as Threshold), has been recognized as the "most significant recent event on the language education scene in Europe" (Alderson, 2005: 275).

The main purpose of the CEFR is to provide a common basis for the elaboration of language syllabuses, examinations, and textbooks, by describing in a comprehensive way what language learners have to learn to do in order to use a language effectively for communication (Council of Europe, 2001: 1). The impact of the Framework on language testing has been wide-spread as the majority of language examination providers claim that their test scores relate to the different levels described in the 2001 volume. However, apart from reporting scores, the CEFR can be a useful tool in developing language tests and other assessment methods in the classroom, as we will illustrate in this chapter.

BACKGROUND TO THE DEVELOPMENT OF THE CEFR

As mentioned earlier, the notion of "plurilingualism" is central in the Council of Europe's approach to language learning. Going beyond multilingualism, that is, the knowledge of a number of languages, plurilingualism emphasizes the use of languages interacting with the cultural context in which they are used. In this cultural context, the language learner builds up communicative competence that leads to effective communication with other individuals.

In 1991, at an intergovernmental symposium in Switzerland, the development of a common framework for learning, teaching, and assessment was deemed desirable in order to:

- promote and facilitate cooperation among educational institutions in different countries;
- provide a sound basis for the mutual recognition of language qualifications;
- assist learners, teachers, course designers, examining bodies, and educational administrators to situate and co-ordinate their efforts. (Council of Europe, 2001: 5)

The authoring group produced an initial version in 1996 and the final version of the CEFR was published after feedback and consultation in 2001, the European Year of Languages, in English and French. To date, the CEFR volume is freely available online from the Council of Europe Web site (www.coe.int/portfolio) in more than 30 languages. These include non-European languages, such as Arabic and Japanese, revealing the strong interest in the document world-wide, not only within Europe.

The CEFR comprises of chapters which are briefly explained below.

Chapter 1: The Common European Framework in its political and educational context

This chapter defines the aims, objectives, and functions of the Framework in relation to the Council of Europe's language policy of plurilingualism.

Chapter 2: Approach adopted

This chapter explains the parameters such as strategies, competences, and domains for description of language use and ability.

Chapter 3: Common Reference Levels

This chapter introduces the Common Reference Levels.

Chapter 4: Language use and the language user / learner

This chapter introduces the categories required to describe language use and users.

Chapter 5: The user / learner's competences

This chapter categorizes in detail the language user's general and communicative competences.

Chapter 6: Language learning and teaching

This chapter explores the relationship between acquisition and learning with a focus on plurilingual competence.

Chapter 7: Tasks and their role in language teaching

This chapter analyzes the role of tasks in language learning and teaching.

Chapter 8: Linguistic diversification and the language curriculum

This chapter deals with the implications of linguistic diversification for curriculum design.

Chapter 9: Assessment

This chapter discusses the various purposes of assessment and types of assessment.

Similar to the wide implementation of the Threshold level in curricula and textbooks in the 1970s, the CEFR started influencing these same areas soon after its publication. It is also clear that the CEFR has been extremely influential in language testing, as evidenced by the 2005 special issue of the *Language Testing* journal on language assessment in Europe (Alderson, 2005). The vast majority of language examinations, both locally and internationally developed, refer to the CEFR primarily to describe the level of language proficiency they assess. The description of language proficiency levels is achieved by referring to what is probably the best-known part of the CEFR, that is, its six main levels of proficiency, illustrated by dozens of performance descriptors. These levels, and the research that led to the construction of their performance descriptors, are briefly described in the next section.

RESEARCH INTO THE DEVELOPMENT OF THE CEFR LEVELS

The CEFR 2001 volume contains dozens of language proficiency scales, describing language activities and competences at six main levels: A1 (the lowest) through A2, B1, B2, C1, and C2 (the highest). These six levels are called "criterion" levels (Council of Europe, 2001: 32) complemented in some scales by "plus" levels: A2+ (between A2 and B1), B1+ (between B1 and B2), and B2+ (between B2 and C1). The CEFR scales comprise statements called "descriptors," which were designed following an action-orientated approach, in accordance with the notion of plurilingualism: language users are seen as members of a society who have tasks to accomplish, including those that are not language-related (Council of Europe, 2001: 9). Given this emphasis on accomplishing tasks the descriptors are also frequently referred to as "can-do statements." The CEFR scales and their descriptors were developed during a large research project in Switzerland (North, 2000). Table 9.1 shows the Overall Listening Comprehension Scale. In some of the scales, the upper descriptors, which are separated by a line, correspond to the "plus" (+) levels A2+, B1+, and B2+.

C2	Has no difficulty in understanding any kind of spoken language, whether live or broadcast, delivered at fast native speed.
C1	Can understand enough to follow extended speech on abstract and complex topics beyond his / her own field, though he / she may need to confirm occasional details, especially if the accent is unfamiliar. Can recognize a wide range of idiomatic expressions and colloquialisms, appreciating register shifts. Can follow extended speech even when it is not clearly structured and when relationships are only implied and not signaled explicitly.
B2	Can understand standard spoken language, live or broadcast, on both familiar and unfamiliar topics normally encountered in personal, social, academic or vocational life. Only extreme background noise, inadequate discourse structure and / or idiomatic usage influences the ability to understand.
	Can understand the main ideas of propositionally and linguistically complex speech on both concrete and abstract topics delivered in a standard dialect, including technical discussions in his / her field of specialization. Can follow extended speech and complex lines of argument provided the topic is reasonably familiar, and the direction of the talk is sign-posted by explicit markers.

(continued overleaf)

(ctd.)	
B1	Can understand straightforward factual information about common everyday or job related topics, identifying both general messages and specific details, provided speech is clearly articulated in a generally familiar accent.
	Can understand the main points of clear standard speech on familiar matters regularly encountered in work, school, leisure etc. including short narratives.
A2	Can understand enough to be able to meet needs of a concrete type provided speech is clearly and slowly articulated.
	Can understand phrases and expressions related to areas of most immediate priority (e.g. very basic personal and family information, shopping, local geography, employment) provided speech is clearly and slowly articulated.
A1	Can follow speech which is very slow and carefully articulated, with long pauses for him / her to assimilate meaning.

Table 9.1   Overall Listening Comprehension (Council of Europe, 2001)

The project applied a variety of qualitative and quantitative methods for the initial analysis and collection of more than 2,000 language descriptors used in proficiency scales around the world, the consequent selection and refinement of 1,000 of these descriptors, and finally, the placement of the descriptors at different proficiency levels that subsequently formed the CEFR levels. A number of studies and research projects such as the DIALANG project (www.dialang.org) have shown that the descriptors can be consistently replicated in a variety of contexts, thus offering validity evidence of the way the descriptors were classified into CEFR levels. Information on the construction of proficiency scales can be found in Appendix A of the CEFR volume.

The proficiency scales of the CEFR have gained popularity because they describe in a comprehensive way objectives that learners can set to achieve at different levels of language proficiency. The descriptors are always phrased positively, as they are intended to motivate learners by describing what they can do when they use the language, rather than what they cannot do (Council of Europe, 2001: 205). What is more, this set of language-learning objectives is available as a common metalanguage to teachers and learners, who can now compare the level of proficiency required by curricula, language courses, and examinations across different educational settings. Thus, the CEFR can be used in many different ways, for example the practical application for language teachers, which is illustrated later in this chapter.

PRACTICAL APPLICATION OF THE CEFR

It is true that most readers of the CEFR will feel overwhelmed by the amount of information and might find some parts containing inaccessible language, as Alderson et al. (2006) point out. This could be the case because one of the main aims of the CEFR is to be comprehensive, thus covering as full a range of language skills and competences as possible. Because of this wide coverage, there is a lot of value in the volume and opportunities for practical uses of the CEFR for assessment in the classroom, as we will explain in this section.

Chapter 9 of the CEFR, entitled "Assessment," is very useful as an introduction to important notions and principles of language assessment. Fundamental terms such as validity and reliability are explained, and different types of assessment are described (e.g., formative versus summative assessment; norm-referencing versus criterion-referencing).

The CEFR provides a lot of support for involving learners in the assessment process (see also Chapter 19 in this volume), through the self-assessment descriptors in Chapter 3 and the DIALANG self-assessment statements in Appendix C (Council of Europe, 2001: 26–27, 205–216). The benefits of engaging learners in self-assessment are significant, as noted by Little (2005), because it fosters collaboration between teachers and learners. In this collaborative process, another Council of Europe project can be of valuable help in the classroom, the European Language Portfolio (ELP), which was developed along with the CEFR and provided the self-assessment descriptors in Chapter 3 of the 2001 volume. The three components of the portfolio (language passport, language biography, and dossier) will also serve a pedagogical function, as they will contribute to the development of learner autonomy, with students recording their language development and collecting their own work.

The proficiency scales in Chapters 4 and 5 of CEFR provide support for the construction of language tests for use in the classroom. They can be used to develop a specification of the content of such tests given that the descriptors provide rich details of what one can do at different levels of proficiency when performing a variety of language activities (see also Chapter 5 in this volume). In addition to the scales, Chapter 2 provides a description of the approach adopted by the CEFR, which will facilitate teachers in their role as test constructors, in particular, the discussion of competences, domains, activities, and tasks.

Language teachers are continuously required to assess their students' oral and written performances in the classroom, and the CEFR offers a variety of oral and writing scales that can form the basis for comprehensive rating criteria (see also Chapter 34 in this volume for a discussion of marking). For example, Table 3 of the CEFR (Council of Europe, 2001: 28–29) presents five aspects of oral language proficiency (range, accuracy, fluency, interaction, and coherence) that can form the basis for the development of rating criteria for formative assessment.

In many language-learning contexts, learners take large-scale examinations, usually in order to obtain a language qualification for further study or employment purposes. The CEFR allows for comparison of such language qualifications in terms of content coverage and proficiency level. Following the publication of the CEFR, the Council of Europe published a Manual (Council of Europe, 2009) to help examination providers relate their examinations to the CEFR. The stages of the suggested linking process in the Manual include an investigation of how the content of a test relates to the CEFR (Specification stage) and how pass / fail decisions are set according to the CEFR levels (Standardization stage). Decisions are made by a panel of trained judges, who need to be familiar with the CEFR scales; for this reason, the Familiarization stage precedes each of the other two stages. Finally, the Empirical Validation stage describes validity evidence that should be provided to support a CEFR linking claim. Based on the results of such a linking process, teachers can provide useful advice to their students as to the language qualification that is more appropriate for them.

CONCLUSION

In this chapter we have presented the Common European Framework of Reference and described its place among the other language projects of the Council of Europe. We have also discussed the development of its proficiency scales and illustrated how the CEFR can be a valuable resource for assessment-related tasks that teachers need to accomplish.

We feel that at this stage it is also important to stress what the CEFR is not, as our professional experience in language-testing projects suggests that even though many teachers have heard about the CEFR, they remain unclear with regard to its goals and potential uses. For example, we have witnessed questions about whether an examination is

"CEFR-based" and how it relates to other CEFR examinations. Two important clarifications need to be made here with regard to these points:

- As clearly stated by North (2004), the CEFR is not a cookbook for language testers. In his article, Weir (2005) actually explains how the CEFR is not very helpful with a number of aspects of the test development process. Thus, we can never expect that a test can be automatically "linked" to the CEFR just because the test developer has read the CEFR. The philosophy of the CEFR as a reference source is, after all, not to dictate what readers should do with regard to testing (as well as teaching), but, as indicated by boxes at the end of each section, readers are encouraged to reflect on the content of the volume and apply the relevant information, where appropriate, to their own professional contexts. The existence of more than one hundred ELP models on the Council of Europe Web site illustrates such a successful adaption in a variety of educational contexts.
- If an examination is claimed to be linked to the CEFR, this does not necessarily make the reported results valid and reliable, as Fulcher (2004) points out. In fact, linkage claims should be supported with evidence from the procedure described in the Manual or other relevant standard-setting procedures. Claims that are not supported by such evidence should be treated with caution. It should be pointed out, however, that for any linking procedure to take place, validity and reliability are prerequisites because "linking a qualitatively poor examination to the CEFR is a wasted enterprise that cannot be saved or repaired by careful standard setting" (Council of Europe, 2009: 90). In addition, even if two examinations are found to be situated on the same CEFR level, this does not indicate that they are similar in terms of content.

The CEFR has offered to the field of language testing the opportunity for a common standard that allows for meaningful comparisons between language examinations, but it does not intend to impose or harmonize testing practices. Similarly, the CEFR can offer teachers support on some of their classroom tasks, as we have attempted to show in this chapter, but it should not be viewed as dictating what or how a language point should be taught.

Suggested resources

Alderson, J. C. (Ed.). (2002). *Common European Framework of Reference for Languages: Learning, teaching, assessment. Case studies.* Strasbourg: Council of Europe.

Figueras, N., & Noijons J. (Eds.). (2004). *Linking to the CEFR levels: Research perspectives.* Arnhem: Cito.

Fulcher, G. (2004). Deluded by artifices? The Common European Framework and harmonization. *Language Assessment Quarterly,* 1(4), 253–266.

Little, D. (2006). The Common European Framework of Reference for Languages: Content, purpose, origin, reception and impact. *Language Teaching,* 39(3), 167–190.

Morrow, K. (Ed.). (2004). *Insights from the Common European Framework.* Oxford: Oxford University Press.

North, B., & Schneider, G. (1998). Scaling descriptors for language proficiency scales. *Language Testing,* 15(2), 217–262.

Takala, S. (Ed.). (2004). *Reference Supplement to the preliminary version of the Manual for relating language examinations to the Common European Framework of Reference for Languages: Learning, teaching and assessment.* Strasbourg: Council of Europe.

Discussion questions

1. How is the CEFR part of the Council of Europe's language policies?
2. How can the CEFR be used for assessment in the classroom?
3. How can the CEFR be used to compare different language tests?
4. What are some of the limitations of the CEFR in the language-testing context?

References

Alderson, J. C. (2005). Editorial. *Language Testing*, 22(3), 257–260.

Alderson, J. C., Figueras, N., Kuijper, H., Nold, G., Takala, S., & Tardieu, C. (2006). Analysing tests of reading and listening in relation to the Common European Framework of Reference: The experience of the Dutch CEFR Construct Project. *Language Assessment Quarterly*, 3(1), 3–30.

Council of Europe. (2001). *Common European Framework of Reference for Languages: Learning, teaching, assessment*. Cambridge: Cambridge University Press.

Council of Europe. (2009). Relating language examinations to the Common European Framework of Reference for Languages: Learning, teaching, assessment. A Manual. Retrieved February 15, 2009, from www.coe.int/T/DG4/Portfolio/documents/Manual%20Revision%20-%20proofread%20-%20FINAL.pdf

Fulcher, G. (2004). Are Europe's tests being built on an 'unsafe' framework? Retrieved September 20, 2006, from http://education.guardian.co.uk/tefl/story/0,5500,1170569,00.html

Little, D. (2005). The Common European Framework of Reference for Languages and the European Language Portfolio: Involving learners and their judgments in the assessment process. *Language Testing*, 22(3), 321–336.

North, B. (2000). *The development of a common framework scale of language proficiency*. New York: Peter Lang.

North, B. (2004). Europe's framework promotes language discussion, not directives. Retrieved January 31, 2007, from http://education.guardian.co.uk/tefl/story/0,1191130,00.html

Van Ek, J. A., & Trim, J. L. M. (1991). *Waystage 1990*. Cambridge: Cambridge University Press.

Van Ek, J. A., & Trim, J. L. M. (1998). *Threshold 1990*. Cambridge: Cambridge University Press.

Van Ek, J. A., & Trim, J. L. M. (2001). *Vantage*. Cambridge: Cambridge University Press.

Weir, C. J. (2005). Limitations of the Common European Framework of Reference for Languages (CEFR) for developing comparable examinations and tests. *Language Testing*, 22(3), 281–300.

Wilkins, D. A. (1976). *Notional syllabuses*. Oxford: Oxford University Press.

CHAPTER 10

Test Impact and Washback: Implications for Teaching and Learning

Liying Cheng and Andy Curtis

DEFINITIONS, IMPORTANCE, AND KEY ISSUES

Testing is never a neutral process. There are always consequences. Therefore, tests are a set of differentiating rituals for students, as: "for every one who advances there will be some who stay behind" (Wall, 2000: 500). This is particularly true for students who are taking high-stakes tests, the results of which will have an important bearing on decisions affecting their future studies, as well as their choices and chances in life.

There is, then, a set of relationships, intended and unintended, positive and negative, between teaching, learning, and testing. Bachman and Palmer (1996) referred to this phenomenon as *test impact* – the effect testing has on individuals (teachers and students), educational systems, and societies at large. Within language testing (see Hamp-Lyons, 1997; McNamara, 2000), two terms are used to distinguish this same phenomenon: *impact* – the effects of language tests on macro-levels of education and society, and *washback* – the effects of language tests on micro-levels of language teaching and learning, i.e., inside the classroom. The differences between impact and washback reside in differences between the scale and scope of the effects of the testing.

Messick (1996) suggested building in validity considerations as an essential part of test design in order to promote positive washback and to avoid construct underrepresentation and construct irrelevant variance. Bailey (1996: 268), however, argued that any test, whether good or bad, in terms of validity, can exert either negative or positive washback depending on whether "it impedes or promotes the accomplishment of educational goals held by learners and / or program personnel," i.e., even good tests can be misused.

In this sense, impact and washback are the effects of testing which have been associated with test validity (consequential validity as in Messick, 1996) and the consequences of test use (Bachman, 2005). In addition, the effects of testing are increasingly discussed from the point of view of critical language testing (Shohamy, 2001), including aspects of social concern, such as ethics and fairness. Research into these aspects also calls for understanding of different stakeholder interpretations of test use. In any given testing context, different stakeholders have different stakes, and therefore have different interpretations of the consequences of test use.

RESEARCH LITERATURE

The work of Alderson and Wall (1993), which explored the potential positive and negative relationship between testing, teaching, and learning, was a significant development in shaping the nature of washback studies in the field of language testing. Alderson and Wall questioned whether washback could be a property of test validity, as suggested by Messick (1996), and they proposed 15 hypotheses regarding the potential influence of language testing on various aspects of language teaching and learning. Their work has directly and indirectly influenced washback studies for the past 15 years.

Cheng and Watanabe's *Washback in language testing: Research contexts and methods* (2004) was the first systematic attempt to capture the essence of the washback phenomenon and has, through its collection of washback studies from around the world, responded to the question "what does washback look like?" (Cheng, Watanabe with Curtis, 2004: ix) – an important step beyond the question "does washback exist?" posed by Alderson and Wall (1993).

We have, therefore, mainly cited the studies reported in Cheng and Watanabe (2004) as examples to illustrate what we have learned so far in addressing and responding to Alderson and Wall's 15 hypotheses. We have used (*) to indicate where there is direct research evidence to support a hypothesis, (*?) to indicate where there is only related evidence, and (?) to indicate that further research evidence needs to be collected to address a particular hypothesis.

> H.1   A test will influence teaching. (*)
>
> H.2   A test will influence learning. (*?)
>
> H.3   A test will influence what teachers teach. (*)
>
> H.4   A test will influence how teachers teach. (*?)
>
> H.5   A test will influence what learners learn. (*?)
>
> H.6   A test will influence how learners learn. (?)
>
> H.7   A test will influence the rate and sequence of teaching. (?)
>
> H.8   A test will influence the rate and sequence of learning. (?)
>
> H.9   A test will influence the degree and depth of teaching. (?)
>
> H.10 A test will influence the degree and depth of learning. (?)
>
> H.11 A test will influence attitudes to the content, method, etc., of teaching and learning. (*?)
>
> H.12 Tests that have important consequences will have washback. (*?)
>
> H.13 Tests that do not have important consequences will have no washback. (*?)
>
> H.14 Tests will have washback effects on all learners and teachers. (?)
>
> H.15 Tests will have washback effects for some learners and some teachers, but not for others. (*)? (Alderson and Wall, 1993: 120–121)

Analyzing the 15 Alderson and Wall (1993) hypotheses, we first consider evidence that testing influences teaching (Hypothesis 1 – H1). Language tests are seen to have a more direct washback effect on teaching content than on teaching methodology. In their study of washback on preparation courses for the Test of English as a Foreign Language (TOEFL), Alderson and Hamp-Lyons (1996) found that the TOEFL test affected both *what* and *how* teachers taught (H3 and H4), but the effect was not the same in degree or kind from teacher to teacher, and the simple difference of TOEFL versus non-TOEFL teaching did not explain why teachers taught the way they did.

Alderson and Hamp-Lyons' (1996) study also indirectly addressed the teacher part of Hypothesis 15, and over the years, many studies have investigated and reported on the influence of testing on teachers (including teaching assistants), teaching, and textbooks (see studies in Cheng, Watanabe with Curtis, 2004). In relation to textbooks, although these were not part of Alderson and Wall's original 15 hypotheses, washback studies using textbooks have indirectly related to Hypotheses 7 to 10. However, these studies have not yet produced sufficient and direct evidence to address these hypotheses.

Watanabe (see Cheng, Watanabe with Curtis, 2004) investigated the effect of a university entrance examination on the prevalent use of the grammar-translation method in Japan. His analyses of past English examinations, classroom observations, and interviews with teachers showed very little relationship between the test content and the use of this particular teaching methodology in teaching English. Rather, teacher factors, including personal beliefs, past education, and academic background seemed to be more important in determining the teaching methodology a teacher employs. These teacher factors are related to the social aspects of testing. In some ways, these results on teacher factors partially addressed Hypothesis 11 – the part related to teaching.

In addition, washback studies have investigated factors such as teacher ability, teacher understanding of the test and the approach the test was based on, classroom conditions, lack of resources, and management practices within the school. Other teaching factors which have been researched and reported on include:

- the status of the subject being tested in the curriculum
- feedback mechanisms between the testing agency and the school
- the time elapsed since the introduction of the test
- the teacher's style, commitment, and willingness to innovate
- the teacher's background
- the general social and political context
- the role of publishers in materials design and teacher training

Shohamy et al. (1996) pointed out that the degree of impact of a test is often influenced by several other factors: the status of the subject matter being tested; the nature of the test (low or high stakes); and the uses to which the test scores are to be put. Shohamy et al.'s (1996) study addressed Hypotheses 12 and 13. Furthermore, the washback effect may change over time and may not last indefinitely within the education system being studied. This is not part of the original 15 hypotheses, but there is research evidence to support this additional "seasonality" hypothesis (Cheng, 2008: 359).

A second major point is that, compared with washback studies on teaching and teachers, the number of studies on learning and learners are limited. Wall (2000) pointed out that while it would be useful to continue to study the effects of tests on teaching, it is extremely important to investigate the effects on student learning, as it is students who are most directly impacted by testing. This reminds us that if we wish to establish the relationship between testing, teaching, and learning, it is not sufficient only to study teaching and the instructional context where learning is studied indirectly along with other instructional variables. Students, and how they are affected by tests, must be an essential part of the equation.

So far, in this very brief overview of the main washback literature, we have summarized a number of studies on the relationship between testing, learners and their learning, students' attitudes toward testing, and test preparation behaviors. These studies have attempted to address Hypotheses 2, 5, 6, 8, and 10; however, more direct research evidence is needed in order to demonstrate the relationship between testing and learning (see a full review in Cheng, 2008).

More recently, Cheng, Klinger, and Zheng (2007) conducted a multiphased study investigating the impact of large-scale literacy testing on second language students in Ontario, Canada. These second language students came to the Ontario secondary school system from other countries and are learning their school subjects via English as their second language. The results of the above study have shown that the following factors impacted second language students and first language students (those who were born and grew up in Canada) differently and significantly:

- reading testing formats (*multiple choice* and *constructed responses*)
- text types (*narrative, informational*, and *graphical*)
- skills (*direct, indirect understanding*, and *making connections*)
- strategies (*vocabulary, syntax, organization*, and *graphical features*)
- different writing tasks (a *summary*, a series of *paragraphs expressing an opinion*, a *news report*, and an *information paragraph*)

In addition, in the Cheng, Klinger, and Zheng (2007) study, these students' after-school reading and writing activities influenced their reading and writing performance differently. The researchers also explored the importance and the influence of students' home language use, home computer use, and their parents' education and income on the students' test performance. In addition to linking learners' variables with their test performance, the researchers also used cognitive verbal protocols to study students' think-aloud accounts of their test-taking processes. This study thus investigated a wide of range of psychometric and social aspects of test impact / washback on students and on their literacy test performance. In doing this, the study researched beyond the original 15 hypotheses of Alderson and Wall (1993), and explored the relationships between testing and learning to inform test validity, test use, and the consequences of test use.

PRACTICAL APPLICATION

Impact and washback are the effects of testing on the macro-levels of society and / or on the micro-levels of classroom teaching and learning. These effects are related to the psychometric aspects of test design and to the social aspects of testing.

Research into the psychometric aspects of test design has been driven by validity theory (e.g., Messick's consequential validity), that is, how to avoid test construct underrepresentation and construct-irrelevant variance. To avoid construct underrepresentation, if you wish to have speaking skills taught and learned, then the curriculum should emphasize speaking and the test should reflect the importance of the speaking construct; for example, sufficient speaking activities should be built into the test design, and the speaking construct should also be reflected in the weighting and in the marking. If, for example, the test designer wanted speaking skills to be taught and learned more, then a greater weighting and more marks should be given to the speaking component than to other skills, such as reading or writing.

To avoid construct-irrelevant variance, if a student were to get a lower mark on a test, this should not be, for example, because the student was late for the test or because the student is a boy, as lateness and gender are not constructs that have been built into the test. In other words, if a student gets a lower test score this should only occur as a result of his / her lower language proficiency, if this were a language test. However, in spite of these points, the impact / washback phenomena do not take place in a linear fashion. As teachers, we know there are many more variables that influence teaching and learning above and beyond the testing.

Research into the social aspects of testing has been limited, and such studies are generally conducted at a more philosophical level rather than an empirical one. In order to understand the ethical, educational, and societal consequences of a test, it is necessary to understand what is valued ethically and educationally by the society within which the testing is taking place. For example, an impact / washback study of a national test of English as a Foreign Language for university students in China will involve different stakeholders and will have different impact on the educational system and the society than a study of a provincial literacy test for first and second language English-speaking students in Ontario, Canada.

Another example of the social aspect of testing is fairness, which is related to impact and washback, as what is deemed fair in one society, country, or community may be interpreted very differently in another. For example, fairness in testing has traditionally been framed in terms of "sameness" (e.g., all students take the same test under the same testing conditions), the practice of which is still considered to be fair. However, is such a practice fair for someone who is hard of hearing, or for someone who needs more time to complete a task due to certain physical and / or psychological conditions or constraints?

CONCLUSION: FUTURE DIRECTIONS

With increasing public accountability in education and the realization of the importance of stakeholders in language testing, we have seen more and more impact / washback research conducted around the world, employing multiple methods of data collection. Over time, attention has been focused increasingly on students as test takers, as among all the various stakeholders in testing events, test takers have the highest stake.

To conclude, we would like to point out a few areas that need to be further strengthened in the impact / washback research. First, we would call on impact / washback researchers to fully analyze the test that they plan to research. They should work backward from the test items and study the test by using, for example, a test fairness framework (Kunnan, 2004) and the social dimension of language testing (McNamara and Roever, 2006), in order to understand the relationship between testing, teaching, and learning – a study into the psychometric aspects of the test.

Second, we would call on these researchers to explore the relationships between test takers' characteristics and their test performance. These characteristics can include: learners' academic background; personal background, including their first language, culture, ethnicity, gender, and age; their learning strategies, learning styles, and personalities; test anxiety; motivation; as well as their attitudes toward the test – to mention just a few characteristics.

Third, researchers should understand the consequences of the test use for stakeholders beyond teachers and students within the testing context of that society, community, or country.

Lastly, impact / washback studies ought to be longitudinal and should involve cross-group studies using higher-level statistical analyses and multiple case studies. As Bachman (2005: 7) pointed out, "the extensive research on validity and validation has tended to ignore test use, on the one hand, while discussions of test use and consequences have tended to ignore validity, on the other." It is, then, essential for researchers to establish the link between test validity and test consequences. Washback researchers need to work together with other language-testing researchers as well as educational policy makers and test agencies to address the issue of validity, and in particular, the fairness and ethics of our tests.

Suggested resources

Alderson, J. C., & Wall, D. (1993). Does washback exist? *Applied Linguistics* 14, 115–129.

Cheng, L. (2008). Washback, impact and consequences. In E. Shohamy & N. H. Hornberger (Eds.), *Encyclopedia of language and education*, (2nd edition), Vol. 7: *Language testing and assessment* (pp. 349–364). New York: Springer.

Cheng, L., & Watanabe, Y., with Curtis, A. (Eds.) (2004). *Washback in language testing: Research contexts and methods*. Mahwah, NJ: Lawrence Erlbaum Associates.

McNamara, T., & Roever, C. (2006). *Language testing: The social dimension*. Malden, MA, and Oxford: Blackwell Publishing.

Messick, S. (1996). Validity and washback in language testing, *Language Testing* 13, 243–256.

Shohamy, E. (2001). *The power of tests: A critical perspective on the uses of language tests*. Harlow: Longman/Pearson.

Wall, D. (2000). The impact of high-stakes testing on teaching and learning: Can this be predicted or controlled? *System*, 28, 499–509.

Discussion questions

1. *Understand the nature of the tests*. What tests are you using in your teaching and what tests are your students taking?

2. *Explore the purposes of test use*. Would you be able to categorize the tests into those that provide information about your students' learning, and those that your students also use for purposes beyond learning, e.g., for admission to a university, for obtaining a job, or for professional certification?

3. *Explore the impact on teaching and/or learning*. How do these purposes of test use (both categories as per Question 2) affect you and your students?

4. *Explore potential differential impact on teachers and students*. What are the consequences (positive, neutral, or negative) of the tests used in your context for you, and for your students?

5. *Explore the role of the teacher in testing*. What can you do as a teacher to make best use of the positive consequences to support your students' learning, and what can you do to minimize the negative consequences?

References

Alderson, J. C., & Hamp-Lyons, L. (1996). TOEFL preparation courses: A case study. *Language Testing* 13, 280–297.

Alderson, J. C., & Wall, D. (1993). Does washback exist? *Applied Linguistic*s 14, 115–129.

Bachman, L. F. (2005). Building and supporting a case for test use. *Language Assessment Quarterly* 2(1), 1–34.

Bachman, L. F., & Palmer, A. S. (1996). *Language testing in practice*. Oxford: Oxford University Press.

Bailey, K. (1996). Working for washback: A review of the washback concept in language testing. *Language Testing* 13, 257–279.

Cheng, L. (2008). Washback, impact and consequences. In E. Shohamy, & N. H. Hornberger (Eds.), *Encyclopedia of language and education* (2nd edition), Vol. 7: *Language testing and assessment* (pp. 349–364). New York: Springer.

Cheng, L., Klinger, D., & Zheng, Y. (2007). The challenges of the Ontario Secondary School Literacy Test for second language students. *Language Testing* 24(2), 185–208.

Cheng, L., & Watanabe, Y., with Curtis, A. (Eds.) (2004). *Washback in language testing: Research contexts and methods*. Mahwah, NJ: Lawrence Erlbaum Associates.

Hamp-Lyons, L. (1997). Washback, impact and validity: Ethical concerns. *Language Testing* 14(3), 295–303.

Kunnan, A. J. (2004). Test fairness. In M. Milanovic, C. Weir, & S. Bolton (Eds.), *Europe language testing in a global context: Selected papers from the ALTE conference in Barcelona*. Cambridge: Cambridge University Press.

McNamara, T. (2000). *Language testing*. Oxford: Oxford University Press.

McNamara, T., & Roever, C. (2006). *Language testing: The social dimension*. Malden, MA, and Oxford, UK: Blackwell.

Messick, S. (1996). Validity and washback in language testing. *Language Testing* 13, 243–256.

Shohamy, E. (2001). *The power of tests: A critical perspective on the uses of language tests*. Harlow: Longman/Pearson.

Shohamy, E., Donitsa-Schmidt, S., & Ferman, I. (1996). Test impact revisited: Washback effect over time. *Language Testing* 13, 298–317.

Wall, D. (2000). The impact of high-stakes testing on teaching and learning: Can this be predicted or controlled? *System* 28, 499–509.

CHAPTER 11

Test-Taking Strategies

Andrew D. Cohen

INTRODUCTION

Language test results may play a highly significant role in the respondents' life, helping to determine whether test takers get into their study program of choice or get offered the job of their dreams. For this reason, it may be crucial that beyond the standard orientation that is available for high-stakes tests, respondents have a sense as to how to enhance their performance on specific types of items and procedures found on such tests. Such knowledge could go a long way toward reducing test anxiety as well. This entry will consider what test-taking strategies are, look briefly at research in this area over the years, identify examples of strategies that emerge from such research, and highlight several topics for future attention.

BACKGROUND

In the past, second language (L2) test validation meant, for the most part, checking on how tests fared in terms of item performance (item difficulty and item discrimination), test reliability, the intercorrelation of subtests and the relationship between the test and other tests or criterion variables (e.g., GPA), and the effects of different test methods. What was missing was the aspect of test validation that related to respondents' behaviors in taking the tests. Little was known about what they were actually doing to produce answers to questions and how this corresponded to the skills that were the target of the assessment.

At that time there was only a small group of assessment specialists who were concerned that claims of test validity required attention to how the respondents arrived at their answers. As formulated in early studies (see Cohen, 2000, for details), this research interest involved attending to the kinds of *strategies* that respondents were drawing upon as they completed language tests – that is, the consciously selected processes that the respondents used for dealing with both the language issues and the item-response demands in the test-taking tasks at hand. There is, however, a debate as to what a language learner strategy is – and therefore by extension, what a test-taking strategy is. A survey of strategy experts as to what language learner strategies are, yielded both consensus and disagreement, such as with regard to how often strategies work in isolation, in sequences, or in clusters; whether there needs to be a metacognitive component (i.e., involving planning, monitoring, and evaluation of the strategy); and the degree of consciousness called for[1] (Cohen, 2007). Nonetheless, there was agreement among experts that the effectiveness of strategy use depends on the particular learners, the learning (and testing) tasks, and the specific context for the tasks.

Thus, concern for strategies in performance on language tests actually involves three types of strategies:

1. *language learner strategies* – the ways that respondents operationalize the basic skills[2] of listening, speaking, reading, and writing, as well as the related skills of vocabulary learning, grammar, and translation. So, for example, with regard to reading skills associated with summarizing, strategies would include distinguishing key points from lesser ones, as well as being able to reconceptualize or paraphrase material at a higher level of generality.

2. *test-management strategies* – strategies for responding meaningfully to the test items and tasks. So strategies on a reading test could deal with how respondents return to the question to obtain more information, how they compare multiple-choice options rigorously to determine the most plausible response, and how they crosscheck with the reading text to make sure their choice seems appropriate.

3. *test-wiseness strategies* – strategies for using knowledge of test formats and other peripheral information to answer test items without going through the expected linguistic and cognitive processes. Again, with regard to a reading test, it would mean using the process of elimination rather blindly (i.e., selecting an option without really understanding it at all, but rather out of a vague sense that the other options are not likely to be correct), using clues in other items to answer an item under consideration, and selecting the option because it appears to have a word or phrase from the passage in it – possibly a keyword.

Hence, in responding to a reading comprehension item, the respondents may well be drawing from their repertoire of reading strategies (e.g., looking for markers of meaning in the passage, such as definitions, examples, indicators of key ideas, guides to paragraph development), test-management strategies (e.g., selecting options through the measured elimination of other options as unreasonable based on paragraph / overall passage meaning), and test-wiseness strategies (e.g., selecting the option simply because it has a word from the passage in it) (adapted from Cohen and Upton, 2006).

RESEARCH

We engage in research on test-taking strategies to help us determine how comparable the results from different test methods and item types are – with regard to the level of difficulty, the strategies elicited, and the abilities actually assessed, depending on the characteristics of the individual respondents or cultural groups. Research can help to determine, for example, whether performance on a given assessment measure is reflective of L2 language behavior in the area assessed or rather represents behaviors employed for the sake of getting through the test. To date, test-taking strategy research has provided insights in the following areas (see Cohen, 2006):

- low-level versus higher-level processing on a test;
- the impact of using authentic versus inauthentic texts in reading tests;

- whether the strategies employed in L2 test taking are more typical of first language (L1) use, common to L1 and L2 use, or more typical of L2 use;
- the more effective strategies for success on tests as well as the least effective ones;
- test takers' versus raters' understandings of and responses to integrated language tasks; and
- the items on a test that would be susceptible to the use of test-wiseness strategies.

It has proved a formidable task to obtain information about what respondents are doing without being obtrusive, while efforts to be unobtrusive often leave us in the realm of speculation. Verbal report became a primary research tool for this endeavor in the early 1980s (see Cohen, 1984). Verbal reports include data reflecting one or more of the following approaches:

1. *self-report* – learners' descriptions of what they do, characterized by generalized statements, in this case, about their test-taking strategies – for example, "On multiple-choice items, I tend to scan the reading passage for possible surface matches between information in the text and that same information appearing in one of the alternative choices;"

2. *self-observation* – the inspection of specific, contextualized language behavior, either introspectively, that is, within 20 seconds of the mental event, or retrospectively – for instance, "What I just did was to skim through the reading passage for possible surface matches between information in the text and that same information appearing in one of the alternative choices;" and

3. *self-revelation* – "think-aloud," stream-of-consciousness disclosure of thought processes while the information is being attended to – for example, "Hmm . . . I wonder if the information in one of these alternative choices also appears in the text."

An early study investigating test method effect in EFL reading testing by Israeli high school students (Gordon, 1987) found a relationship between proficiency and strategy use, comparing multiple-choice and open-ended questions in English and in Hebrew. Low-proficiency students were found to process information at a local (sentence / word) level, not relating isolated bits of information to the whole text. They used individual word-centered strategies, like matching words in alternatives to text, copying words out of text, word-for-word translation, formulating global impressions of text content on the basis of keywords or isolated lexical items in the text or in the test questions. High-proficiency students were found to comprehend the text at a global level – predicting information accurately in context, using lexical and structural knowledge to cope with linguistic difficulties.

A theme highlighted in a number of more recent studies relates to whether the strategies employed in L2 test taking are specific to first-language (L1) use, common to L1 and L2 use, or more typical of L2 use. One study found, for instance, that while two-thirds of a group of intermediate L2 learners of French at the college level had their essays rated better if they were written directly in French (with only occasional mental translation from English), one-third of the group fared better if they wrote their essay in English first and then translated it into French (Cohen and Brooks-Carson, 2001).

While verbal report continues to play a key role in test-taking strategy research, there have been changes in procedures for conducting such verbal reports aimed at improving the reliability and validity of the results. One has been to model for the respondents the kinds of responses that are considered appropriate (see, for example, Cohen and Upton, 2006), rather than to simply let them respond however they wish, which has often failed to produce enough relevant data. In addition, researchers now may intrude and ask probing questions during data collection (something that they tended not to do in the past), in order to make sure, for instance, that the respondents indicate not just their rationale for selecting "b" as the correct alternative in multiple choice, but also their reasons for rejecting "a," "c," and "d." Respondents have also been asked to listen to a tape recording or read a transcript of their verbal report session in order to complement those data with any further insights they may have (Nyhus, 1994).

Educational Testing Service commissioned the above-cited process-oriented study to describe the reading and test-taking strategies that test takers used with different item types on the Reading section of the *LanguEdge Courseware* (2002) materials developed to familiarize prospective respondents with the Internet-based TOEFL (Cohen and Upton, 2006). The investigation focused on strategies used to respond to more traditional "single selection" multiple-choice formats (i.e., *basic comprehension* and *inferencing* questions) versus the new selected-response (multiple selection, drag-and-drop) *reading-to-learn* items. The latter were designed to simulate the academic task of forming a comprehensive and coherent representation of an entire text, rather than focusing on discrete points in the text. Results showed that working through the Reading sections of the *LanguEdge* test did not fully constitute an academic reading task for these respondents, but rather a test-taking task with academic-like aspects to it. While the respondents were found to use an array of test-taking strategies, these were primarily test-management strategies.[3]

Another study conducted with the Internet-based TOEFL involved the Listening Comprehension section and represented an innovative approach to collecting data (Douglas and Hegelheimer, 2007). The procedures involved the use of the software application Morae (by Techsmith), which allowed for remotely monitoring, recording, and analyzing the data produced by users in front of a monitor, including audio recording of the verbal protocol, screen capturing (recording everything the participants do on the computer, namely, selecting and changing answers or attempting to proceed without having completed a question), and video capturing (recording facial expressions and note-taking behavior). The analysis revealed among other things various types of strategies for approaching the response task:

- recalling elements of the test input, including the instructions, the question, the input text, or a previous question;
- working with the response options by reviewing them in order, narrowing the options to the two or three most plausible, and stopping the review of options without considering the rest when one is deemed correct;
- making a hypothesis about the likely answer; and
- referring to notes before reviewing options.

The picture that emerges from test validation studies such as these is that the field has progressed beyond the days when tests were validated simply by statistical analysis of correct and incorrect responses. At present, crucial questions about what these tests are actually measuring are being asked, and impressive strides are being taken to determine what it actually entails for respondents to arrive at answers to various language assessment measures.

PRACTICAL APPLICATION

A primary purpose of conducting test-taking strategy research is to arrive at a series of empirically validated suggestions for what respondents need to do in order to enhance their performance on tests. In this section, let us look at just a few illustrative test-taking strategies that emerge from this work with respect to a few of the prominent formats for assessing language.

I. STRATEGIES IN TAKING CLOZE TESTS

Respondents are asked to complete a cloze test – namely, to supply the original or a plausible alternative for every *n*-th word which has been deleted from a text. While there are often clues within the sentence having the blank that help the respondent find the right answer, there are also items where the clue is in another sentence. More often than not, this sentence is further along in the passage. Some sample strategies for the cloze include the following:

- looking both at words and phrases immediately preceding and following a blank, as well as at the extended context for clues as to how to fill it in
- rephrasing sentences in the mind to get at the intended meaning
- recalling knowledge of the passage and any other prior knowledge that could be of use in completing the blanks

2. STRATEGIES IN DEALING WITH MULTIPLE-CHOICE READING COMPREHENSION ITEMS

a. Test-management strategies

The following are sample strategies for responding meaningfully to the test items and tasks:

- going back to the question for clarification – rereading it carefully or paraphrasing it in order to verify or confirm understanding of the question or task, as the necessary clue may be in the wording of the question
- reading the question(s) first and then reading the passage / portion in order to expedite the search for the material in the text needed to answer the question
- selecting or eliminating options based on vocabulary knowledge or on the meaning of the sentence, paragraph, overall passage, or discourse structure
- performing a mental translation of parts of the text to see if the material makes sense in the L1, and then summarizing the passage as a check for comprehension

b. Test-wiseness strategies (based largely on Allan, 1992)

Whereas, as test constructors, we may wish to avoid items where test-wiseness can produce correct answers, we have to assume that such items will continue to be written and so here are some illustrative examples:

- checking for identical or similar words or phrases in the stem and in one of the multiple-choice options as a giveaway to the answer
- looking for grammatical cues, where only one alternative matches the stem grammatically
- eliminating several distractors because they essentially say the same thing
- seeing if a previous item supplies a sufficient clue to answering a subsequent item correctly
- using knowledge of the world to eliminate multiple-choice distractors that are patently false or involve an illogical inference

3. MULTIPLE-CHOICE LISTENING COMPREHENSION ITEMS

- verifying if the options match elements of the listening text or the question in terms of keywords, specific details, inferences about details, level of specificity (which may constitute a test-wiseness strategy if the matching does not require understanding the language)
- checking back to part or all of a prior question as a guide to selecting a response to the item at hand
- determining the level of detail required in answering a question so as to reject an option that is either too general or too specific
- identifying relevant background knowledge and then utilizing it in an appropriate way
- when uncertainty prevails, making an educated guess drawing on a combination of strategies such as those listed above

CURRENT TRENDS AND FUTURE DIRECTIONS

The picture emerging from current work on test-taking strategies, often involving highly sophisticated data analysis techniques (e.g., structural equation modeling), is that more proficient learners are better able to utilize such strategies to their advantage than are less proficient students. Even if two groups of respondents are using the very same strategies, there is likely to be a qualitative difference in how they use them. In addition, there may be differences among respondents at different proficiency levels, depending on the manner in which they approach the test (for example, comparing more process-oriented with more product-oriented respondents; Purpura, 1999). It has been found, for example, that highly successful test takers are more likely to use metacognitive strategies than moderately successful ones, who in turn use these strategies more than unsuccessful test takers (Phakiti, 2003).

In addition, it would appear that instruction in the use of test-taking strategies may have a somewhat differential impact on the performance of prospective test takers on high-stakes standardized tests, depending in part on their language proficiency as well as on a variety of other factors. In a study of 43 students at a coaching school in Taiwan, for example, it was found that high scorers tended to focus on their understanding of the passages, to use the strategies taught by the coaching school only as an auxiliary to comprehension, and to stress the need to personalize these strategies (Tian, 2000). The low scorers, on the other hand, tended to focus on word-level strategies, to use the suggested strategies as a way of circumventing comprehension, and to follow the test-taking strategy instruction from the coaching school staff mechanically. These findings should serve as a warning that strategy instruction materials may not necessarily help those who need it the most, and perhaps most benefit those who least need assistance.

Looking to future directions for test-taking strategy work, there can be value in describing test-taking strategies in terms of the interaction among the following factors:

- the respondents' characteristics (such as L2 proficiency level);
- the nature of the testing task at hand;
- the array of strategy use by subtest;
- the method for data collection; and
- how all of these factors impact test performance.

One issue in this regard that still seems unresolved is the directionality – that is, the extent to which test takers who adopt strategies to fit the demands of the assessment tasks perform better on the assessment. Another lingering question is the extent to which findings from research on test-taking strategies have contributed to making language tests more valid.

Suggested resources

Cohen, A. D. (1994). The process of responding to an assessment instrument. In *Assessing language ability in the classroom* (2nd ed.) (pp. 115–159). Boston: Heinle & Heinle.

This chapter from my book looks at the process of responding to an assessment instrument, considering both issues of research and practice, focusing on what respondents actually do to respond to different kinds of language assessment measures.

Nevo, N. (1989). Test-taking strategies on a multiple-choice test of reading comprehension. *Language Testing*, 6(2), 199–215.

Forty-two 10th-grade Hebrew L1 students of French took an MC reading comprehension test given in both languages. The researchers were getting feedback from subjects immediately after each item concerning their test-taking strategies.

Purpura, J. E. (1998). Investigating the effects of strategy use and second language test performance with high- and low-ability test takers: A structural equation modeling approach. *Language Testing*, 15(3), 333–379.

Strategy questionnaires and a language test, the First Certificate in English, were administered to 1,382 respondents. The sections included: grammar, vocabulary, passage comprehension, word formation, cloze, and sentence formation. A cognitive strategy questionnaire checked for inductive analysis, clarification, inference, association, linking to prior knowledge, repeating / rehearsing, summarizing, applying rules, practicing naturalistically, and transferring from L1 to L2. A metacognitive strategy questionnaire looked for self-testing, assessing the situation, self-evaluating, and monitoring.

Turner, C. E. (1989). The underlying factor structure of L2 close test performance in francophone, university-level students: Causal modeling as an approach to construct validation. *Language Testing*, 6(2), 172–197.

This article looks at the extent to which performance on L2 cloze tests depends upon cloze-taking ability, knowledge of the L1 and L2, the content domain, and local and global contextual constraints. Eight cloze tests were designed such that four were in English and four in French, with two each on "sleep and dreams" and two each on "physical conditioning," with two of the English cloze texts having words deleted that could be restored using the local context and two having blanks intended to be restored through more global reading of the text. The study found that performance on an ESL cloze was dependent upon an L2 factor and upon cloze-taking ability, the latter making more of a contribution. Findings for French L1 cloze performance would suggest that success is based on performance at the whole text (global) level.

Warren, J. (1996). How students pick the right answer: A "think aloud" study of the French CAT. In J. Burston, M. Monville-Burston, & J. Warren (Eds.), Special issue: Issues and innovations in the teaching of French. *Australian Review of Applied Linguistics Occasional Paper* No. 15, pp. 79–94.

A French Computer Adaptive Test (CAT) with 124 items was developed in Australia and administered to 20 college students. Warren categorized strategies as being automatic, using a grammar rule, using a grammar cue, determining if a choice looked or sounded right, guessing, translating, or taking an "off-the-wall" approach.

Yamashita, S. (2001). Using pictures for research in pragmatics: Eliciting pragmatic strategies by picture response tests. In T. Hudson & J. D. Brown (Eds.), *A focus on language test development* (pp. 35–56). Honolulu, HI: University of Hawai'i, Second Language Teaching and Curriculum Center.

The researcher developed a pragmatic test without written descriptions – a Picture Response Test (PRT) – partly to avoid the reactive effects of the written prompt on the output. Two hundred and forty-four respondents equally representing four groups (native speakers of Japanese in Tokyo, native speakers of English in Chicago and Los Angeles, English-speaking Americans in Tokyo, and Japanese learners of English in Tokyo) responded to six apology situations. The results illustrated the challenges in developing such a test.

Discussion questions

1. What are the three types of strategies of concern when dealing with so-called test-taking strategies? What would an example be of each kind?

2. What do you think would be the potential benefit of having test respondents draw on such strategies when taking high-stakes tests?

3. What does it mean that a respondent could be getting an item wrong for the right reasons or right for the wrong reasons? Provide examples of test-taking strategies (especially test-wiseness ones) that students might use to answer multiple-choice items correctly on reading passages even when they do not understand the passage.

4. In what ways has verbal report been used as a tool in such research?

5. What examples are given in the article of ways in which test-taking strategies may be beneficial in taking cloze tests, and in responding to multiple-choice reading comprehension and listening items?

References

Allan, A. (1992). Development and validation of a scale to measure test-wiseness in EFL / ESL reading test-takers. *Language Testing*, 9(2), 101–122.

Cohen, A. D. (1984). On taking language tests: What the students report. *Language Testing*, 1(1), 70–81.

Cohen, A. D. (2000). Exploring strategies in test-taking: Fine-tuning verbal reports from respondents. In G. Ekbatani & H. Pierson (Eds.), *Learner-directed assessment in ESL* (pp. 127–150), Mahwah, NJ: Lawrence Erlbaum.

Cohen, A. D. (2006). The coming of age of research on test-taking strategies. *Language Assessment Quarterly*, 3(4), 307–331.

Cohen, A. D. (2007). Coming to terms with language learner strategies: Surveying the experts. In A. D. Cohen & E. Macaro (Eds.), *Language learner strategies: 30 years of research and practice* (pp. 29–45). Oxford: Oxford University Press.

Cohen, A. D., & Brooks-Carson, A. (2001). Research on direct vs. translated writing: Students' strategies and their results. *Modern Language Journal*, 85(2), 169–188.

Cohen, A. D., & Upton, T. A. (2006). *Strategies in responding to the new TOEFL reading tasks* [Monograph No. 33]. Princeton, NJ: ETS. Retrieved June 7, 2009, from www.ets.org/Media/Research/pdf/RR-06-06.pdf.

Douglas, D., & Hegelheimer, V. (2007). *Strategies and use of knowledge in performing New TOEFL listening tasks*. Final Report to the Educational Testing Service. Ames, IA: Department of English, Iowa State University.

Gordon, C. (1987). "The effect of testing method on achievement in reading comprehension tests in English as a foreign language." Unpublished M.A. Thesis, Tel-Aviv, Israel: School of Education, Tel-Aviv University, Ramat-Aviv.

Nyhus, S. E. (1994). *Attitudes of non-native speakers of English toward the use of verbal report to elicit their reading comprehension strategies.* Unpublished Plan B Masters Paper, Minneapolis, MN: Department of English as a Second Language, University of Minnesota.

Phakiti, A. (2003). A closer look at the relationship of cognitive and metacognitive strategy use to EFL reading achievement test performance. *Language Testing*, 20(1), 26–56.

Purpura, J. E. (1999). *Learner strategy use and performance on language tests: A structural equation modeling approach.* Cambridge: Cambridge University Press.

Tian, S. (2000). TOEFL reading comprehension: Strategies used by Taiwanese Students with coaching-school training. Unpublished doctoral dissertation. Teachers College, Columbia University.

Notes

[1] In reality, the level of conscious attention in the selection of strategies can be on a continuum from high focus to some attention to just general awareness.

[2] Note that for the purposes of this chapter, a skill constitutes the ability to do something (such as looking up a word in a dictionary or paraphrasing a text) and that strategies are the means used to operationalize this skill.

[3] The respondents were perhaps reluctant to use test-wiseness strategies because they knew we were observing their behavior closely.

CHAPTER 12

What Teachers Need to Know About Test Analysis

James Dean Brown

INTRODUCTION

Classical Test Theory (CTT) is the basis for most of the developments in testing today. Indeed language-testing books ranging from Lado (1961) to Brown (2005) focus largely on CTT, which includes such concepts as item analysis (item facility and discrimination), descriptive statistics (mean, mode, median, range, standard deviation, etc.), reliability (test–retest, parallel forms, and internal consistency), and validity (content, criterion-related, and construct). These CTT concepts and the statistics that accompany them are clearly explained in Chapter 4, and they are certainly helpful for understanding the manuals provided with many standardized tests of proficiency and placement. At the institutional level, CTT is most useful for developing placement tests for use in making decisions about who should study at what level upon entering the program. In contrast, the purpose of this chapter is to consider what *teachers* need to know about classroom test analysis and what they can learn about their classroom tests before, during, and after they have been administered.

BACKGROUND

I have argued elsewhere (e.g., Brown, 1990, 1992, 1993, 2005; Brown and Hudson, 2002; Chapter 15) that classroom tests are quite different from standardized tests. One central issue is that CTT notions of reliability and validity may not be appropriate for analyzing the classroom quizzes / tests that teachers develop and use. Technically, classroom tests belong in a category called Criterion-Referenced Tests (CRTs), a concept that only appeared in the educational testing literature in the mid-1960s. CRT theory showed how concepts like reliability and criterion-related validity were not appropriate for analyzing classroom quiz / test scores. Indeed, the whole area of reliability was replaced for CRTs with the notion of *dependability* (Brown and Hudson, 2002).

RESEARCH

I have often found that classroom teachers find concepts like *reliability* and *dependability* esoteric and boring. As a result, I decided to avoid jargon and statistics in this chapter as much as possible and allow only those aspects to filter through that are practical and directly applicable for teachers doing classroom testing. To those ends, I am framing these issues as a series of questions.

CTT concept	Standardized testing concerns	Analogous CRT concerns	Teacher / classroom questions of interest
CTT reliability	NRT reliability – test–retest, parallel forms, internal consistency (K-R20 & 21, alpha, etc.)	CRT dependability – threshold-loss agreement, squared-error lost agreement, domain-score dependability	Are the scores on my quiz / test consistent?
CTT validity	Content validity – test map, item planning, analysis by expert opinion	Content validity – item specifications, expert analysis for matching to objectives	Does the content of my quiz / test match the objectives of the class and the material covered? Do my course objectives meet the needs of the students?
CTT validity	Construct validity – analysis of differential groups and intervention studies, factor analysis, structural equation modeling, etc.	Construct validity – analysis of intervention or mastery / non-mastery studies	Do my quizzes / tests show that my students are learning something in my course?
CTT validity	Criterion-related validity – analysis of concurrent and predictive correlations	NA	NA
CTT validity	Face validity – analysis of whether the test looks as expected by stakeholders		Will my students think my quiz / test matches the material I am teaching them?
Values implications in validity	Values implications – analysis of the values (and whose values they are) underlie the testing content, purpose, method, etc.		How do the values that underlie my quiz / test scores match my values? My students' values? Their parents' values? My boss's values? The values of others?
Consequential validity	Social consequences – analysis of the intended and unintended repercussions of decisions based on the test scores for all stakeholders		What are the consequences of the decisions I base on my quiz / test scores for my students, their parents, me, my boss, others?

Table 12.1   Standardized testing concerns, analogous CRT concerns, and questions of interest to teachers

The first column of Table 12.1 shows the main conceptual categories of CTT reliability and validity as well as recent developments like values implications and consequential validity. The second column shows how they are technically framed in standardized testing; the third column shows the analogous CRT framing; and the last column shows the parallel questions I hope teachers will find intriguing enough to address when they are doing their own classroom testing.

PRACTICAL APPLICATIONS

ARE THE SCORES ON MY QUIZ / TEST CONSISTENT?

Teachers already attend to this issue when they find obvious problems with test consistency. For example, if their best student, who usually scores 100 percent, suddenly fails a test with 45 percent, the teacher notices and will probably investigate. Was the student sick? Are there problems at home? Score consistency centers on this idea that a student's scores should be steady, consistent, reliable, dependable, and so on, as opposed to unsteady, inconsistent, unreliable, undependable, and so on. Thus, students' scores should not vary for random reasons (sickness, family problems, etc.) unrelated to the material being tested. Most teachers agree that dependable variation in scores is desirable. The degree to which the scores on a test are consistent can be estimated by calculating a reliability estimate for standardized tests or a dependability estimate for classroom tests. Fortunately, Brown (2005: 209) showed that the Kuder-Richardson formula 21 (K-R21) is applicable for classroom tests because it is "a conservative 'rough and ready' underestimate of the domain-referenced dependability." This is fortunate because K-R21 is also easy to calculate:

$$K\text{-}R21 = \frac{k}{k-1}\left(1 - \frac{M(k-M)}{kS^2}\right)$$

where: K-R21 = Kuder-Richardson formula 21

k = number of items

M = mean of the test scores

S = standard deviation of the test scores

Figure 12.1   The Kuder-Richardson formula 21 (K-R21)

You only need to know the number of items, the mean, and the standard deviation on the test. Calculating the mean and standard deviation by hand is explained by Brown (2005, 2009).

With these three statistics in hand, the rest is easy. For example, to calculate K-R21 for a test with 50 test items, a mean of 35, and a standard deviation of 5, you need only do the following:

$$K\text{-}R21 = \frac{k}{k-1}\left(1 - \frac{M(k-M)}{kS^2}\right) = \frac{50}{49}\left(1 - \frac{35(50-35)}{50 \times 7^2}\right) = 1.02\left(1 - \frac{525}{2450}\right)$$

$$= 1.02(1 - .2143) = 1.02 \times .8014 = \approx .80$$

That .80 can be converted to a percent by moving the decimal two places to the right (.80 → 80%). It means that the scores on the test were 80 percent consistent. That is a good result for a classroom test, but it could be made better by increasing the quality of the items, insuring maximal testing conditions, making sure that the students are well prepared, and so on. (For those who care, the K-R21 estimates the *dependability* of the scores on your quizzes / tests.)

DOES THE CONTENT OF MY QUIZ / TEST MATCH THE OBJECTIVES OF THE CLASS AND THE MATERIAL COVERED? DO MY COURSE OBJECTIVES MEET THE NEEDS OF THE STUDENTS?

Unless your teaching is completely unplanned, you have some form of instructional objectives, learning outcomes, or just things you want students to be able to do by the end of your course (I will refer to these collectively as *objectives*). Such objectives may come from your ministry or department of education, school district, school, or textbook, or you may have determined them yourself. Regardless, the first step in examining the content of your tests is to identify, locate, and print out your objectives. With the objectives in front of you, identify which objective(s) each quiz / test item is assessing. Then, write the objective(s) that you think you are testing next to each item.

Now carefully compare the list of objectives you wrote on your test with the list of your actual course objectives, and ask yourself a series of questions: Are all of my test items assessing course objectives? Or, are they testing something else? Do I want to eliminate those items that are testing something else? Are all of my objectives assessed somewhere on my test, or at least a representative cross-section of those objectives? Are the objectives weighted with the same degrees of relative importance in my course and on my test? And, how well do my objectives and test items match the real-world language needs of my students? Should I revise my test and my objectives according to what I have learned here?

All of these questions are important for teachers to answer. If you are feeling particularly adventuresome, you might ask a colleague to go through your objectives and tests in the same steps to see if they come to the same conclusions.

Either way, you should recognize that analyzing your test items and objectives in this way is not a one-way street. This process may indeed lead to changing, dropping, or even adding items on your test, but it can equally well lead to modifying, dropping, or adding objectives. (For those who care, the strategies explained in this subsection can enhance or provide arguments for the *content validity* of the scores on your quizzes / tests.)

DO MY QUIZZES / TESTS SHOW THAT MY STUDENTS ARE LEARNING SOMETHING IN MY COURSE?

Even if the test items perfectly match the content of your course, you cannot be sure that your students are learning any of it unless you check to see if students have relatively low scores at the beginning of the course and higher scores at the end. In ideal situations, where I have been with teachers who work together on their diagnostic and achievement tests, we have been able to compare our students' scores at the beginning of the course (i.e., their diagnostic test scores) with their scores at the end (i.e., their achievement test scores). We developed two parallel tests, Form A and Form B, based on the course objectives that we had all agreed to. Then at the beginning of the course, we administered Form A to half the students (randomly selected) and Form B to the other half as a diagnostic test. At the end of the course, we administered the opposite form to the students as an achievement test. We were then able to compare beginning and end total scores and even scores on individual objectives. Initially, we found 10 to 15 percent gains in overall scores between the beginning and end of 45-hour courses, which we found disappointing. However, after we eliminated objectives that most students already knew at the beginning and after we revised and fine-tuned our tests and objectives, we were able to demonstrate 25 to 30 percent average gains, which were much more gratifying. That is what a group of teachers working together can accomplish.

But what about the teacher who is working alone? Of course, a teacher who puts in 27-hour days can accomplish anything, but perhaps more focused strategies will be more useful for real teachers. Consider, for example, giving your final exam (i.e., your achievement test) at the beginning of the course as a diagnostic test. If you use the same test for both diagnostic and achievement testing purposes, you won't be able to disentangle the effect on the final exam scores of simply having taken the first test and remembering the items. However, if you consider the diagnostic test a part of the teaching / learning process, the testing effect may not be a major concern for you. In any case, administering your test at the beginning will allow you to give your students diagnostic feedback for the course objectives included on the diagnostic test. Another benefit: If you notice that students generally score very high on two or three of the objectives at the beginning of the course, you can eliminate those objectives and use the time that you save for teaching things the students actually needed to learn.

Later, after the final examination, you can compare the total scores on the diagnostic test with those on the final achievement test to see if any learning has occurred. If you find all of this an intimidating prospect, consider administering a small subset of objectives / items at the beginning and end, then treating them as explained earlier in this chapter. (For those who care, the strategies explained in this subsection can enhance or provide arguments for the *construct validity* of the scores on your quizzes / tests.)

WILL MY STUDENTS THINK MY QUIZ / TEST MATCHES THE MATERIAL I AM TEACHING THEM?

If your students do not feel that the items you included on a quiz, midterm, or final examination match the material you covered in class, they will be justifiably upset. That is why it is important that you assess what you teach and do so in the same way that you teach it. If you teach functions like giving and seeking information by doing pair work, you should use pair work to assess them (perhaps, this time, with you as one half of the pair). If you teach writing with a task like filling out forms, then students should find themselves filling out a form on your classroom quiz / test. This may seem self-evident, but many teachers fail to do this, some in the belief that what we teach with one type of activity should "transfer" to other sorts of activities. Personally, I think they are wrong because (a) such transferability is poorly understood if it exists at all; in any case, (b) assessing for transferability is a poor use of the washback effect; and, (c) assessing with activities that are different from the teaching activities may be viewed as unfair by students and their parents. If you assess a particular knowledge, skill, or language point using the same activity used to teach and practice it, all of the above problems will disappear. Similarly, if you use a variety of activities to teach a particular objective and then assess it using one of those activities, you will also avoid the problems listed above because you will be perceived as sampling from the material you taught. (For those who care, the concerns explained in this subsection can enhance or provide arguments for the *content validity* and *face validity* of the scores on your quizzes / tests.)

HOW DO THE VALUES THAT UNDERLIE MY QUIZ / TEST SCORES MATCH MY VALUES? MY STUDENTS' VALUES? THEIR PARENTS' VALUES? MY BOSS'S VALUES? THE VALUES OF OTHERS?

It is nearly impossible to do teaching or assessment that is not laden with cultural values. We are all products of our background, upbringing, and training, who carry with us belief systems that may be quite different from the belief systems of our students. There is nothing wrong with this, it just *is*. However, it might be worth thinking about and taking into consideration the values of your students, their parents' values, your boss's values, and so on, and how their values differ from your own, especially with regard to the roles of teachers and students, what teaching is, what language learning is, what good assessment is, and so on. You can gather information on such issues by reading up on them, or by gathering more direct information in interviews with your students, parents, other teachers, administrators, and others. Armed with such knowledge, you can then incorporate both the good characteristics of your own values and those of the local values into your teaching and assessment practices. Why is this important? Considering all stakeholders' underlying values will help you adjust your teaching and assessment practices so that you increase buy-in from the stakeholders, and unless you are absolutely sure that your own values are the only values worth believing in (a foolish stance indeed), then buy-in from stakeholders will make your teaching easier and more effective.

I am not arguing that you should simply adopt the values of the students, parents, or administrators. Indeed, you need to recognize that some of your values, especially the ones based on your training and experience as a language teacher, may be worth arguing for. In such cases, you may have to do a selling job, that is, you may have to explain respectfully that your training and experience as a language teacher tell you that it is good to X, Y, and Z. For example, I have taught EFL students who firmly believed in grammar–translation as the only way to learn a language, and I eventually succeeded in cajoling, convincing, and shifting their views by respectfully asking them to try doing some fluency exercises and then including pair work and a fluency rubric in my assessment of them. (For those who care, the concerns explained in this subsection can enhance or provide arguments for the *values implications* in the validity of the scores on your quizzes / tests.)

WHAT ARE THE CONSEQUENCES OF THE DECISIONS I BASE ON MY QUIZ / TEST SCORES FOR MY STUDENTS, THEIR PARENTS, ME, MY BOSS, OTHERS?

Certainly the consequences of decisions based on most classroom assessment are not as dire as those in the high-stakes proficiency tests (for example, those used to determine whether a student should be admitted to a university) or placement tests (for example, those used to determine how much time and tuition students will have to spend on language instruction). Nor are the consequences of teachers' assessment-based decisions negligible. Negative consequences tend to center on assessment that results in grading decisions. For instance, what will the consequences be of failing a student based on a teacher's assessments, or of passing a student who should have failed? Failing a student can have a very negative effect on that student's life and get a strong negative reaction from the student, parents, boss, and others. But passing a student who should have failed may get that student into a situation that is way above their ability level, and get a strong negative reaction from the teacher at the next level, for example, who must deal with this weak student.

Positive consequences can also occur. Many students see their test results as a reward for their hard work. In addition, positive washback from tests can serve as motivation for many students. For example, in the EFL situation I mentioned in the previous subsection, I watched students who wanted nothing more than to learn more grammar and vocabulary completely reverse their attitudes toward communicative teaching, in no small part because we matched our communicative teaching with communicative assessments that they had to prepare for and pass. Thus our tests had positive consequences.

In short, assessment can have social consequences, both positive and negative, and teachers need to be aware of these possibilities and harness them as much as possible to foster student learning. (For those who care, the concerns explained in this subsection can enhance or provide arguments for the *consequential validity* of the decisions based on the scores of your quizzes / tests.)

CONCLUSION

So, what do teachers need to know about test analysis? They need to know that test analysis is not some distant set of esoteric statistical concepts and practices that only apply to the large-scale standardized tests that have nothing to do with their everyday professional lives.

By way of a summary, let me reverse the issues covered in this chapter by asking a corollary question: Why bother doing test analysis before, during, or after the exam is over? A number of reasons should now pop to mind:

1. to make sure that your quiz / test is functioning consistently and fairly for your students, and to improve that consistency and fairness

2. to insure that you are testing the same material you are teaching, and to improve both the relevance of that material and the degree to which you are assessing it

3. to understand the degree to which students are learning the material and improve that learning

4. to understand your values and the values of all stakeholders and how those values affect your classroom teaching and quizzes / tests

5. to consider both the negative and positive consequences of your assessments and use that understanding to help foster student learning

To twist Socrates's famous saying a bit, the bottom line is that "the unexamined quiz / test isn't worth giving."

Suggested resources

Bachman, L. (2004). *Statistical analysis in language assessment*. Cambridge: Cambridge University Press.

Brown, J. D. (2005). *Testing in language programs: A comprehensive guide to English language assessment* (new ed.). New York: McGraw-Hill.

Discussion questions

1. How are standardized and classroom assessment different? Which of these two types of assessments is more likely to be of interest to busy classroom teachers?

2. How can you determine if your test scores are consistent?

3. How can you find out if the content of your test matches the objectives of your class and the material you covered? How can you determine whether your objectives meet the needs of the students?

4. How can you know if your tests indicate that students are learning something in your course?

5. How can you find out if your students think your test matches the material you taught them?

6. How do your values affect your quizzes / tests? And what is the effect of your students' values? Their parents' values? Your boss's values? The values of others?

7. How can you come to understand both the positive and negative consequences of your assessment-based decisions for your students, their parents, your boss, and others?

8. Why should you bother with analyzing your tests before, during, and after they are administered?

References

Brown, J. D. (1990). Where do tests fit into language programs? *JALT Journal*, 12, 121–140.

Brown, J. D. (1992). Classroom-centered language testing. *TESOL Journal*, 1, 12–15.

Brown, J. D. (1993). A comprehensive criterion-referenced language testing project. In D. Douglas & C. Chapelle (Eds.), *A new decade of language testing research* (pp. 163–184). Washington, DC: TESOL (also available from ERIC: ED 365 138).

Brown, J. D. (2005). *Testing in language programs: A comprehensive guide to English language assessment* (new ed.). New York: McGraw-Hill.

Brown, J. D. (2009). Using a spreadsheet program to record, organize, analyze, and understand your classroom assessments. In C. Coombe, P. Davidson, & D. Lloyd (Eds.) (2009), *The Fundamentals of language assessment: A practical guide for teachers* (2nd ed.) (pp. 59–70). Dubai, UAE: TESOL Arabia Publications.

Brown, J. D., & Hudson, T. (2002). *Criterion-referenced language testing*. Cambridge: Cambridge University Press.

Lado, R. (1961). *Language testing: The construction and use of foreign language tests*. London: Longmans.

CHAPTER 13

Ethics in Language Testing and Assessment

Annie Brown

INTRODUCTION

Language tests are used for many purposes and in many contexts and are often the basis for high-stakes decision making. Language test scores are used to make many types of decisions about people and programs. They are used to screen, place, and classify students, to hire, promote, or even dismiss employees, to allow entry into a profession or a country, to award citizenship, to determine language interventions, to evaluate the effectiveness of language programs, and to act as tools for data gathering in research. This increasing use of language tests as a means of making decisions about individuals and programs, and the growth of language testing as an industry in the 20th century, have led to increasing awareness of and concern about appropriate and inappropriate uses of tests and ethical action on the part of testers and testing organizations.

In the *Dictionary of Language Testing*, Davies et al. (1999) define ethics as "the agreed rules of conduct of a group, profession or society." The increasing concern of language testers with the ethics of the activity of language testing is reflected in the development over the last decade or so of professional codes of ethics or practice, such as those of the Association of Language Testers in Europe (ALTE, 1994), the International Language Testing Association (2000, 2007), and Japan Language Testing Association (2001/2003), and is, according to Davies et al. (1999), a consequence of the language-testing community's "growing sense of professionalism." Davies sees the need for a code of practice to "provide a contract for the profession and the individual with the public, thereby safeguarding all three (1997: 333). To McNamara and Roever (2006: 137), the increasing interest in a professional ethics for language testers specifically is also "a sign of language testing coming into its own as a profession rather than being a subordinate component of language teaching or general psychometrics."

In contrast with this perspective, which, according to McNamara (2006: 43) "holds that language-testing practice can be made ethical and stresses the individual responsibility of testers to ensure that it is," and which he terms *ethical language testing*, is a more radical perspective, known as *critical language testing* (Lynch, 2001; Shohamy, 1998, 2001a, b), following the model of critical applied linguistics (Pennycook, 2001), and critical theory in general. In this conceptualization, given that tests are "embedded in political, social, educational, ideological and economic contexts" (Shohamy, 2001a: 114), there is, it is argued, a need to refuse to accept language test constructs as value-free givens, but instead to subject them to critique in terms of the values they embody (McNamara, 2006), and to recognize that testing is a political act and to challenge the status quo in order to "protect [society] from undemocratic principles" (Shohamy, 2001b: 373).

The notion of ethicality has long been linked with that of validity. In fact, it could be argued that validation is all about establishing the ethicality of assessment practices, ensuring that the use of a test for a particular purpose is justified and that the inferences drawn and decisions made about test takers on the basis of that test are both meaningful and fair. Schwandt and Jang (2004: 268) argue that "[b]ecause tests are tools created for various social purposes (e.g., selection, placement, classification), validity can never be merely a technical matter but is also always an ethical-political matter of the intended and actual use of a test. Therefore, we cannot treat issues of reliability and validity as fundamentally distinct from issues of use and fairness that are taken up in discussions of language testing practices in society."

However, it is only recently that conceptualizations of validity, such as that of Messick (e.g., 1989, 1996), have made the link between validity and ethics explicit, through the inclusion of the *consequences* of test use as an integral aspect of construct validity. In other words the responsibilities of the language tester go beyond developing a good test to a responsibility for how it is used. Within language testing, the consequences of test use, or consequential validity, have been engaged with to the greatest extent through discussion of and research into *test impact* and *washback* (see Chapter 9 in this volume). Indeed, Alderson, Clapham, and Wall (1995) argue that ethics is made up of a combination of validity and washback.

A term that is frequently linked with that of ethics is *fairness* (e.g., Bachman, 2000; Fulcher and Davidson, 2007; Hamp-Lyons, 2001; Kunnan, 2006). Fairness has traditionally been interpreted as the need to ensure that tests are not biased against particular groups of test takers. In the context of performance testing, facets of the testing situation, such as tasks, raters, interlocutors or rating scales, would be investigated in order to determine the existence and causes of bias (McNamara, 2008). More recent conceptualizations of fairness have broadened its scope, however. Lynch (1997) expands the notion of fairness to refer not only to giving everyone a fair chance to demonstrate their abilities, but also to the consequences of language-testing decisions. Kunnan (2000) extends the meaning of fairness further to embrace *validity*, *access* (e.g., financially and educationally), and *justice* (in terms of societal equity and legal challenges) as its three main concerns. He subsequently (2004, 2006) brought together the traditional concerns of validity and reliability with newer ones – absence of bias, access, test administration, and test consequences – to create a *Test Fairness Framework* for evaluating tests.

BACKGROUND

The first papers on ethics in language testing appeared in the late 1970s and early 1980s, but it was not until the late 1990s and early 2000s that the question of ethics really came to the fore with the publication of a collection of papers on the ethics of language testing in a special issue of *Language Testing* (1997), following a symposium on the topic at the 1996 meeting of the Association Internationale de Linguistique Appliquée in Finland. Subsequently, *Language Assessment Quarterly* (2004) published a special issue containing papers from a Language Assessment Ethics Conference held in Pasadena, California, in May 2002. The engagement of the language-testing community with the question of ethics is evidenced by the ILTA bibliography of language testing (Brown, 2010), which contains 74 entries under the heading "Ethics" for the period 2000–2010.

According to McNamara (2006: 43), the growing interest in ethics is a "response within language testing to Messick's concern for the consequences of test use." Messick defines the consequential aspect of test validation as "evidence and rationales for evaluating the intended and unintended consequences of score interpretation and use in both the short- and long-term . . . [and] unfairness in test use, and positive or negative washback effects on teaching and learning" (Messick, 1996: 251). This broadening of the concept of validity to include test consequences is referenced also as *decision-based interpretations* in the work of Kane (2001) and included as *impact* within Bachman and Palmer's (1996) concept of *test usefulness*, and as *impact–consequential validity* within Lynch's (2001) validity framework, developed from the perspective of critical theory and a qualitative research tradition.

Weir (2005) considers consequential validity to have three main aspects: differential validity (that is, test bias); washback validity (the impact of tests on teaching and learning); and effect on society. The first of the three – differential validity – is concerned with the fairness of tests for subgroups of test takers. Fairness reviews, that is the review of potential items, texts, or tasks against a set of item-writing guidelines (e.g., Educational Testing Service, 2007) and their statistical correlate, differential item functioning (DIF) (Holland and Wainer, 1993), along with investigations using quantitative or qualitative methods to investigate the impact of test method facets in performance tests, are all ways to ensure that differential group performance is due to *bona fide* differences in ability on the trait being measured, and not to a bias within the measurement process itself. The last two of Weir's validities – washback validity and effect on society – reference Hamp-Lyons' (1997) distinction between *impact*, as a macrolevel societal effect, and *washback*, which operates at the microlevel on teachers, students, and the classroom.

At the impact level – that is, the effect of tests *outside* the classroom – the issues are engaged with as much through debate and discussion of case studies as through research (see, for example, Kunnan and Davidson, 2004), in order to develop principles of ethical behavior, or an *ethical milieu* (Davies, 1997) for language testing. In the next section we will consider three of the current most hotly debated ethical issues, bearing in mind that this selection is necessarily limited due to space. Other issues, such as the roles of standardized assessment and alternative assessment, or the involvement of stakeholders, might equally well have been included.

KEY ISSUES

1. THE LIMITS OF THE TESTER'S RESPONSIBILITIES

A number of researchers (e.g., Davies, 1997; Hamp-Lyons 1997; Kunnan, 2000) have raised the question of whether, or to what extent, testing specialists should take any responsibility for decisions about nonintended use of tests or for unintended consequences of test use. In other words, at what point does the test developer's responsibility end? What if, for example, a test that is used to determine resources across a school system is ultimately used to close certain schools down? Or, what if the threshold on a test used to determine whether prospective immigrants have sufficient English is raised in order to limit the number of entrants during an economic downturn? Whereas the American Psychological Association (Joint Committee on Testing Practices, 2004) states that test developers should provide specific information about the potential limitations of the test, including situations in which the use of the test scores would be inappropriate, Davies (2008) argues that it is not possible for a test developer to foresee all possible uses and social consequences, and seeks therefore to limit responsibility to the more traditional validity concerns such as internal (technical) bias analysis and accountability for a test's "fairness." Certainly, in the case of the immigrant language test, if the test has been properly validated the test developer should have empirical data to support the original threshold. However, and this is also increasingly a concern, what if it is testing organizations themselves who are guilty of using tests developed for one purpose in other, less obviously relevant contexts?

2. THE POLITICS OF LANGUAGE TEST USE

Much has been written on the social and political consequences of test use and the use of tests as instruments of social control, for example to determine immigration, citizenship, professional entry, and progress (Blackledge, 2009; Fulcher and Davidson, 2007; Hawthorne, 2005; McNamara, 2008; Shohamy, 2001a). From the critical perspective, it is argued that tests should be seen not as neutral measures but as instruments of power and control, designed to further the policies of those in power. McNamara and Roever (2006) point out that the question of the "rightness" of what the test results are used for stands against the appropriateness of the test itself (its reliability / validity). However, although one cannot argue with the view that "the professional language tester is responsible for conscious, self-critical reflection and analysis of the social, cultural, historical, political, and economic conditions within which tests are designed and administered and the interests they serve" (Schwandt and Jang, 2004), McNamara questions not only whether language testers are willing to do this but, whether "the lack of an appropriate model of the broader social context in which to consider the social and political functions of tests" (2008: 423) means they do not have the tools to effectively engage with testing as a social and political practice. What is needed, he argues, is for validity theory to engage with broader social theory.

3. THE ETHICALITY OF SCHOOL TESTING PROGRAMS

In the United States, the federal "No Child Left Behind" (NCLB) legislation requires that all school students must meet a certain threshold of learning outcomes. The consequences of students not meeting these thresholds are great: Funding may be withheld from so-called "failed" schools or school districts. Other than the ethicality of holding schools accountable on the basis of standardized tests and of punishing failing schools as if they have somehow abused their responsibility (Bishop, 2004), and the question of the impact of these penalties on the quality of education, of particular concern to language testers is the ethicality of testing English language learners (ELLs) and English-proficient students with the same content tests (Abedi, 2004; Bailey, 2007; Bailey and Butler, 2004; Butler and Bailey, 2002). Bailey and Butler argue that unless ELLs have the requisite academic language skills, different constructs will be measured for the two groups. They propose that the ethical approach is to define academic language, develop tests of academic language, and determine on the basis of student performance on these tests whether students are equipped with the requisite language to take content-area assessments or, if not, what content-area test accommodations are appropriate. They conclude: "The notion of ethics in this assessment arena is primarily articulated as equitable treatment of EL students given our increasing knowledge, as well as remaining gaps in knowledge, of the complexities involved in assessing students as they simultaneously acquire English language skills and learn content-area material . . . We also invoke other notions of ethical behavior in assessment practices such as fiscal responsibility and humane treatment of individuals when we consider the logic of implementing statewide assessment of students in a language they have yet to master" (Bailey and Butler, 2004: 178).

While the U.S. context of school-based testing is currently the most widely discussed, the issues raised there – of standardized assessment and fair treatment of different groups – have also been raised in other contexts. Lynch (1997) and Elder (2000), for example, deal with the same issues in the Australian context.

PRACTICAL APPLICATION: THE ILTA CODE OF ETHICS

One of the ways in which professions deal with ethical questions and make public their adherence to a policy of ethical behavior and social responsibility is through a code of ethics. A code of ethics is a set of principles of conduct intended to guide professional decision making and behavior. The possession of a code of ethics can enhance the status of a profession and, by setting standards, also reduce the need for remediation through, for example, courtroom defense of actions. According to McNamara and Roever (2006: 139), "One function of a code of ethics is that it gives members a moral guideline for action and helps them to resolve ethical conflicts. It is also recourse for members when they are asked by employers or other stakeholders to participate in work that violates ethical or professional standards."

The International Language Testing Association (ILTA), as the leading professional organization for language testers, began the development of a code of ethics in the late 1990s, following on from discussions of ethicality and the responsibility of the profession. The ILTA Code of Ethics consists of "nine fundamental principles, each elaborated on by a series of annotations which generally clarify the nature of the principles; they prescribe what ILTA members ought or ought not do, or more generally how they ought to comport themselves or what they, or the profession, ought to aspire to; and they identify the difficulties and exceptions inherent in the application of the principles" (ILTA, 2000: 1). The principles deal with issues such as respect for the humanity and dignity of test takers, confidentiality, experimentation and research, misuse of language testers' skills, development and sharing of knowledge, upholding the integrity of the profession, the societal role of testers, mindfulness of obligations to the society within which they work, and awareness of the impact of their work on stakeholders.

While the development of a code of ethics is widely viewed as a step in the right direction for the profession, there has been some questioning of its value, particularly its enforceability. McNamara and Roever (2006: 253) comment, "[w]e are relatively less convinced of the beneficial impact of codes of ethics in language testing . . . The lack of enforceability for any code in a profession like language testing makes codes of ethics or practice little more than broad aspirational document. . . . we are uncertain whether the codification of ethical principle will have any measureable impact on the field." To Bishop, however, the question of enforcement and the application of sanctions misses the point. She takes issue with a view of ethical standards as aspirational, as they are not something that one can strive for and fail to attain: Failure is a failure to be ethical. In her words, "[t]o fail to respect a person's rights or dignity is, however, a grave fault. It marks a failure to be ethical; it misses the very bedrock of ethical life. In short, I must not aspire to be ethical, I must be ethical . . . I must be professional, not aspire to be" (Bishop, 2004: 116–117). She argues that enforceability is irrelevant because the principles are too general and unspecified, and that what is required is an interpretation of these general principles which will lead to their implementation in policies and activities in daily life, an interpretation, in other words, which will instantiate them.

In fact, this interpretation is underway. Whereas there is some debate as to whether one set of guidelines for good testing practice can be applied in different countries, not least because of different levels of expertise available in language testing, ILTA has developed a set of Guidelines for Practice (ILTA, 2007), which includes more specific direction on good testing practice and conduct, and which complements and elaborates the set of moral principles in the Code of Ethics. According to ILTA (2007: 1), "[w]hile the Code of Ethics focuses on the morals and ideals of the profession, the Code of Practice identifies the minimum requirements for practice in the profession and focuses on the clarification of professional misconduct and unprofessional conduct." Sections include: Basic considerations for good testing practice in all situations; Responsibilities of test designers and test writers; Obligations of institutions preparing or administering high stakes examinations; Obligations of those preparing and administering publicly available tests; Responsibilities of users of test results; Special considerations; and Rights and responsibilities of test takers. It is anticipated by the authors that it will act as a starting point for the development of more localized Codes of Practice.

CONCLUSION: FUTURE DIRECTIONS

Whereas the development of codes of ethics and practice reflects a move toward the professionalization of language testing, they are essentially statements of the desired state of field. On a more practical level, professional training is one way of ensuring that these standards are met. The Association of Language Testers in Europe (ALTE) has gone some way to dealing with this through the publication on its Web site of materials for test item writers (ALTE, 2005). However, there is scope for further provision of materials, online and face-to-face training. Language testers, represented through their professional organizations, need to continue not only the academic training but also the professional development of language testers.

Also needed is clearer direction on how issues such as consequences, fairness, impact, and values can be addressed within a test validation framework. While the consequences of test use and other ethical considerations are increasingly included in models and frameworks, there is little guidance on how these can be developed into a set of procedures for test developers to follow. Bachman's work in this area on the development of an assessment utilization argument is a start. Bachman (2005) proposes a framework with a set of principles and procedures for linking test performance to score-based inferences to test use through the articulation of an assessment use argument alongside a validity argument.

Testing organizations will continue to be challenged to defend their tests and their testing practices, particularly from a political and ethical standpoint. At the same time recognition of the leadership they have often provided in the development of codes of practice or in documenting principles of test development, in the training of test writers, and in the funding of research into ethical issues, such as fairness and impact, is also in order. Important also is the increasing engagement of testers with policy decisions at a national political level.

Given that it is not possible to envisage or provide an answer to every possible ethical dilemma in language testing, continued discussion of individual cases is one way for individuals and the profession as a whole to clarify right and wrong, ethical and unethical behavior. Whether one approaches this from the view of the language-testing professional as part of a community, and uses debate as a means to reach consensus, or whether one comes from a critical perspective which sees it as the responsibility of each individual to question what they do and why they do it, debate must continue in order for the ethicality of language-testing practice to progress.

Suggested resources

Bachman, L. F. (2005). Building and supporting a case for test use. *Language Assessment Quarterly* 2, 1: 1–34.

Kunnan, A. J. (2006). Towards a model of test evaluation: Using the test fairness and wider context frameworks. In M. Milanovic & C. Weir (Eds.), *Selected Papers from the Association of Language Testers of Europe Conference, Berlin, Germany*, Cambridge: Cambridge University Press.

Language Testing 14, 3 (1997). Special issue on *Ethics in language testing*.

Language Assessment Quarterly 1, 2/3 (2004). Special issue on *The ethics of language assessment*.

Lynch, B. K. (2001). Rethinking assessment from a critical perspective. *Language Testing*, 18, 4: 351–372.

McNamara, T., & Roever, C. (2006). *Language testing: The social dimension*. Malden, MA: Blackwell Publishing.

Schwandt, T. A., & Jang, E. E. (2004). Linking validity and ethics in language testing: Insights from the hermeneutic turn in social science. *Studies in Educational Evaluation*, 30: 265–280.

Discussion questions

1. Download and read the ILTA code of ethics (see References). Is it comprehensive enough? Is there anything missing? Is there anything in there that you think should not be included?

2. To what extent are questions of ethicality in language testing likely to vary from country to country or culture to culture?

3. Take a test that you work with. What is its impact? How can you ensure that its use is ethical? What are the limits of your responsibility?

4. Fairness reviews typically focus on the identification and removal of culturally sensitive or upsetting content, content that is biased against one group, or material that is too specialized or technical and requires other than language knowledge. This approach has led to accusations of blandness in test content. To what extent should test content be "tamed"?

References

Abedi, J. (2004). The No Child Left Behind Act and English language learners: Assessment and accountability issues. *Educational Researcher*, 33: 4–14.

Alderson, J. C., Clapham, C., & Wall, D. (1995). *Language test construction and evaluation*. Cambridge: Cambridge University Press.

Association of Language Testers in Europe. (1994). *The ALTE Code of Practice*. Retrieved from www.alte.org/downloads/index.php

Association of Language Testers in Europe. (2005). ALTE materials for the guidance of test item writers. Retrieved from www.alte.org/downloads/index.php

Bachman, L. F. (2000). What, if any, are the limits of our responsibility for fairness in language testing? In A. J. Kunnan (Ed.), *Fairness and validation in language assessment: Selected papers from the 19th language testing research colloquium, Orlando, Florida*. Cambridge: Cambridge University Press.

Bachman, L. F. (2005). Building and supporting a case for test use. *Language Assessment Quarterly* 2,1: 1–34.

Bachman, L. F. & Palmer, A. (1996). *Language testing in practice*, Oxford: Oxford University Press.

Bailey, A. L. (2007). *The language demands of school: Putting Academic English to the test*. New Haven and London: Yale University Press.

Bailey, A. L., & Butler, F. A. (2004). Ethical considerations in the assessment of the language and content knowledge of English language learners K-12. *Language Assessment Quarterly* 1: 177–193.

Bishop, S. (2004). Thinking about a professional ethics. *Language Assessment Quarterly* 1, (2&3): 109–122.

Blackledge, A. (2009). "As a country we do expect": The further extension of language testing regimes in the United Kingdom. *Language Assessment Quarterly* 6,1: 6–16.

Brown, A. (2010). *ILTA Language Testing Bibliography 1999–2010*. Available at www.iltaonline.com

Butler, F. A., & Bailey, A. L. (2002). *Equity in the assessment of English language learners K- 12*, New York: Teachers of English to Speakers of Other Languages (TESOL).

Davies, A. (1997). Demands of being professional in language testing. *Language Testing* 14: 328–39.

Davies, A. (2008). Ethics, professionalism, rights and codes. In E. Shohamy & N. H. Hornberger (Eds.), *Encyclopedia of Language and Education* (2nd ed.), Vol. 7: *Language Testing and Assessment*, 429–443. New York: Springer.

Davies, A., Brown, A., Elder, C., Hill, K., Lumley, T., & McNamara, T. (1999). *Dictionary of language testing*. Cambridge: Cambridge University Press.

Educational Testing Service. (2007). *International principles for fairness review of assessments*. Princeton, NJ: Educational Testing Service.

Elder, C. (2000). Is it fair to assess native and non native speakers in common on school 'foreign' language examinations? In A. Kunnan (Ed.), *Fairness and validation in language assessment: Selected papers from the 19th language testing research colloquium*, Orlando, Florida, Cambridge: Cambridge University Press.

Fulcher, G., & Davidson, F. (2007). *Language testing and assessment*. London & New York: Routledge.

Hamp-Lyons, L. (1997).Washback, impact and validity: Ethical concerns. *Language Testing*, 14,3: 295–303.

Hamp-Lyons, L. (2001). Ethics, fairness(es) and developments in language testing. In C. Elder, A. Brown, K. Hill, N. Iwashita, T. Lumley, T. McNamara, and K. O'Loughlin (Eds.), *Experimenting with uncertainty: language testing essays in honour of Alan Davies*. Cambridge: Cambridge University Press.

Hawthorne, L. (2005). 'Picking winners': The recent transformation of Australia's skilled migration policy. *International Migration Review*, 39,3: 663–696.

Holland, P. W., & Wainer, H. (1993). *Differential item functioning*. Hillsdale, NJ: Lawrence Erlbaum.

International Language Testing Association. (2000). *Code of Ethics for ILTA*. Retrieved from www.iltaonline.com/index.php?option=com_content&view=article&id =57&

International Language Testing Association. (2007). ILTA Guidelines for Practice. Retrieved from www.iltaonline.com/index.php?option=com_content& Itemid=47

Japan Language Testing Association. (2001/2003). *JLTA Code of Practice*. Retrieved from www.avis.ne.jp/~youichi/COP.html

Joint Committee on Testing Practices. (2004). *Code of fair testing practices in education.* Washington, DC: American Psychological Association.

Kane, M. T. (2001). Current concerns in validity theory. *Journal of Educational Measurement*, 38, 4: 319–342.

Kunnan, A. J. (2000). Fairness and justice for all. In A. J. Kunnan (Ed.), *Fairness and validation in language assessment*, Cambridge: Cambridge University Press.

Kunnan, A. J. (2004). Test fairness. In M. Milanovic & C. Weir (Eds.), *European language testing in a global context*, Cambridge: Cambridge University Press.

Kunnan, A. J. (2006). Towards a model of test evaluation: Using the test fairness and wider context frameworks. In M. Milanovic & C. Weir (Eds.), *Selected papers from the association of language testers of Europe conference, Berlin, Germany*, Cambridge: Cambridge University Press.

Kunnan, A. J., & Davidson, F. (2004). Situated ethics in language assessment. In D. Douglas (Ed.), *English language tests and testing practice.* Washington, D.C.: National Association for Foreign Students Affairs.

Lynch, B. K. (1997). In search of the ethical test. *Language Testing*, 14,3: 315–527.

Lynch, B. K. (2001). Rethinking assessment from a critical perspective, *Language Testing*, 18, 4: 351–372.

McNamara, T. (2006). Validity in language testing: The challenge of Sam Messick's legacy. *Language Assessment Quarterly*, 3,1: 31–51.

McNamara, T. (2008). The socio-political and power dimensions of tests. In E. Shohamy & N. H. Hornberger (Eds.), *Encyclopedia of language and education* (2nd ed.), Vol. 7: *Language Testing and Assessment*, 415–427. New York and London: Springer.

McNamara, T., & Roever, C. (2006). *Language testing: The social dimension.* Malden, MA: Blackwell Publishing.

Messick, S. (1989). Validity. In R. L. Linn (Ed.), *Educational Measurement* (3rd ed., pp. 13–103). New York: Macmillan.

Messick, S. (1996). Validity and washback in language testing. *Language Testing*, 13, 241–256.

Pennycook, A. (2001). *Critical applied linguistics: A critical introduction.* Mahwah. NJ: Lawrence Erlbaum.

Schwandt, T. A., & Jang, E. E. (2004). Linking validity and ethics in language testing: Insights from the hermeneutic turn in social science. *Studies in Educational Evaluation*, 30: 265–280.

Shohamy, E. (1998). Critical language testing and beyond. *Studies in Educational Evaluation*, 24, 331–345.

Shohamy, E. (2001a). *The power of tests: A critical perspective on the uses of language tests.* London: Pearson.

Shohamy, E. (2001b). Democratic assessment as an alternative. *Language Testing*, 18, 4: 373–391.

Weir, C. J. (2005). *Language testing and validation: An evidence based approach.* Oxford: Palgrave Macmillan.

CHAPTER 14

Professional Development in Language Assessment

Stephen Stoynoff and Christine Coombe

INTRODUCTION

Knowledge of assessment is increasingly considered an essential aspect of the knowledge base in our discipline. Language teachers are expected to choose or construct, administer, and interpret the results of assessments designed for a variety of purposes and situations. Although the impetus for language teachers to attain and sustain expertise in language assessment varies, developments such as the establishment of standards by professional groups, the implementation of government policies, and the introduction of educational change are some of the factors prompting teachers to pursue professional development in language assessment.

In the United States, for example, the National Council for the Accreditation of Teacher Education (NCATE) and the TESOL association established assessment as one of five professional knowledge domains for ESOL teachers, and the NCATE/TESOL standards also codified the expectation that teachers will "participate in professional growth opportunities" (TESOL/NCATE Standards for the Recognition of Initial TESOL Programs in P-12 ESL Teacher Education, 2010: 72). The strategic plan for English and foreign language learning that is being implemented by the 21 member nations of the Asia-Pacific Economic Cooperation consortium is a multilateral agreement with implications for language teachers. The plan acknowledges the central role of assessment in second language learning and calls for additional professional development of language teachers (Chen et al., 2008; Duff, 2008). In Europe, Edelenbos and Kubanek-German (2004) found that educational changes precipitated by the introduction of the Common European Framework of Reference for Languages (CFER) and the European Portfolio for Modern Languages have led language teachers to explore new ways of assessing language ability. As these examples demonstrate, professional groups, government policymakers, and practitioners recognize the importance of language assessment to language teaching.

BACKGROUND

Some of the key terms relevant to discussions of teacher professional development in language assessment include professionalism, teacher development, professional development, and language assessment literacy. Davies argues that the field of language testing has "sought to professionalize itself" (2008a: 431) over the past few decades and this effort has been manifest in numerous ways, including the establishment of professional organizations, publications, conferences, and codes. These activities in turn have increased the perceived status and professionalism of the field of language testing and given language-testing specialists the authority to advocate for particular standards in assessment. The assessment standards advocated by authoritative groups like the Joint Committee on Testing Practices in the United States and the International Language Testing Association (ILTA) are intended to promote sound test development and proper test use practices among testing specialists and practitioners.

Crandall (2000) contends that "teacher development is a lifelong process of growth which may involve collaboration and / or autonomous learning, but the important distinction is that teachers are engaged in the process and they actively reflect on their practices" (p. 36). If teacher development is a process, professional development represents one of the ways teachers engage in it. Accordingly, those in language teacher preparation programs as well as practicing teachers can benefit from professional development activities that contribute to insights and improved professional performance.

A number of assessment specialists believe that developments in educational practices, measurement, and assessment research require teachers to be more *assessment literate* (see Chapter 2 of this volume for a fuller consideration of this issue) than in the past and this means being able to choose and use assessments for all their purposes (Shepard, 2000; Stiggins, 1997; Stoynoff and Chapelle, 2005). Inbar-Lourie (2008) defines *language assessment literacy* as the current assessment knowledge base and believes it is comprised of "assessment literacy skills combined with language specific competencies" (pp. 389–390).

RESEARCH

Several issues discussed in the professional literature have implications for the development of teachers' language assessment literacy. The first is the shift in the content of language assessment textbooks over the past few decades. Davies (2008b) examined a sample of language-testing textbooks that were published between 1961 and 2007, and he determined the texts have evolved from an emphasis on the skills needed to develop and use language assessments to the "skills + knowledge" and more recently to the "skills + knowledge + principles" needed to develop and use assessments (p. 335). Malone (2008) also reviewed a sample of widely used language assessment texts and concluded that a trend has emerged over the past few decades: Authors are incorporating practical considerations into their books to complement the theoretical aspects of assessment typically covered in language-testing textbooks. If this is indeed the case, language teachers have access to books that provide both comprehensive and practical introductions to the current assessment knowledge base.

Another issue has to do with the extent to which teachers have completed coursework in language assessment. Bachman (2000) reported that a survey of the TESOL organization membership conducted in the 1990s found only about half of the respondents had completed a course in language testing. More recently Stoynoff (2007) determined that about half of the graduate programs in the 2005 edition of the *Directory of Teacher Preparation Programs in TESOL* (Christopher, 2005) required candidates to complete coursework in language assessment, although two-thirds of the programs offered one or more courses in the subject. For a recent account of the content of language assessment courses, see Brown and Bailey (2008). Their study included a sample of 97 instructors representing 29 different countries and more than half of the respondents resided outside the United States. Based on a comparison of the data collected in the 2008 study and a previous one published in 1996, the researchers concluded there is "a stable knowledge base that is evolving and expanding" (p. 371). However, many ESOL teachers may not have acquired sufficient expertise in assessment during their preparation programs, and those who have acquired it will need to update their expertise as the knowledge base gradually changes.

A third issue is the emergence of a new perspective that acknowledges the role of assessment in teaching and learning and that reflects a cognitive and social-constructivist view of learning (Shepard, 2000). According to Shepard, past beliefs about learning, curriculum, instruction, and measurement have led to current educational practices that separate assessment from instruction. However, if a new perspective of assessment is to be fully realized, language teachers will need to consider how their current beliefs, knowledge, and skills affect their assessment practices, and they will need to stay abreast of developments in the assessment knowledge base. Inbar-Lourie (2008) has proposed how the language assessment literacy of classroom teachers might be developed from this new social-constructivist perspective. The focus would be on establishing "the reason for assessment (the "why"), describing the trait to be assessed (the "what"), and organizing the assessment process (the "how")" (p. 390). Teachers would engage in a process of "learning, negotiating, discussing, experiencing and researching" a set of core competencies developed from the professional literature in the disciplines of "education, linguistics, and applied linguistics" (p. 396).

PRACTICE

Resources for professional development can be categorized in a variety of ways. Malone (2008) divided professional development in language assessment into "text-based" and "technology-mediated materials" (p. 229). Richards and Farrell (2005), on the other hand, described professional development in terms of the kinds of activities (e.g., "individual," "one-to-one," "group-based," or "institutional") that teachers elect to pursue (p. 14).

The following description of professional development resources is grouped in terms of medium (print and Web-based), sponsors (professional associations, nonprofit organizations, and government-supported entities), and teacher-based activities. Given the limitations of space, it is not possible to include more than a small sample of the resources available for professional development in assessment.

PUBLICATIONS

This resource includes the professional reference books, textbooks, and journals produced by commercial, academic, and nonprofit publishers. There has been a dramatic increase in the number of publications devoted to language assessment in the past decade. In addition to the release of many individual titles, there are now several series that provide comprehensive coverage of language assessment issues. One example is the Cambridge Language Assessment Series that has seen the publication of eleven books since 2000. These books contain much of the essential practical and special knowledge language teachers need to use large-scale assessments or to develop classroom assessments. The Cambridge Studies in Language Testing series is another collection that considers developments in language assessment over the past fifteen years.

Volume 7 (Shohamy and Hornberger, 2008) of the second edition of the *Encyclopedia of Language and Education* provides a concise yet comprehensive overview of many of the most significant issues in language assessment. The 29 chapters in Language Testing and Assessment (Vol. 7) are grouped into four sections: assessing language domains, methods of assessment, assessment in education, and assessment in society. Because single volumes are not available for purchase and there are ten volumes in the set, this resource may not be available in all academic libraries.

Two journals in our field focus exclusively on language assessment: *Language Testing* (*LT*) and *Language Assessment Quarterly* (*LAQ*). Although assessment specialists are the primary audience for *LT* and *LAQ*, the journals publish articles that some language teachers will find accessible and informative. Additionally, many journals publish occasional papers that are intended for a general teacher audience, including the *Annual Review of Applied Linguistics*, *Applied Linguistics*, *ELT Journal*, *Modern Language Journal*, *TESOL Quarterly*, and the relatively new *International Journal of Testing*.

Government agencies, university research centers, and nonprofit organizations are important sources of information on language assessment. Two notable examples of university research centers in the United States are the Center for Research on Education, Diversity and Excellence (CREDE, www.crede.org) at the University of California, Santa Cruz, and the National Center for Research on Evaluation, Standards, and Student Testing (CRESST) at the University of California, Los Angeles (www.cse.ucla.edu). CREDE researchers investigate assessment issues of particular interest to ESOL teachers and many of the center's reports contain guidelines on how the findings can be applied to improve language teaching. CRESST researchers also investigate assessment issues and disseminate the results in reports intended for assessment specialists and language teachers.

There are similar national and international research centers throughout the world. The National Centre for English Language at the University of Melbourne, Australia (www.ltrc. unimelb.edu.au/resources/index.html), conducts research and publishes papers on language assessment. It also produced a professional development series titled *Mark my words* that consists of six 20–25-minute videos; the topics include language proficiency assessment, principles of test development, objective and subjective assessment, stages of test analysis, performance assessment, and classroom-based assessment. The Regional English Language Centre (RELC) of the Southeast Asian Ministers of Education Organization (SEAMEO) is a multilateral, government-supported resource center located in Singapore (www.relc. org.sg).

The University of Cambridge ESOL Examinations (www.cambridgeesol.org) and Educational Testing Service (www.ets.org) are global leaders in language test development and research. In addition to providing extensive information on their tests, both centers publish serial publications and reports that address many of the most significant issues in language assessment. Language teachers can gain useful insights into the standards and practices applied to the development and use of high-stakes ESOL assessments by reviewing the contents of the Cambridge and ETS Web sites.

Whenever commercially produced language tests are used to assess students, language teachers ought to be familiar with the tests. Most academic libraries have reference publications such as the Buros Institute's *Tests in Print* and *Mental Measurements Yearbook* and Pro-Ed's *Tests: A Comprehensive Reference for Assessments in Psychology, Education, and Business* and *Test Critiques*. These publications are excellent sources of impartial information on tests. Other credible resources include the test reviews published in the journals *Language Testing* and *Language Assessment Quarterly* and a recent volume edited by Stoynoff and Chapelle (2005).

WEB-BASED

The World Wide Web has expanded teachers' access to language assessment resources and professional development activities. Many test publishers, academic research centers, nonprofit organizations, government agencies, and professional associations host elaborate Web sites with extensive resources and links to additional resources. For example, the Center for Applied Linguistics site (www.cal.org) includes a free online tutorial titled *Understanding Assessment* that prepares teachers for selecting assessments that are suitable for their assessment purpose and target population. For a fee, visitors to the TESOL association Web site can access a live or after-the-fact 1.5–2-hour Web cast (*virtual seminar*). A 2009 seminar led by O'Sullivan addressed classroom-based assessment. Visitors to the International Language Testing Association (ILTA) site have the ability to view streaming video of interviews conducted with prominent language-testing specialists.

Some personal Web sites also contain useful resources. Glenn Fulcher's *Resources in Language Testing Page* (http://languagetesting.info) provides extensive information on language assessment as well as links to other resources. A noteworthy feature of Fulcher's site is the option of viewing streaming video of language-testing specialists addressing frequently asked questions about key concepts in language assessment, including reliability, validity, and test impact.

Professional organizations sometimes host a Wiki (a forum where visitors are permitted to view and edit the content on the site). The APEC Human Resources Working Group Wiki is a language assessment site where language assessment issues in APEC nations are discussed and language assessment reports and resources are posted (www.hrd. apecwiki.org/index.php/Language_Assessment). Visitors have access to the site and are able to download the content, but they must obtain permission from the APEC Secretariat to edit the content.

PROFESSIONAL ASSOCIATIONS

International, national, and regional professional associations regularly sponsor professional development events. The TESOL association (www.tesol.org) and its international affiliates hold conferences, institutes, workshops and other face-to-face events in which language assessment issues are on the program. This is also true of the International Association for Applied Linguistics (or Association Internationale de Linguistique Appliquée, AILA: www.aila.info). In terms of major annual meetings devoted exclusively to language assessment issues, the ILTA (www.iltaonline.com) sponsored Language Testing Research Colloquium (LTRC: www.ltrc.org), the Association of Language Testers in Europe (ALTE: www.alte.org) meetings, and the Current Trends in English Language Testing (CTELT) conference (Dubai, UAE) are among those events with the most extensive programs. In some cases, associations publish conference proceedings and may make some or all of their conference sessions available in various forms of media (e.g., audio or videotape, DVD, CD-ROM, podcasts, or streaming video).

EDUCATIONAL INSTITUTIONS

Many colleges and universities deliver courses to students at a distance. However, Henrichsen (2001) cautioned that *distance education* includes everything from taking a course by correspondence (using the postal system to exchange materials) to taking a computer-mediated, Internet-based course that uses state-of-the-art videoconferencing technology. In the 2005 *Directory of Teacher Preparation Programs in TESOL* (Christopher, 2005) more than 40 assessment courses were available via distance education. With the proliferation of personal computers and advances in computer technology, it is now possible for language teachers to complete coursework in assessment regardless of where they reside.

If teachers are unable to take courses during the academic year, there are short-term summer courses available at some institutions. Lancaster University's (UK) Language Testing at Lancaster program (www.testdevelopmenttrainingandanalysis.com/Language_Testing_at_Lancaster_LTL1.html) is one example. It provides a two-week intensive course in language assessment for participants with the option to extend the program another week or two and to focus on test theory. The American University in Washington, D.C., hosts a summer institute on teaching ESOL each year and it often includes a course on language assessment.

PEER-BASED

Colleagues represent a valuable but frequently overlooked resource in professional development in language assessment. One Web-based way to draw on the knowledge and experience of peers is to join an existing network of professionals who subscribe to a distribution list. The LTEST-L list is maintained by ILTA and peers use it to discuss current issues in assessment. TESL-L is a broader-based group of language teachers with over 10,000 subscribers. While the topics posed on TESL-L are not limited to assessment, it is a forum in which assessment issues are regularly discussed.

In some cases, it may be more useful and practical to form a learning community of local or regional peers. One possibility is to form a study group in which members select books, reports, or other assessment materials and agree to read and discuss them on a regular basis. Discussions can be conducted online or in person. Another option is to form a peer support group and to share assessment resources, discuss assessment challenges, and offer feedback on each other's assessment practices. The feedback can be based on a review of the teacher's classroom assessments or a classroom observation. Although some teachers consider peer observation threatening, it can prompt reflections on classroom practices that in turn lead to new understandings of the teacher's purposes for and methods of assessment.

CONCLUSION

Taylor (2009) observes that the current perspective toward professional preparation in language assessment involves achieving "an appropriate balance of technical know-how, practical skills, theoretical knowledge, and understanding of principles, but all firmly contextualized within a sound understanding of the role and function of assessment within education and society" (p. 270). The optimal balance among the various aspects of the knowledge base and the degree of professional expertise required in each will depend somewhat upon the stage of the teacher's career, employment context, and professional responsibilities. Therefore, language teachers ought to view professional development in assessment as part of an ongoing process of professional growth and not a static competence to be mastered. This chapter has highlighted some of the resources available and ways language teachers can attain and maintain their expertise in language assessment.

Suggested resources

Crandall, J. (2001). Keeping up to date as an ESL or EFL professional. In M. Celce-Murcia (Ed.) (1997), *Teaching English as a Second or Foreign Language* (3rd ed.), (pp. 535–552). Boston: Heinle and Heinle.

Fulcher, G., & Davidson, F. (2007). *Language testing and assessment: An advanced resource book*. London: Routledge.

Richards, J. C., & Farrell, T. S. C. (2005). *Professional development for language teachers*. Cambridge: Cambridge University Press.

Shohamy, E., & Hornberger, N. H. (Eds.) (2008). *Encyclopedia of language education* (2nd ed.) Vol. 7: *Language testing and assessment*. New York: Springer.

Discussion questions

1. How does professional development in assessment enhance the effectiveness of language teachers?

2. What factors are likely to affect the kinds of professional development activities language teachers choose to pursue?

3. Propose a professional development plan that includes specific activities and resources that will increase your expertise in language assessment.

References

Bachman, L. F. (2000). Modern language testing at the turn of the century: Assuring that what we count counts. *Language Testing*, 17.1, 1–42.

Brown, J. D., & Bailey, K. M. (2008). Language testing courses: What are they in 2007? *Language Testing*, 25.3, 349–383.

Chen, H., Sinclair, P., Huang, S.-Y., & Eyerman, L. (January 2008). APEC EDNET project seminar on language standards and their assessment: Background research paper. Symposium conducted at the APEC EDNET meeting, Xi'an, China.

Christopher, V. (Ed.). (2005). *Directory of teacher preparation programs in TESOL*. Alexandria, VA: TESOL.

Crandall, J. (2000). Language teacher education. *Annual Review of Applied Linguistics*, 20, 34–55.

Davies, A. (2008a). Ethics, professionalism, rights and codes. In E. Shohamy & N. H. Hornberger (Eds.) (2nd ed.), *Encyclopedia of language and education;* Vol. 7: *Language testing and assessment* (pp. 429–443), New York: Springer.

Davies, A. (2008b). Textbook trends in teaching language testing. *Language Testing*, 25.3, 327–347.

Duff, P. A. (January 2008). APEC second / foreign language standards and their assessment: Trends, opportunities, and implications. Symposium conducted at the APEC EDNET meeting, Xi'an, China.

Edelenbos, P., & Kubanek-German, A. (2004). Teacher assessment: The concept of 'diagnostic competence.' *Language Testing*, 21.3, 259–283.

Henrichsen, L. E. (ed.) (2001). *Distance-learning programs*. Alexandria, VA: TESOL.

Inbar-Lourie, O. (2008). Constructing a language assessment knowledge base: A focus on language assessment courses. *Language Testing*, 25.3, 385–402.

Malone, M. E. (2008). Training in language assessment. In E. Shohamy & N. H. Hornberger (Eds.), *Encyclopedia of language and education* (2nd ed.), Vol. 7: *Language testing and assessment* (pp 225-239). New York: Springer.

Richards, J. C., & Farrell, T. S. C. (2005). *Professional development for language teachers: Strategies for teacher learning.* Cambridge: Cambridge University Press.

Shepard, L. A. (2000). The role of classroom assessment in teaching and learning. Santa Cruz, CA: University of California, Center for Research on Education, Diversity & Excellence (CREDE).

Shohamy, E., & Hornberger, N. H. (2008) (Eds.). *Encyclopedia of language education* (2nd ed.) Vol. 7: *Language testing and assessment.* New York: Springer.

Stiggins, R. J. (1997). *Student-centered classroom assessment* (2nd ed.). Upper Saddle River, NJ: Merrill Prentice-Hall.

Stoynoff, S. J. (2007). A survey of recent developments in ESOL testing. *Proceedings of the 9th and 10th Current Trends in English Language Testing (CTELT) Conferences,* 5, 115–128.

Stoynoff, S. J., & Chapelle, C. A. (Eds.) (2005). *ESOL tests and testing: A resource for teachers and administrators,* Alexandria, VA: TESOL.

Taylor, L. (2009). Developing assessment literacy. *Annual Review of Applied Linguistics,* 29, 21–36.

TESOL/NCATE (2010). TESOL/NCATE Standards for the Recognition of Initial TESOL Programs in P-12 ESL Teacher Education. Alexandria, VA: TESOL.

SECTION 2

ASSESSMENT PURPOSES AND APPROACHES

This section looks to the fundamentals of the development process by focusing on particular types of assessment and also on the uses of assessments with specific learners and for specific learning-related goals.

In Chapter 15, JD Brown argues that teachers and language program administrators need to be able to choose the right type of assessment to reflect the decisions being made and the curriculum with which it is being used. The chapter presents the different "families" of assessment purposes, focusing on both standardized and classroom-based assessment, and suggests examples of how assessment tasks can be designed to reflect the classroom activities they are meant to assess.

Morrow begins Chapter 16 by suggesting that "the most interesting thing about the phrase *communicative language testing* is that it belongs very clearly to history." He then delves into the emergence of the movement and reflects on how the communicative testing "revolution" continues to exert a significant impact on how language is tested today. The changes to assessment practice championed by the drivers of the communicative movement are reflected in the two following chapters. The first of these, Chapter 17 by Coombe, Purmensky, and Davidson, addresses the area of alternative assessment. The chapter provides a rationale for alternative assessment, arguing that it offers a perspective on learning that is not possible with standardized tests as it involves both the learner and the teacher. The chapter also discusses some common alternative assessment techniques, specifically projects and portfolios, offering practical advice on both content and how these might be assessed.

Shehadeh, in Chapter 18, then discusses the area of task-based language assessment, stressing its focus on performance and value as both a summative and formative assessment tool. He also follows the example of other authors in this Guide in arguing that assessment must be closely linked to the type of tasks undertaken by learners in the classroom, and should be seen as supporting as well as assessing learning.

The area of placement testing is the focus of Green, in Chapter 19. The types of tests used for placement purposes are described in terms of the practical decisions made in their construction. In presenting the argument for assessment instruments that focus on language use (production) or language knowledge (e.g., of grammar or vocabulary), Green suggests that ideally both should be used where practical, though he also emphasizes the importance of knowing the test taker and of quality control when developing such instruments.

Moving away from the discussion of a test used for a specific purpose (i.e., placement), in Chapter 20 Hasselgreen focuses instead on the testing of a specific population, that of young learners. This chapter emphasizes the differences between the assessment of older learners (who typically require a summative / judgmental assessment of their language ability) and the assessment of young learners (who typically require a formative / developmental assessment to aid their individual learning process) and offers a number of practical solutions to the many issues highlighted.

In Chapter 21, Greenberg looks at how needs analysis for language use in the workplace should reflect the specific needs of the client company, stressing also the differences in focus between typical classroom-based assessments. Greenberg goes on to demonstrate how Swale's (1990) framework for studying writing might also be applied to the other skills, exemplifying her argument using three key elements: discourse community, genre, and language learning task.

The final two chapters in the section turn to issues of more immediate concern to the classroom language teacher. In Chapter 22, Anderson argues that for self-assessment to work, the learner must be both metacognitively aware of his / her own learning processes and also of the process of assessment. He also suggests that this awareness of the assessment process is equally critical to the success of peer assessment. He then suggests a number of practical self- and peer assessment activities which are designed to promote learner awareness of the processes of both learning and assessment and which have the additional benefit of locating assessment within the learning system.

Finally, Eslami and Mirzaei argue in Chapter 23 that whereas the teaching of second language pragmatics is quite well established, its assessment is still relatively limited. They outline the complexities involved in designing assessment instruments for L2 pragmatics and present examples of assessment items and scoring criteria designed for the assessment of two aspects of pragmatic competence: pragmatic comprehension and pragmatic production.

CHAPTER 15

Choosing the Right Type of Assessment

James Dean Brown

INTRODUCTION

Choosing the right type of assessment requires matching the purpose and type of the assessment to the decisions that are being made with it and the curriculum in which it is being used. More precisely, the assessment purpose should match the decisions that are being made, and the assessment type should match the curriculum objectives or learning points being taught in the context of the decision making. For instance, an assessment instrument designed for purposes of measuring students' aptitudes for learning languages should *not* be used to make achievement decisions at the end of an ESL course because the purpose of the assessment and the decision making do not match. Similarly, a multiple-choice assessment type should *not* be used to assess students in a process-writing course because the multiple-choice assessment does not match the process-writing curriculum in which the assessment is being used.

BACKGROUND

Choosing the right type of assessment is crucial because assessments are used to make important decisions (e.g., whether or not students are admitted to a program, what level of language they will study, what they need to focus on, whether or not they will pass the course, etc.) that can dramatically affect students' lives. Picking the wrong type of assessment is professionally irresponsible because the assessment will provide useless or misleading information, and may lead to erroneous decisions that will harm students. The key issues that administrators and teachers need to understand in order to choose the right type of assessment are the distinction between two families of assessment purposes (standardized and classroom) and the differences among three common language assessment types (selected-response, productive-response, and personal-response).

FAMILIES OF ASSESSMENT PURPOSES

In brief, *standardized assessments* are general in nature because students vary greatly in the abilities measured on such assessments; are primarily of interest to administrators because they are designed for purposes of deciding who should be admitted into a program or how students should be grouped into course levels; are usually made up of a few large subtests; and have scores that are interpreted in terms of each student's relative position in the distribution of scores for all students in a population. Standardized assessments are designed for purposes of measuring:

1. *Aptitude* – Very general: aptitude assessments are designed for all students interested in studying foreign languages for purposes of measuring their relative overall abilities to learn languages (i.e., language aptitude). The purpose is usually to decide who will benefit most from language instruction (or who will be the best investment for studying a language) – especially for selection or admissions decisions when resources are limited.

2. *Proficiency* – Also very general: proficiency assessments are designed for all students of a particular language for purposes of measuring their relative overall abilities in that language (i.e., proficiency) – especially for deciding who should be admitted to a particular institution.

3. *Placement* – Tailored to the ability levels of students in a particular institution, placement assessments are designed for measuring the language abilities of students who are already part of a particular institution so they can be put in the appropriate levels of language study (i.e., placement) – especially for deciding who should study at which levels (sometimes assessing different skill areas separately).

In contrast, *classroom assessments* are specific in nature because students are likely to vary much less on these measures (especially if they have been put into more-or-less homogeneous groups by the admissions and placement assessments); are primarily interesting to teachers because they are used for deciding what percentage of material the students already know or can do in relation to a particular course; are therefore designed to measure specific course objectives or teaching points; usually have a fairly large number of short subtests measuring different things; and have scores that are interpreted in terms of the percentage of the course material the students know or can do. Classroom assessments are designed for purposes of measuring:

4. *Diagnostic information* – Administered at the beginning of a course, these assessments are designed for gauging individual students' strengths and weaknesses with regard to the specific objectives or language points addressed in a particular language course – especially for providing information to students and teachers about how much the students already know or can do and where they should concentrate their energies.

5. *Progress* – Administered in the middle of a course, these assessments are designed for measuring students' progress with respect to the objectives or language points addressed in a particular language course – especially for providing information to the students and teachers about how they are doing so far in the course and where they should re-focus their energies.

6. *Achievement* – Administered at the end of a course, these assessments are designed for evaluating how much students have accomplished with respect to the objectives or learning points in a particular language course – especially for grading students and informing them and other interested parties about how the students did in the course in terms of what they know or can do.

MATCHING ASSESSMENT TYPES TO CLASSROOM ACTIVITIES

Ideally, standardized assessments should be closely matched to the sorts of things instructors are teaching to students. However, teachers typically have little direct control over the types of aptitude or proficiency assessments used in their institutions for two reasons: First, since the types of instruction vary widely from country to country, institution to institution, and even classroom to classroom, matching any aptitude or proficiency assessment to all those situations would be impossible; and second, given that aptitude and proficiency assessments must, as far as possible, not favor any particular institution or type of student, they must remain more or less neutral with regard to particular curricula.

Fortunately, teachers *can* control the sorts of standardized assessments used for placement as well as those used for classroom assessment for diagnosis, progress, and achievement. Whenever such opportunities for teachers to control assessment arise, they should be seized, with the goal of matching the assessment types as closely as possible to the sorts of classroom activities the instructors are using in their classrooms to teach the language.

Assessment types and classroom-activity types can and should both vary in several ways. Table 15.1 summarizes the relationships between assessment types and corresponding classroom activities by showing three main types of assessments; what they are appropriate for assessing; example items; and corresponding classroom activities. (For more on the three types of assessments and the item types in each, see Brown, 2005; Brown and Hudson, 2002.)

Assessment types	Appropriate for assessing	Example items	Corresponding classroom activities
Selected-response	knowledge (vocabulary, grammar, sound contrasts, etc.) or receptive skills of listening and reading	true–false, multiple-choice, matching, etc.	explicit learning of receptive grammar, vocabulary, and pronunciation knowledge exercises; all kinds of listening or reading activities in isolation, etc.
Productive-response	productive skills of speaking and writing or their interactions with other skills, or task performance	fill-in, short-answer, task-performance, etc.	productive knowledge of grammar, vocabulary, and pronunciation exercises; pair work, group work; role plays; speaking and writing performance tasks of all kinds, etc.
Personal-response	all four skills simultaneously, or higher-order thinking skills, or for motivating students to speak or write	self- / peer-assessments, portfolios, conferences, etc.	all of the activities immediately above, plus introspection and reflection activities, individualized instruction, project work, etc.

Table 15.1   Relationships between assessment types and corresponding classroom activities

One important role of teachers in any placement, diagnostic, progress, or achievement assessments should be to insure that these sorts of assessments match the sorts of things students are learning and practicing in their classroom activities (using information like that presented in Table 15.1). The result of matching assessments to classroom activities will be a much closer match of those assessments to the belief systems of the teachers, to the syllabuses being used to organize the teaching, and to the techniques and exercises that teachers are using to foster learning in their classrooms.

What often goes on today is the reverse: Instead of matching the assessments to the classroom activities, the classroom activities are adjusted to the assessments, in the guise of TOEFL or TOEIC (Test of English for International Communication) preparation, or getting ready for the university entrance examinations, and so on. In other words, the teaching activities are changed to match the assessment instruments. Shouldn't it be the other way around? Shouldn't the assessment tools be changed to match the teaching activities?

RESEARCH

The best sources of information on choosing the right type of assessments tend to be those articles and books that focus on criterion-referenced tests (CRTs are what I am labeling classroom assessments in this chapter), in contrast with norm-referenced tests (NRTs are what I am calling standardized assessments here). Key books on CRTs in language assessment include Brown and Hudson (2002) and Davidson and Lynch (2002). In addition, the Brown (1993) paper provides a description of an actual CRT development project in the English Language Institute at the University of Hawai'i at Manōa.

PRACTICAL APPLICATIONS

The most egregious case I know about where the wrong types of assessment were chosen surfaced in Childs (1995), who described a Japanese company that was administering a series of TOEIC examinations for purposes of (a) assessing their overall English proficiency (i.e., proficiency assessment); (b) comparing the gains made in the different schools within the company (i.e., proficiency-level comparisons); (c) assessing average learning gains of groups of students (i.e., proficiency gain assessment); (d) counseling individuals on their courses of study (i.e., diagnostic assessment); (e) measuring their progress in learning English as individuals (i.e., progress assessment); and (f) assessing the learning gains of individuals (i.e., assessment of achievement).

Based on the results of 113 students who took the TOEIC four times, Childs concluded that it might be appropriate to use the TOEIC for the purposes listed in (a), (b), and (c) above, that is for purposes of *proficiency* assessment, *proficiency*-level comparisons, and *proficiency* gain assessment "with the caveats that careful measurement of statistical significance is necessary in order to distinguish real gains from illusory ones, and that, even if the significance of gains is established, the causes of gains may remain problematic" (1995: 74). These proficiency uses of the TOEIC make sense; after all it is a *proficiency* assessment.

However, Childs also pointed out the inappropriateness of using the TOEIC for the purposes listed in (d), (e), and (f) above, that is, for purposes of *diagnostic* assessment and counseling individuals, assessing the *progress* of individuals, and assessing the learning gains (i.e., *achievement*) of individuals. In Childs' own words:

> TOEIC is not a diagnostic test, and it cannot pinpoint learners' strengths and weaknesses. It can be a rough guide for gauging a learner's overall level, if the administrator clearly understands the statistical variability of the results, but TOEIC cannot help the administrator determine *what* a specific learner needs to be taught.... We have seen that, in a teaching program that totaled 53 hours, the variability of TOEIC results defeated their usefulness in measuring learning gains because the SEM of TOEIC was in the range of expected individual gains.... Indeed the lower results

that are frequently encountered in successive tests can have the unfortunate side effect of demotivating learners. (Childs, 1995: 74)

The sort of administrator that Childs faced was one who really wanted a single proficiency–placement–diagnostic–progress–achievement assessment procedure that is short, easy-to-administer, and cheap. Such administrators clearly do not understand the different types of assessments and their mutually exclusive purposes, nor that some of those purposes require matching the assessment to the relevant classroom activities.

Fortunately, I also know of situations where assessments and classroom activities have been well matched. One day in my speaking class at the Guangzhou English Language Center in China, a student asked me, "Why is it that I can understand you, teacher, when you talk to us in class, but I cannot understand you when you talk to the other American teachers?" My American colleagues and I decided that the answer to his question was that we used clearly enunciated teacher talk when we spoke to the students, but used *reduced forms* when conversing with each other. We collected a total of 68 reduced forms that we all agreed we were using. Here is a sampling of eight of them:

Howarya (How are you?)
c'mon (come on)
in' (-ing)
gonna, goin'ta (going to)
jus' (just)
Whatser (What is her . . .)
mighta (might have)
there's, there're (there is, there are)

We then classified and taught these 68 forms systematically for 5–10 minutes in each of 50 speaking-class meetings. To help the students practice listening to and understanding this sort of reduced speech, we developed a classroom activity that we called *reduced-forms dictations*, which were read as follows:

Directions: Write the full forms of the words you will hear three times; the second reading will have pauses to give you time to write:

Jack: *Whenerya goin' ta Princeton?*
Mary: *I'm gonna go on Monday.*
Jack: *Boy! I wish I were gettin' ouda here fer awhile. Ya gotcher train ticket?*

The following is the answer key for this abbreviated example:

Jack: *When are you going to Princeton?*
Mary: *I am going to go on Monday.*
Jack: *Boy! I wish I were getting out of here for awhile. You got your train ticket?*

This example has 17 possible points (counting only the underlined words); the operational versions were longer with 50 points possible.

If we were going to teach these reduced forms, we felt that we should develop assessment procedures that would match those classroom activities. In order to assess the degree to which students had learned to process the reduced forms, we used two parallel 50-point reduced-forms dictations with half the students taking each form at the beginning of instruction and taking the other form at the end. On average, the students scored 35 percent at the beginning of instruction and 68 percent at the end (Brown and Hilferty, 2006), indicating considerable gain: 33 percent.

Similarly in the same course, since we were doing pair work and role-play activities to help the students learn how to use selected functions in different registers, we did role-play interview assessment. At the beginning, middle, and end of the course, we recorded these role-play interviews and rated them for fluency, meaning, gambits, register, and intonation / stress. In the first week of instruction, we gave students a copy of our scoring rubric, and then after the first two interview role plays, we sat down with them individually to give them diagnostic and progress feedback at the beginning and middle of the course. At the end of the course, the scores on the role-play interview, their reduced-forms dictation scores, and other factors went into grading the students. Clearly, we had done our best to match diagnostic, progress, and achievement assessments in this speaking class to our classroom activities.

CONCLUSION

Willful ignorance of sound assessment practices is no excuse for the sorts of damage administrators can cause to teachers, students, and the language-learning process by not matching assessment purposes with decisions and not matching assessment types with classroom activities. Somehow, language program administrators need to learn that a single aptitude–proficiency–placement–diagnostic–progress–achievement assessment is a pipedream. They need to understand the differences between the various purposes and types of assessments. They need to learn to give teachers more control over placement, diagnostic, progress, and achievement assessments – all of which should match the existing classroom activities to the highest degree possible. Perhaps teachers can gently inform those administrators who are unwilling to learn. Perhaps teachers can quietly become more involved in the development of assessments, especially for placement, diagnostic, progress, and achievement purposes. Perhaps teachers who are reading this article will someday become administrators. When that day comes, I beg you to recall what I have argued here and remember what it was like to see assessment from the teacher's point of view.

Suggested resources

Brown, J. D. (2005). *Testing in language programs: A comprehensive guide to English language assessment* (new edition). New York: McGraw-Hill.

Coombe, C., Folse, K., & Hubley, N. (2007). *A practical guide to assessing English language learners*. Ann Arbor, MI: University of Michigan Press.

Norris, J. (2000). Purposeful language assessment: Selecting the right alternative test. *Forum*, Vol. 38/No. 1, Jan–Mar 2000.

Discussion questions

1. What are the purposes of *standardized* aptitude, proficiency, and placement assessments? How are they similar to each other? And, how are they different?

2. What are the purposes of *classroom* diagnostic, progress, and achievement assessments? How are they similar to each other? And, how are they different?

3. What are selected-response, productive-response, and personal-response assessments appropriate for measuring? What are at least three sorts of example items for each? What sorts of classroom activities match with selected-response assessments? Productive-response assessments? And, personal-response assessments?

4. Why is it impossible to create a single aptitude–proficiency–placement–diagnostic–progress–achievement assessment procedure?

5. Which types of assessments do administrators control (and teachers *not* control)? Why is that true? Which types of assessments should teachers have control over? Why is that true?

6. In your teaching situation, what are the purposes of assessment? What types of decisions are made wholly or partly on the basis of assessments? How well do the purposes of the assessments match the decisions that are being made?

7. In your teaching situation, what assessment types are used? What types of classroom activities are used? How well do the assessment types match the classroom activities?

References

Brown, J. D. (1993). A comprehensive criterion-referenced language testing project. In D. Douglas & C. Chapelle (Eds.), *A new decade of language testing research* (pp. 163–184). Washington, DC: TESOL (also available from ERIC: ED 365 138).

Brown, J. D. (2005). *Testing in language programs: A comprehensive guide to English language assessment* (2nd ed.). New York: McGraw-Hill.

Brown, J. D., & Hilferty, A. (2006). The effectiveness of teaching reduced forms for listening comprehension. In J. D. Brown & K. Kondo-Brown (Eds.), *Perspectives on teaching connected speech to second language speakers* (pp. 51–58). Honolulu, HI: University of Hawaii Press. Reprinted by permission from the original article: Brown, J. D., & Hilferty, A. (1987). The effectiveness of teaching reduced forms for listening comprehension. *RELC Journal*, 17(2), 59–70.

Brown, J. D., & Hudson, T. (2002). *Criterion-referenced language testing*. Cambridge: Cambridge University Press.

Childs, M. (1995). Good and bad uses of TOEIC by Japanese companies. In J. D. Brown & S. O. Yamashita (Eds.), *Language testing in Japan* (pp. 66–75). Tokyo: Japan Association for Language Teaching. Retrieved from http://eric.ed.gov/ERICDocs/data/ericdocs2sql/content_storage_01/0000019b/80/14/c0/9e.pdf

Davidson, F., & Lynch, B. K. (2002). *Testcraft: A teacher's guide to writing and using language test specifications*. New Haven, CT: Yale University Press.

CHAPTER 16

Communicative Language Testing

Keith Morrow

INTRODUCTION

Perhaps the most interesting thing about the phrase "communicative language testing" is that it belongs very clearly to history. Its time was the 1970s and 1980s, when it was part of the broader movement to develop "communicative" language teaching (CLT); but whereas CLT has gone on to become the default position for language teachers in classrooms all over the world, very few testers these days would claim to adopt an overtly "communicative" perspective. To do so would be to risk being seen as a romantic, out of touch with the realities of the modern world of testing and test design. The reasons for this are revealing about the nature of language testing as it is viewed in the early 21st century, and about the power structures that support and maintain this view.

In broad terms, a communicative test aims to find out what a learner can "do" with the language, rather than to establish how much of the grammatical / lexical / phonological resources of the language he / she knows. In this sense, a key feature of a communicative test is the focus on "use" rather than "usage"; related to this is the notion of purpose. A communicative test involves the student in using the language for some explicit purpose. This purpose may relate to the everyday: to explain to a visitor how to get to the airport (in a speaking test); to find out about the facilities in a hotel (in a reading or listening test); to complete a customer satisfaction survey (in a writing test). Or it may relate to some more specialized area of use: to make a sales presentation; to compare different reports of the same event in order to research an article on media bias; to write an application letter for a job.

A communicative test is thus a direct test of the learner's ability to use the language. It consists of a set of purposeful tasks, designed to be relevant and appropriate to the test taker.

BACKGROUND

In his overview paper "Language testing, art or science," Spolsky (1975) identifies three phases in the history of language testing to date: prescientific, psychometric-structuralist, and psycholinguistic-sociolinguistic. It is tempting to see the latter two movements not just as linear developments, but also as reactions against what had gone before, and certainly there was a very strong sense in the mid-1970s of a movement away from the structuralist basis of much then-current language testing. One manifestation of this had been the interest of researchers such as Oller (1973; Oller and Streiff, 1975) in "integrative" approaches to testing such as dictation and cloze, but although these tapped the psycholinguistic dimension which Spolsky identified ("analysis through synthesis," in Oller's terms), they did not take account of the social dimension of language use. It was a focus on this area that became the main hallmark of the development of communicative tests. Hitherto the main focus of tests had been on the accuracy with which students could demonstrate their control of the language systems; in communicative tests, weight was also given to the "appropriacy" of the language used to achieve the purpose underlying the contextualized task that the student was asked to carry out.

So what were the key issues in the design of communicative tests? The first is implicit in the previous paragraph – rather than being a test of the language system (grammar, vocabulary, etc.) from which inferences could be made about actual performance, a communicative test was a direct test of performance in areas of language use (speaking, writing, reading, listening). The role of these "skills" was therefore quite different in a communicative test. Instead of being the medium through which grammar and vocabulary were tested, they became the focus of the test, which concentrated on how well the student could convey or understand meaning.

The issues emerge starkly:

1. Tests cease to be tests of "language" and become instead tests of speaking, reading, and so on. So how do we achieve a single measure of proficiency – of how "good" somebody is "at the language," given that performance in the different areas may vary markedly? And how do we disentangle all the other variables (personality, mood, culture, etc.) that may influence actual performance of a communicative task?

2. What do we mean by "reading" and "listening"? What do they consist of? How do we show that someone has "understood" a text? What does "understand" mean if understanding any nontrivial text is a process of negotiation between reader / listener and author? How, in other words, do we ensure the validity of our tests?

3. How do we decide whether a piece of writing or of spoken production has achieved its purpose? What sort of factors do we base this decision on? And how do we ensure consistency in these decisions? How, in other words, do we ensure the reliability of our tests? If we decide that we are going to achieve reliability by making our tests criterion-referenced and basing these decisions on explicit criteria (e.g., accuracy, appropriacy, range, complexity), we face the validity issue of where these criteria come from, and the reliability issue of ensuring that different markers understand and apply the criteria in the same way.

4. Any language test can only work by sampling aspects of the language. It is impossible to test the whole – there is just too much of it. In constructing grammar and vocabulary tests, we can be fairly confident of what it is that we are sampling, but if we want to test the ability of students to use language purposefully, where do we start? How many "purposes" are there? And how are they realized in language? In the absence of answers to questions like these, how can we generalize from students' performance on a particular set of tasks to their performance on other possible tasks. In other words, what can we say about their performance in general on the basis of their performance on the particular?

This seems a rather daunting list of problems, and many of them are still far from being completely resolved. But perhaps the most important insight that came from the attempts to develop tests along these lines is that at the heart of the design of any test is the need to make compromises.

Most obvious is the compromise between reliability and validity. Psychometric-structural testing (most typically in the form of multiple-choice grammar tests) laid great stress on reliability, and developed the idea of language testing as "measurement." This was "language testing as science" as in the title of Spolsky's paper referred to earlier. But in practical terms, it was only when the idea of "communicative" tests was mooted that people began to question the validity of discrete-item grammar tests. What, after all, do they actually test? For communicative tests, this question could on one level be answered very simply and clearly: *What does this listening test test?* It tests how well the student can understand this news bulletin. *What does this writing test test?* It tests how well s/he can write an e-mail complaining that the computer s/he ordered last week has not arrived. Content validity can therefore be fairly easily established, as can face validity. Construct validity is rather trickier, at least until the construct itself is fully developed, but the main problem is reliability. How do you mark the writing? How do you ensure that the listening test you offer in this session of the test is "the same" as the one you offered in the last one?

There are answers to this last set of questions – or at least there are steps that can be taken to minimize the inherent lack of reliability in communicative formats, but it has to be recognized that the degree of reliability found in multiple-choice grammar tests will never be achieved by a communicative test. In this sense, communicative testing will always have the aura of "language testing as art" attached to it. But what is interesting in retrospect is how the powerful discourse of "science" has been mobilized over the last 30 years to ensure that reliability (the key selling point of major commercial testing interests such as ETS and Cambridge ESOL) has remained at the forefront of attention. It has become something of a truism nowadays to say that a test cannot be valid if it is not reliable; it is often forgotten that a test that sacrifices any part of its validity in order to achieve or increase its reliability is sacrificing its reason for being.

RESEARCH

It is interesting to note that very little research was carried out into the design, construction, or implementation of communicative tests. There was a considerable amount of discussion and assertion, but little that one could describe as "research."

As far as I am aware, the first article published where the words "communicative language testing" were used in the title was my own "Communicative language testing: Revolution or evolution" (Morrow, 1979). This was usefully reprinted two years later (Alderson and Hughes, 1981) with comments and reactions from a number of testing specialists.

The ideas put forward in the paper grew out of a monograph I had produced for the Royal Society of Arts called "Techniques of Evaluation for a Notional Syllabus," on the basis of which they had decided to develop a series of examinations called CUEFL, the Communicative Use of English as a Foreign Language. I was the leader of the working party set up to oversee this project, and it was the experience of the background work that had gone into the monograph, and the work with colleagues on the working party that fed into the article. Although the monograph had a research element, in terms of a review and critique of then-current approaches to language testing, the working party was guided largely by intuition and enthusiasm, rather than by a research agenda. But like the 1979 article, it focused on three key areas:

1. A move away from an "atomistic" view of language learning that prioritized knowledge of discrete elements of the language system.

2. A focus on capturing in tests a number of aspects of language use not found in existing tests, such as context, purpose, authenticity, and focus on behavior.

3. An emphasis on developing qualitative as opposed to simply quantitative methods for the assessment of language.

In the volume containing the 1981 reprint of the article, there were three "reaction" papers (by Weir, Moller, and Alderson) and a summary of the discussion held by the participants. A range of issues were raised but the general tone was one of cautious welcome for the approach, although with concern about the lack of precision involved in some of the areas (e.g., authenticity), and a desire to see much more hard evidence to support some of the claims that were made.

A particular area where developments were soon made was the production of "scales of performance" defining levels in relation to the British Council ETS (later IELTS) tests of English for Academic Purposes. The first scales were drawn up (like the scales for the CUEFL tests) on the basis of introspection and expert judgment. These were criticized on the grounds of "relativity" (i.e., each level was defined by reference to the level above or below it) and a more sophisticated approach was developed by North in the production of the scales underlying the *Common European Framework of Reference* (Council of Europe, 2000). The "can do" scales contained in this book are the most comprehensive "behavior-based" set of descriptions available for the characterization of language proficiency, and represent the most fully developed outcome in this area of the work started in connection with the CUEFL tests back in the 1970s. In this connection, mention must also be made of the descriptions developed by ALTE (Association of Language Testers in Europe) to show what candidates "can do" at different levels in tests devised by their members.

Criticisms of communicative approaches to testing started early, and rumbled on for some time. Davies (1978) suggested that a criterion-referenced test was just a norm-referenced test in disguise, since the criteria could only be developed from norms. By 2003, communicative testing was one of "Three heresies of language testing research" (Davies, 2003). In his review of Nic Underhill's *Testing Spoken Language: A Handbook of Oral Testing Techniques*, Fulcher (1991) professed disappointment with the view of oral testing it put forward. The ideas in Underhill's book drew heavily on his work as an oral test designer and examiner for the CUEFL tests. Nearly ten years later, Fulcher (1999: 221) critiqued the notion of content validity as the basis of test design: "[This article argues that] using content validity as a major criterion in test design and evaluation has been mistaken."

PRACTICAL APPLICATION

The most obvious, and perhaps extreme, example of the application of a communicative approach to language testing is the set of tests referred to earlier. The CUEFL suite was administered by the Royal Society of Arts between 1981 and 1988, when it was taken over by the University of Cambridge Local Examinations Syndicate (now Cambridge ESOL).

After a review, they were re-launched as Certificates in Communicative Skills in English (CCSE) in 1990 and then amalgamated with the English language tests offered by the University of Oxford Delegacy, when this too was taken over by UCLES in the late 1990s. These continued to be available as the *Certificates in English Language Skills* until 2006, when they were withdrawn.

Throughout their various incarnations, these tests had a number of characteristic features:

1. *Modular structure*: Tests were at four levels, and at each level they consisted of four independent modules (listening, speaking, reading, writing). Candidates could enter whichever modules they liked at whatever level and, if successful, would receive certification in that module at that level (though a module could only be entered at one level in each session of the exam). Candidates would only be graded at the level they entered, that is, you could not get a lower level pass by "poor" performance on a higher level test (or vice versa).

2. Tests were task-based, reflecting the type of language use that the target audience (young adults learning English at language schools or colleges) would be likely to engage in.

3. Production tests were marked by reference to assessment criteria defined for each level.

4. Receptive tests were based on authentic input (i.e., "real" texts or recordings not originally produced for testing purposes).

For more details of these tests, see Hawkey (2005).

CONCLUSION

As noted at the beginning of this article, the label "communicative language testing" is now largely history. But like all history, its influence is still discernible in the present, and in some respects it is now an unremarked, and unremarkable, feature of the mainstream. Here is a short list of some features of mainstream tests that owe their origin to ideas first developed in the communicative context.

1. The use in oral testing of pairs of candidates, and of a separate "interlocutor" and "assessor."

2. The use of tasks in speaking and writing tests, requiring candidates to produce language appropriate to a range of specified purposes.

3. The use of criteria to define the type of production expected from candidates in speaking and writing tests at different levels.

4. The use in reading and listening tests of "authentic" material.

5. The recognition (e.g., in IELTS though not yet in Cambridge main-suite exams) that a test can yield valid results without the inclusion of a "language in use" component (i.e., grammar / vocabulary).

6. The ubiquitous linking of tests to the "can do" statements of the Common European Framework.

The revolution was a velvet one. But things have certainly evolved!

Suggested resources

Alderson, J. C. (1991). Bands and scores in J. C. Alderson and B. North (Eds.), *Language testing in the 1990s*, London: British Council / Macmillan.

Canale, M., & Swain, M. (1980). Theoretical bases of communicative approaches to second language teaching and testing. *Applied Linguistics* 1/1.

Morrow, K. E. (1991). Evaluating communicative tests. In S. Anivan (Ed.), *Current developments in language testing*. Singapore: SEAMEO Regional Language Centre.

Skehan, P. (1984). Issues in the testing of English for specific purposes. *Language Testing* 1/2.

Weir, C. J. (1991). *Communicative language testing*. New York: Prentice Hall.

Weir C. J. (1993). *Understanding and developing language tests*. New York: Prentice Hall.

Discussion questions

1. Was communicative language testing a revolution? Has there been evolution? Apart from the ones identified by the author, are there any other features of current mainstream tests that have a "communicative" dimension?

2. Do you agree with the author's implied criticism that current testing orthodoxy prioritizes reliability at the expense of validity? Is there a solution to the tension between these two requirements in test design?

3. You can never replicate in a test a real-life situation where a learner wants to use language for a real and immediate purpose. So is it worth trying to incorporate aspects of "authenticity" into test formats and procedures, or is this just a distraction from the design of a "real" test?

References

Alderson, J. C., & Hughes, A. (1981). *ELT Documents 111 – Issues in Language Testing*. London: British Council.

Council of Europe. (2000). *The Common European Framework of Reference for Languages: Learning, Teaching, Assessment*. Cambridge: Cambridge University Press.

Davies, A. (1978). Language testing. *Language Teaching and Linguistics Abstracts* 11(3–4).

Davies, A. (2003). Three heresies of language testing research. *Language Testing* 20(4).

Fulcher G. (1991). Review of *Testing spoken language: A handbook of oral testing techniques* (by N. Underhill). *ELT Journal* 44(1).

Fulcher, G. (1999). Assessment in English for Academic Purposes: Putting content validity in its place. *Applied Linguistics* 20(4).

Hawkey, R. (2005). *A modular approach to testing English language skills*. Cambridge: Cambridge University Press.

Morrow, K. E. (1979). Communicative language testing: Revolution or evolution? In C. J. Brumfit & K. Johnson (Eds.), *The communicative approach to language teaching*. Oxford: Oxford University Press.

Oller, J. (1973). Cloze Tests of second language proficiency and what they measure. *Language Learning* 23(1).

Oller, J., & Streiff, V. (1975). Dictation: A test of grammar-based expectancies. *English Language Teaching* 30(1).

Spolsky, B. (1975). Language testing: Art or science? Paper presented at the Fourth AILA International Congress, Stuttgart 1975. In Nickel G. (Ed.), *Proceedings of the Fourth International Congress of Applied Linguistics*, Vol. 3. Stuttgart, Germany: Hochschulverlag.

Alternative Assessment in Language Education

Christine Coombe, Kerry Purmensky, and Peter Davidson

INTRODUCTION

Until recently, assessment in many parts of the world has focused primarily on high-stakes examinations. However, with the increased popularity of multiple-measures assessment, institutions worldwide are adopting alternative forms of assessment. This chapter provides a rationale for alternative assessment in EF/SL testing and discusses some common alternative assessment techniques, namely projects and portfolios.

WHAT IS ALTERNATIVE ASSESSMENT?

In the past decade, educators have come to realize that alternative assessments are an important means of gaining a dynamic picture of students' academic and linguistic development. Alternative assessment is defined as the ongoing process involving the student and teacher in making judgments about the student's progress in language using nonconventional strategies (Hancock, 1994). Hamayan (1995) describes alternative assessment procedures as those techniques which can be used within the context of instruction and can be easily incorporated into the daily activities of the school or classroom. The purpose of alternative assessment is to gather data about how students are processing and completing authentic tasks in the target language. In general, alternative assessments meet these common criteria:

- focus is on documenting student growth over time, rather than on comparing students with one another (Stiggins, 1987; O'Malley and Valdez Pierce, 1996)
- emphasis is on students' strengths (what they know and can do with the language), rather than on their weaknesses (Tannenbaum, 1996)
- consideration is given to the learning styles, language proficiencies, cultural and educational backgrounds, and grade levels of students (Tannenbaum, 1996)

- they are authentic because they are based on activities that represent actual progress toward instructional goals and reflect tasks typical of classrooms and real-life settings (Stiggins, 1987; Tierney, Carter, and Desai, 1991)

The need to go beyond standardized tests has recently given prominence to the concept of alternative assessment, an approach that aims at integrating learning, teaching, and evaluation. For some there is good reason for the emergence of alternative assessment measures in developing effective assessment procedures. Until recently, control over the collection and interpretation of assessment information was kept by school administrators and a centralized authority. Now, however, this control has shifted toward classrooms where assessment occurs on a regular and continual basis. As teachers and students become more involved in the assessment process, the ways of measuring progress in a language have become less prescribed and more straightforward.

TRADITIONAL AND ALTERNATIVE ASSESSMENT

Alternative assessment is often viewed as being an "alternative" to traditional types of assessment, but this is not necessarily the case. Alternative assessment should be used in conjunction with traditional assessment, as part of a comprehensive multiple-measures assessment scheme. Perhaps a more suitable term for alternative assessment would be "additional assessment," as it should be used in addition to, rather than instead of, traditional testing. However, having established that alternative assessment and traditional assessment are not mutually exclusive, to better understand the essence of alternative assessment it is helpful to contrast it with traditional assessment.

Alternative assessment is different from traditional assessment in that it utilizes different task types. With traditional assessment students are often required to answer multiple-choice questions, true–false questions, or short-answer questions. In contrast, with alternative assessment, students are evaluated on what they integrate and produce rather than on what they are able to recall and reproduce. As noted by Huerta-Macias (1995), alternative assessment provides alternatives to traditional testing in that it:

- does not intrude on regular classroom activities
- reflects the curriculum that is actually being implemented in the classroom
- provides information on the strengths and weaknesses of each individual student
- provides multiple indices that can be used to gauge student progress
- is more multiculturally sensitive and free of the norm, linguistic, and cultural biases found in traditional testing

Bailey (1998: 207) provides us with a very useful chart that effectively contrasts traditional and alternative assessment (see Table 17.1).

Authentic assessment, as mentioned in Table 17.1, refers to the type of assessment that requires the test candidates to carry out some kind of performance or task. The key requirement of an authentic assessment is that it requires the test taker to demonstrate that they are able to complete a particular task or tasks that resemble something that they are likely to have to do in real life (O'Malley and Valdez Pierce, 1996), for example, getting students to complete a visa application form, or buy something from a store, or make a hotel booking, are all examples of authentic assessment. According to Hamp-Lyons (1996), assessment tasks that are the same as or closely resemble the tasks to be carried out in actual language-in-use situations will provide a more accurate measure of the language learners' abilities.

Traditional assessment	Alternative assessment
one-shot tests	continuous, longitudinal assessment
indirect tests	direct tests
inauthentic tests	authentic assessment
individual projects	group projects
no feedback provided to learners	feedback provided to learners
timed exams	untimed exams
decontextualized test tasks	contextualized test tasks
norm-referenced score interpretation	criterion-referenced score interpretation
standardized tests	classroom-based tests

Table 17.1 Contrasting traditional and alternative assessment (Bailey, 1998: 207)

PRACTICAL APPLICATION – PROJECTS

Project work creates opportunities for language learning through problem solving, cooperative learning, collaboration, and negotiation of meaning-processes which are central to the second language acquisition process. Projects are a very effective means of mixing classroom practices with long-term assessment. Whereas some projects can last the entire length of the class, other projects can be accomplished within days, weeks, or months. Some of the most important considerations to keep in mind when using projects as alternative assessments are that they must be closely tied to curricular objectives; they should have clear language and academic goals; and they ought to have unique qualities that encourage students to higher levels of thinking. Projects should engage students with their creative nature, and encourage students to produce language that is both accurate and authentic. Projects can come in many forms, and students can work as individuals or in groups. They can be based in reading, writing, listening, speaking, or integrate all four language skills.

Some teachers equate project work with group work but it is much more than that. When incorporating projects into their classes, educators can create a vibrant learning environment that requires active student involvement, stimulates higher-level thinking skills, gives students responsibility for their own learning (Stoller, 2002), and involves multiskill activities that focus on a theme of interest rather than specific language tasks. When doing projects, students work together to achieve a common goal, purpose, or concrete outcome (i.e., a brochure, a report, a display, or an article, etc.). In recent years, educators have turned to content-based instruction (CBI) and project work to promote meaningful student engagement with language and content learning. CBI seeks to use content, rather than the task, as the vehicle for developing language skills.

Project work has been described by a number of second language educators and has been found to have the following features (Stoller, 1997: 2):

- focuses on content learning rather than on specific language targets
- is student-centered (though the teacher plays a major role to support / guide students)

- is cooperative rather than competitive
- leads to authentic integration of skills and processing of information from varied sources
- mirrors real-life tasks
- culminates in an end product that can be shared with others
- has both a process and product orientation
- is potentially motivating, stimulating, empowering and challenging
- usually results in building student self-confidence, self-esteem, and autonomy as well as building language skills and content learning

TYPES OF PROJECTS

Projects can be classified by the way in which they are structured, by the data collection procedures they utilize, and by the way the information is reported. Henry (1994) describes the three major types of projects that ES/FL teachers use in their classrooms: structured, unstructured, and semistructured. Structured projects are determined, specified, and organized by the teacher in terms of topic, materials, methodology, and presentation. Unstructured projects, however, are defined largely by the students themselves. Semistructured projects represent the middle ground as they are defined and organized by both teacher and students.

Projects can also differ in the type of data collection procedures they employ. Stoller (2002) classifies projects into research, text, correspondence, survey, and encounter projects. Each of these project types differs in terms of the data collection procedures that students need to employ as they engage in project work. Research projects require students to gather information through library / Internet research. Text projects are similar in that they involve encounters with "texts" (i.e., literature, reports, newspaper articles, etc.). Correspondence projects involve students communicating with individuals (i.e., government agencies, businesses, schools) to solicit information by mail or e-mail. Survey projects call for students to create a survey and then collect and analyze data. Encounter projects necessitate face-to-face contact with guest speakers or individuals outside the classroom.

Another way to classify projects is by the way the information is reported. Production projects involve the creation of something (i.e., bulletin board, display, video, photo essay, travel itinerary, etc.). Performance projects call for students to "perform" something (i.e., debate, oral presentation, play, skit, etc.). Organizational projects require students to plan or organize something (i.e., a club, conversation table, special interest group, or special event).

INCORPORATING PROJECTS INTO THE EF/SL CLASSROOM

To be successful, teachers need to systematically implement projects into their classrooms. Teachers need to first decide the time frame of the project. Another decision teachers need to make is whether they want their students to work individually, in groups or pairs, or as a class. Yet another consideration is whether the project will be completed inside the classroom or whether it should extend outside the walls of the classroom or school. Once decisions to these questions have been made, teachers need to decide on the format of the project. The most suitable format for a project can depend on a number of factors, including:

- curricular objectives
- course expectations / outcomes
- students' proficiency level
- student interests
- time constraints
- availability of materials / resources

To introduce project work effectively multiple stages of development are required. Sheppard and Stoller (1995: 2) propose a 10-step sequence of activities for incorporating project work into the classroom.

1. Students and teacher agree on a theme for the project (establishing starting point).
2. Students and teacher determine the final outcome (defining an endpoint).
3. Students and teacher structure the project.
4. Teacher prepares students for language demands of research / information gathering.
5. Students gather information or conduct research.
6. Teacher prepares students for language demands of compiling and analyzing data.
7. Students compile and analyze information.
8. Teacher prepares students for language demands of culminating activity.
9. Students present final product.
10. Students evaluate the project.

Language intervention steps (4, 6, 8) are optional and are intended to provide explicit language instruction at critical moments during the project. These steps would of course depend on the language proficiency level of the students engaged in the project work.

ASSESSING THE PROJECT

Projects should be assessed in the same way that writing samples are assessed in EF/SL. In other words, teachers have the option of using either a holistic banding scale or an analytical one that separates out important categories. Figure 17.1 provides an example of an analytical marking scale for a project.

Student Name: _____ ID No.: _____

English Teacher: _____ Group: _____

Scale:	5-Excellent	4-Good	3-Satisfactory	2-Needs improvement	1-Weak	0-Omitted/Not valid
	10	8	6	4	2	0
	15	12	9	6	3	0

1.	**Presentation** appearance format	5	4	3	2	1	0
2.	**Organization** introduction / development / conclusion	10	8	6	4	2	0
3.	**Correctness** sentence structure / grammar / punctuation / spelling	10	8	6	4	2	0
4.	**Research** sources used visual aids (maps, photos, charts)	10	8	6	4	2	0
5.	**Information / Content** coverage of major / minor details	15	12	9	6	3	0
	TOTAL /50						

Figure 17.1 Project-marking criteria (HD English, Dubai Men's College, Higher Colleges of Technology)

PRACTICAL APPLICATION – REFLECTIVE WRITTEN PORTFOLIOS

Another common form of alternative assessment is the writing portfolio. In simple terms, a portfolio is a collection of student work. As far as portfolios are defined in writing assessment, it is a purposive collection of student writing over time that shows the stages in the writing process a text has gone through and the stages of the writer's growth. Portfolio-based assessment examines multiple pieces of writing produced over time under different constraints rather than an assessment of a single essay written under a specified time frame. Increasingly, portfolios are being compiled in a way that allows the student to provide evidence of self-reflection. Portfolios reflect accomplishment relative to specific instructional goals or objectives. Key elements of portfolios are student reflection and self-monitoring.

Since the 1970s considerable progress has been made in introducing the direct assessment of writing to colleges and universities. A frequent complaint about traditional measures of writing ability is that they undermine regular classroom instruction. These days many writing teachers like to teach using a process approach in which students spend time selecting the subjects they will write about, deciding on a viewpoint, finding materials to include in their essays, drafting, and revising before submitting a finished essay. Portfolios reflect the kinds of instruction valued in composition and therefore judgments made of portfolios are claimed to be inherently more meaningful.

CHARACTERISTICS OF A PORTFOLIO

Several well-known testers have put forth lists of characteristics that exemplify good portfolios. Paulson, Paulson, and Meyer (1991: 60) state that portfolios must include student participation in four important areas: (1) the selection of portfolio contents; (2) the guidelines for selection; (3) the criteria for judging merit; and (4) evidence of student reflection. Hamp-Lyons and Condon (2000) offer nine characteristics of good portfolios. They stress, however, that these characteristics may or may not be found in all portfolio systems equally.

1. Collection: The portfolio judges more than a single performance.
2. Range: The writer is able to use different genres that show off different areas of expertise.
3. Context richness: Writers bring their experiences with them into the assessment.
4. Delayed evaluation: Students can go back and revise their work.
5. Selection: Students participate in the selection process.
6. Student-centered control: The learner is responsible for his / her success.
7. Reflection and self-assessment: The learner self assesses and / or reflects on what he / she has learned.
8. Growth along specific parameters: Portfolios allow evaluators to ask specific questions such as "Has the writer developed over time / become a better speller?"
9. Development over time: Readers can trace the development of each piece.

Moya and O'Malley (1994: 1) state that five characteristics typify a model portfolio. They maintain that portfolios must display comprehensiveness and be predetermined, systematic, informative, tailored, and authentic. A brief description of these qualities follows.

1. Comprehensiveness: The potential for determining the depth and breath of a student's capabilities can be realized through comprehensive data collection and analysis.

2. Predetermined and systematic: A sound portfolio is planned prior to implementation. This includes information such as the purpose, contents, data collection schedule, and student grading criteria.

3. Informative: The information in the portfolio must be meaningful to all stakeholders in the process (i.e., teachers, students, staff, and parents).

4. Tailored: An exemplary portfolio is tailored to the purpose for which it will be used, classroom goals and objectives, and individual student assessment needs.

5. Authentic: A good portfolio provides student information based on assessment tasks that reflect authentic activities used during classroom instruction.

ASSESSING THE PORTFOLIO

It is generally recognized that one of the main benefits of portfolio assessment is the promotion of learner reflection (O'Malley and Valdez-Pierce, 1996), and this forms a critical element in the assessment of portfolios. By having reflection as part of the portfolio process, students are asked to think about their needs, goals, weaknesses, and strengths in language learning. They are also asked to select their best work and to explain why that work was beneficial to them. By having a reflective element in a portfolio, the process is more personalized. Learner reflection allows students to contribute their own insights about their learning to the assessment process. It enhances feelings of learner ownership of their work and increases opportunities for dialogues between students and teachers about curricular goals and learner progress. As noted by Santos (1997: 10) "Without reflection, the portfolio remains 'a folder of all my papers.'"

We feel that the most effective way to grade a portfolio is through an analytical marking scale like the one featured in Figure 17.2. This scale separates out a number of important criteria that focus on areas like content, organization, language accuracy, and fluency, as well as formatting conventions. Note that evidence of reflection in the form of a reflective statement figures prominently in this sample assessment criteria.

CONCLUSION: FUTURE DIRECTIONS

For a variety of reasons, some students simply do not perform well on traditional tests. Because language performance depends heavily on the purpose for language use and the context in which it is used, it makes sense to provide students with assessment opportunities that reflect these practices. In the real world, we must demonstrate that we can complete tasks using the English language effectively both at work and in social settings. Our assessment practices must reflect the importance of using language both in and outside of the language classroom. Alternative assessment should not be used as an alternative to traditional language assessment, but it should be used in conjunction with it. It should also be held to the same standards in terms of validity and reliability as traditional types of testing. Alternative assessment provides rich data that enhances the data generated from traditional tests, and together this data allows us to make more informed assessment decisions.

Student Name: _____		ID No.: _____			
English Teacher: _____		Group: _____			

5	4	3	2	1	0
Excellent	Good	Satisfactory	Needs improvement	Weak	Omitted / Not valid

		5	4	3	2	1	0
1	**Selection** of relevant material & completeness • Inclusion of **final** as well as draft material, if needed • Appropriate headers and footers, titles, file names • 3 = minimum materials included as required by teacher	5	4	3	2	1	0
2	**Language accuracy** Sentence structure, grammar, punctuation, spelling Evidence of editing in Draft 2, if required	5	4	3	2	1	0
3	**Language fluency** Cohesion and coherence Content	5	4	3	2	1	0
4	**Presentation of work** Word processing, bound if required. Appropriate cover sheet & contents page Paragraphing & formatting conventions followed	5	4	3	2	1	0
5	**Evidence of reflection on portfolio** Student includes 100 word evaluation of own progress in writing and the focus of future efforts.	5	4	3	2	1	0
	TOTAL /25						
	= %						

Figure 17.2 Sample writing portfolio assessment criteria (adapted from Dubai Men's College Portfolio Assessment Criteria, 2009)

Suggested resources

Herman, J. L., Aschbacher, P. R., & Winters, L. (1992). *A practical guide to alternative assessment*. Alexandria, VA: Association for Supervision and Curriculum Development.

Miller, W. (1995). Alternative assessment techniques for reading and writing. San Francisco, CA: Jossey-Bass.

O'Malley, J., & Valdez Pierce, L. (1996). *Authentic assessment for English language learners: Practical approaches for teachers*, Reading, MA: Addison-Wesley.

Discussion questions

1. What are the advantages of using alternative assessments in language assessment?
2. What would be the washback effect of using alternative assessment?
3. Can you think of any disadvantages associated with this type of assessment?
4. How can you ensure validity and reliability when using alternative assessment?
5. What is the purpose of the "reflective element" in a written portfolio?

References

Bailey, K. M. (1998). *Learning about language assessment: Dilemmas, decisions, and directions*. Boston: Heinle & Heinle Publishers.

Hamayan, E. V. (1995). Approaches to alternative assessment. *Annual Review of Applied Linguistics*, 15: 212–226.

Hamp-Lyons, L. (1996). Applying ethical standards to portfolio assessment of writing in English as a foreign language. *Studies in Language Testing #3: Performance Testing, Cognition and Assessment*. Selected papers from the 15th Annual LTRC Conference.

Hamp-Lyons, L., & Condon, W. (2000). *Assessing the portfolio: Principles for practice, theory, and research*. Cresskill, NJ: Hampton Press.

Hancock, C. R. (1994). Alternative assessment and second language study: What and why? *ERIC Clearinghouse on languages and Linguistics*, Washington, DC: Center for Applied Linguistics.

Henry, J. (1994). *Teaching through projects*. London: Kogan Page.

Huerta-Macias, A. (1995). Alternative assessment: Answers to commonly asked questions, *TESOL Journal*, 5(1): 8–10.

Moya, S., & O'Malley, J. (1994). A portfolio assessment model for ESL. *The Journal of Educational Issues of Language Minority Students*, 13: 13–36.

O'Malley, J., & Valdez Pierce, L. (1996). *Authentic assessment for English language learners: Practical approaches for teachers*. Upper Saddle River, NJ: Pearson.

Paulson, F., Paulson, P., & Meyer, C. (1991). What makes a portfolio a portfolio? *Educational Leadership*, 48(5): 60–63.

Santos, M. (1997). Portfolio assessment and the role of learner reflection. *English Language Teaching Forum*, 35(2): 10.

Sheppard, K., & Stoller, F. (1995). Guidelines for the integration of students' projects in ESP classrooms. *English Teaching Forum*, 33(2): 10–15.

Stiggins, R. J. (1987). Design and development of performance assessments. *Educational Measurement: Issues and Practices*, 6(1), 33–42.

Stoller, F. (1997). Project work: A means to promote language content. *English Teaching Forum*, 35(4): 2–16.

Stoller, F. (2002). Project work: A means to promote language content. In J. C. Richards & W. Renandya (Eds), *Methodology in language teaching: An anthology of current practice* (pp. 107–20). Cambridge: Cambridge University Press.

Tannenbaum, J.-E. (1996). Practical ideas on alternative assessment for ESL students. *ERIC Digest*: Center for Applied Linguistics.

Tierney, R. J., Carter, M. A., & Desai, L. E. (1991). *Portfolio assessment in the reading–writing classroom*. Norwood, MA: Christopher Gordon Publishers.

CHAPTER 18

Task-Based Language Assessment: Components, Development, and Implementation

Ali Shehadeh

INTRODUCTION

The main purpose of this chapter is to explain testing / assessment within the framework of task-based language assessment (TBLA) and the wider context of task-based language teaching (TBLT). The chapter will describe TBLA and its characterizing features, illustrating the main components of TBLA, its development, and its classroom implementation and utilization. In order to properly understand and contextualize TBLA, however, we must first understand TBLT.

WHAT IS TASK-BASED LANGUAGE TEACHING, OR TBLT?

TBLT is an educational framework and an approach for the theory and practice of second / foreign language (L2) learning and teaching, and a teaching methodology in which classroom tasks constitute the main focus of instruction (Richards et al., 2003). A classroom task is defined as an activity that is (1) goal-oriented, (2) content-focused, (3) has a real outcome, and (4) reflects real-life language use and language need (Shehadeh, 2005). The syllabus in TBLT is organized around activities and tasks rather than in terms of grammar or vocabulary (Richards et al., 2003).

The interest in TBLT is based on the strong belief that it facilitates second language acquisition (SLA) and makes L2 learning and teaching more principled and more effective. This interest arose from a constellation of ideas issuing from philosophy of education, theories of SLA, empirical findings on effective instructional techniques, and the exigencies of language learning in contemporary society (Van den Branden et al., 2009). It is beyond the limits of this chapter to illustrate the various perspectives on TBLT and ways of implementing and utilizing it in the L2 classroom. (For reviews, see, for instance, Ellis, 2003; Shehadeh and Coombe, 2010; Van den Branden et al., 2009.)

Indeed, tasks are now viewed as "the devices that provide learners with the data they need for learning" (Ellis, 2000: 193). No wonder, therefore, that many teachers around the world are moving toward TBLT, and no wonder that task-based pair and group work is now considered a standard teaching / learning strategy in many language classrooms around the world (Shehadeh and Coombe, 2010).

After this brief introduction to TBLT, it is now possible to describe task-based language assessment, its defining characteristics, its basic components, the basic steps in its development and implementation, and its classroom application and utilization.

WHAT IS TASK-BASED LANGUAGE ASSESSMENT, OR TBLA?

TBLA is a framework for language testing / assessment that takes the task as the fundamental unit for assessment and testing. It is based on the same underlying principles as TBLT, but extends them from the learning-and-teaching domain to the testing domain. Specifically, as in TBLT methodology, testing / assessment in TBLA is also organized around tasks rather than in terms of grammar or vocabulary. For instance, Long and Norris (2000: 600) state that "genuinely task-based language assessment takes the task itself as the fundamental unit of analysis, motivating item selection, test instrument construction and the rating of task performance." As in TBLT methodology too, the main goal and validity of TBLA is measured against the extent to which it can successfully achieve a close link between the testee's performance during the test and his / her performance in the real world. For instance, Ellis (2003: 279) states that "task-based testing is seen as a way of achieving a close correlation between the test performance, i.e. what the testee does during the test, and the criterion of performance, i.e. what the testee has to do in the real world." Assessment tasks are thus viewed as "devices for eliciting and evaluating communicative performances from learners in the context of language use that is meaning-focused and directed towards some specific goal" (ibid.).

Four main features characterize TBLA. *First*, it is a formative assessment; that is, it is an assessment undertaken as part of an instructional program for the purpose of improving learning and teaching. *Second*, it is a performance-referenced assessment; that is, it is an assessment that seeks to provide information about learners' abilities to use the language in specific contexts, that is directed at assessing a particular performance of learners, and that seeks to ascertain whether learners can use the L2 to accomplish real target tasks. *Third*, it is a direct assessment; that is, it is an assessment that involves a measurement of language abilities that involves tasks where the measure of the testee's performance is incorporated into the task itself, like information-transfer test tasks such as information-gap, opinion-gap, and reasoning-gap tasks. It must be noted, however, that direct assessment still involves some level of inferring because it is necessary to observe performance and then infer ability from that performance. Put differently, you can measure outcomes, but you are still left with inferring the ability that produced the outcome. *Fourth*, it is an authentic assessment; that is, it is an assessment that involves either real-world language use (or as close as possible to this), or the kinds of language processing found in real-world language use, that is, the test task's characteristics must match those of the target-language task (Ellis, 2003: 285).

COMPONENTS OF TASK-BASED LANGUAGE ASSESSMENT

Task-based language assessments consist of three basic components: a test task, an implementation procedure, and a performance measure:

TEST TASK DESIGN AND SELECTION

It is possible to identify two approaches to test task design and selection within the framework of TBLA: The first is called the *construct-centered approach* or the direct system-referenced tests. This approach entails the identification of a theory of language learning and language use as a basis for the test task design and selection. This approach is used with tasks that seek "to establish the general nature of the testees' language proficiency" (Ellis, 2003: 286). The second approach is called the *work-sample approach* or the direct performance-referenced tests. This approach involves analysis of the target situation to determine what tasks the testee will need to perform in the real world. This approach is used with tasks that seek "to find out what a learner can do in a particular situation" (Ellis, 2003: 286). It should be noted, however, that the two approaches must be seen as complementary rather than mutually exclusive because any successful TBLA ideally requires both approaches.

IMPLEMENTATION PROCEDURES

There are two implementation procedures: The first is *planning time*. Planning time must be adopted as a key implementation procedure because it can improve the test taker's performance. The second procedure is the *interlocutor* (on oral test tasks). The role of the addressee (familiar or unfamiliar, native speaker or nonnative speaker) plays a significant role in the performance of the testee on an assessment task. For instance, some researchers have shown that if you want to elicit the "best performance" from the testee, it may be preferable to set up a testing situation where the candidates interact with another nonnative speaker than with a native speaker (e.g., Wigglesworth, 2001). Along the same lines, one wonders whether it is also possible to have real recipients for writing tasks, analogous to the interlocutor in oral tasks. This is an important question for further exploring the implementation of TBLA in the L2 classroom.

MEASURING PERFORMANCE

How do we assess the performance elicited from the testee in TBLA tests? Two principal methods for measuring learner performance are used in TBLA contexts. The first is the *direct assessment of task outcomes*. This method involves either the assessor observing a performance of a task and making a judgment, or no judgment on the part of the assessor (i.e., judgment / measurement is objective – the testee did or did not succeed in performing the task) because it results in solutions that are either right or wrong. A good example of direct assessment of task outcomes is a closed task that results in a solution that is either right or wrong, like locating a journal article relating to a particular topic in a library (Robinson and Ross, 1996: 474–475). The main advantages of this method are that "it affords an objective measurement, involving no judgment on the part of the assessor, and it is easy and quick" (Ellis, 2003: 296).

The second performance measure is *external ratings*. This method involves external judgment which is more subjective (but efforts are being made to make it more reliable). This measure also involves a holistic measure (scale) or an analytic measure (scale) of linguistic ability (e.g., paragraph or essay evaluation; overall linguistic ability versus the four language skills identified for rating separately). Examples of this assessment include judging that the learner's speaking ability is at the "expert" level in the oral interview component of the old ELTS test which specifies that the learner "can speak with authority on a variety of topics; can initiate, expand, and develop a theme" (Ellis, 2003: 300). The main advantage of this method is that it enables the assessor to specify the learner's competencies to be measured in more functional terms. Competencies in external ratings are determined in terms of learner performance levels or checklists (for fuller discussion, see Ellis, 2003: 296 ff.)

Along the same lines, Long and Norris, bearing in mind language professionals and classroom teachers, specify six practical steps for developing and implementing task-based language tests as follows:

1. The *intended use(s)* for task-based assessment within the language programme must be specified, minimally addressing the following four issues: who uses information from the assessment? [. . .]; what information is the assessment supposed to provide? [. . .]; what are the purposes for the assessment? [. . .]; and who or what is affected, and what are the consequences of the assessment?

2. Target tasks or task-types emerging from the needs analysis are analyzed and classified according to a variety of *task features*. Analysis is undertaken in order to understand exactly what real-world conditions are associated with target tasks and should therefore be replicated under assessment conditions.

3. Based on information from the analysis of task features, *test and item specifications* are developed. . . . Specifications delineate the formats tests should take, procedures involved, tasks or task-types to be sampled, format for test tasks (items), and how performance on the task-based test should be evaluated.

4. [Carrying out] identification and specification of *rating criteria*, which form the basis for interpretations of examinee performance and task accomplishment . . . Real-world criterial elements (aspects of task performance that will be evaluated) and levels (descriptions of what success looks like on these aspects of task performance) should be identified within initial needs analysis, with a view toward providing students and teachers with clear learning objectives.

5. Task items, test instruments and procedures and rating criteria need to be *evaluated* (involving pilot-testing and revision) according to their efficiency, appropriacy and effectiveness with respect to the intended assessment uses.

6. Finally, task-based language assessment should incorporate procedures for systematic and ongoing *validation* of its intended use within the language programme. Validation should minimally consider: to what extent test instruments and procedures are providing appropriate, trustworthy and useful information; to what extent particular uses for the assessment are warranted, . . . and to what extent the consequences of assessment use can be justified, given the impact on students, teachers, language programmes and any other relevant stakeholders in the assessment process. (Long and Norris, 2000: 600–601)

UTILIZATION AND CLASSROOM APPLICATIONS OF TASK-BASED LANGUAGE ASSESSMENT

TBLA has been utilized by language teachers in the L2 classroom in a broad range of formal and informal educational settings that serve a wide range of language learners who come from different age groups, different proficiency levels, and different educational and cultural backgrounds. For space limitations, I will only cite in this section selective, but illustrative, examples that demonstrate recent applications of TBLA in the L2 classroom.

Gan, Davison, and Hamp-Lyons (2009) analyzed the discourse derived from a task, which in their particular case was based on choosing a gift for the main character in the movie *Forrest Gump*. They found that peer group discussion as an oral assessment format has the potential to provide opportunities for students to demonstrate "real-life" spoken interactional abilities. Yeh (2010) describes a blended task-based activity designed for intermediate- and advanced-level students in speech or oral training classes. She describes a number of assessment tools used to evaluate student performance. Winke (2010) explains how to use online tasks for formative language assessment, which is defined as assessment that is used in "evaluating students in the process of 'forming' their competencies and skills" (Brown, 2004: 6). She demonstrates how these tasks provide continuous feedback to the teacher and learners, and how this feedback can be used for making decisions about ongoing instructional procedures and classroom tasks.

In a new collection of studies on TBLT and TBLA (see Shehadeh and Coombe, forthcoming, 2012), Weaver (forthcoming), like Winke (2010) above, provides an account of incorporating a formative assessment cycle into a TBLT curriculum in relation to a task for Japanese business students with a strong sense of authenticity.

It is important to note that in all these contexts, and in line with the underlying principles of TBLT and TBLA, assessment has been utilized and implemented not as an isolated component, but rather as *part and parcel* of the learning-and-teaching process. That is, assessment was intended to both facilitate learning and provide feedback that can be used for making further decisions about instructional procedures and teaching methodology. More specifically, assessment has been undertaken as part of the instructional program for the purpose of improving learning and teaching. At the same time, such assessments are both authentic and involve a measurement of language abilities that involve tasks where the measure of the testee's performance is incorporated into the task itself (see characteristics of TBLA earlier in the chapter).

CONCLUSIONS: FUTURE DIRECTIONS

Carless (forthcoming) argues that "the use of teacher assessment in a traditionally examination-oriented system is both a powerful impetus for change and a challenge to teachers' workloads and mindsets." It is a challenge because traditionally examination-oriented systems have a long history of public assessment. In such systems, the uniform test, which emphasizes grammar, vocabulary, and reading comprehension, can be an obstacle to the implementation of TBLA (Ng and Tang, 1997). Language tests in these systems play a key part in success in the pursuit of personal well-being and future employment opportunities. According to Cheng (2008), for instance, the high status of English tests in China does not support teaching but drives it. Carless points out that in such settings, "there is a likelihood that test takers (often with the assistance of the ubiquitous after-hours tutorial sector) may seek to subvert the aims of the test developers." He cites an example from a recent study (Luk, 2010) which reveals that "a careful analysis of the discourse of test interaction . . . shows how students colluded in producing utterances aimed at creating the impression of being effective interlocutors for the purpose of scoring marks rather than for authentic communication" (Carless, forthcoming).

The use of teacher assessment in traditionally examination-oriented systems, on the other hand, can be an impetus for changing teachers' mindsets because it is proving again and again its futility and thus falling into disfavor, instead favoring TBLA which is a more powerful assessment tool, as described above. No wonder, therefore, that high-stakes examinations have over the last twenty years increased the weighting awarded to oral performance and the examinations have become increasingly task-based (Carless, forthcoming).

Nonetheless, more research still needs to be done into TBLA. On the research side, we still need to know, for instance, to what extent does a formative assessment cycle support the development of wider student learning capacities, or more narrowly help them to improve their performance (Carless, forthcoming). As Black and Wiliam (2003) have argued, an assessment sequence can only be said to have acted formatively if it advances student learning. It may be that a way forward for formative assessment in relation to TBLA is to engage more with the expanding educational literature on formative assessment (e.g., Andrade and Cizek, 2010) and developments in dynamic assessment (e.g., Poehner, 2008).

On the pedagogical side, TBLA – as well as its underlying principles – should be made more accessible to practicing teachers. One reason why traditional, examination-oriented systems still persist in many parts of the world is because many teachers do not know how to utilize TBLA in their practices. Another reason is that not many teachers or instructors, when pressed hard, know what exactly is meant by TBLA and why it is more conducive to L2 learning. Also, many teachers, particularly in EFL / ESL contexts, believe that tasks are another face of the traditional exercises. Finally, many teachers consider TBLA to be an "alien theoretical concept" that is not applicable to their specific teaching context or educational setting.

Obviously, more work and more research need to be done to combat these hindrances in the design, implementation, application, and utilization of TBLA. As Brindley stated more than fifteen years ago (Brindley, 1994: 90), the challenge for researchers and test designers in TBLA is to develop a method that provides valid and reliable measurements in assessments that are "complex, qualitative, and multidimensional, rather than uniform and standardized." This challenge continues to manifest itself in one form or another. Nevertheless, it is worth doing in order to arrive at an accurate assessment of the test taker's ability, which is a crucial aspect of task-based language assessment.

Suggested resources

Brindley, G. (2008). Educational reform and language testing. In E. Shohamy & N. Hornberger (Eds.), *Encyclopedia of language and education*. Vol. 7: *Language testing and assessment* (pp. 365–378). New York: Springer.

Brown, J. D., Hudson, T., Norris, J., & Bonk, W. (2002). *An investigation of second language task-based performance assessments*. Honolulu, Hawai'i: University of Hawai'i Press.

Long, M. H., & Norris, J. M. (2000). Task-based language teaching and assessment. In M. Byram (Ed.), *Encyclopedia of language teaching* (pp. 597–603). London: Routledge.

Norris, J. M. (Ed.) (2002). Special issue: Task-based language assessment. *Language Testing*, Vol. 19, Issue 4.

Norris, J. M. (2009). Task-based teaching and testing. In M. Long & C. Doughty (Eds.), *Handbook of second and foreign language teaching*. Cambridge: Blackwell.

Shehadeh, A., & Coombe, C. (Eds.) (2010). *Applications of task-based learning in TESOL*. Alexandria, VA: TESOL Publications.

Van den Branden, K., Bygate, M., & Norris, J. M. (Eds.) (2009). *Task-based language teaching: A reader*. Amsterdam: John Benjamin's.

Wigglesworth, G. (2008). Tasks and performance-based assessment. In E. Shohamy & N. Hornberger (Eds.), *Encyclopedia of language and education: Language testing and assessment.* Vol. 7: *Language testing and assessment* (pp. 111–122) (2nd ed.). New York: Springer.

Discussion questions

1. Do you utilize TBLA in your specific educational context? Why? Why not? What are the challenges?

2. Does your institution encourage assessment procedures alternative to an examination-oriented system? Why? Why not?

3. Design an open-ended, but well-planned activity in which students in pairs or groups carry out a specific task to their liking or interest (e.g., summarizing a book chapter, evaluating a course textbook, convincing a partner to invest in a certain company, making a hotel reservation on the telephone, etc.). On completion of the task, ask students to report to the class on their findings individually or collectively, orally, and / or in writing. After that, ask them to self-evaluate and / or other-evaluate their performance using specific rubrics or criteria. Survey your students on how much they feel they have benefited from the task itself as well as from self-evaluation and /or other-evaluation.

4. Compare the performance and achievements of students in a traditional language-centered, teacher-centered class with those of students in a learner-centered TBLT and TBLA class. Do you see any differences? Specify the main difference you have observed between the two contexts. Discuss the major differences you have observed with your colleagues or students.

References

Andrade, H., & Cizek, G. (Eds.) (2010). *Handbook of formative assessment.* New York: Routledge.

Black, P., & Wiliam, D. (2003). In praise of educational research: Formative assessment. *British Educational Research Journal*, 29(5), pp. 623–637.

Brindley, G. (1994). Task-centred assessment in language learning programs: The promise and the challenge. In N. Bird, P. Falvey, A. Tsui, D. Allison, A. & McNeill (Eds.), *Language and learning* (pp. 73–94). Hong Kong: Institute of Language in Education.

Brown, H. D. (2004). *Language assessment: Principles and classroom practice.* White Plains, NY: Pearson ESL.

Carless, D. (forthcoming). TBLT in EFL settings: Looking back and moving forward. In A. Shehadeh & C. Coombe (Eds.), *Researching and implementing task-based language learning and teaching in EFL contexts.* Amsterdam: John Benjamin's.

Cheng, L. (2008). The key to success: English language testing in China. *Language Testing* 25(1), pp. 15–37.

Ellis, R. (2000). Task-based research and language pedagogy. *Language Teaching Research*, 4, pp. 193–220.

Ellis, R. (2003). *Task-based language learning and teaching.* Oxford: Oxford University Press.

Gan, Z., Davison, C., & Hamp-Lyons, L. (2009). Topic negotiation in peer group oral assessment situations: A conversation analytic approach. *Applied Linguistics*, 30(3), pp. 315–334.

Long, M. H., & Norris, J. M. (2000). Task-based language teaching and assessment. In M. Byram (Ed.), *Encyclopedia of language teaching* (pp. 597–603). London: Routledge.

Luk, J. (2010). Talking to score: Impression management in L2 oral assessment and the co-construction of a test discourse genre. *Language Assessment Quarterly*, 7(1), pp. 25–53.

Ng, C., & Tang, E. (1997). Teachers' needs in the process of EFL reform in China: A report from Shanghai. *Perspective* 9, pp. 63–85.

Poehner, M. (2008). *Dynamic assessment: A Vygotskian approach to understanding and promoting L2 development*. Berlin: Springer.

Richards, J., Schmidt, R., Platt, H., & Schmidt, M. (2003). *Longman dictionary of applied linguistics*. London: Longman.

Robinson, P., & Ross, S. (1996). The development of task-based assessment in English for academic purpose programs. *Applied Linguistics*, 17, pp. 455–476.

Shehadeh, A. (2005). Task-based language learning and teaching: Theories and applications. In C. Edwards & J. Willis (Eds.), *Teachers exploring tasks in English language teaching* (pp. 13–30). London: Palgrave Macmillan.

Shehadeh, A., & Coombe, C. (Eds.) (2010). *Applications of task-based learning in TESOL*. Alexandria, VA: TESOL.

Shehadeh, A., & Coombe, C. (Eds.) (forthcoming, 2012). *Researching and implementing task-based language learning and teaching in EFL contexts*. Amsterdam: John Benjamin's.

Van den Branden, K., Bygate, M., & Norris, J. (Eds.) (2009). *Task-based language teaching: A reader*. Amsterdam: John Benjamin's.

Weaver, C. (forthcoming). Incorporating a formative assessment cycle into task-based language teaching. In A. Shehadeh & C. Coombe (Eds.), *Researching and implementing task-based language learning and teaching in EFL contexts*. Amsterdam: John Benjamin's.

Wigglesworth, G. (2001). Influences on performance in task-based oral assessments. In M. Bygate, P. Skehan, & M. Swain (Eds.), *Researching pedagogic tasks: Second language learning, teaching, and testing* (pp. 186–209). Harlow, England: Longman.

Winke, P. (2010). Using online tasks for formative language assessment. In A. Shehadeh & C. Coombe (Eds.), *Applications of task-based learning in TESOL* (pp. 173–185). Alexandria, VA: TESOL.

Yeh, A. (2010). Assessing task-based activity in a speech training class. In A. Shehadeh & C. Coombe (Eds.), *Applications of task-based learning in TESOL* (pp. 161–171). Alexandria, VA: TESOL.

CHAPTER 19

Placement Testing

Anthony Green

INTRODUCTION

In language programs, placement means matching a learner to the most suitable class or group. Often this is done on the basis of language ability as measured by a test, but there are many other kinds of information that are used. Here are some examples (you will probably be able to add to this list):

- learner preferences
- nationality and first language
- gender
- age
- friendship groups
- personality
- discipline
- motivation
- academic subjects that language learners follow in other classes
- institutional and regulatory restrictions on class sizes

Where such considerations are felt to be relevant, these will need to be balanced with evidence concerning language ability.

Placement tests are most frequently used when students first enter an educational institution because at that point teachers will have little other evidence of their abilities. However, tests are sometimes also used in preference to or in addition to teacher judgments in deciding on how learners should progress within a program. Placement tests may also be used to inform decisions about whether learners should be exempt from a course; at some universities international students will not need to attend language support courses if they score above a threshold level on a placement test.

Although this depends on the context and should not be assumed, placement is generally seen as a comparatively *low-stakes* decision. In other words, placement decisions often have only limited impact on the life chances of the test taker. Although mistakes in placement are inconvenient, frustrating, and potentially demotivating for teachers and learners, once detected they can usually be put right: The incorrectly placed student can be moved to a more suitable class.

Additionally, placement can often be an administrative and logistical challenge for an institution. When they arrive to begin a program, perhaps in very large numbers, learners will typically need to be assigned to classes very quickly. In these circumstances, efficiency of administration and scoring are paramount. For these reasons, stakeholders are not generally as concerned to see evidence for the quality of a test used for placement purposes as they would be for higher-stakes tests used in employment selection or for determining access to educational opportunities such as university courses or training programs.

TYPES OF TESTS USED IN PLACEMENT

When considering the most appropriate form of test to use for placement decisions, it is useful to think about two interpretations of the word "place." Firstly, tests can help to *place* students relative to each other: to separate more able from less able students. Doing this allows us to create groups of roughly equal language ability, which may help to make teaching and learning more efficient. Secondly, we might *place* each student in relation to our learning materials. We can use a test to find out how much students already know of what we intend to teach them – and so what they might most need to focus on in their learning.

The first interpretation of place implies the use of a test of language-learning aptitude or of general language proficiency. Although proficiency tests are widely used where students have different levels of ability, aptitude tests can be used to discriminate between learners before they begin studying a language (and so have little or no measurable ability). The second interpretation of place requires a test that closely reflects the content of the program: in effect a variation of a terminal achievement test that is given before the course rather than at the end.

In settings where course objectives can be clearly defined, enough resources are available, and learners are already familiar with relevant task types, tests based on course content are potentially more useful (provided that they are of good quality) because they can give us diagnostic information about the aspects of the course that require the most attention for each learner. In courses intended to develop general language abilities in students at a range of proficiency levels, more generic tests, not closely linked to the specific course, may prove to be more suitable and will certainly be more practical to administer and score. Whichever type of test is used, it will need to provide a sensitive measure of differences in ability between more and less able learners.

In practice, the weight given to administrative flexibility and cost effectiveness often limits a developer's options in designing a placement test. Many institutions simply don't have, or don't prioritize, the resources to support test development, complex administrative arrangements, or rater training. Pressure for quick results at a reasonable cost means that, except where there are few students and extensive resources, institutions are limited to certain testing methods. Because they are easily scored, selected response formats (such as multiple choice or matching) will generally be more practical than test formats that involve extended responses (essays, interviews, etc.).

Although locally made tests can be shaped to meet the specific needs of a course, restrictions on resources and lack of expertise in test development can have unfortunate consequences. Where objectively scored tests are used, insufficient attention to design issues and pretesting of items can lead to the development of poor-quality tests that fail to measure relevant abilities. Where tests of written or spoken production are used, lack of support for training and monitoring may result in unacceptably low levels of reliability: Variations in interviewers' questions and behavior or differences in the severity of the raters scoring the tests can lead to inconsistent results.

RESEARCH INTO PLACEMENT TESTS

Placement testing is, as Wall et al. (1994) observe, among the most common reasons for taking a language test and the instruments are often made locally. There is therefore a need for advice and guidance for placement test developers (who will often be classroom teachers rather than full-time testing professionals). As a result, placement testing is widely discussed in practical language-testing handbooks such as Hughes (2003) and Heaton (1989).

Ultimately, for a placement test to fulfill its purpose its use must result in a satisfactory assignment of learners to classes – at least in terms of language level. As a result of using the test, the course of study should be well targeted to the level of the learners and the materials should be appropriate to their learning needs. On this basis, Hughes (2003) recommends that the starting point for validating placement procedures should be the proportions of learners judged by their teachers to have been appropriately or inappropriately assigned to a class. Unfortunately, although simple checks on learner and teacher satisfaction with placement decisions or comparisons with results at the end of the course are straightforward and demand few resources, it remains the case that the use of placement tests is not often formally validated.

Placement testing also receives comparatively little attention in the language testing research literature (however, see Green and Weir, 2004). Placement tests tend to be conservative in design as this makes them both familiar to learners and relatively inexpensive to develop. We have seen that they attract relatively little scrutiny and as a result, there is little to attract funding for research. Published studies involving placement testing have more often concerned wider testing issues, such as differences in test performance across groups or the impact of computerization, than the kinds of validation on the basis of teacher judgments about the suitability of placement decisions suggested by Hughes (2003) and cited in the previous paragraph.

Heaton (1989: 15) argues that placement tests can provide valuable information about students' abilities to inform teaching. He explains this in relation to a grammar-based syllabus: "if students are going to learn about ways of using the past perfect tense to talk about past events, we should include items on the past simple tense (and possibly the present perfect tense) in our test as mastery of these areas will clearly be important before past perfect is taught."

Given the evidence from second language acquisition research that learning to use one tense does not require full control of any other, Heaton's assumption that learners need to master the past simple before learning about past perfect may seem wide of the mark. Nonetheless, the potential for placement tests to provide additional diagnostic information has been asserted in a number of research studies.

As a strong advocate of the diagnostic value of placement tests, Brown (1988) suggests a means of evaluating what a test and the course to which it relates have in common whereas Wall et al. (1994) and Wesche et al. (1996) are among the few published research studies to investigate whether language placement tests actually lead to accurate placement decisions. As a means of aligning a test with the curriculum and so to improve its potential for placement purposes, Brown (1988, and in this volume) describes giving the same test at the beginning and end of a course, then using statistical tools to identify items on which performance fails to improve following instruction. Lack of improvement in scores on an item suggests that it fails to reflect what has been learned in the course. Either the item should be removed from the test or more attention given to teaching the point being tested. Wall et al. (1994) describe the use of a placement test in an EAP setting to diagnose particular areas of weakness. Based on their results, learners are encouraged to attend remedial courses in grammar, writing, reading, or listening. However, neither of these studies provides any examples of teachers or learners using information from a test to guide learning at the level of specificity envisaged by Heaton (1989).

Arguing that Heaton's (1989) recommendations are overly simplistic, Green and Weir (2004) question whether placement tests that meet requirements for efficiency can also adequately reflect both course materials and the range of conditions that apply when learners undertake tasks in the language classroom. Knowing that a particular linguistic form is required to fill a gap on a test is not the same as being able to use that form appropriately in writing or speech. Green and Weir's study compared results from a test based on course materials that used a single-word gap-fill format *(Lucy ____ gone to New York so she's not in the office this week)* with results from the same learners on an alternative format that required the test takers to transform a given verb to the appropriate form *(Lucy ____ (go) to New York so she's not in the office this week)*. Learners who were able to respond correctly to items on the gap-fill test were less likely to be able to answer similar questions on the more open-ended transformation task, which more closely resembled the course materials on which the test was based. This suggests that where information is required about how well learners can perform the tasks that they will encounter in the classroom, a large number of well-designed test tasks will be needed and these must reflect classroom tasks very closely. Meeting these requirements may not be practical within the constraints on time and resources.

In spite of the objection that the skills or knowledge that they test are limited or unclear and although their diagnostic value has been questioned, indirect tests of language ability, such as cloze tests, dictations, and tests of grammar and vocabulary, often appear to work rather well as placement tests for general language courses. Wesche et al. (1996) investigated four alternative placement procedures and found that a general-purpose dictation test correlated well both with text-based tests of reading and listening skills, based on course content and on final placement decisions additionally based on teacher judgments. Similarly, the series of studies into the use of a grammar-based placement test described in Green and Weir (2004), together with evidence from Wall et al. (1994), suggest that such tests also have the potential to support consistent placement decisions. Wall et al. found higher correlations between language teacher ratings of their students and the grammar component of their test than with any other test component. A number of studies including Fountain and Nation (2000) have found tests of vocabulary knowledge to be another useful and relatively easily constructed indirect means of placing students into suitable classes perhaps because, like grammatical knowledge, it is fundamental to the wide range of ways in which we use language.

Self-assessment procedures also seem to have potential value for placement decisions. A key advantage of self-assessment is that it encourages learners to reflect on their own abilities, acknowledging and fostering an active role in the learning process. Although the use of self-assessment for high-stakes purposes raises obvious concerns, learners may recognize that they have more to gain from accurate placement decisions than from overstating their abilities. Wesche et al. (1996) found that their self-assessment instrument did not work well as an alternative to their course content-based tests, but other research, such as LeBlanc and Painchaud (1985), indicates that under certain conditions – when well designed and used in conjunction with other measures – self-assessment can provide a reasonably accurate basis for placement.

There is a general consensus among researchers that multiple measures are preferable to single-format tests and this is supported by both the Wesche et al. (1996) and Wall et al. (1994) studies. If a single method is used, we may bias the test in favor of learners who are better at taking tests of that type. Introducing different test methods reduces this risk.

Indirect tests that focus on grammar, vocabulary, or dictation skills can be highly reliable (if well designed), but may be limited because they fail to reflect realistic communication. Tests of comprehension, interviews, and essays (again, if well designed and carefully linked to course content) may better reflect the tasks that learners will need to be able to carry out. However, more direct tests tend to be less reliable and so are restricted in the extent to which they are able to measure the ability to perform these tasks. Perhaps because of limited training and standardization of raters, Wall et al. (1994) found an unacceptably low interrater correlation on the essay component of the test they investigated, while the grammar component was acceptably reliable. In short, a combination of methods should be used.

PRACTICAL APPLICATIONS

Although placement may not be a particularly high-stakes issue, it is not trivial and deserves investment of time and resources. Mistakes in allocating learners to classes can result in real disadvantage if they are not corrected and can cause considerable inconvenience and disaffection even when they are. Mistakes are perhaps inevitable, but they can certainly be minimized through carefully considered placement procedures.

The best placement decisions are those that take account of relevant information about learners. This will vary according to the context, but will usually include information from tests. There is need for a balance to be struck between competing demands for accuracy of decision making and for cost effectiveness. For tests, greater accuracy means including more tasks that reflect the variety of skills to be taught on the course. The longer the placement test the more likely it is to be accurate, sensitive, and diagnostically useful. Unfortunately, it is also likely to be more challenging to develop, more expensive and time consuming to administer and score, and more difficult to maintain over time as new material and new test forms become necessary.

For specialized courses with well-defined content and relatively homogenous learner populations, it is worth considering tests that closely reflect the course and can provide diagnostic information. For courses that cover more general language skills, there may be published tests available that will meet placement requirements, or in-house tests can be developed that reflect course content more loosely, perhaps employing easily scorable item formats.

Whatever test is used, quality control is vital to its success. Editorial reviews of material, item piloting, and analysis are essential tools in evaluating whether the test is addressing relevant abilities and whether items are working to discriminate effectively between more and less able learners in the way intended. If raters are used to score essays or interviews, at least two should score each performance, levels of agreement should be reported, and cases of disagreement should be referred to a third rater. Unless acceptable levels of agreement between raters can be reached, it is difficult to argue that a test is measuring anything. Surveys of teachers and learners together with comparisons between placement decisions and outcomes are straightforward means of evaluating the accuracy of placement and should be used routinely.

FUTURE DIRECTIONS

Ongoing changes in the design of tests used for placement purposes and in the technology used to deliver them are both likely to continue to impact on placement testing practices over the coming decade. The growth of freely accessible Internet-based testing options, such as DIALANG (www.dialang.org), may help to build shared understandings of levels so that learners begin language programs with a clearer sense of their own abilities.

To arrive at a more satisfactory balance between requirements for efficiency and for relevance to a specific course, some recent placement tests have adopted a staged approach in which test takers are given a series of tests, targeted at increasingly specific levels of ability. The results of the first test are used to determine the level of the test that should be administered next. A low score on the first test would lead the test taker to an easier second test, and a high score to a more challenging second test. As the test taker advances through the process, the tests provide an increasingly sensitive and reliable indication of the level. Different item formats can be used at each stage to support this increasing sensitivity. In this approach, learners may begin by responding to a brief self-assessment questionnaire or a cloze test to provide a broad indication of level before being directed to a second and perhaps a third stage test that reflects the content of courses at their level of ability.

As in other areas of testing and assessment, computers are playing a growing role in tests used for placement and their impact can be seen in a number of areas. Computer adaptive tests (CAT) provide another means of tailoring a test to the ability of the test taker. In a CAT, when a test taker responds correctly to one item, the next item presented will be more difficult; if the first response is incorrect, the next item presented will be easier. By selecting items targeted to the test taker's level, the CAT is able to more quickly arrive at an estimate of the learner's level without presenting large numbers of items that are either too easy or too difficult for that individual. In spite of the obvious attractions of CATs, they are not very widely used in institutional placement testing because they are complex to compile (it is difficult to ensure that all test takers are provided with a similar range of content), require quite sophisticated computing and statistical knowledge to construct, and need large numbers of questions to cater for the possible routes through the test (see Chapter 30, this volume, for further discussion of CATs).

Delivering tests on computer also allows for instant automated scoring of responses (at least for selected response items), which can greatly reduce costs and has the potential to generate instant results. Automated scoring of writing (see for example the Criterion software from Educational Testing Service), and more controversially speaking (see, for example, the Versant tests from Pearson Language Assessment), is also becoming established in large-scale testing programs and could minimize some of the problems of interrater reliability identified in this chapter. Unfortunately, the costs involved and the need for large numbers of example performances to train automated scoring machines mean that they do not yet provide a practical option for most locally developed tests.

Whatever changes may occur in the technology of placement testing, it is to be hoped that growing awareness of language-testing issues will lead to greater attention to the quality of placement test instruments in the future on the part of the teachers and institutions that use them.

Suggested resources

Huhta, A. (2007). The vocabulary size placement test In DIALANG – Why do users love and hate it? In C. Carlsen & M. Moe (Eds.), *A human touch to language testing*. Oslo: Novus Publishers.

Hughes, A. (2003). *Testing for language teachers* (2nd ed.). Cambridge: Cambridge University Press.

Green, A. (2011). A case of testing L2 English reading for class level placement. In B. O'Sullivan (Ed.), *Language testing: Theories and practices*. Basingstoke: Palgrave.

Whitney, D. R. (1993). Educational admissions and placement. In R. L. Linn (Ed.), *Educational measurement* (3rd ed.), Phoenix, AZ: The Oryx Press.

Discussion questions

1. Should language learners be divided into classes according to ability? What might be the advantages of mixing students?

2. What alternative methods, other than using a test, might you use to place students into classes?

3. Placement is often said to be a low-stakes decision, but what are the problems that can occur if you make a mistake in placing students?

4. How long should a placement test be? What are the advantages of longer and shorter procedures?

5. Do you think it is better to develop your own placement test, or to buy one from a recognized testing agency?

6. Should you include tests of writing and speaking abilities on a placement test (if the course teaches these skills)? What problems might this cause and what problems might it avoid?

References

Brown, J. D. (1988). Improving ESL placement tests using two perspectives. *TESOL Quarterly* 23(1), 65–83.

Fountain, R. L., & Nation, I. S. P. (2000). A vocabulary-based graded dictation test. *RELC Journal*, 31(1), 29–44.

Green, A., & Weir, C. (2004). Can placement testing inform instructional decisions? *Language Testing*, 21(4), 467–494.

Heaton, J. B. (1989). *Writing English language tests*. Harlow: Longman.

Hughes, A. (2003). *Testing for language teachers* (2nd ed.). Cambridge: Cambridge University Press.

LeBlanc, R., & Painchaud, O. (1985). Self-Assessment as a Second Language Instrument. *TESOL Quarterly*, 19(4), 673–687.

Wall, D., Clapham, C., & Alderson, J. C. (1994). Evaluating a placement test. *Language Testing* 11(3), 321–344.

Wesche, M., Paribakht, S. T., & Ready, D. (1996). A comparative study of four placement instruments. In M. Milanovic & N. Saville (Eds.), *Performance testing, cognition and assessment* (pp. 199–210). Cambridge: Cambridge University Press.

CHAPTER 20

Assessing Young Learners

Angela Hasselgreen

INTRODUCTION

This chapter is devoted to the assessment of Young Language Learners (YLLs), defined here as children from about five to 12 years old, who are learning any language other than their mother tongue(s).

The issues presented in the chapter relate to the particular situation of YLL assessment; these include characteristics of the learners themselves, the focus of the assessment purpose, the tasks YLLs can carry out and language ability they can be expected to demonstrate, as well as their teachers' competence as assessors. The section on research focuses on the kind of studies carried out, drawing attention to the relatively slow emergence of YLL assessment research. The section on practical applications offers suggestions for dealing with the implications of the issues that have been highlighted, and the conclusion points to ways of meeting some of the many challenges in the area of YLL assessment.

BACKGROUND

YLLs tend to have rather different assessment needs from older learners, who often need documentation of their ability for external purposes, such as study or work. However, this does not diminish the relative importance of YLL assessment. Younger and older learners alike need well-founded and helpful feedback on their strengths and weaknesses. Children generally need more help and support in understanding what and how they need to learn. They need to be kept interested in a task and are more likely to become demotivated in the face of failure or adverse feedback. The very nature of YLLs thus places heavy demands on the assessment of their language, and the task is made more complex by a number of key issues.

The focus of the assessment purpose varies widely in the YLL classroom, and this in turn affects the forms that assessment can take. Summative assessment, which will normally take the form of testing, may take place systematically at a national, regional, or school level, although many YLLs will not be subjected to formal testing of this kind, which is more the domain of secondary schooling. However, summative testing of individuals or groups may be required for particular reasons, for example, to see if a child is ready for mainstream teaching, or to sum up the effects of a teaching program or method.

Formative assessment, on the other hand, should be an integral part of YLL teaching and can be carried out in many forms. Teachers may use a small test to see if a child has reached a target (but unless the result of this feeds back into and affects the subsequent teaching / learning, it cannot be considered formative). Formative assessment of tasks should ideally involve both teacher and child, and can be in the form of written teacher feedback, self-assessment comments, or checklists, or as a short dialogue. Both teachers and pupils should be aware of the criteria used in judging what has been done. A natural way of giving formative feedback is in the everyday questioning of pupils by the teacher. However, in their investigation of practices used in teacher assessment in UK infant schools, Torrance and Pryor (1998) have found that this questioning does not automatically elicit the most revealing answers nor provide the best support to learning.

Tasks used in assessment should be those that lead to learning, particularly if the assessment is to be formative. The tasks that YLLs can carry out will depend on their level of language, but Cameron (2001) warns of other demands that may put a task beyond the ability of a child. She cites six types of demand that a task may impose:

- cognitive (involving the child's readiness to deal with the concepts involved);
- language (involving whether this is spoken or written language, and its familiarity / complexity);
- interactional (involving the child's ability to take part in pair work, teacher interactions, etc.);
- metalinguistic (involving the language used about the task, e.g., instructions);
- involvement (involving time, interest, game-element, humor, etc., which may influence the degree of engagement with the task); and
- physical (involving the ability to sit still, the actions needed and motor skills required). (adapted from Cameron, 2001: 25)

When designing tasks for assessment, these should be taken into account, to ensure that the nonlanguage demands do not prevent the child from demonstrating his / her language ability. It can be argued that the help given should extend to some support (scaffolding) in coping with the language itself, in order to show what the child has the potential to achieve.

The language ability being assessed will depend on the purpose of the assessment. As for any learner group, the assessment should, over time, cover the spoken and written language, receptive and productive skills, and language used in a near-authentic range of communicative situations as well as in narrower, form-focused contexts on occasion. The range of communicative abilities will expand as the learner progresses.

However, in the case of YLLs, these assessment "norms" are complicated. A younger child is still in the process of learning his / her first language, and mastering the nonlinguistic skills involved in using it. It is increasingly usual for children to begin learning a foreign or second language very young – often on entering school. This means that they do not have the advantage of being able to use the written language to assist in their language learning or communication. It is common in these situations to begin with the spoken language, that is, through songs, rhymes, and dramatization. Written language use may be restricted to familiar word recognition and the production of a few formulae. Assessment should reflect this; a young child who can write nothing and say little independently may understand a great deal, and should be given the opportunity to demonstrate this.

The level of language ability reached by YLLs in today's language classrooms can vary greatly. The child's background and what is picked up outside school can have a greater influence than a couple of hours a week in class. This ability may also be "skewed" toward an interest, for example, one pursued over the Internet. This means that assessment should, at times at least, be designed to allow children to show *what* they can do, rather than *if* they can do a prescribed "x." These two approaches are termed *divergent* and *convergent* by Torrance and Pryor (1998), who believe the former to be the most truly formative kind of assessment. A child's mother-tongue competence is also a complicating factor. Cameron maintains, for instance, that "the full use of coordinators, including *but* and *yet*, is still to be developed after the age of 11 years, and clauses introduced with *although* or *unless* can cause problems even for 15 year olds" (Cameron, 2001: 12). Additionally, the world knowledge of a child is much smaller than that of an adult, which in turn limits the range of elements, such as vocabulary and skills of a sociolinguistic nature. This has repercussions for those who wish to place YLLs on a scale designed for lifelong learning, such as the Council of Europe's CEFR (Common European Framework of Reference, 2001). A child may have near-native competence in a language, yet cannot be placed anywhere near the top of the CEFR scale. In the light of the recent widespread adoption of the European Language Portfolio (ELP) in European schools, this is of some concern.

Teacher competence as assessors can be problematic in the YLL context. In many countries, the systems of teacher training and conventions for appointing teachers have combined to place the least specialized (in linguistics and language pedagogy) teachers at the lowest end of the school. This has not changed in pace with the lowering of the age of learning languages. Moreover, language assessment has traditionally been given low priority in teacher training. The result is that the assessment of YLLs is largely in the hands of teachers who do not have the benefit of training in language assessment.

RESEARCH

As a research field, YLL assessment is modest. Tradition has neglected it. Language assessment research has its roots in high-stakes testing, which has rarely involved children. Studies and research in language assessment have generally been the preserve of postgraduate study, which traditionally has not fed back into primary schools. Those involved in YLL research often come from a background in primary school teaching, with little grounding in assessment theory. However, since the 1990s, YLL assessment research has begun to make an impact, perhaps partly due to the recognition of forms of assessment "other" than testing. At major conferences, such as those of EALTA (European Association for Language Testing and Assessment) and IATEFL (International Association of Teachers of English as a Foreign Language), presentations on YLL assessment are increasingly common.

The periodical *Language Testing* has published a special edition with articles devoted to research on assessing young learners. In her editorial, Rea-Dickins (2000) summarizes these articles, and comments:

> There are clearly common themes running throughout the contributions presented here, which are also of concern more generally in North America, as elsewhere [. . .]. Of key importance in the assessment of early language learning are issues of: 1) processes and procedures used by teachers to inform teaching and learning; 2) assessment of achievement at the end of the primary phase of education; and 3) teachers' professional development. (Rea-Dickins, 2000: 116).

The *Cambridge Language Assessment Series* has produced a volume on YLL assessment (MacKay, 2006). This book gives a comprehensive overview of the field, combining a practical and a theoretical approach. In McKay's chapter on research, she comments:

> There are challenges for researchers of young learner assessment, with variability of programmes, lack of consensus about proficiency and variable teacher expertise most evident. These challenges make it difficult for researchers in both foreign language and second language research to carry out research. (McKay, 2006: 95)

McKay goes on to identify four main types of research: (1) to investigate and share information on current practices; (2) to ensure fair and valid assessment practices; (3) to find out more about the nature of young learner language proficiency and language growth; and (4) to investigate and improve the impact of assessment on YLLs. The research she identifies is not extensive, although some peaks seem to exist, for example in Area (2) where she maintains: "Assessment carried out by the teacher in the classroom is a rapidly growing area of research . . . Research interest in this area has developed as standard documents require teacher-based assessment and reporting" (McKay, 2006: 96). It would seem then, that YLL assessment research has had a late and slow start, although the recent focus on formative classroom assessment by the teacher may be acting as a catalyst in research activity. What is being researched involves both learners and their teachers.

YLL assessment is also gradually becoming visible in the literature for teachers. In his revised book on language testing for teachers, Hughes (2003) has included a chapter on YLLs. Similarly, books on teaching YLLs, such as by Cameron (2001), contain a chapter on assessment. There is a growing amount of teacher material in the field of formative assessment, which can be applied to YLLs. Torrance and Pryor (1998) present the findings of an empirical investigation of classroom assessment practice through the analysis of teacher–pupil interactions in infant schools. Drawing on theories of learning and the sociology of the classroom, they are able to draw conclusions about the effectiveness of this interaction in formative assessment.

PRACTICAL APPLICATIONS

Let us now consider the practical implications of what has been presented so far for those involved in YLL assessment.

YLL assessment is more often formative than summative, and more in the hands of the classroom teacher than an external assessor. Thus it is crucial that teachers are given training in assessment, through initial or in-service courses, and through access to good tools (see Chapters 2 and 14 in this volume). It is worth noting that even if no formal testing takes place, all teachers use some testing in class, as part of formative assessment, and they should therefore be familiar with the basic principles and practice of testing. Hughes (2003), for example, offers this grounding. Many software programs are available for teachers to "make" tests, but these only provide a format; the content and how the test result is interpreted are in the teacher's hands! To carry out systematic formative classroom assessment, teachers need practical advice on such issues as planning, target setting, feedback, questioning, and pupils' self-assessment, which is offered, for example, by Clarke (2001).

The tasks given to YLLs as part of assessment, whether in a test or informal classroom activity, should be designed to minimize the potential "non-language" demands and to maximize engagement, so that the pupil can perform at his / her best. MacKay (2006) discusses this in detail, and Cameron (2001) gives many examples of tasks that are suitable for both learning and assessment. Pictures are generally essential in YLL tasks, and hiring the services of an illustrator is an invaluable investment for widespread testing. Computerized testing can bring tasks further to life, for example with clicking, dragging, matching, and coloring.

The skills and language to be assessed will depend on such factors as a national curriculum or simply what a teacher feels a need to assess at any time. In the early stages, listening may be the most relevant skill to assess, which can simply involve pupils identifying pictures, or following instructions. As pupils may be struggling to read, it can be worth giving simple tests of whether they can recognize a written word when they hear it.

The actual language ability of YLLs may be very diverse within a group, but will never be beyond that of a pupil's first language ability. It is common to use a scale of descriptors to assess the "level" of a pupil, whether in testing or everyday classroom assessment. MacKay discusses the development of such scales, or "standards." In European education systems, the CEFR has been widely adopted and has found its way into many primary schools, largely through the ELP. This makes it possible for teachers to chart the progress of individuals, and to describe the ability of learners at very diverse levels. However, the scale should be used in an adapted YLL form. The original CEFR wording is influenced by what adults "do" with their language, which is very different from what children do. The upper levels (from around B2) are generally beyond what a primary school pupil (even in his / her first language) could achieve. These issues appear to have been recognized to a varying degree by those making primary school versions of the ELP, which are now in widespread use across Europe. Hasselgreen (2003) gives an account of a process by which CEFR linked "can do" statements were empirically developed for 10 to 15-year-olds in Nordic and Baltic countries.

Finally, a word about criteria and feedback: It is important that children are aware of what they are being judged on and how to interpret feedback. Torrance and Pryor (1998) demonstrate that this is frequently not the case. Children can be over-focused on a "reward" as an end in itself and can interpret suggestions for improvement as failure. When a pupil is given a task s/he should know what will rate the performance as "good." The ELP can be a useful tool for giving children criteria, and to show their progress, through "can do" checklists and a collection of their own work over time. Material for target setting, self-assessment, and teacher feedback can also be found in Clarke (2001) and in Hasselgreen (2003). As regards teacher questioning in the classroom, Torrance and Pryor (1998) advocate movement away from questioning of the type question–answer–evaluation to a more genuine, open type of question, which should allow the pupils to engage in a dialogue, informing the teacher more about what a pupil knows, and turning the questioning into a formative learning exercise.

CONCLUSION

As this chapter will hopefully have made clear, the assessment of YLLs is special. Many challenges face those of us involved in this field.

The assessment of children's language needs to take into account the characteristics which make this group delightful to work with, which shape the kind of tasks they can perform at their best, and the feedback which will help them learn. It must also take into account the language and skills children can be expected to acquire, as well as the particular assessment purposes in primary education.

As the age of learning new languages has been consciously lowered by education policymakers, additional assessment demands have been placed on primary school teachers. Investment and research are needed to ensure that these teachers have training and tools to effectively carry out a wide range of assessment practices.

The field of YLL assessment research is still emerging from the backwaters of both assessment and language pedagogy. Traditionally, researchers in language assessment have neglected YLLs, and YLL specialists have shied away from assessment. This is changing, particularly as classroom assessment is attracting more attention as a research field. However, it is difficult to find any area of YLL assessment where research is not badly needed. Perhaps the most pressing need is research into the actual language that YLLs of different ages can be expected to acquire, across a range of levels from beginning to near-native. Only with real insight into this can we hope to do justice to this deserving and ever-growing group of language learners.

Suggested resources

Cameron, L. (2001). *Teaching language to young learners*. Cambridge: Cambridge University Press.
An introduction to the principles and practices for those involved in teaching YLLs

Clarke, S. (2001). *Unlocking formative assessment: Practical strategies for enhancing pupils' learning in the primary classroom*. London: Hodder Murray.
A practical handbook on formative assessment, generally for primary school teachers

Hughes, A. (2003). *Testing for language teachers*. Cambridge: Cambridge University Press.
An introduction to the principles and practices of language testing for teachers

Ioannou-Georgiou, S., & Pavlou, P. (2003). *Assessing young learners (Resource Books for Teachers)*. Oxford: Oxford University Press.
A collection of methods and photocopiable material for assessment in the primary school language classroom

McKay, P. (2006). *Assessing young learners*. Cambridge: Cambridge University Press.
An overview of the field, for researchers and practitioners of YLL assessment

Web sites:

ECML's AYLLIT (Assessment of Young Learner Literacy) Project – descriptors adapted from CEFR for assessing young learners' writing:
http://ayllit.ecml.at/Resources/tabid/1189/language/en-GB/Default.aspx

ECML's "can do" project – material for use in teacher- and self-assessment of young learners' language skills:
http://archive.ecml.at/cando/

CILT, the National Centre for Languages – Junior ELP:
www.primarylanguages.org.uk/resources/assessment_and_recording/european_languages_portfolio.aspx

Discussion questions

1. Do primary school teachers in your region get the necessary support / training to implement good assessment practice?

2. Do you have access to a YLL research network, and, if so, is assessment represented in its research topics?

3. Are the tools (including criteria) used in YLL assessment, in your experience, appropriate for children?

References

Cameron, L. (2001). *Teaching language to young learners.* Cambridge: Cambridge University Press.

Clarke, S. (2001). *Unlocking formative assessment: Practical strategies for enhancing Pupils' learning in the primary classroom.* London: Hodder Murray.

Council of Europe. (2001). *Common European Framework of Reference for Languages, Learning, Teaching and Assessment.* Cambridge: Cambridge University Press.

Hasselgreen, A. (2003). The Bergen 'Can Do' project. Graz, Austria: ECML publications.

Hughes, A. (2003). *Testing for language teachers.* Cambridge: Cambridge University Press.

McKay, P. (2006). *Assessing young learners.* Cambridge: Cambridge University Press.

Rea-Dickins, P. (2000). Assessment in early years language learning contexts. *Language Testing* 17/2, pp. 115–122.

Torrance, H., & Pryor, J. (1998). *Investigating formative assessment.* Maidenhead, UK: Open University Press.

CHAPTER 21

ESL Needs Analysis and Assessment in the Workplace

Ingrid Greenberg

INTRODUCTION

English language assessment in the workplace differs from classroom-based testing in many regards. Firstly, most of the stakeholders work outside of the education arena in business environments and they are numerous. They can include managers, union representatives, human resource personnel, subject matter experts, and regional Workforce Investment Board (WIB) members. Secondly, there are ESL (English as a Second Language) workplace-specific tests that address the language skills that employees use in the context of their jobs, such as hard skills (math, technology, and science) and soft skills (team work, customer service, and clarification). Language specialists must select ESL tests to match employees' backgrounds and / or pick from these workplace-specific tests (Douglas, 2000; Long, 2005). Thirdly, needs analysis is essential for identifying learning outcomes (Douglas, 2000; Friedenberg et al., 2003; Greenberg, 1993; Long, 2005). Also, many workplace language tasks that need to be measured are often performance based. These language tasks require increasing competence in speaking and writing. Thus, workplace ESL practitioners must often implement performance-based assessments to measure oral aptitude (e.g., safety speech, train a coworker, interview and report, give feedback) and writing aptitude (e.g., write hazard reports, e-mail next shift, list missing parts). Results from the workplace needs analysis and language tests often shape a program and curriculum that are very different from the ones found in traditional schools.

BACKGROUND

In the United States, when a business decides to offer English training to its workers, the training needs to be customized to the language needs of the company. A language specialist needs to identify high-priority learning outcomes and may ask the employers questions such as the following: Do the employees need safety and OSHA training (Occupational

Safety & Health Administration, United States Department of Labor)? Is worker retention important, calling for career-ladder training? Has new technology been introduced, calling for technical training? Additionally, within an industry, different companies may request very different learning goals. For example, in the shipyard industry, two different companies approached me for two different training goals. One company requested OSHA and safety training, whereas the second one asked for writing and grammar training. Each of these trainings requires customization, which is labor and time intensive to design, develop, and implement. Needs analyses, including language assessment, play an important role in targeting the level and content of the customized curriculum (Douglas, 2000; Friedenberg et al., 2003; Long, 2005). Additionally, tests must be matched appropriately to the language tasks in the workplace.

Employers use assessment for a variety of reasons. Technical assistance, curriculum, and assessments presented in this article are for educational and training purposes only. This chapter and its contents must not be used for employment decisions. Be aware that assessment, confidentiality, and data collection agreements between an educational management team and the employer(s) and other stakeholders must be defined prior to starting implementation. Please consult your legal and human resource advisors for a complete understanding of local, regional, and national rules, regulations, and laws that apply to workplace training, curriculum, and assessment. This chapter will focus exclusively on assessing English as a second language acquisition for non-hiring and non-high-stakes decisions. Furthermore, the chapter will discuss assessment in the adult education arena, for workers in entry-level positions who are seeking advancement on the career ladder to supervisory or management positions and beyond.

TRENDS

In the workplace, training is frequently delivered with a blended face-to-face and computer format. Thus, workplace language assessment is often accompanied by surveys of employees' computer and technology skills. Additionally, job promotions often require increased computer competence. Thus, workplace evaluation should include an analysis of learners' technology skills. The results of a technology survey can provide valuable feedback to the trainer who is charged with designing ESL instruction that includes a variety of delivery methods (e.g., computer lab, face-to-face) and types of media (e.g., print, PowerPoint).

RESEARCH: BRIEF LITERATURE REVIEW

When comparing language evaluation in the traditional classroom and in the workplace, there are similarities and differences. The similarities are numerous. Practitioners in both the classroom and workplace are most effective (Genesee and Upshur, 1996; Long, 2005) when they:

- utilize multiple measures;
- rely on both qualitative and quantitative information;
- administer tests that are reliable and valid;
- collect basic demographic data (e.g., number of years of education and level of education);
- use formative, ongoing evaluation; and
- implement performance-based assessment such as writing and speaking portfolios.

The differences between traditional classroom-based assessment and workplace assessment will be covered in the remainder of this section. These differences are driven mostly by the workplace stakeholders and the workplace language tasks. This chapter will cover criteria for the selection of published tests, number of hours of instruction for significant learning gain, needs analysis, and a genre / discourse community approach to identifying, selecting, and creating performance-based assessments and curriculum.

Traditional language assessments for the classroom typically address students who seek to advance to the next level of education. Genesee and Upshur (1996: 8) state that language evaluation is "classroom based and teacher driven." Whereas school-based language teachers are the primary drivers of test selection, workplace ESL specialists must take into consideration many more stakeholders and dynamics. For example, one-on-one speaking tests are time consuming (e.g., up to 15 minutes per student) and usually cost prohibitive for large public education institutions that serve thousands of learners annually. However, most employees are seeking to improve their confidence with their performance skills: writing and speaking, and thus, these oral and written tests are often essential in the workplace.

There are a number of reliable assessments for the workplace, including these widely used systems: CASAS's (Comprehensive Adult Student Assessment System, 1980–2001) Workplace Learning System (2003), ACT's (American College Testing) WorkKeys (1992–2011), and CAL's (Center for Applied Linguistics) BEST test (1984, 1989). When reviewing assessments, it is advisable to use tests that have been field-tested in a workplace environment with native and nonnative speakers. After more than 25 years of data collection in adult literacy and workplace ESL programs, national standards regarding number of hours of instruction and intensity of instruction for adult education have become widely recognized. Most educators recognize that significant learning gains can be achieved after 80 to 100 instructional hours between pretesting and post-testing standardized tests (California Department of Education, 2004; Young, 2007). Once employees have taken the placement tests, scores are collected and analyzed. I also suggest surveying students for number of years of education and degrees attained. The scores and demographic data will inform instructional goals and objectives which shape curriculum development.

While the tests provide important data regarding students' level, a variety of needs analysis methods still remain to be completed. Depending on the size and scope of the project and budget, needs analysis can include a variety of procedures, from formal questionnaires to diaries to open-ended interviews with language students (Douglas, 2000; Friedenberg et al., 2003; Greenberg, 1991; Long, 2005). Long recommends a "carefully sequenced use of two or more [needs analysis] procedures can be expected to produce better quality information." (2005: 33).

Whether the scope of the project is large or small, interviewing subject-matter experts is essential. Douglas (2000: 99) describes the strengths and weaknesses of working with a subject-matter expert also known as a subject specialist informant (SSI). He notes that while an SSI can competently identify technical terminology and grammatical choices relevant to their field, "[i]t is also the case that working with informants can be a very time consuming process." Douglas continues, "The optimal use of a subject specialist informant is first to help the researcher achieve a top-down understanding of the purpose of the . . . text or interaction." Given the importance of working with SSIs, texts, and other materials, I utilize John Swales's (1990) and Ann Johns's (1993) approaches for analyzing the genre and discourse communities.

Swales (1990) analyzed English in academic and research settings to identify language-based tasks and how workers accomplished these tasks. He demonstrates that workers interacted with tasks such as written reports that were defined by the institution. As Greenberg (1993) summarized in her master's thesis, Swales further argues that each institution forms a discourse community by which it defines the parameters for a task to be completed. Although Swales provides a comprehensive framework to study writing, this framework can also be applied to listening, speaking, and reading tasks. Swales's framework can be applied to workplace training by discussing three key elements: discourse community, genre, and language learning task. Swales suggests that each workplace discourse community has a number of written and spoken genres that can be taught through language-learning tasks. I include his definition of discourse community in full with my comments about its relevance to workplace ESL assessment:

1. A discourse community has a broadly agreed set of common public goals. [Some goals are tacit, unfortunately. Even when obviously posted or published, semiliterate nonnative speakers might not be able to know them.]

2. A discourse community has mechanisms for intercommunication among its members. [E-mail allows employees to send and read messages. At one utility company, for example, senior janitors are expected to e-mail duties to the next shift.]

3. A discourse community uses its participatory mechanisms primarily to provide information and feedback. [Monthly newsletters, bulletin boards, and flyers inform employees about benefits, holidays, and awards.]

4. A discourse community utilizes and hence possesses one or more genres in the communicative furtherance of its aim. [Genres come in a variety of forms. Workplaces have posted notices, online computer memos, whiteboard checklists, and employee appraisal forms.]

5. The discourse community has some specific vocabulary. [A machine shop tooler, for example, uses jargon to make notes in a daily journal about parts, sizes, temperature, and problems.]

6. A discourse community has a threshold level of members with a suitable degree of relevant content and discoursal expertise. [Machine manuals often provide expert information for apprentices.]
    (Swales, 1990: 24–27)

Understanding discourse community elements mentioned in the above list helps nonnative speakers make linguistic and rhetorical decisions about language tasks in the workplace. However, discovering the discourse community's goals is not always obvious or easily understood. Workplace ESL trainers must conduct needs analysis to identify these goals and deliver lessons to make them transparent (Friedenberg et al., 2003; Greenberg, 1993; Long, 2005).

Swales recommends performing a number of language-learning tasks to help students come closer to understanding the role of genres in their discourse communities. For example, Swales (1990) provides three letters which request a reprint or copy of an article. He assigns critical thinking and reference questions, which provoke the students to evaluate the audience, purpose, context, and appropriateness of each letter:

1. What changes might you make to letter (a) to make it more effective?

2. Are there . . . reasons why (c) may not have been answered? And if so, how would you change the letter? Redraft in pairs.
    (Swales, 1990: 80)

Johns (1993) also seeks to guide her students to discover the criteria valued by a discourse community. She describes an assignment where she asked her ESL students to "conduct research" on their target discourse community and audience, the board of trustees of the California State University system, before writing letters to argue against a fee hike. The questions helped identify arguments, which would appeal to the trustees:

1. What does my reader value?

2. Which values are most important to this audience? Which are least important?

(Johns, 1993: 86)

Workplace ESL assessment data and needs analysis results can help the trainer target language-learning tasks which prompt students to discuss discourse community and genre characteristics. Swales's framework for developing workplace ESL courses can be useful for the goal to:

mov[e] [learners] toward membership of a chosen discourse community via effective use of established genres within that community.... A genre-centered approach is likely to focus student attention on rhetorical action and on the organizations and linguistic means of its accomplishment.

(Swales, 1990: 81–82)

A genre-centered approach is likely to introduce workplace ESL students, who are typically linguistic and cultural outsiders, to unfamiliar discourse communities.

IMPLICATIONS OF A GENRE APPROACH FOR NEEDS ANALYSIS AND ASSESSMENT IN THE WORKPLACE

Swales's (1990) and Johns's (1993) methods of analyzing academic discourse communities can prove useful in identifying language tasks and genres which nonnative speakers may be required to produce in a business environment. I have conducted needs analyses of several workplaces in the construction, shipyard, hospitality, and utilities industries between 1991 and 2010. These needs analysis observations indicate that language tasks commonly found in industry sometimes contrast sharply with content found in widely used general ESL textbooks and multiple-choice lifeskills assessments. In order to maintain content validity of assessments, practitioners must match the language tasks found during needs analysis with workplace-oriented materials and assessments. For example, one restaurant chain required advanced speaking skills for a promotion from a position in food preparation to one in shift management. Given the oral demands of the management position, an oral assessment, BEST Plus (2002) by CAL, was included in the list of measurements used for placement, pre-test, and post-tests.

PRACTICAL APPLICATIONS

In this section I will discuss the size and scope of needs analysis and assessment in a nine-step process to research, develop, and implement effective workplace ESL and VESL (Vocational English as a Second Language) programs for an industry.

Developing a curriculum for industry is different than writing a course outline for a traditional classroom. We must use workplace-related assessments, collaborate with stake-holders in the local industries, and match the learning goals to the students' / workers' language task goals. Below I outline the steps and then I elaborate on each point.

1. needs analysis: identify priority learning goals / outcomes
2. identify levels: appraisals and demographics
3. identify content
4. write course outline
5. write curriculum
6. deliver content pre-tests and instruction
7. revise curriculum; make adjustments
8. deliver content post-tests; publish / reflect / acknowledge
9. program evaluation

The first step is to identify the priority learning outcomes during a comprehensive needs analysis. As Long (2005: 64) elucidates on the importance of needs analysis, he states: "It is difficult to over-emphasize the likelihood that use of multiple methods of data-collection and analysis will increase the quality, not just the quantity, of information obtained." I performed needs analysis of several entry-level positions in the following industries: construction, entrepreneurism, health care, shipyards, and warehousing. I conducted unstructured interviews of employees, supervisors, and subject-matter experts. I asked for copies of training and safety manuals (language audits), and I took notes while I observed workers on the job. Based on these needs analyses, I identified these commonly found learning outcomes.

- career ladder
- computer literacy
- listening, speaking, reading, and writing
- math
- customer service
- safety

It is important to prioritize the learning outcomes because in many cases, a company will tell you that you only have 60 to 100 hours to deliver a course. The priority learning outcomes will shape the curriculum. On a construction job site, for example, a safety director informed me that the No. 1 cause of injury is falls from ladders. Based on that interview, one of the top learning objectives was ladder safety. I also discovered numerous learning resources including a video describing safe ladder usage. This video provided practical advice as well as mathematical formulae for calculating the safe distance to prop a ladder from a wall. It became apparent that some basic math and geometry skills, as well as memorization of OSHA safety guidelines, were required. As part of the needs analysis, I also interviewed apprentices who said they needed oral skills to become supervisors. Specifically, the apprentices said they needed to train other workers on the safety, materials, and tools used in a given project. Based on these interviews and observations, I developed a performance-based project that would allow all members of the class to participate in math, safety, tools, and materials activities. A team of framers, dry-wall hangers, plasterers, and painters coordinated the building of a wall over the course of two weeks. The learning objectives were as follows.

Each team member will be able to:

1. Construct a part of a wall: framing, dry-wall, plaster, or paint.

2. Identify and demonstrate tools and materials for each stage of construction.

3. Identify and demonstrate OSHA guidelines for each stage.

To prepare for the demonstrations, students practiced conversations from *Day by Day* (Molinsky and Bliss, 2000) and practiced dialogues from customized handouts based on the needs analysis. Students also learned vocabulary and verbs related to tools and materials by using the *Oxford Picture Dictionary* (Adelson-Goldstein and Shapiro, 1998).

I also guided the apprentices to take notes during the demonstrations. During the literacy audit, I discovered that taking notes is an important skill for apprentices because they also take safety, math, carpentry, dry-wall, and other craft classes consisting of lecture and reading materials. As students watched the demonstrations, they took notes in a customized graphic organizer designed to support low-literacy students who usually require more time and support in taking notes. We also drilled the clarification and confirmation phrases, "Can you please repeat?", "How do you spell _____?", "What does _____ mean?"

While learning basic English and being safe on the job were two primary goals identified by employers, the customized course also facilitated the apprentices' desire to become more competent in demonstrating their crafts in English. They developed confidence in training others as they firmly grasped the vocabulary of their crafts. They replaced feelings of inadequacy and self-deprecating remarks about their language learning with renewed confidence in their fluency. They stopped editing themselves and apologizing for not knowing a word or verb. Students stopped saying, "I'm not smart," or "I'm sorry." While they described the safety, tools, and materials for their crafts, they spoke English with less hesitation and doubt. Yes, they made grammatical and vocabulary mistakes; however, these errors were not interfering with communication. Even the apprentices with the most limited ability in English took on a confident persona as they demonstrated the proper use of a pick ax, shovel, and paintbrush. The hours of hard work of practicing industry-specific conversations drills and vocabulary contributed to their new competence.

In summary, by using a genre / discourse community approach in analyzing a workplace, the ESL practitioner can identify performance-based language tasks and assessments (e.g., portfolios, team projects, simulations, interviews, speeches) that can be used alongside paper and pencil or oral tests. The content-based performance tasks can help learners set individual goals, are industry-related, and help learners strengthen oral and written confidence.

In conclusion, language assessments are used in the workplace in the phases as follows. Needs analysis of a workplace is conducted to identify priority learning outcomes. Placement tests are used in the analysis phase to identify learners' listening, speaking, reading, and writing skills. Results from the needs analysis, placement tests, and pre-tests play an important role in designing curriculum, lesson plans, and performance-based tasks. Finally, post-tests and portfolios can help to identify student progress.

CONCLUSION: FUTURE DIRECTIONS

Computers are playing a larger role in assessment. Publishers are developing computer-based tests, computer-adaptive tests, and touch-screen tests. While computer testing can be found at one-stop centers and career centers, it is often not mobile enough to transport to work sites. Future research is recommended in this arena.

Suggested resources

Blake, R. J. (2008). *Brave new digital classroom: Technology and foreign language learning*. Washington, D.C.: Georgetown University Press.

Crystal, D. (2008). *Txting: The gr8 db8*. Oxford: Oxford University Press.

Fotos, S., & Browne, C. M. (2004). *New perspectives on CALL for second language classrooms*. Mahwah, New Jersey, USA: Lawrence Erlbaum Associates, Publishers.

Warschauer, M., & Liaw, M. (2010). Emerging Technologies in Adult Literacy and Language Education. National Institute for Literacy. Washington D.C. Available at http://lincs.ed.gov/publications/pdf/technology_paper_2010.pdf

Discussion questions

1. As distance-learning technology such as Web-conferencing becomes more affordable and widely available, how might workplace ESL trainers utilize these tools to deliver training?

2. As computer technology becomes seamlessly integrated into entry-level workplace tasks (e.g., menu orders alert cooks in food service), how can workplace ESL trainers integrate technology training into the curriculum?

3. As publishers develop more language tests online, how might workplace ESL trainers take advantage of these tools?

4. How might teachers go about performing a needs assessment of a particular industry? How can they use the information they obtain to create a curriculum?

5. What kind of projects / activities would be appropriate in a workplace classroom versus a traditional classroom?

References

Adelson-Goldstein, J., & Shapiro, N. (1998 & 2008). *Oxford picture dictionary*. New York: Oxford University Press.

ACT (American College Testing), Inc. (no date). Iowa City, Iowa. www.act.org/workkeys/.

ACT (American College Testing), Inc. (August, 2000). Workplace essential skills: Resources related to the scans competencies and foundation skills. Presented to the United States Department of Labor, Employment and Training Administration. Available online at: http://wdr.doleta.gov/opr/fulltext/00-wes.pdf.

CAL (Center for Applied Linguistics) BEST oral English proficiency assessment for adults. (1984, 1989) and BEST Plus (2002). Washington, D.C. www.cal.org.

California Department of Education (August 2004). The Relationship of Adult ESL Reading Performance to Instructional Time. Research Brief No. 2: Learner Persistence and Achievement. Department of Education, State of California.

CASAS (Comprehensive Adult Student Assessment System) Workplace Learning System. (2003) San Diego, CA. www.CASAS.org.

Douglas, D. (2000). *Assessing language for specific purposes*. Cambridge: Cambridge University Press.

Friedenberg, J., Kennedy, D., Lomperis, A., Martin, W., & Westerfield, K. (2003). *Effective practices in workplace language training: Guidelines for providers of workplace English language training services*. Alexandria: Teachers of English to Speakers of Other Languages, Inc.

Genesee, F., & Upshur, J. A. (1996). *Classroom-based evaluation in second language education.* Series editor: J. Richards. New York: Cambridge University Press.

Greenberg, I. A. (1993). Building on the past, looking toward the future: An ESL teacher reference for writing instruction in adult education. Unpublished Master's Thesis. San Diego, CA: California State University.

Johns, A. M. (1993). Written argumentation for real audiences: Suggestions for teacher research and classroom practice. *TESOL Quarterly*, 27, 75–90.

Long, M. H. (2005). Methodological issues in learner needs analysis. In M. Long (Ed.), *Second language needs analysis.* New York: Cambridge University Press.

Molinsky, S., & Bliss, R. (2000). *Day by Day: English communication skills.* Plains, NY: Longman, Pearson.

Swales, J. M. (1990). *Genre analysis: English in academic and research settings.* New York: Cambridge University Press.

Young, S. (2007). Effects of instructional hours and intensity of instruction on NRS level gain in listening and speaking. Available at www.cal.org/resources/digest/levelgain. html, Washington, D.C.: Center for Applied Linguistics.

CHAPTER 22

Student Involvement in Assessment: Healthy Self-Assessment and Effective Peer Assessment

Neil J Anderson

INTRODUCTION

Student involvement in assessment is a vital and often overlooked part of the assessment process. If we want to gather the best possible assessment data to improve language teaching and learning, we must include students in that process. This chapter will address two ways to engage students in the assessment process: healthy self-assessment and effective peer assessment. As we include students in the assessment process, both in self-assessment and in peer assessment, it is vital to begin by teaching them how to engage in healthy self-assessment and then teach them how to engage in effective peer assessment. Healthy self-assessment can be defined by viewing it at the center of a continuum with super-ficial self-assessment on one end and hypercritical self-assessment on the other. Perhaps you have had students who are *superficial* in their self-assessment. They have a firm belief that their performance in class is near-perfect and they do not feel challenged. In response to self-assessment questions about how they believe they are performing in class, these students quickly respond that they are doing well and that sometimes they find the class boring. These learners often *overestimate* their ability to perform well in a second language. As will be pointed out in this chapter, most learners who overestimate their language performance actually score in the bottom quartile on exams of language abilities. At the other end of the continuum we have learners who are *hypercritical* of their performance. They give very thoughtful consideration of their performance and then they tell you all the reasons why they do not believe that they are performing well in the language. These learners often *underestimate* their performance. As will be pointed out here, these usually include the learners who score in the top quartile on tests of language ability. We want to help both of these types of learners to engage in healthy, but critical self-assessment.

In order for learners to engage in critical but healthy self-assessment and effective peer assessment, they must be metacognitively aware of their learning processes. Metacognition can be defined as thinking about your learning (Anderson, 2002, 2005, 2007). Awareness of their preferred learning style can assist in improving learners' metacognitive awareness. Also, increased awareness of the wide range of learner strategies available to effectively learn a second language and how to evaluate the successful use of those strategies is an essential part of developing metacognitively aware learners who can successfully engage in self- and peer assessment.

This chapter will first provide a brief background based on findings from key research studies of why student involvement in assessment is of value. Next, practical applications to engage students in healthy self-assessment and effective peer assessment will be given. Finally, suggestions for future research will be reviewed. These suggestions can inform us on how the important role that student involvement plays in assessment can be improved.

KEY RESEARCH STUDIES ON HEALTHY SELF- AND EFFECTIVE PEER ASSESSMENT

There are many studies that have examined the impact of healthy self-assessment and effective peer assessment (self-assessment studies: Anderson and Vandergrift, 1996; Bachman and Palmer, 1989; Blanche, 1990; Heilenman, 1990; Mokhtari and Sheorey, 2002; Nunan, 1996, 1997; Oscarson, 1989; Riley and Harsch, 1999; Ross, 1998; Strong-Krause, 2000; peer assessment studies: Berg, 1999; Ferris, 2003; Guerrero and Villamil, 1994; Lockhart and Ng, 1995; Mendonca and Johnson, 1994; Min, 2005; Paulus, 1999; Stanley, 1992; Tsui and Ng, 2000; Zhu, 1995). Due to space restrictions in this chapter we are not able to address all of these studies. I would like to review two key research studies that can provide a foundation of the main points that teachers and researchers should understand in terms of healthy self- and effective peer assessment.

RESEARCH ON SELF-ASSESSMENT

Strong-Krause (2000) suggests that self-assessments can be used in combination with or in place of the traditional placement test, which she reminds us can be expensive in terms of both the development of the instruments as well as the costs associated with printing them. She reports on a study that she conducted in an intensive English as a Second Language program in the United States. The study included 81 students from three language backgrounds: Japanese, Korean, and Spanish. The students responded to two parts of a self-assessment survey. Part 1 included background information questions, whereas Part 2 elicited self-assessment information on the students' self-perceived abilities in the language skills of listening, speaking, reading, and writing. In order to facilitate the collection of accurate information, the questionnaire was administered in the students' first language. Following the suggestion from Bachman and Palmer (1989), the questions were presented from the perspective of the task's difficulty. Students were asked to respond to three tasks for each of the four language skills. Task 1 asked students for a general assessment of their ability in English, Task 2 included a description of 10 specific tasks, and Task 3 included three actual tasks. In addition to the self-assessment tasks, students took a traditional placement test examining their performance in each language skill.

Strong-Krause (2000) analyzed the data through a stepwise regression for each language skill to determine which of the three tasks was the best predictor of a student's abilities. The self-assessment of the actual task was the best predictor for each of the four language skills. For the writing skill, learners performed almost equally on both the actual task and the global task. The major finding from her study was that learners should be given actual tasks with a detailed description and asked to self-assess their ability to perform such tasks. For writing, since both the actual and the global task were similar, using the global task could be easier for gathering self-assessments. Another major finding was that self-assessments of students' reading ability were the most difficult. Strong-Krause suggests that perhaps self-assessments of this skill should be avoided.

What we learn from this study is that self-assessments are challenging and that the better we prepare the learner to reflect on their abilities, the more likely they are to make better predictions of their own abilities.

Anderson (in press) carried out a study with language learners in Costa Rica. This study focused on comparing learners' self-assessments with their actual performance on the end-of-course tests. He was particularly interested in identifying whether the language learners in the top quartile and the bottom quartile were equally skilled at providing self-assessments. Kruger and Dunning (1999) suggest that learners who are most skilled (as measured by performing in the top quartile on an assessment) underestimate their performance while learners who are least skilled (as measured by performing in the bottom quartile on an assessment) overestimate their performance on the test. In order to see how accurate learners were in providing self-assessments, learners took a test and then were immediately asked to evaluate their performance on each of the items of the test. Learners participated in an integrated skills test of listening, reading, and writing. They also participated in a one-on-one oral interview. After each test they were asked whether they thought the answer they had provided on the test was correct, incorrect, or if they were not sure.

The data from Anderson (in press) were analyzed through ANOVA and t-tests. The results support the original research hypothesis that learners who are more skilled under-estimate their performance while those learners who are less skilled overestimate their performance on tests of their language abilities.

This self-assessment study suggests that learners, both those who perform well and those who do not perform well, would benefit from a strong curricular component on self-assessment. Language teachers can play a significant role in preparing learners to be better self-assessors. In particular, see Example No. 1 in the section on Practical Application of this chapter.

RESEARCH ON PEER ASSESSMENT

Peer assessment in language learning is most frequently associated with peer reviews of the writing process. Min (2006) provides an excellent example of research on the role of peer assessment in language learning. The power of her research is that she takes into account not just the number and kinds of revisions that students make in their compositions but also the impact that the peer-review comments have in improving the final quality of the compositions.

Min (2006) gathered data from 18 EFL university writers in Taiwan. A pre-training assessment was made. The students wrote the first draft of an essay and then engaged in peer review. The comments from the peer review led to a second draft of the essay. Based on the peer feedback, students made a total of only 80 revisions in the final draft of their compositions. Of the 80 revisions, 54 (or 68%) could be traced directly to the feedback provided by the peers. The quality of the revisions was evaluated by trained raters – 78% of the content in the pre-training compositions remained unchanged, 13% of the revisions were rated as increasing the quality of the final composition, and 9% of the revisions were rated as actually negatively influencing the quality of the final product.

The students then participated in two 2-hour in-class demonstration / modeling sessions and two 30-minute after-class reviewer-teacher conferences. The focus of the training sessions was on how to provide effective peer feedback on writing. The focus of the reviewer-teacher conference was to help reviewers understand how to make their feedback more useful to their peers. All of the individual comments that the reviewers provided were graded by Min. This is one point that enhances this research over prior peer review studies (Berg, 1999; Ferris, 2003; Liu and Hansen, 2002; Min, 2005; Paulus, 1999).

Min found that after receiving reviewer training, students made a total of 165 revisions in final drafts of their compositions, double the number from before the training. Of the 165 revisions, 149 revisions (90%) could be traced to feedback received from the peer evaluation. The impact of the quality of these revisions was again evaluated by the trained raters – 72% of the changes made after receiving the reviewer training contributed to a higher quality composition, 19% of the changes were judged as decreasing the quality of the final product, and 9% as unchanged.

The results of Min's research have significance for increasing our understanding of peer assessment. The combination of teacher modeling and training reviewers, as well as the individual reviewer-teacher conferences in which the reviewers' comments are graded by the teacher, have a greater impact on the quality of the final product.

Perhaps writers are also influenced through the reviewer training. The training as a reviewer may cause the writer to be more aware of his / her own writing during first drafts and also on how to use the peer feedback to make improvements. It may be an added value that writers benefit as much from the training sessions as a reviewer in their future writing tasks.

I want to explicitly point out the great importance of Min's research (as well as that of the other peer-review researchers mentioned in this chapter) in narrowing the gap between a writer's intentions in early drafts of compositions with the actual meaning that is perceived by the reader. As teachers we need to help learners narrow the gap between their perceived intentions in writing and the actual meaning that readers receive.

PRACTICAL APPLICATIONS

In order to narrow the gap between a learner's self-perception and reality, one centrally agreed upon finding from research studies is that learners must receive explicit training in the classroom (Ferris, 2003, 2009; Liu and Hansen, 2002; Min 2005, 2006; Paltridge et al., 2009; Paulus, 1999; Strong-Krause, 2000). Training learners in critical but healthy self-assessment of their own skills and how to effectively provide peer feedback is a very important part of our teaching responsibilities. Let me share two examples of practical ways that you can help learners.

EXAMPLE NO. 1: NARROWING THE GAP OF SELF-ASSESSMENT

When I administer a test (diagnostic, progress, or achievement) or a classroom quiz, I ask the students to review their performance on each of the test items. For this example let's assume that I have just administered a mid-term exam on which I assessed students on the following reading skills: scanning, skimming for the main idea, predicting, identifying the meaning of unknown vocabulary in context, and identifying main ideas. While they still have their copy of the test booklet, I give them a handout like the one in Table 22.1a and ask them to complete Parts A, B, and C.

Name: _____

Self-Assessment of Performance on the Mid-Term Exam

Part A

How do you think your score on this mid-term exam will compare with that of other students in the class?

| 0 | 25 | 50 | 75 | 99 |

| I'd be at the very bottom | I'd be exactly average | I'd be at the very top |

Part B

Go back over *each* of the questions on this mid-term exam and provide a self-assessment of your performance. How well do you think you did on *each* item?

Item	Do you believe you will receive *full* credit for your response on this item?		
	Yes	No	I'm not sure
		(circle one)	
Section 1. Scanning			
1.	Yes	No	I'm not sure
2.	Yes	No	I'm not sure
3.	Yes	No	I'm not sure
4.	Yes	No	I'm not sure
5.	Yes	No	I'm not sure
Section 2. Skimming for the Main Idea			
6.	Yes	No	I'm not sure
7.	Yes	No	I'm not sure
8.	Yes	No	I'm not sure
9.	Yes	No	I'm not sure
10.	Yes	No	I'm not sure

(ctd.)

(ctd.)			
Section 3. Predicting			
11.	Yes	No	I'm not sure
12.	Yes	No	I'm not sure
13.	Yes	No	I'm not sure
14.	Yes	No	I'm not sure
15.	Yes	No	I'm not sure
Section 4. Identifying the Meaning of Unknown Vocabulary in Context			
16.	Yes	No	I'm not sure
17.	Yes	No	I'm not sure
18.	Yes	No	I'm not sure
19.	Yes	No	I'm not sure
20.	Yes	No	I'm not sure
Section 5. Identifying Main Ideas			
21.	Yes	No	I'm not sure
22.	Yes	No	I'm not sure
23.	Yes	No	I'm not sure
24.	Yes	No	I'm not sure
25.	Yes	No	I'm not sure
Part C			
There are a total of 25 points on this test. What do you estimate will be your score? _____ of the 25 points			

Table 22.1a   Self-assessment form (Parts A, B, and C)

After the exam is corrected, I return it to the students along with the self-assessment sheet. I then ask them to complete Part D of the form (Table 22.1b). This self-assessment activity provides explicit practice for the students in being more aware of how they are performing on a test. Through this type of activity, teachers can begin to make students more aware of the connections between the questions on the test and their ability to assess their skills. This type of self-assessment activity also allows teachers to help learners become more aware of their strengths and weaknesses in self-assessment.

EXAMPLE NO. 2: SELF- AND PEER ASSESSMENT

In relationship to peer assessment we have discussed primarily its use in peer reviews of writing. In this example let me share one way that you can combine self- and peer assessment in a group speaking activity.

Part D (to be completed after receiving the results of the test)

My actual score was _____ / 25 points

I _____ my score on this test.

   A. overestimated (I estimated my score would be more than _____ points.)

   B. correctly estimated (I estimated my score would be between _____ points.)

   C. underestimated (I estimated my score would be lower than _____ points.)

In preparation for the next test, I will do the following things to improve my score:

_____

_____

_____

Table 22.1b   Self-assessment form (Part D)

Many teachers use group work to provide more opportunities for learners to use the language. Rarely do teachers evaluate the effectiveness of the group work to see if it is meeting the needs of the learners. Here is one way that you can use both self- and peer assessment in a group work activity. This evaluation works particularly well for group work activities that will last for more than a single class session.

Let's assume that you have formed groups to work on a project and then present the project to the class. Students work with each other for several class sessions. After completing the presentations from all of the groups, the administration of the group work evaluation form (Table 22.2 overleaf) would be appropriate. This form was proposed by Angelo and Cross (1993: 349–351).

Notice that this form combines elements of both peer assessment (Questions 1, 2, 3, and 6) and self-assessment (Questions 4 and 5). As I have used this particular assessment tool in my classes I share the results of the anonymous responses. I assign students a group number and then ask that they use the group number in providing me the responses to these questions. I then tabulate the results to the questions and return feedback to the students and have them meet one more time as a group to review the responses. We then discuss as a class what has been learned from the results of the group work evaluation form.

FUTURE DIRECTIONS

There are rich possibilities for future research on the roles of self- and peer assessment in language learning. First, from the results of my research on the self-assessment continuum, it is clear that learners underestimate and overestimate their performance on tests. The next step in the research on self-assessment would be to train a group of learners to narrow the gap between their perceived and actual performance, using training such as that suggested in Example No. 1. Following a period of intensive training on self-assessment, data could be gathered to see if learners are able to more accurately self-assess their performance.

Group # _____

1. Overall, **how effectively** did your group work together on this assignment? (circle the appropriate response)

1	2	3	4	5
not at all	poorly	adequately	well	extremely well

2. How many of the five group members participated actively most of the time? (circle the appropriate number)

   1   2   3   4   5

3. How many of you were fully prepared for the group work most of the time? (circle the appropriate number)

   1   2   3   4   5

4. Give one specific example of *something you learned from the group* that you probably wouldn't have learned on your own.

5. Give one specific example of *something the other group members learned from you* that they probably wouldn't have learned without you.

6. Suggest *one specific, practical change* the group could make that would help improve everyone's learning.

Table 22.2   Group work evaluation form

In terms of peer assessment, based on the research from Min (2006) the next step she suggests is a replication of her training for reviewers with the addition of interviews with "student writers to examine their own revisions and discuss the effects of peer review comments on their decision making" (2006: 136). In this way we can learn more about the source of the changes in writing (self, peer, teacher, reviewer training, etc.) and what decision process writers actually go through to improve their writing.

I think also that there must be an exploration of the role of learner motivation in the process of engaging in healthy self- and effective peer assessment. Do learners see the value of self- and peer assessment? If so, why? If not, why not? How can taking responsibility for one's own learning lead to better, more successful learning outcomes?

CONCLUSION

Classroom assessment is a central part of every teacher's role in the classroom. Teachers, administrators, and learners all need to understand how to use the results from well-designed assessments to improve learning. In addition to using the results of standard assessments of learning, I propose that educators establish a classroom culture of collaboration and evaluation of each other's work as well as one's own performance in the classroom. Increased metacognitive awareness of one's learning and engaging in critical but healthy self-assessment and effective peer assessment can lead to greater improvement in language learning.

Suggested resources

The following articles or book sections may be of interest to those wishing to learn more about self- and peer assessments.

Chamot, A. U. (2009). *The CALLA handbook: Implementing the Cognitive Academic Language Learning Approach* (2nd ed.). White Plains, NY: Pearson Education.

On pages 82–83, Chamot provides a brief discussion on self-assessment.

Dörnyei, Z., & Ushioda, E. (2009). *Motivation, language identity and the L2 self*. Bristol: Multilingual Matters.

As we continue to improve self- and peer assessment in language learning, we need to make connections with the literature on motivation. Dörnyei and Ushioda provide the most current and extensive look at the literature on motivation. Teachers and researchers interested in assessment would benefit a great deal from this literature.

Hedgcock, J. S., & Ferris, D. R. (2009). *Teaching readers of English: Students, texts, and contexts*. New York: Routledge.

See in particular pages 367–369.

Hyland, K. (2003). *Second language writing*. New York: Cambridge University Press.

See in particular pages 198–207 for suggestions on training students to participate in peer review of writing.

Kroll, B. (2003). *Exploring the dynamics of second language writing*. New York: Cambridge University Press.

See pages 129–136 for a strong discussion on the value of peer assessment.

Nation, I. S. P. (2009). *Teaching ESL/EFL reading and writing*. New York: Routledge.

On page 144, Nation provides a suggestion of a self-evaluation checklist that could be of benefit in teaching learners to self-assess prior to engaging in peer assessment.

Discussion questions

1. Over- or underestimation of language abilities in the classroom is a common problem. What factors do you think contribute to learners over- or underestimating their language abilities?

2. What self- and peer assessment training have you previously provided for learners in your classes? What successes or failures have you experienced? Based on what you have read in this chapter, what changes could you make to self- and peer assessments that you use?

3. How could you use the self-assessment provided in Table 22.1? What benefits do you see from using such a self-assessment?

4. How could you use the group work evaluation form provided in Table 22.2? What benefits do you see from using such an assessment?

5. Given all that you have learned in this chapter, what steps will you take to engage learners in critical but healthy self- and peer assessment?

References

Anderson, N. J. (2002). The role of metacognition in second / foreign language teaching and learning. *ERIC Digest*. Retrieved from www.cal.org/resources/digest/0110anderson .html

Anderson, N. J. (2005). L2 strategy research. In E. Hinkel (Ed.), *Handbook of research in second language teaching and learning* (pp. 757–772). Mahwah, NJ: Lawrence Erlbaum Associates.

Anderson, N. J. (2007). Metacognition in writing: Facilitating writer awareness. In A. Stubbs (Ed.), *Rhetoric, uncertainty, and the university as text: How students construct the academic experience* (pp. 19–43). Regina, Saskatchewan, Canada: Canadian Plains Research Center, University of Regina.

Anderson, N. J. (in press). Metacognition. In S. Mercer, S. Ryan, & M. Williams (Eds.), *Language learning psychology: Research, theory & pedagogy*.

Anderson, N. J., & Vandergrift, L. (1996). Increasing metacognitive awareness in the L2 classroom by using think-aloud protocols and other verbal report formats. In R. L. Oxford (Ed.), *Language learning strategies around the world: Cross-cultural perspectives* (pp. 3–18). Manoa, HI: University of Hawai'i Press.

Angelo, T. A., & Cross, K. P. (1993). *Classroom assessment techniques: A handbook for college teachers*. San Francisco: Jossey-Bass.

Bachman, L. F., & Palmer, A. S. (1989). The construct validation of self-ratings of communicative language ability. *Language Testing*, 7, 14–29.

Berg, B. C. (1999). The effects of trained peer response on ESL students'; revision types and writing quality. *Journal of Second Language Writing*, 8, 215–241.

Blanche, P. (1990). Using standardized achievement and oral proficiency tests for self-assessment purposes: The DLIFLC study. *Language Testing*, 7, 202–229.

Ferris, D. (2003). *Response to student writing: Implications for second language students*. Mahwah, NJ: Lawrence Erlbaum Associates.

Ferris, D. (2009). *Teaching college writing to diverse student populations*. Ann Arbor, MI: The University of Michigan Press.

Guerrero, M. D., & Villamil, O. (1994). Social cognitive dimensions of interation in L2 peer revision. *The Modern Language Journal*, 78, 484–496.

Heilenman, L. K. (1990). Self-assessment of second language ability: The role of response effects. *Language Testing*, 7, 174–210.

Kruger, J., & Dunning, D. (1999). Unskilled and unaware of it: How difficulties in recognizing one's own incompetence lead to inflated self-assessments. *Journal of Personality and Social Psychology*, 77, 1121–1134.

Liu, J., & Hansen, J. G. (2002). *Peer response in second language writing classrooms*. Ann Arbor, MI: The University of Michigan Press.

Lockhart, C., & Ng, P. (1995). Analyzing talk in ESL peer response groups: Stances, functions, and content. *Language Learning*, 45, 605–655.

Mendonca, C. O., & Johnson, K. E. (1994). Peer review negotiations: Revisions activities in ESL writing instruction. *TESOL Quarterly*, 28, 745–769.

Min, H.-T. (2005). Training students to become successful peer reviewers. *System: An International Journal of Educational Technology and Applied Linguistics*, 33, 293–308.

Min, H.-T. (2006). The effects of trained peer review on EFL students' revision types and writing quality. *The Journal of Second Language Writing*, 15, 118–141.

Mokhtari, K., & Sheorey, R. (2002). Measuring ESL students' awareness of reading strategies. *Journal of Developmental Education*, 25(3), 2–10.

Nunan, D. (1996). Learner strategy training in the classroom: An action research study. *TESOL Journal*, 6(1), 35–41.

Nunan, D. (1997). Does learner strategy training make a difference? *Lenguas Modernas*, 24, 123–142.

Oscarson, M. (1989). Self-assessment of language proficiency: Rationale and applications. *Language Testing*, 6, 1–13.

Paltridge, B., Harbon, L., Hirsch, D., Shen, H., Stevenson, M., Phakiti, A., & Woodrow, L. (2009). *Teaching academic writing: An introduction for teachers of second language writers*. Ann Arbor, MI: The University of Michigan Press.

Paulus, T. (1999). The effect of peer and teacher feedback on student writing. *Journal of Second Language Writing*, 8, 265–289.

Riley, L. D., & Harsch, K. (1999). *Enhancing the learning experience with strategy journals: Supporting the diverse learning styles of ESL/EFL students*. Paper presented at the The Higher Education Research and Development Society of Australia Annual International Conference, Melbourne, Australia.

Ross, S. (1998). Self-assessment in second language testing: A meta-analysis and analysis of experiential factors. *Language Testing*, 15, 1–20.

Stanley, J. (1992). Coaching student writers to be effective peer evaluators. *Journal of Second Language Writing*, 1, 217–233.

Strong-Krause, D. (2000). Exploring the effectiveness of self-assessment strategies in ESL placement. In G. Ekbatani & H. Pierson (Eds.), *Learner-directed assessment in ESL* (pp. 49–73). Mahwah, NJ: Lawrence Erlbaum.

Tsui, A. B. M., & Ng, M. (2000). Do secondary L2 writers benefit from peer comments? *Journal of Second Language Writing*, 9, 78–88.

Zhu, W. (1995). Effects of training for peer response on students' comments and interaction. *Written Communication*, 1, 492–528.

CHAPTER 23

Assessment of Second Language Pragmatics

Zohreh R. Eslami and Azizullah Mirzaei

INTRODUCTION

Although pragmatic competence has been proposed and included as an integral component of communicative competence by most prominent models of language ability (e.g., Bachman, 1990; Bachman and Palmer, 1996), its development and assessment in the L2 (second language) classroom have only fairly recently attracted second language acquisition researchers' serious attention (Ishihara, 2009). Despite the fact that the necessity of teaching pragmatics has been recognized, assessment of L2 pragmatics is still a very young field of inquiry, awaiting further research and development (McNamara and Roever, 2006).

Utilizing research-based information, this chapter presents different instruments and techniques for the assessment of L2 pragmatics. We will first give a brief description of L2 pragmatics. Next we will discuss some of the persistent issues and challenges faced when we deal with the assessment of L2 pragmatics. Following that, different classroom-based measures for assessment of learners' pragmatic ability will be presented. We will integrate the role of learners' agency and identity preservation in the assessment instruments, and highlight the importance of learners' self-assessment and input in order to provide culturally responsive assessment of pragmatics. The chapter will conclude with some practical ideas for teachers.

WHAT IS PRAGMATICS?

Pragmatics is a rich interdisciplinary research domain that deals with "how language is used in communication" (Leech, 1996: 1). A definition that has largely appealed to the field of instructional pragmatics has been offered by Crystal (2003), who defines pragmatics as "the study of language from the point of view of users, especially of the choices they make, the constraints they encounter in using language in social interaction and the effects their use of language has on other participants in the act of communication" (p. 364). More simply put, pragmatics deals with communicative action in its sociocultural context as well as interpersonal rhetoric (i.e., the way interlocutors accomplish goals as social actors who do not just need to get things done but must attend to their interpersonal relationships at the same time).

According to Leech (1983), pragmatics encompasses two components, *pragmalinguistics* and *sociopragmatics*. Pragmalinguistics refers to the resources for conveying communicative acts and relational and interpersonal meanings. Pragmalinguistic resources include pragmatic strategies such as directness and indirectness, routines, and a large range of linguistic forms which can intensify or soften communicative acts. For instance, compare "I'm sorry" with "I'm absolutely devastated – could you possibly find it in your heart to forgive me?" as two versions of an apology. Each of these pragmalinguistic choices serves the function of apologizing, while, at the same time, conveying a very different attitude and social relationship in each of the apologies, which is where sociopragmatics comes into play. According to Leech (1983), sociopragmatics is "the sociological interface of pragmatics" (p. 10). It refers to the social perceptions underlying participants' comprehension and production of communicative action. Despite the fact that descriptions of L2 pragmatic behavior began to appear as early as the 1960s, we have witnessed efforts and interest in teaching and assessment of L2 pragmatics only recently. If pragmatics is to be integrated into L2 instruction, learners' pragmatic knowledge needs to be assessed in the classroom context. However, assessment of pragmatic knowledge within instructional contexts poses a number of challenges to be noted.

CHALLENGES IN THE ASSESSMENT OF L2 PRAGMATICS

Although there has been a growing interest in the teaching of L2 pragmatics (e.g., Eslami-Rasekh, 2005; Ishihara, 2007), assessment of learners' pragmatic skills seems to have received less emphasis, even though assessment is an essential part of the instruction. The reason for the lack of emphasis on the assessment of pragmatic knowledge could be related to the complexities associated with this task.

First, there is an inherent complexity involved in the assessment of second language pragmatics that arises from the highly contextualized or social nature of what is intended to be tested. If the purpose of assessing L2 pragmatics is to test L2 use in real-world or simulated social settings, this important goal then leads to significant tension between the construction of such social settings through authentic assessment procedures and practicality (McNamara and Roever, 2006). That is, the usual "discourse completion tasks" can never be viewed as simulations of real-world social settings. Making use of "face-to-face interaction" (e.g., authentic discourse, elicited conversation, or open role-plays) as the assessment procedure carries its own practicality problems.

A second challenge facing SLA researchers when they come to assess L2 users' pragmatic competence in terms of the sociopragmatic and pragmalinguistic knowledge is the close connection between the two components that often makes them so inseparable that it becomes difficult in practice to judge which component deficiency is involved in a typical pragmatic failure (McNamara and Roever, 2006).

Third, pragmatic ability is challenging to measure due to inherent variability in pragmatic norms. Research shows that pragmatic behavior is realized differently due to social, individual, and contextual variations (Barron, 2005; Ishihara, 2009; McNamara and Roever, 2006). An appropriate range of norms of linguistic behavior may be realized differently based on the interlocutors' individual personalities and social experiences (McNamara and Roever, 2006). Context-specific factors, such as social status of interlocutors, social distance, and degree of imposition, may lead to pragmatic variation as well (Barron, 2005; Ishihara, 2009).

Finally, another source of complexity stems from learners' subjectivity. Researchers have found that pragmatic choices are intertwined with one's identity and values, and learners may intentionally diverge from native speakers' pragmatic norms for identity assertion (Ishihara, 2006; LoCastro, 2001). In a culturally responsive teaching and assessment of pragmatics, learners' goals and intentions and their strategic choices should be taken into consideration by the teachers. Teachers must be careful not to impose native-speaker norms upon learners' pragmatic choices and penalize them in assessment for nontarget pragmatic behavior when they have made an informed and intentional choice (Kasper and Rose, 2002; Ishihara, 2006).

Despite the challenges and complexities related to the assessment of pragmatics, since the 1990s, the field of L2 pragmatics has witnessed the use of different assessment methods for testing L2 pragmatics (e.g., Hudson et al., 1995; Liu, 2006; Roever, 2005, 2006). However, literature on the assessment of learners' pragmatic knowledge in the context of classrooms lags behind (exceptions are Cohen, 2004; Ishihara, 2009). Ishihara's (2009) study seems to be the only prominent teacher-based assessment of L2 pragmatics. In her study, the instructor utilized collaboratively developed authentic assessment tools, such as reflective writing, rubrics, role-plays, and self-assessment.

In what follows we will present different pragmatic assessment instruments that can be utilized by teachers. The assessment strategies proposed promote culturally responsive assessment and consider learners' role of agency. Learners' intentions and strategic choices are taken into consideration and used as a basis for evaluation. Collaborative assessment is promoted by using self-assessment, peer assessment, and teacher assessment in the evaluation process.

ASSESSMENT OF L2 PRAGMATICS

Since instruction and assessment of L2 pragmatics have mainly focused on speech acts, this chapter limits itself to speech acts and uses examples from the most frequently used speech acts (e.g., requesting and apologizing). A speech act refers to the ways in which people carry out specific social functions such as requesting, apologizing, or complaining in speaking or in writing. A speech act is considered to be a functional unit in communication (Cohen, 2004).

Assessment of pragmatics should include productive and receptive skills. Productive skills involve examination of learners' ability to know, for example, "what to say" and "how to say," and receptive skills involve the ability to interpret what others say as it is normally interpreted in the community. When assessing learners' comprehension of pragmatics, the focus is on receptive pragmatic skills. The learners may be involved in the assessment of someone else's (peer assessment) or their own pragmatic production (self-assessment).

A DCT is an item describing a situation requiring a speech act (e.g., request, apology, etc.) in one of the possible combinations of the sociopragmatic variables of power (i.e., power or social-institutional rank of the speaker with respect to the hearer), social distance (i.e., degree of familiarity and solidarity the interlocutors share), and degree of imposition (i.e., expenditure of goods or services by the hearer, or the obligation of the speaker to perform the act) (Hudson, 2001). According to Kasper and Rose (2002), DCT formats vary in a number of ways, for instance, whether the situations are followed by spaces for the test takers to provide their responses, whether they also include a brief dialogue with an open slot to be completed by the respondents, and, in the case of dialogues, whether they include a first-pair part or rejoinder, rejoinder type, or the participants have to provide both discourse turns, such as a compliment-and-compliment response. Still another variant of a discourse completion test is whether the instructions allow the test takers to opt out, that is, choose not to perform the act, thus revealing sociopragmatic differences in the appropriateness of communicative acts.

MEASURING PRAGMATIC COMPREHENSION

In comprehension of the pragmatics, learners are mainly asked to assess how well they think someone else has performed pragmatically. Assessment could entail looking at learners' reactions to a videotaped role-play, a multiple-choice discourse completion test, and a scaled-response DCT (Ishihara and Cohen, 2010).

After learners are instructed about pragmatics and have improved their pragmatic language use they can be asked to do self- or peer assessment of pragmatic performance. Based on Ishihara (2009: 452), an example is developed and provided in Figure 23.1 to show how learners' pragmatic comprehension can be assessed by using a scaled-response discourse completion test.

The class assignment is due, but Hassan hasn't finished it yet. He wants to ask his teacher for an extension.

Hassan: I could not finish the assignment. Can I finish and bring it to your office tomorrow?

Indicate with an X how you would rate the appropriateness of Hassan's request based on the following criteria:

Overall directness, politeness, and formality:

1. Appropriate   2. Somewhat appropriate   3. Inappropriate

Choice and use of requesting strategies (e.g., offering a reason for the request, checking availability, promising to compensate, showing consideration for the listener, expressing apology / thanks):

1. Appropriate   2. Somewhat appropriate   3. Inappropriate

Overall comprehensibility of the speaker's intention (in terms of appropriateness, not grammatical accuracy):

1. Comprehensible   2. Somewhat comprehensible   3. Incomprehensible

Figure 23.1   DCT item to assess pragmatic comprehension of requesting

Learners can also be asked to provide an explanation for giving a certain ranking. Learners' disagreements may result from differences in their subjectivity, and this potential difference in reaction can be a natural indication of pragmatic variability and lead to insightful class discussions related to cross-cultural and individual differences.

Teachers can assess additional related pragmatic components of the above situation and ask learners about their perception of contextual factors, as shown in Figure 23.2 overleaf.

Indicate your analysis of the situation above by placing an X on the lines.

Social status (your professor's status relative to yours)   lower_____X_____higher

Distance (how well you know the professor)   close_____X_____distant

Amount of the imposition of the request   low_____X_____high

How would the teacher interpret Hassan's utterance?

What suggestions would you give to Hassan about the way he spoke?

Teacher's evaluation and comments: . . . .

Figure 23.2   Awareness of contextual factors and collaborative assessment (Ishihara, 2009: 453)

Contextual factors have some bearing on pragmatic performance and therefore are worthy of attention. Students from different cultural backgrounds may rate these contextual variables differently, and therefore increase or decrease the level of formality, directness, and politeness of their speech act performance accordingly. A teacher using culturally responsive teaching should respect students' choices if it is in accordance with their assessment of contextual variables and if they are making an informed choice. Thus, scaled-response DCTs can preferably be used to assess different L2 learners' perception (or appraisal) of sociopragmatic variables that is assumed to underlie their varying pragmatic performance in similar contexts of use.

A Multiple-Choice Discourse Completion Task (MDCT) is similar to a written DCT in terms of its description of the situational context and the prompt (if any) for a response, but rather than leaving the response production to the test takers, the test specifies several response choices from which one must be chosen. The responses are usually scored right or wrong. The right option will take full points and distractors will take no points. Kasper and Rose (2002) maintain that the construction of such tasks should rely on previous research on the communicative act in question in order to make principled selections from the alternative responses. Some instances of such valid sources can be speech act realization strategies collected through DCTs, spoken discourse exchanges, and free responses to comprehension questionnaires. In Hudson et al.'s (1995) case, high-frequency native speaker (NS) responses were employed as correct answers and dissimilar nonnative speaker (NNS) responses were included as distractors. MDCTs are generally preferred over the other forms of assessing pragmatic comprehension when the ease of administration and consistency of scoring are the users' major concerns. An example MDCT (with one correct answer and two distractors) follows in Figure 23.3.

You are a student. You forgot to do the assignment for your Human Resources course. When your teacher whom you have known for some years asks for your assignment, you apologize to your teacher.

A. I'm sorry, but I forgot the deadline for the assignment. Can I bring it to you at the end of the day?

B. Pardon me, sir, I forgot about that. Shall I do the assignment at once? So sorry! It's my fault!

C. I've completed my assignment but forgot to bring it with me. I'll hand it in tomorrow.

Figure 23.3   MDCT item to elicit an apology (Liu, 2006: 5)

Measuring Pragmatic Production

Different types of DCTs are used in the pragmatic assessment literature to assess the pragmatic production of the students. A *Written DCT* (WDCT) is the paper and pencil version of a DCT that requires the students to read the situations and write their responses in the spaces provided after each situation on the paper. An example of a WDCT item is given in Figure 23.4.

> You have borrowed a book from your friend (Mina), which you promised to return today. When meeting Mina, however, you realize that you forgot to bring it along.
>
> Mina: I hope you brought the book I lent you.
> You: ....

Figure 23.4 WDCT item to elicit an apology

An *Oral DCT* (ODCT) is similar to a WDCT but the productions are audio- or video-recorded, sometimes using computers. The learners, after listening to or seeing each (situational) description, are required to audio-record their oral responses of what they would say in each situation.

A *Discourse Role-Play Task* (DRPT) item resembles the items of previous types of DCTs in terms of providing the test takers with a predefined social framework or situational blueprint (a "scenario"). For the responses, however, the test takers are expected to play a specified role with an interlocutor within the situation, which may be audio- or video-recorded (Hudson et al., 1995; Kasper and Rose, 2002). A distinction is sometimes made between "closed" and "open" role-play tasks. In the former, the test takers respond to the description of a situation or produce the required speech act in reply to a partner's standard initiation. In the latter, however, the situation description as well as each participant's role and goal(s) are specified on individual "role cards" without determining the course and outcome of the interaction. Communicative events and acts may evolve over multiple turns and different discourse phases within the context. An example of a DRPT follows in Figure 23.5.

> **Situation:**
>
> Background One: Last week you had trouble with your company van and took it to the company mechanic. The mechanic promised to have it ready by tomorrow at noon. However, you just found out that you have to go on a business trip tomorrow morning and have lots of display materials and samples to bring with you. *So, you need your van to be ready early tomorrow morning.*
>
> Now: You go to the shop and walk over to the head mechanic who is eating lunch and say:

Figure 23.5 A discourse role-play task for making a request (taken and adapted from Hudson et al., 1995: 69)

A *Self-Assessment Instrument* (SAI) is more participant-oriented and requires the test takers to either prepare a self-report on their pragmatic performance or assess their pragmatic ability to perform in some situations after reading the descriptions of each one by rating themselves on a Likert scale based on different assessment criteria (pragmalinguistic aspects, sociopragmatic aspects, and cultural aspects).

As mentioned before, in a culturally responsive assessment, learners should be given the option to follow their own locally developed norms and practice their agency if they are making informed choices intentionally. They may decide to follow the target community's norms or, at times, they may intentionally behave uniquely in order to maintain their cultural identity even when they know what the normative pragmatic behavior is (Ishihara, 2006). Learners reflect on their own language production with guiding prompts and assess their pragmatic production in terms of directness, politeness, and formality in context and show their awareness of a hearer's interpretation of their pragmatic production. Self-assessment pragmatic instruments and provision of rationale by learners give the teachers a chance to work with their students in detecting the nuances learners are likely to convey intentionally in their pragmatic behavior. To accommodate learners' goals in the assessment of their pragmatic production, teachers can collaborate with learners in the assessment process. The example in Figure 23.6 incorporates the learner's self-assessment with the teacher's assessment and feedback.

Scenario: You are a university student and want to apply for jobs after graduation. To do so, you need a letter of recommendation from one of your professors. You go to him / her after class and ask:

Learner

You: *When you have time, I would really appreciate if you could write a letter of recommendation for me because I have started my job research.*

a)   Your intention / goal as a speaker: How do you want to sound, and what do you want to achieve through your request? [**learner writes**]
     Nice, polite, and not pushy to get a nice recommendation through this polite conversation.

b)   Professor's most probable interpretation: [**teacher writes**]
     You made a fairly polite request using various strategies. Since your intention to be polite is clear, your professor will probably ask you more questions about the job, the deadline and format of the letter, etc. and agree to write the letter. S/he may expect more background information first (the way you start with the request may sound a bit too forward).

Match between a) and b): [**teacher evaluates**]

excellent   (good   fair)   poor

Figure 23.6   Example of a collaborative pragmatic assessment (taken from Ishihara, 2010: 218)

As shown here, we can assess learners based on their intentions and goals, their awareness of contextual factors, and, at the same time, probe their linguistic ability to produce native-like utterances and assess their awareness of the most likely community interpretations of their pragmatic performance. In doing this, we give our students the choice to express themselves in the way they choose to – rudely, tactfully, or in an elaborately polite manner. What we want to prevent is for them to be inadvertently rude or subservient (Thomas, 1983).

SCORING CRITERIA

Teachers can use different checklists (rubrics) to evaluate learners' pragmatic performance. Different criteria can be selected in the assessment rubric based on the instructional goals. Areas of focus can include linguistic and cultural aspects.

The linguistic aspects (pragmalinguistics) can include the effectiveness of the language used in conveying the speaker's intentions. The following dimensions can be considered (based on Ishihara, 2009):

- the choice of strategy or set of strategies for the intended speech act (e.g., expressing an apology, giving an explanation, offering repair);
- the typicality of the expressions used and their formulaic nature;
- the choice of syntactic strategies used for a speech act (sorry, I apologize . . .); and
- the choice of intensifiers.

It should be noted that this list represents some possible assessment criteria. Teachers should choose the ones that correspond to their instructional focus. If their focus is on linguistic aspects of pragmatics (pragmalinguistic) and not social aspects then they may employ the above criteria for assessment of students' pragmatic ability.

The cultural aspects (sociopragmatics) include pragmatic aspects related to the appropriateness of the pragmatic performance as it is perceived by L2 community members or the extent it is effective in conveying the speaker's intentions. Teachers can choose from the criteria listed below or add their own if so desired.

- the appropriateness of the amount of information provided;
- the appropriateness of the number of supportive moves and intensifiers used; and
- the appropriateness of the level of formality.

We should keep in mind that what teachers decide to consider as more or less important to include in the assessment rubric depends on the purpose of assessment and also the focus of instruction.

CONCLUSION

This chapter has attempted to review and describe how pragmatic performance can be assessed in a classroom context. It has shown some measures and highlighted some of the challenges associated with this task. There are some other pragmatic assessment measures such as interviews, observation of naturally occurring performance instruments, think-aloud protocols, diaries, and reflective journals available in the literature. However, in this chapter we have tried to present the most practical classroom-based measures that can be used by teachers.

As mentioned before, pragmatic behavior is variable. Therefore, there mainly will be tendencies in pragmatic performance rather than strictly "right" or "wrong" answers (Cohen, 2004).The variable nature of pragmatic behavior has made assessment of pragmatics more complicated. However, if pragmatics is to be included in the classroom curriculum and instruction, then teachers need to engage in its assessment as well. Doing so indicates to the learners that the pragmatic performance and the ability to make requests, apologies, and complaints, for example, has enough significance to warrant attention and is worthy of assessment. As shown in the self-assessment tools in Figure 23.6, the students and teachers can collaborate in this evaluation process and students themselves could engage in this endeavor to share the responsibility.

Some pedagogical suggestions for teachers to consider include using culturally relevant scenarios. If the students are from Middle Eastern countries for example, it may not be realistic and appropriate to use a situation in which a female student asks a male student for a ride home. One suggested approach is "exemplar generation," used by Liu (2006), in which a group of students with similar sociocultural background to the target test takers are asked to write the most recently occurring events in their lives which necessitated the use of the intended speech act, and assessment scenarios are then constructed based on the students' input. Using the events and situations based on students' daily experience can help teachers to provide teaching and assessment scenarios that are culturally relevant and appropriate to the students.

To respect learners' sense of identity and at the same time assess their awareness of a target community's norms, teachers should have students provide their rationale for why they responded as they did in given scenarios. Students' responses can then be used for class discussion on cultural norms and diversity with implications for intercultural communication.

If pragmatic assessment is going to be part of the instruction, we need to think about practicality and feasibility (construction time, administration time, and scoring time). More work is required by L2 practitioners and researchers to illustrate which pragmatic assessment instruments are the most effective and efficient for the language classroom focusing on both comprehension and production skills and on different proficiency levels in different instructional contexts. Without a doubt, more work needs to be done but the rewards can be great in that pragmatic performance is vital for successful communication in an increasingly globalized world.

Suggested resources

Ishihara, N., & Cohen, A. D. (2010). *Teaching and learning pragmatics: Where language and culture meet*. Harlow, Essex, England: Longman / Pearson Education.

Kasper, G., & Rose, K. R. (2002). *Pragmatic development in a second language*. Malden, MA: Blackwell Publishing.

McNamara, T., & C. Roever, C. (2006). *Language testing: The social dimension*. Malden, MA: Blackwell.

Tatsuki, D. H., & Houck, N. R. (2010) (Eds). *Pragmatics: Teaching speech acts*. TESOL Classroom Practice Series. Alexandria, VA: TESOL.

Discussion questions

1. Pragmatic competence includes two components of "pragmalinguistic" and "sociopragmatics," as discussed in this chapter. Explain what each component encompasses and give one example for each component to illustrate your point.

2. Discuss the reasons why the assessment of learners' pragmatic skills has received less emphasis in the literature compared to linguistic skills.

3. Present and discuss two techniques for measuring learners' productive pragmatic skills.

4. Present and discuss two techniques for measuring learners' receptive pragmatic skills.

5. Discuss the importance of respecting learners' sense of identity and culture in teaching and measuring pragmatic aspects of language. Use some examples to illustrate your point.

References

Bachman, L. F. (1990). *Fundamental consideration in language testing*. Oxford: Oxford University Press.

Bachman, L. F., & Palmer, A. S. (1996). *Language testing in practice: Designing and developing useful language tests*. Oxford: Oxford University Press.

Barron, A. (2005). Variational pragmatics in the foreign language classroom. *System*, 33, 519–536.

Cohen, A. D. (2004). Assessing speech acts in a second language. In D. Boxer & A. D. Cohen (Eds.), *Studying speaking to inform second language learning* (pp. 302–327). Clevedon: Multilingual Matters.

Crystal, D. (2003). *A dictionary of linguistics and phonetics*. (5th ed.). Oxford: Blackwell Publishing.

Eslami-Rasekh, Z. (2005). Raising the pragmatic awareness of language learners. *ELT Journal*, 59, 199–208.

Hudson, T. (2001). Indicators for pragmatic instruction: Some quantitative tools. In K. G. Rose & G. Kasper (Eds.), *Pragmatics in language teaching* (pp. 283–300). New York: Cambridge University Press.

Hudson, T., Detmer, E., & Brown, J. D. (1995). Developing prototypic measures of cross-cultural pragmatics (Technical Report #7). Honolulu, HI: Second Language Teaching & Curriculum Center, University of Hawai'i at Manoa.

Ishihara, N. (2006). *Subjectivity, second / foreign language pragmatic use, and instruction: Evidence of accommodation and resistance*. Unpublished Doctoral dissertation, University of Minnesota, Minneapolis, MN.

Ishihara, N. (2007). Web-based curriculum for pragmatics instruction in Japanese as a foreign language: An explicit awareness-raising approach. *Language Awareness*, 16(1), 21–40.

Ishihara, N. (2009). Teacher-based assessment for foreign language pragmatics. *TESOL Quarterly*, 43(3), 445–470.

Ishihara, N. (2010). Assessing Learners' Pragmatic Ability in the Classroom. In D. H. Tatsuki & N. R. Houck (Eds), *Pragmatics: Teaching speech acts* (pp. 209–227). Alexandira, VA: TESOL.

Ishihara, N., & Cohen, A. D. (2010). *Teaching and learning pragmatics: Where language and culture meet*. Harlow, Essex, England: Longman / Pearson Education.

Kasper, G., & Rose, K. R. (2002). Pragmatic development in a second language. Malden, MA: Blackwell Publishing.

Leech, G. (1983). Principles of pragmatics. London: Longman.

Liu, J. (2006). Assessing EFL learners' interlanguage pragmatic knowledge: Implications for testers and teachers. *Reflections on English Language Teaching*, 5(1), 1–22.

LoCastro, V. (2001). Individual differences in second language acquisition: Attitudes, learner subjectivity, and L2 pragmatic norms. *System* 29, 69–89.

McNamara, T., & C. Roever, C. (2006). Language testing: The social dimension. Malden, MA: Blackwell.

Roever, C. (2005). *Testing ESL pragmatics: Development and validation of a web-based assessment battery (language testing and evaluation)*. Frankfurt: Peter Lang Publishing.

Roever, C. (2006). Validation of a web-based test of ESL pragmalinguistics. *Language Testing*, 23(2), 229–256.

Thomas, J. (1983). Cross-cultural pragmatic failure. *Applied Linguistics*, 4, 91–112.

SECTION 3

ASSESSING SECOND LANGUAGE SKILLS

Communicative L2 ability is widely viewed as consisting of a set of multiple competencies. Whereas many factors contribute to L2 users' ability to communicate, reading, writing, listening, speaking, grammar, and vocabulary are considered important parts of the general ability construct. This section offers teachers insights into the assessment of these different aspects of L2 ability as well as an introduction to some of the developments related to each of these underlying constructs.

In Chapter 24, Hubley traces developments in the conceptualization of reading ability and highlights the array of underlying skills that contribute to a reader's ability to process texts. She acknowledges the role of major test development organizations in the development of new types of assessment tasks, but she also cautions us that the nature of L2 reading ability is not completely understood and that this partly accounts for the diversity of approaches to assessing it. Additionally, the author offers a set of considerations that will assist teachers in improving the quality of their reading assessments. Finally, Hubley concludes by noting the impact of technology on the kinds of reading skills that are called for in a world that is more interrelated and interconnected.

As Weigle rightly observes, assessing L2 writing ability in classroom contexts is not as simple as it might appear to be, and teachers can benefit from an understanding of the research and best practices associated with the assessment of writing. She emphasizes the importance of construct definition as a crucial step in the process of determining what to assess and how to assess it. Weigle believes timed in-class writing tests may not be the most appropriate form of assessment or pedagogy in classroom situations, and that portfolio assessment represents a viable alternative to both developing and assessing students' writing ability. However, in cases where writing tests are required, Weigle encourages teachers to take into consideration key test qualities, including reliability, validity, and practicality. She also emphasizes the need to recognize how writing tasks can vary based on such factors as the subject matter, cognitive demands, and characteristics of the prompt, the response mode, and scoring procedures. The chapter concludes with the caveat that we need to have a clearer understanding of the effect of technology on the process and product of writing and also its effect on the scoring of writing.

Flowerdew and Miller take up L2 listening ability, which they contend is the "Cinderella" skill, a language skill that is taken for granted and underappreciated by both teachers and learners. After presenting a brief overview of general approaches to assessing listening ability, the authors discuss the practical challenges to developing listening assessments. These include the need to determine the purpose of the assessment, the kinds of items to include in it, and key context-related considerations that are likely to affect both the design and administration of the test. Flowerdew and Miller note the importance of being clear about the construct that is being measured, and they describe how teachers can develop better listening tests by considering the test, the skills that are being assessed, and the role of reliability and validity in assessment. Finally, the authors discuss some of the scoring options available and how to formulate performance descriptors.

In Chapter 27, O'Sullivan summarizes the results of research on the assessment of speaking ability and this is followed by a description of the key considerations in developing speaking tests, including features of the task, test taker, and scoring procedure. O'Sullivan's detailed explication of the salient factors, the range of options available, and the questions to address in developing credible speaking assessments provides teachers with a theory-based approach to putting "together the various pieces of the assessment jigsaw."

Whereas grammar remains an important consideration in L2 teaching and learning, how it is defined and assessed in terms of communicative language ability has evolved in the past few decades. Jones reviews key theoretical developments and how they have influenced the design of several high-stakes L2 proficiency assessments developed by Cambridge ESOL and Educational Testing Service. He goes on to consider the practical implications of these developments for L2 teaching and learning and the use of particular tasks for assessing grammar ability. Jones concludes with caveats regarding the kinds of assessment tasks that are suitable given current conceptualizations of the L2 grammar construct and the need for a more complete understanding of the effect of different test methods on performance.

In the final chapter in this section, Read explores the nature of vocabulary ability and provides a thorough review of key considerations and relevant research. Based on what is known about L2 vocabulary ability, the author submits vocabulary assessments that are helpful for placement and diagnostic purposes. Read describes different types of vocabulary assessment tasks and recommends using a combination of them, including recognition, recall, and communicative tasks. The author concludes by noting several limitations in the study of vocabulary assessment to date. These include the emphasis on assessing vocabulary in the context of reading written texts and the tendency to focus on single words; however, the author observes this appears to be changing.

CHAPTER 24

Assessing Reading

Nancy J. Hubley

INTRODUCTION

The receptive skill of reading cannot be directly observed. In fact, there is ongoing discussion about how the component subskills and strategies involved in the process of reading actually work together so that a person creates meaning. However, there is consensus that reading is an essential language skill, perhaps the paramount skill since so much information comes from written sources. *Literacy*, the ability to comprehend and produce written material, entails understanding an enormous variety of texts ranging from instructions for preparing breakfast to traffic signs, technical reports at work, e-mails from friends, bank statements, and the day's stock market news. Language students need to comprehend information in textbooks, evaluate articles for research projects, and follow instructions and prompts on examinations, including those that test other language skills, such as listening or speaking.

This chapter reviews the main components that underlie the construct of reading and how these features are assessed. The chapter then explores recent developments in the testing of reading as well as challenges for assessing reading in the future.

BACKGROUND

Students learning to read in English as a second or subsequent language vary greatly. Some are mature students who are already fluent readers in their first languages. Others are young learners who are simultaneously developing initial reading ability in their own language and in English. Yet others may be economic migrants who never achieved literacy in their first language, but now must learn to read and write in English. All of these learners require appropriate assessment to evaluate and support their progress.

The traditional literature on teaching reading – hence assessing it – made assumptions that all English learners went through similar stages in developing literacy, assuming a single, unitary reading process. Gradually, more attention has been paid to sociocultural differences in the languages of first learning and cultural attitudes toward literacy. Grabe (1986: 29–33) covered the main issues and early research. In the area of language assessment, Alderson (2000) drew attention to the sociocultural dimensions of reading. More recently, Part IV of the *Cambridge Handbook on Literacy* (2009) examined the comparative ethnography of writing and reading. It then focused on the experiences of Chinese and Arabic learners who not only have a new orthography to learn, but also have cultural traditions that prioritize the precise rendition of written symbols instead of gist comprehension or paraphrasing. Teachers and testers need to be sensitive to these issues in teaching and assessing reading.

Since the process of reading is not directly observable, reading assessments are based indirectly on what are commonly believed to be the component subskills. These subskills are in turn associated with prevailing models of how people process written information. The oldest of these models is the "bottom-up" approach, as espoused by Bloomfield and other structural linguists in the 1930s. It focused on decoding the smallest written bits, such as letters, morphemes, words, and grammatical structures at the sentence level. The concomitant teaching method was *phonics*, in which students sounded out the letters and recognized them as words. Assessment focused on testing these microskills.

In the mid-20th century psycholinguistic theorists, such as Goodman (1967), presented the "top-down" model in which readers actively worked with larger amounts of text that they used to check predictions about meaning. Assessment foci were on skimming an entire passage for gist comprehension and identifying main ideas and supporting details.

By the 1980s, a third model integrated the two previous approaches. The "interactive" model posited that the reader is simultaneously engaged in finding meaning in the larger, global text while attending to details at a local level. The interactive aspect also describes the reader's relationship with the text, bringing to it both background knowledge on the topic as well as schemata about text types and genres. Testing tasks may require students to recognize how parts of the text are interconnected with discourse markers or to detect shifts in opinion that are supported with specific details.

To this day, the interactive model or paradigm has determined the teaching of reading, the development of instructional materials, and assessment of reading. Associated with the interactive model is the pedagogical practice of teaching stages of reading. In *pre-reading*, students' background knowledge is activated and they quickly skim or scan the passage to become familiar with it or find specific information. *While-reading* is a more intensive stage that features attention to both detail and larger structure. In *post-reading*, comprehension questions are posed and students analyze the passage. Most testing focuses on the middle and last stages of reading, although students generally understand that they may have to read a passage several times for different reasons and at different degrees of intensity.

In the literature on reading assessment, subskills are usually categorized according to whether they apply to local aspects of a text (decoding or sentence-level features) or to larger segments of the passage. Table 24.1 is a sample of such subskills arranged from top to bottom with examples of ways they are often assessed.

Additional lists of subskills arranged by somewhat different criteria are found in Alderson (2000: 10–11), Hughes (2003: 138–139), and Brown (2004: 187–189). Hughes (2003) and Brown (2004) have particularly helpful suggestions for testing subskills at the local level, appropriate for beginner readers.

English teachers encourage students to develop strategies to address these subskills so that using the strategies becomes automatic. Han and Anderson (2009) have advocated a teaching system that encourages increasing reading rate for fluency as well as self-evaluation of progress in using strategies. Both of these enhance student performance on exams.

Level	Subskill	Typical way to test
Whole passage	comprehend the main idea or gist meaning	What is the best title for this passage? What is the reading mainly about?
	recognize structure, genre	What is the source of this text? Possible options: a blog, a letter, a textbook, a commercial.
	identify audience for text	Which of the following groups is meant to read this text? Possible options: graduate students, teenagers, grandparents, single fathers.
	understand the purpose of the writing passage (narrative, argument, explanation)	What is the author trying to do in this text? Options include: Tell how something works, convince people that they should vote, recall a favorite holiday, etc.
	recognize author's attitude and biases	With which of the following statements would the author mostly closely agree?
	sequence events	Formally: Scramble items to be numbered (use anchor numbers for several items). Classroom: Create a timeline.
	summarize key information	Select 4 sentences from 7 options that best summarize the passage.
	distinguish fact from opinion	Formally: Which of the following is not a fact? Classroom: Retell the story and guess which statement is not true.
Section	understand headers	Here are five new sentences. Under which headers would you place them?
	understand logical organization	Where would be the best place for this sentence? (Give 4 lettered insert places marked in the passage.)
	categorize information	Formally: Put the characteristics under each type of camel. Classroom: Create Venn diagrams with shared characteristics in overlap area.
Paragraph	identify main idea and supporting details	List main ideas and match with paragraphs (allow extra options that will not be used).
	understand topic sentences	The most important idea in Paragraph 5 is . . .
	infer content	What did the man really feel about the film?
	distinguish between statements and examples	Which of the following is an example of severe weather? Options: temperature, blizzard, clouds, rainfall.
Across sentence boundaries	understand the function of discourse markers	In Line 21, what does "in addition" mean?
	identify pronoun reference	What does "its" in Line 14 refer to?

(ctd.)

(ctd.)

Level	Subskill	Typical way to test
Sentence level	guess the meaning of unknown words in context	Which word is closest to the meaning of "nomadic" in Line 37?
	understand cohesive devices signaling relationships between clauses	Roger wanted to play soccer, but he didn't finish his homework in time. Did Roger play soccer?
	interpret word order	"I wonder how expensive it is." Does Mrs. Wright know how much the pen costs?
	paraphrase wording	Which phrase means the same as "your brothers and sisters" in Line 10?
	recognize and distinguish graphemes	Circle the word from the second sentence: dog bog fog log

Table 24.1   Sample of subskills

RESEARCH

The preparation, administration, and analysis of standardized reading tests constitute a major industry. Yet, despite the enormous amounts of research on how to best assess reading, there is still debate about the very nature of reading. Alderson (2000: 93–97) questions whether reading is one unitary skill or a group of "empirically distinguishable skills" that can be meaningfully assessed. Research based on think-aloud protocols has not provided much insight. In Han and Anderson's recent book (2009), the authors are skeptical that a coherent understanding of L2 reading exists, let alone a preferred instructional approach. When the very construct of reading is questioned, small wonder that so many diverse approaches to reading assessment exist.

However, a brief overview of standardized reading examinations presents some new approaches. In the past, vocabulary and reading formed one section of the TOEFL examination. Target vocabulary was underlined in decontextualized sentences and students had to choose a synonym from four multiple-choice (MCQ) options. The reading section featured two-paragraph texts followed by five MCQ comprehension questions, at least one of which was a word to identify in context. Tasks seemed separate from real-life academic reading and the student's purpose in reading was to get a good score.

In the last decade, serious revisions have occurred to the way reading is assessed in the TOEFL examination. In 2000, a team of testing experts redesigned the reading section to be more communicative and authentic (Enright et al., 2000). The team identified purposes for academic reading, including reading to learn and reading to integrate information across multiple texts. In the Internet-based TOEFL or iBT, students categorize or summarize information, employing higher-level thinking skills identified by Bloom half a century ago. In ways that reflect realistic academic scenarios, students integrate reading, listening, and speaking about a topic. Other reading tasks focus on lexical cohesion where students insert sentences into a longer passage, a testing technique already in use by Cambridge ESOL in their suite of exams.

Sometimes testing organizations are in the vanguard by introducing new techniques for testing aspects of reading that are taught but not always assessed. When high-stakes examinations include these reading tasks, it produces positive washback and publishers, teachers, and students take notice. Note, for example, Pearson Longman's *Northstar* reading series that uses TOEFL-iBT-type tasks. Regularly check the Web sites of Educational Testing Service, Cambridge ESOL, and IELTS for current techniques for assessing reading.

PRACTICAL APPLICATION

Teachers can find useful information on creating reading tasks in Alderson (2000) as well as in general books on assessment such as Brown (2004) and Hughes (2003). They all contain many examples of techniques and formats. The article by Lloyd and Davidson (2009) provides helpful suggestions on choosing and modifying a text, checking it for readability and vocabulary, and providing students with diagnostic feedback.

The most common subskill tested is the ability to identify main ideas and discriminate between them and supporting details. This is often tested in the multiple-choice format with four options, only one of which is the key. Experienced item writers often use a "Goldilocks formula" to develop the options. The nickname derives from the three bears in the fairytale saying items in Goldilock's house are too big, too small, or just right. The options represent:

- one option – the key – at just the right level of specificity
- one option that is too general for a main idea
- one option that is too narrow, often citing a supporting detail or example
- one option that is related, but off topic

When teachers explain these options to students, they often have an "ah-ha" moment when they start to discriminate between concepts and are better able to identify main ideas.

Here are some of the main practical considerations to keep in mind for reading assessment:

- Determine what reading skills are important for students in your program.
- Develop test specifications for each level of your program and follow them.
- Choose appropriate texts, check them for length and readability, and modify them if necessary so they are suitable for the learners' language level.
- Do not use texts that students have encountered before, but do choose familiar topics.
- Restrict the number of unfamiliar words in the passage to 5–10 percent.
- Develop questions in the order of the passage, and space carefully for coverage.
- Make the level of the questions less difficult than the reading passage.
- Use a variety of formats, but avoid changing formats within one section of the exam.
- Test a range of subskills, not just what is easy to assess.
- After administration, analyze your test and provide constructive feedback to teachers and students.
- Assess reading in the classroom, emphasizing reading strategies.

CONCLUSION: FUTURE DIRECTIONS

Until the last decade, most reading was of printed material. The Internet has changed the availability of written information, the range of sources, and the ways in which people read. Now, a huge amount of information is available to anyone with an Internet connection. People suffer from "information overload" in their attempts to evaluate and make use of so much input. Search engines yield hundreds of possible sources for each inquiry and the user must quickly decide which sites are appropriate for the task at hand. Skimming and scanning are no longer primarily classroom strategies, but essential tools in deciding what information to use.

Other skills that previously seemed most appropriate to academic contexts now are used in everyday life. Subskills such as identifying keywords for searching, understanding the source of a text, discerning the author's perspective, and separating fact from opinion are now relevant every time you are online. This is especially true for students who must learn to quickly evaluate sources as to whether they are germane and appropriate for their purposes. In fact, anthropologist Michael Wesch has attracted considerable media attention with his view that digital media have changed how we learn. He asserts that we have moved from knowing information to knowing how to find information (http://ksuanth.weebly.com/wesch.html).

A byproduct of digital information is that it is frequently multimodal with ideas presented in different forms. Written texts are often accompanied by photographs, maps, graphs, diagrams, and videos. More than ever, students need to comprehend information in these forms as well as through the written word. Although some examinations, such as IELTS, have long asked students to interpret and explain information presented in graphic form, most other language examinations have yet to encompass visual literacy. Some publishers have recently developed reading textbooks that explicitly teach students to interpret nonlinear texts (for example, see Heinle's *Reading Explorer* series).

Another epiphenomenon of technological change in communications and transportation is the massive growth of English as an international language. People read material that originates all over the world, much of it free from the editorial conventions that made reading texts more standardized in the past. Moreover, on social networking sites and with e-mail, new, abbreviated forms of English are widespread. People read more than ever before, but with far fewer constraints. Millions of people who use English for effective communication have never taken a reading course or examination.

With the mass of information in various forms available online, the challenge will be to define anew what reading skills are relevant and how to assess them. Perhaps this is the greatest opportunity since Gutenberg to re-evaluate the reading process and identify what teachers can do to enhance their students' skills.

Suggested resources

Alderson, J. C. (2000). *Assessing reading.* New York: Cambridge University Press.

Coombe, C., Folse, K., & Hubley, N. (2007). *A practical guide to assessing English language learners.* Ann Arbor, MI: University of Michigan Press.

Lloyd, D., & Davidson, P. (2009). Guidelines for developing a reading test. In C. Coombe, P. Davidson, & D. Lloyd (Eds.), *The fundamentals of language assessment: A practical guide for teachers* (2nd ed.). Dubai, UAE: TESOL Arabia Publications.

Discussion questions

1. Do you think that reading is a single unitary skill or can it be divided into many subskills? If it is a single skill, how can it be assessed?

2. What types of reading are important for your students? How can you design assessments that help them to become stronger readers?

3. English teachers devote a great deal of class time to reading strategies such as skimming, scanning, and predicting. Do you think these strategies can be effectively assessed? Support your opinion with examples.

4. Do you agree that teachers should explicitly promote test-taking skills for reading in the classroom? For example, should you share the "formula" for writing main-idea answer options?

5. The literature on teaching reading promotes extensive reading of longer texts outside of class. What are some ways to assess this type of reading?

6. In everyday reading, people need to comprehend maps, charts, diagrams, and photographs. What are some ways to assess visual literacy?

7. What are the advantages and disadvantages of using computers to assess reading?

References

Alderson, J. C. (2000). *Assessing reading*. New York: Cambridge University Press.

Brown, H. D. (2004). *Language assessment: Principles and classroom practices*. White Plains, NY: Pearson Education.

Enright, M. K., Grabe, W., Koda, K., Mosenthal, P., Mulcahy-Ernt, P., & Schedl, M. (2000). TOEFL® 2000 Reading Framework: A Working Paper. Research Report RM-00-04, TOEFL-MS-17. Princeton, NJ: TOEFL.

Goodman, K. (1967). Reading: A psycholinguistic guess game. *Journal of the Reading Specialist*, May, 126–135.

Grabe, W. (1986). The transition from theory to practice in teaching reading. In F. Dubin, D. E. Eskey, & W. Grabe (Eds.), *Teaching second language reading for academic purposes*. Reading, MA: Addison-Wesley.

Han, Z., & Anderson, N. (Eds.) (2009). *Second language reading research and instruction*. Ann Arbor, MI: University of Michigan Press.

Hughes, A. (2003). *Testing for language teachers* (2nd ed). New York: Cambridge University Press.

Lloyd, D., & Davidson, P. (2009). Guidelines for developing a reading test. In C. Coombe, P. Davidson, & D. Lloyd (Eds.), *The fundamentals of language assessment: A practical guide for teachers* (2nd ed.). Dubai, UAE: TESOL Arabia Publications.

Olsen, D. R., & Torrance, N. (Eds.) (2009). *The Cambridge handbook of literacy*. New York: Cambridge University Press.

CHAPTER 25

Assessing Writing

Sara Cushing Weigle

INTRODUCTION

At first glance, it might seem that assessing writing in the classroom is a simple matter: Just give students a topic (or prompt) and ask them to write about it. As for scoring, experienced teachers often feel they know their students well enough to score the resulting essays fairly and consistently. However, even very experienced teachers often have questions about assessing their students' writing. These questions include the following: (a) Will students perform better on one type of prompt than another? (b) Should I focus on content, language, or some combination in scoring essays? (c) How accurately does a writing test really represent how well my students can write? By considering some of the research and best practices in these areas, language teachers are able to make informed decisions about how – and indeed whether – to assess writing in their classes.

BACKGROUND

In order to improve classroom writing assessment, it is important to understand some fundamental issues. These issues include the nature of writing ability, whether and when to test writing in the classroom and what the alternatives are, the qualities of good tests in general, and what research tells us about the two key elements to any writing assessment: the task (what we ask students to do) and the scoring.

WRITING ABILITY

Scholars do not all agree about whether second language (L2) proficiency or first language writing ability is more important in L2 writing ability. This is a particularly important issue for L2 writing teachers, because they need to know whether to focus more on writing strategies or vocabulary and structure development in their classes. Similarly, in assessing writing it is critical to define writing so that we can make informed decisions about tasks and scoring. Language proficiency and writing ability are highly interrelated and often inseparable, but frequently a student shows a fluent command of the second language – at least at the sentence level – without being able to organize their writing or address a writing task adequately, or a student may address the task adequately and use an appropriate organizational scheme but have weaknesses in grammar or vocabulary.

Thus, the central issue in writing assessment is defining the construct – are we more interested in the students' control of the building blocks of the language, or are we interested primarily in their rhetorical abilities, e.g., the ability to formulate and support a strong argument or to write in a specific style? The answer to this question is largely determined by the context and the proficiency level of the students. At lower levels of instruction, and in many foreign language (as opposed to second language) contexts, writing is often seen as a support skill for practicing the structures and vocabulary taught in class. In such situations test tasks need to be simple and not require students to generate new ideas or come up with their own organizational pattern. The scoring, likewise, will focus on the use of specific language items that have been taught. At higher levels of proficiency, particularly in situations where students will be expected to write in the L2 for school or work, the task itself will be more demanding and the scoring criteria are likely to place an emphasis on content development and organization of ideas, with linguistic criteria that include range and precision of language structures rather than accurate use of specific grammatical and lexical forms. When deciding how to evaluate writing – whether in a testing situation or through some other means – it is therefore crucial to consider both the proficiency level of the students and the importance of writing in the course and in the students' lives outside of class.

TO TEST OR NOT TO TEST?

One fundamental issue in writing assessment, particularly for classroom teachers, is whether or not to give writing tests at all. Most real-world writing is not done under timed conditions, and teachers may wonder how timed writings relate to writing performance under other circumstances. Furthermore, teachers may not want to devote limited class time to writing assessment and prefer to have students do their writing outside of class, when feasible. However, there are at least three reasons why teachers may choose to assess writing in this way. First, teachers may want to see what students can do without help and to ensure that the writing they submit is their own. Second, students may be faced with high-stakes tests, such as the TOEFL or IELTS, in which they will need to perform on a timed writing assessment. Third, from the perspective of second language acquisition, a writing test may function as a measure of automatized language knowledge and may thus give a truer picture of a student's proficiency than other means for evaluating writing.

At the same time, there may be legitimate reasons for evaluating students' writing abilities without administering timed examinations. A writing test generally consists of a limited number of tasks (often only one or two) and thus may not always be the appropriate way to judge whether a student has the appropriate skills to write on different topics or in different genres. It may be more appropriate for many classroom settings to evaluate writing that is not done under time pressure, as this is generally more authentic in terms of real-world writing. In non-classroom writing situations generally we have time to reflect, to consult sources such as dictionaries or reference materials, and to seek help and feedback from others. Thus, for many writing teachers, the idea of portfolio assessment, where students submit for evaluation several papers that have been revised based on teacher and peer feedback, is an attractive alternative to in-class tests.

QUALITIES OF GOOD TESTS

Once one has decided to test writing, it is important to understand the range of possibilities for assessing students, what the essential qualities of a good test are, and how to develop tests that maximize these essential qualities within the limitations of available time and resources. Thus, as in all tests, issues of reliability, validity, and practicality must be considered, both in terms of the task or prompt and in terms of scoring.

Reliability has to do with consistency of measurement. So, in terms of tasks, reliability concerns include making sure that the testing conditions are the same for all students (for example, students should be given the same amount of time to complete the task) and, if different topics are given to different students, they should be as similar as possible so that a student's chances of success do not depend on which topic they happen to be asked to write about. In terms of scoring, one of the most important reliability concerns is that scorers apply the criteria consistently to all students, and that, if there is more than one person scoring the assessment, all scorers apply the criteria in the same way.

Validity means making sure that the test is really measuring what we are trying to measure. To put it more precisely, validity involves making sure that the decisions made on the basis of test results are appropriate. In writing assessment, this means that high scores on a test are due to a student's writing ability and not, for example, the characteristics of the exam grader or the student's familiarity or interest in the topic. In terms of task, the most important validity concern is that the content of the test (what students are asked to write about) is representative of the skill(s) and knowledge being taught. There are two aspects of this concern: first, that students are not asked to demonstrate skills they have not been taught, and second, that the test covers an adequate range of skills. In terms of scoring, one important validity concern has to do with making sure that the criteria used to evaluate the written product are both stated clearly in the scoring rubric and are actually used by the person or people scoring the test.

Finally, a test needs to be practical; that is, the resources required to develop, administer, and score the test cannot exceed the resources available. For classroom teachers this will involve setting realistic expectations about how much time they can devote to developing test prompts and how long it will take to score the responses, as well as the amount of time that will be used for the actual test administration.

TASKS IN WRITING ASSESSMENT

In order to design appropriate assessment tasks, it is important to consider the many ways in which writing tasks can differ and how those differences may affect performance on writing tests. Weigle (2002: 63) provides a list of dimensions across which writing assessment tasks vary. These dimensions include factors such as the subject matter (what we are asking students to write about); whether students are writing from a "bare" prompt or in response to a reading passage, picture, or other input material; the cognitive demands of the prompt; how long students have to respond to the prompt; whether they are given a choice of prompt or not; and whether they write on paper or on a computer. Research on these aspects of writing has demonstrated that all prompts are not alike: Students perform differently on different task types; thus it is especially important to recognize which of these variables is most important in any given situation. For example, research tells us that prompts that are personal (i.e., prompts that require students to write about their own experience) are easier to respond to for many students but sometimes more difficult to score reliably than non-personal prompts. There are advantages to both types of prompts: Teachers will need to decide which is most appropriate for their own situation given the needs of their own students. As another example, research has consistently shown that students prefer to be given a choice of prompts to write on, but that they do not always make the best decisions, and giving a choice of prompts has the potential for making the results less reliable, since different students may be writing on different topics.

SCORING

The most important considerations in scoring include (a) designing or selecting a rating scale or scoring rubric and (b) selecting and training the people who will be doing the rating. Scoring an assessment can be either holistic or analytic (sometimes called multi-trait): That is, raters can either give a single score based on their overall impression of a piece of writing or can evaluate different aspects of performance separately – for example, by giving one score for content, another for organization, and still another for language use. A single score is usually preferred in situations where a large number of tests need to be scored in a short time, such as in placement testing. On the other hand, for classroom purposes, it is often more informative to give students separate scores for different aspects of writing such as content, organization, and use of language. A thorough discussion of different types of rating scales can be found in Weigle (2002, Chapter 6).

For classroom assessment, of course, the instructor will ordinarily be the person who evaluates student writing, but in many language programs, such as intensive English programs where there are either several sections of the same course or levels that students need to pass through, it makes sense for tests to be scored by people other than the classroom teacher. Whoever scores the assessment must be careful to be as consistent as possible in rating, so that the rating is fair to all students. It is common practice in large-scale assessments to have written responses scored by at least two trained raters, using a third rater if the first two raters disagree by a wide margin.

Research on raters has focused primarily on raters' background and experience; for example, scholars have looked at the differences between raters from different cultural and educational backgrounds, or raters with and without specific training. This research, summarized in Weigle (2002, Chapter 4) and Shaw and Weir (2007, Chapter 5) has shown consistently that these characteristics of raters can have significant effects on their scoring. That is, one rater group may tend to be more severe or more consistent in their rating than another group, or may tend to focus more on one set of concerns in rating than another. Since raters are human beings with their own biases, experiences, personality traits, and other differences, this research highlights the importance of minimizing the effects of these differences through the use of clear and appropriate criteria for rating and training raters to adhere to these criteria.

RESEARCH

Writing assessment as an area of research inquiry has expanded substantially in the past 30 years. Barkaoui (2007) provides a comprehensive review of research on essay tests, noting that the majority of such studies focus on the effects of writing tasks, features of the written product, and rater characteristics on test scores. The effects of task and rater have traditionally been viewed as factors that need to be controlled for valid and reliable scoring, whereas the characteristics of the essay itself are seen as the main focus of the assessment. However, recent scholars (e.g., Deville and Chalhoub-Deville, 2006) have proposed that variation in tasks and raters is natural and needs to be "understood and mapped" (p. 16) rather than suppressed. Underresearched areas, according to Barkaoui, include the participants (test takers) themselves, scoring methods, and contexts of assessment; these factors also affect scores but are less well understood.

Useful information about designing writing tests can be found in Weigle (2002) and other general test development books, such as Hughes (2003), particularly for foreign language / lower-proficiency testing. Hamp-Lyons (1991) has an edited volume that provides a good introduction to research on second language writing assessment. Two recent volumes on the development of major international tests include Shaw and Weir (2007), which provides an overview of writing assessment in the Cambridge suite of tests, and Chapelle et al. (2008), which gives information about the TOEFL examination. Teachers who are involved in portfolio assessment may be interested in Hamp-Lyons and Condon (2000). For a summary of the history of academic writing assessment, see Cumming (2009). Finally, for a comprehensive overview of the role of raters in writing assessment see Lumley (2005).

PRACTICAL APPLICATION

Much of the research on writing assessment has been carried out on large-scale tests rather than classroom tests. However, it is possible in classroom settings to combine what we have learned from large-scale testing with the advantages of the classroom. There is a lot of good information and research-based advice available on designing writing prompts and scoring procedures; much of this research is directly applicable to classroom testing even if it was conducted in large-scale tests. This knowledge can help teachers write better and more reliable tests. In addition, classroom teachers have advantages that are not available in large-scale testing situations. Specifically, teachers can evaluate writing that is done in class along with writing that is done outside of class to get a fuller picture of what students are capable of in both timed and untimed settings and in a variety of genres and formats. Furthermore, it is possible to prepare students to write on a specific topic by providing readings, discussion materials, and other input rather than simply giving them an impromptu topic to write on with little or no time for preparation, as is typically done in large-scale assessments. Finally, classroom teachers can use scoring rubrics that are specific to the assignment and to the instructional focus of the class and that provide useful feedback for students. Teachers can (and should) also supplement numerical scores with oral or written comments, and ideally an opportunity for students to revise their writing. In addition, instructors can share their rubrics with their students to enhance their understanding of the criteria by which they are being evaluated.

CONCLUSION: FUTURE DIRECTIONS

Writing is becoming an increasingly important skill for second language learners, especially in major world languages such as English. Therefore the need to assess writing ability in academic and specific work contexts is becoming ever more important. While there is still much that needs to be done in terms of increasing our understanding of writing assessment, one issue that is particularly pertinent is the impact of technology on writing assessment. This issue has two key components: First, to what extent is technology changing the process and product of writing? And second, what is the impact of technology on the scoring of writing? To address the first question, researchers have looked at both the process of writing on computer versus paper and at the quality of the written product (see Lee, 2002; Wolfe and Manalo, 2005). This research suggests that, in those places where computers are widely accessible, students generally produce higher quality essays on computer than on paper, although raters sometimes evaluate handwritten essays higher than otherwise identical word-processed ones (Powers et al., 1994). The implications of this development for writing assessment are twofold. First, as writing on computer becomes more and more common, it becomes more important to use computers for writing assessment so that writing in a test situation is as close to writing in non-test situations as possible. Second, in terms of scoring, rater training needs to address the differences between handwritten and word-processed writing so that the scoring process is fair and reliable.

As for the second question, there has been a great deal of interest, particularly within large test development companies, in creating automated scoring systems for writing. Research has demonstrated that, within a narrow range of prompt types, existing automated scoring systems are at least as reliable as human raters in scoring essays (see, for example, Chodorow and Burstein, 2004). However, this development has caused quite a bit of controversy and even suspicion among writing teachers, who are quick to point out that the computer cannot "read" the essay for meaning: In essence, it only counts things. While it is impossible to predict the future, it seems likely that automated scoring systems will continue to be refined, improved, and made more accessible to a broader audience. However, there is a general consensus among both researchers and practitioners that automated scoring will not, and should not, replace human raters in writing assessment; at best it is a tool that can assist people with the time- and labor-intensive work of making responsible decisions based on student writing.

Suggested resources

Crusan, D. (2010). *Assessment in the second language writing classroom*. Ann Arbor: University of Michigan Press.

Douglas, D. (2000). Specific purpose tests of reading and writing. *Assessing languages for specific purposes* (pp. 189–245). Cambridge: Cambridge University Press.

Hamp-Lyons, L., & Condon, W. (2000). *Assessing the portfolio: Principles for practice, theory, and research*. Cresskill, NJ: Hampton Press.

Kroll, B., & Reid, J. (1994). Guidelines for designing writing prompts: Clarifications, caveats, and cautions. *Journal of Second Language Writing*, 3, 231–255.

Weigle, S. C. (2002). *Assessing writing*. Cambridge: Cambridge University Press.

Discussion questions

1. What is the relationship between second language proficiency and writing ability? Considering your own teaching context, is it more important to focus on language ability or writing strategies?

2. What are some of the advantages and disadvantages of evaluating writing through timed tests as opposed to other means?

3. What are some of the considerations in improving reliability and validity of writing tests?

4. Consider the following two writing prompts, taken from a test of writing for academic purposes at a U.S. university. In what ways do they differ? How might these differences affect student performance?
(a) "Human rights" is a term frequently used but seldom defined. What rights should belong to every human being? Discuss.
(b) Name your favorite game or sport and explain why you find it enjoyable.

5. In your own testing or teaching context, is holistic or analytic scoring more appropriate?

6. What are some of the similarities and differences between large-scale and classroom writing assessment?

7. What are the advantages and potential problems of automated writing assessment?

References

Barkaoui, K. (2007). Participants, text, and processes in ESL/EFL essay tests: A narrative review of the literature. *The Canadian Modern Language Review*, 64, 1, 99–134.

Chapelle, C., Enright, M., & Jamieson, J. (Eds.) (2008). *Building a validity argument for the Test of English as a Foreign Language*. New York: Routledge.

Chodorow, M., & Burstein, J. (2004). Beyond essay length: Evaluating e-rater®'s performance on TOEFL® essays (TOEFL Research Report RR-04-73). Princeton, NJ: Educational Testing Service.

Cumming, A. (2009). Research timeline: Assessing academic writing in foreign and second languages. *Language Teaching*, 42:1, 95–107.

Deville, C., & Chalhoub-Deville, M. (2006). Old and new thoughts on test score variability: Implications for reliability and validity. In M. Chalhoub-Deville, C. Chapelle & P. Duff (Eds.), *Inference and generalizability in applied linguistics*, 9–25. Amsterdam, Netherlands: John Benjamins.

Hamp-Lyons, L. (1991). *Assessing second language writing in academic contexts*. Norwood, NJ: Ablex.

Hamp-Lyons, L., & Condon, W. (2000). *Assessing the portfolio: Principles for practice, theory, and research*. Cresskill: Hampton Press.

Hughes, A. (2003). *Testing for language teachers* (2nd ed.). Cambridge: Cambridge University Press.

Lee, Y. (2002). A comparison of composing processes and written products in timed-essay tests across paper-and-pencil and computer modes. *Assessing Writing*, 8, 135–157.

Lumley, T. (2005). *Assessing second language writing: The rater's perspective*. Frankfurt am Main: Peter Lang.

Powers, D. E., Fowles, M. E., Farnum, M., & Ramsey, P. (1994). Will they think less of my handwritten essay if others word process theirs? *Journal of Educational Measurement*, 3, 220–233.

Shaw, S. D. & Weir, C. (2007). Examining writing: Research and practice in assessing second language writing. Studies in Language Testing 26, Cambridge: UCLES and Cambridge University Press.

Weigle, S. C. (2002). *Assessing writing*. Cambridge: Cambridge University Press.

Wolfe, E. W., & Manalo, J. R. (2005). An investigation of the impact of composition medium on the quality of TOEFL writing scores (TOEFL Research Report RR-04-29). Princeton, NJ: Educational Testing Service.

CHAPTER 26

Assessing Listening

John Flowerdew and Lindsay Miller

INTRODUCTION

Listening has often been described as the "Cinderella" skill (Flowerdew, 1994; Flowerdew and Miller, 2005; Nunan and Miller, 1995). It is the language skill most teachers take for granted, and the skills many students spend less time on actively developing. The impression, from both teachers and students, is that listening is a language skill that can take care of itself. However, research in the past thirty years or so has demonstrated that good listening skills are fundamental to the development of the other language skills and the ability to develop good listening tests is important for the washback effect this has on teaching.

In this chapter[1] we present some of the main ways in which listening can be assessed. Many of the types of questions associated with assessment, or testing, also appear in the teaching of listening. However, there are significant differences, or at least there should be, in how questions are used to elicit comprehension, and how similar types of questions are asked to test comprehension. This chapter is necessarily brief; more complete discussions can be found in Brindley (1998), Buck (2001), Heaton (1990), and Thomson (1995).

BACKGROUND

Buck (2001) tells us that there have been three historical developments in testing listening. These developments correspond to the theories of language learning and to the different methods used to teach English over the past 60 years or so. The three approaches are:

- the discrete-point approach
- the integrative approach
- the communicative approach

The discrete-point approach is derived from structuralism and behaviorism. The focus of testing listening here is on the identification of isolated items of the language. That is, separate parts of the language are tested independently of each other; for instance, segmental phonemes, grammatical structures, and lexis are all treated as separate entities. The types of tests that can be used with the discrete-point approach are phonemic discrimination (identifying differences between phonemes), paraphrase recognition (reformulating what was heard), and response evaluation (responding appropriately to what was heard). The assumptions behind this type of approach to testing listening are that spoken text is the same as written text and that it can be isolated and tested as individual parts of the language. This is clearly not what listening is about and is rather artificial.

The integrative approach attempted to move away from the discrete measuring of language items by testing more than one item of language at a time. The main real difference between the discrete-point approach to testing and the integrative approach is that whereas in the former the product is the focus of the assessment, in the latter it is the process that becomes important. The techniques used with this approach are mainly: gap-filling exercises; dictation; sentence repetition activities; statement evaluation; and translation. With the integrated approach listeners have to process spoken text and demonstrate that they understand the literal meaning of what is said. The main criticism here is that this type of test does not move much above the sentence level. Language is rarely tested within a wider context.

The communicative approach to testing attempted to account for listening and understanding in a wide range of contexts. It takes as its main orientation a demonstration by the listeners that they are able do something with the information they have comprehended, that is, apply it to a wider communicative context. Language proficiency is now seen as being able to demonstrate a degree of communicative competence (Hymes, 1972). The characteristics of the communicative approach to testing are:

- focus on communicative performance as opposed to linguistic accuracy
- tests replicate as closely as possible conditions of actual performance
- need to identify skills and performance conditions of language use in specific contexts
- importance of sampling of relevant activities
- importance of authenticity of task and genuineness of texts
- use of un-simplified language
- need for a range of tests according to communicative purposes
- tests will closely resemble communicative teaching activities, except there will be no peer or teacher help (adapted from Weir, 1990: 10–14)

Although the communicative approach is well used in teaching and testing there are some problems with it. There are an enormous number of communicative events, and it is impossible to test them all. Also, there are many ways to react to a situation, many more than it is possible to test. Being able to perform in one test situation would not necessarily mean that the test taker could perform well in other communicative situations. Furthermore, communicative tests are more difficult to prepare compared with discrete-point or integrative tests. However, communicative tests have had a significant influence on language testing in recent decades and the basis of this type of testing is the most appropriate one we have at the moment. Two of the most important features of communicative tests are that the language of the tests and the requirements of the tasks are contextualized and that they are more authentic than the other types reviewed thus far; good communicative tests put the students into the sort of situations they might find in real life and ask them to do purposeful activities that they might also find in real life.

Understanding the approaches used in testing helps to frame our ideas about what and how to test. In this short chapter it is difficult to give a full account on all the possible ins and outs of listening tests. Here we will consider four practical issues: what to test, how to test, what to measure, and what grading system to use.

PRACTICAL CONSIDERATIONS

WHAT TO TEST

The type of listening test used will very much depend on the overall type of tests being administered. In *proficiency* and *placement* tests, the focus is on trying to discover what the learners know about the language. This is often done so as to admit students into specific courses. Therefore the test designer will prepare general listening-type test items. A number of different test items are required in order for the learner to demonstrate overall listening abilities. There should also be degrees of difficulty in the test items as the characteristics of such tests are to determine where the learner is in terms of proficiency level with respect to other learners, that is, it is *norm-referenced*.

With *achievement* and *diagnostic* tests the test designer has a different job. An achievement test aims to measure what the learners know after a course of instruction, that is, how much learning has been achieved. A diagnostic test acts more like a needs analysis. The learners demonstrate what they can already do, and then the course designer develops material to raise their proficiency to the next level. Both achievement and diagnostic tests are *criterion-referenced*. A criterion-referenced test means that learners are assessed on a pre-agreed standard. They must reach a certain level or standard in order to pass the test. The learner's test score is interpreted with respect to the set criteria and is not measured against the scores of other students.

Once the type of test has been decided upon, the test designer can begin to prepare test items. The first thing the tester has to do is make decisions about the most suitable types of questions that will be used in the test. There is a wide range of questions the tester can use, and so decisions have to be made about the question type, for instance:

- display versus referential questions
- focused versus open questions
- pre-, while-, and post-listening questions
- first language versus second language questions
- visual supported questions versus non-visual supported questions
- individual versus group questions

An important point to note is that achievement and diagnostic tests usually take place within existing language programs. As such, the teacher should make use of types of test questions that the learners have been exposed to during the course. It would not be appropriate to use certain types of questions in the teaching of a course, then use completely different types of questions in the tests – basically the learners would then be tested on their ability to handle unknown testing procedures.

HOW TO TEST

How to administer a listening test often relies on what the teaching environment is like. In privileged educational environments the teacher most probably will have access to language laboratories or high-quality sound-systems. In addition to this, the classrooms will be comfortable with little or no outside noise to disturb the learners. On the other hand, many secondary school contexts, especially in developing countries, have little or no technology available, and the conditions under which the learners have to take tests may be physically challenging. Consideration needs to be made as to what technical support is available, and how the test can effectively be administered to the learners so as to reduce the possibility of external factors affecting the learners' performance. Before preparing listening tests some of the following questions need to be considered:

- What approach to testing will be taken?
- What type of test is being developed (proficiency, placement, achievement, diagnostic)?
- What technology is available or required?
- What will happen in case of technical problems (is there a back-up plan)?
- Where will the texts come from: commercial, adapted, or self-produced texts?
- Will the learners have access to visual support as well as the audio message? How will this affect the comprehension?
- Will the learners be presented with authentic texts or not?
- What types of spoken text will the learners listen to: spoken by native or nonnative English speakers?
- How will learners demonstrate their comprehension (type of test items)?
- Who will take the test?
- How many learners will take the test?
- How will the learners take the test – whole group listens together, or in language lab with earphones?
- Who will supervise the test?
- What are the test conditions likely to be?
- Can physical factors, which might affect performance, be eliminated (e.g., closing windows, turning off noisy air conditioners)?
- How will the test be collected?
- How will the test be marked?

WHAT TO MEASURE

In developing listening tests the checklist of questions above may prove useful. However, the test designer needs to seriously consider if it is only listening that the test measures. In many instances the learners are tested on other skills and if students happen to be weak in say, reading, this may have an adverse affect on their ability to demonstrate their listening skills. Table 26.1 illustrates some common types of tests that are used to measure "listening," and what language skills are actually involved.

As can be seen from Table 26.1, it is very easy for the tester to think that the only skill being tested is listening. However, the learners' ability to handle other language skills is also important and the success or failure of learners on the test may rest not so much with their listening ability but with their reading, writing, or speaking proficiencies.

Thompson (1995) outlines some factors to consider when preparing listening tests:

- The closer the text is to oral than written text, the more appropriate it is for testing listening.
- Visual support is particularly helpful for lower-proficiency learners.
- Test passages should be short, around two or three minutes.
- Consideration should be given to the amount of prior knowledge that learners may require to comprehend the text.
- Specialized vocabulary needs to be avoided in general listening tests.

- Simplification of oral texts does not necessarily help the learner.
- Insertion of macro-markers may aid comprehension (e.g., *Today I am going to talk about . . .*).
- Speech rates that are very fast (above 200 wpm) should be avoided. (adapted from Thompson, 1995: 4–5)

Description of test	What skills it is testing
Learners listen to a description while they look at several pictures. They choose the picture that is being described.	Listening
The learner has a conversation with an examiner, or in a group with other test takers. The student's ability to interact and respond appropriately to the dialogue is measured.	Listening / Speaking
Learners listen to a dialogue and then choose the best answers from multiple-choice statements.	Listening / Reading
Learners listen to a story and then write a summary of the story.	Listening / Writing
Learners listen to an oral text. They read questions about the text. Then they write full-sentence answers to the questions.	Listening / Reading / Writing

Table 26.1   A selection of tests and the skills they test

In any discussion about what is being measured in language testing we come across the words *validity* and *reliability* (see Chapters 3 and 4 of this volume). Test validity refers to whether or not the test appears to test what it is intended to test. If, for example, we ask learners in West Africa to listen to a description of a Hawai'ian wedding, and the learner does not even know where Hawai'i was, then we are testing more than simple comprehension: we are testing world knowledge, the ability to deal with a lot of new vocabulary, and unfamiliar concepts. Table 26.2 overleaf illustrates the different types of validity we have to consider in test construction.

Test reliability refers to the consistency of the test. That is, if two different markers mark the test, will they get the same scores? Or, if the same marker marks the test on two different occasions will the same result be given? Or, if the test taker takes the exam twice will the scores be the same? Some of the factors which can affect test reliability are:

- The number of test items: Is there a big enough range of test items in the test to measure listening skills, or is the test only a measure of one particular aspect of listening?
- The administration of the test: Is the test administered in the same way each time it is given?
- Test instructions: Are all the instructions clear so that all test takers can follow them?

- Personal / environmental factors: Are the conditions for taking the test appropriate, that is, no one is sick, and the room is adequate for the purpose of a test?
- Scoring: What kind of scoring techniques are used? Objective tests – that is, tests which have agreed-upon answers, usually have higher reliability levels than subjectively marked tests – that is, tests where individual markers decide on the correctness of the answer.

Validity	
Face validity	This basically means: Does a listening test look like a listening test? If a test looks like it has been designed to test listening skills then it has face validity. The easiest way to check this is to ask a colleague to look at a test and tell you what it is measuring. Their answer will either confirm or nullify the face validity of the test.
Content validity	This refers to the degree to which the test actually measures the language it is intended to measure. With achievement and diagnostic tests, the test items must be in the course content. With placement and proficiency tests, then the content should try to measure different facets of listening, e.g., if a test had a lot of phonemic discrimination but no items on stress and intonation, then it probably would not have high content validity.
Construct validity	This refers to the relationship of the test to the approaches of language learning in a course. For instance, if a course approach is based on behaviorism, then a communicative listening test would not have construct validity.
Empirical validity	The empirical validity is the relationship of the test results to some other form of measurement such as: • other valid test scores • teacher's ratings • later performance on other tests In this way, if test scores match some other criteria for measurement, then the test is considered empirically valid.

Table 26.2 Types of test validity

WHAT GRADING SCALE TO USE

There are many ways in which to mark tests: percentage points, number scales, grade points, descriptors, and performance criteria. Whereas the discrete-point and the integrative approaches favor more detailed marking by numbers or grades, the communicative approach tends toward more holistic marking, such as descriptors (also known as performance indicators, or task criteria).

Carroll and West (1989) provide details of how to construct test descriptors, which they refer to as "yardsticks." The authors suggest twenty-two yardsticks, of which four are specific to listening, and use a nine-point scale with descriptions of what the listener should be able to do at each level. For example, at Level 9, the listener should be able to handle "all general listening operations, as well as those in their own specialist areas, with confidence and competence similar to that in their own mother tongue" and extract "the full content of the message without undue need for repetition or repair," among other things. At Level 5, the listener is expected to handle "moderate-level listening operations with competence and confidence" and to extract "major points of message but with frequent loss of detail and subtlety." At Level 1, a listener can handle "only the simplest listening operations such as short isolated exchanges (e.g. greetings, giving times, prices) and with little confidence" and extract "only basic or predicted messages or those translated using a dictionary or phrase book" (1989: 26–7).

CONCLUSION

This chapter has highlighted some of the important issues related to testing listening comprehension. Developing valid and reliable listening language tests is a complex process. This is because the processes of listening are hidden from the tester and so the ways to measure the ability to handle spoken text are more demanding. Three main approaches have been used to test listening and there are many ways in which listening tests can be devised. We maintain that the communicative approach offers the most opportunity for learners to demonstrate their comprehension ability.

Suggested resources

FCE

www.cambridgeesol.org/resources/teacher/fce.html
This site allows learners access to sample listening tests for the First Certificate of English test. The materials on this site are accompanied by answers so that learners can check their results immediately. The listening tests on this site follow the examination procedure so that learners get access to how the test will be conducted. Learners can save the listening tests onto their computer and practice listening to the tests more than once to get familiar with the type of listening involved in such a test.

TOEFL / IELTS

www.ehow.com/how_5883230_study-toefl-listening-test.html
www.ielts-worldwide.com/ielts-example.htm
There are many sites on the Web where learners can access TOEFL / IELTS listening test practice. These sites can be explored by the learners on their own and most of the listening material can be downloaded so that the learner can listen more than once to become more familiar with the type of listening involved. Or, the teacher can use such material in class and give students some "real" practice in taking the listening part of the test.

Young learners

www.123listening.com
The 123listening Web site contains listening material that can easily be used to help younger learners practice their listening.

Other Web sites

The following resources, although not directly related to testing listening, can easily be used as listening materials to prepare learners for their listening tests, or could be used as listening tests themselves.

Teachers Without Borders

http://teacherswithoutborders.org/resources

This Web site provides a space mostly for teachers who want to share their resources with others. Some sections of the site can be utilized for listening practice in or out of class. For instance, there are podcasts about recent news events, and video interviews with prominent people about issues in education.

TED

www.ted.com

TED is a free Web site offering short talks on a variety of topics by international experts. The talks are all highly entertaining and informative: The variety of topics ensures that there is something there to cater to everyone's interests. Teachers could employ this material for high-proficiency learners and apart from good listening practice, students are also exposed to excellent presentation skills. Most of the talks have links to the scripts of the talks so the teacher could use these in class for further language practice.

The British Council

www.teachingenglish.org.uk

The British Council Web site for teachers offers free downloadable materials. An example of what is available is the section on "Using traditional songs in class" (primary level). After explaining the rationale for using such songs in a language class there is a link for the teacher to follow and examples of some songs to utilize in class. There are also free listening lesson plans for teachers to examine.

Self-Access Learning

www2.elc.polyu.edu.hk/CILL/listenin.htm

Many universities now have dedicated Self-Access Centers, and they put a lot of their materials online for their own students and other students to use. A good example of this is the Polytechnic University of Hong Kong. The English Centre at the PolyU has a dedicated Centre for Independent Language Learning (CILL) and their Web site has some excellent listening material. This material can be used with a variety of students of differing proficiencies.

Discussion questions

1. For a group of learners you are familiar with, discuss what you believe are their main problems when taking listening tests.

2. How do you prepare your learners for any listening tests? Are your learners sophisticated about taking tests or do they need coaching beforehand?

3. Look at the list of questions in the section on "How to test." Think of a listening test you have recently given to your learners and discuss if you were able to meet all the challenges in making the conditions of the test suitable for your learners.

4. Look at a listening test you have recently given your learners, or look at one from a textbook. Is the test only about listening, or are other skills also tested? How could you change the test to ensure that the focus was only on testing listening skills?

5. Look at Thompson's (1995) factors to consider when preparing listening tests. Then apply them to a listening test you are familiar with, or take one from a textbook. Discuss the merits of the test based on Thompson's factors.

6. How can grading affect the feedback given to learners on a listening test? What type of grades / feedback do your learners expect?

References

Brindley, G. (1998). Assessing listening abilities. *Annual Review of Applied Linguistics*, 18, 171–191.

Buck, G. (2001). *Assessing listening*. Cambridge: Cambridge University Press.

Carroll, J. B., & West, R. (1989). *ESU framework: Performance scales for English language testing*, Harlow: Longman.

Flowerdew, J. (Ed.) (1994). *Academic listening: Research perspectives*. Cambridge: Cambridge University Press.

Flowerdew, J., & Miller, L. (2005). *Second language listening: Theory and practice*. New York: Cambridge University Press.

Heaton, J. B. (1990). *Writing English language tests* (2nd ed.). London: Longman.

Hymes, D. (1972). On communicative competence. Extracts in J. B. Pride & J. Holmes (Eds.), *Sociolinguistics* (pp. 269-293). Harmondsworth: Penguin.

Nunan, D., & Miller, L. (1995). *New ways in teaching listening*. Alexandria, VA: TESOL.

Thompson, I. (1995). Assessment of second / foreign language listening comprehension. In D. J. Mendelson & J. Rubin (Eds.), *A guide for the teaching of second language listening*. San Diego, CA: Dominie Press.

Weir, C. (1990). *Communicative language testing*. Hemel Hempstead: Prentice Hall.

Note

[1] This chapter is adapted from Chapter 11 of *Second Language Listening: Theory and Practice*, by John Flowerdew and Lindsay Miller, Cambridge: Cambridge University Press, 2005

CHAPTER 27

Assessing Speaking

Barry O'Sullivan

INTRODUCTION

This chapter begins with a brief overview of the area of assessing speaking before moving on to take a primarily practical look at the main issues related to task types and performance scoring. As with my earlier chapter on the test development process (Chapter 5) I will begin by focusing on larger-scale tests, but I will also present and discuss the type of test tasks that may be useful to you in the classroom.

BACKGROUND

It is commonly believed that tests of spoken language ability are the most difficult to develop and administer. Despite a growing understanding of spoken discourse over the past decade, there remain a number of areas of great concern to the test writer. Most notable of these concerns are the effect on performance of characteristics of the test taker and of the interlocutor, construct definition (what is it we are actually trying to test?), the predictability of task response, the validity, and the consistency of the scoring system.

RESEARCH

Although there has been relatively little research conducted in recent years into those aspects of spoken language testing referred to above, some really interesting work has been done to investigate the impact on performance of characteristics of the test taker (Berry, 2004; Kunnan, 1995; O'Loughlin, 2001; Purpura, 1999); of the interlocutor (O'Sullivan, 1995, 2000, 2002, 2008); of manipulating task performance conditions (Foster and Skehan, 1996, 1999; Norris et al.,1998; O'Sullivan et al., 2006; Ortega, 1999; Wigglesworth, 1997); of the development and use of different types of rating scales (or rubrics) (Fulcher, 1996; North, 1995); and of rater or marker performance (McNamara, 1996; McNamara and Lumley, 1997; O'Sullivan, 2000; O'Sullivan and Rignall, 2007; Wigglesworth, 1993).

You may now be thinking that this is just a long list of things that you will never get round to reading! Since you are probably right, I should briefly summarize what these researchers tell us; see Table 27.1.

Research Focus	Findings
Test Taker Characteristics	Obviously characteristics such as language ability impact on performance, but it also seems that things like test taker personality (introversion / extraversion); test taker age, gender, etc. impact when responding to particular topics.
Interlocutor Effect	When we consider the interlocutor in a test event, we should consider all of the above characteristics, as the person who takes on this role will be very likely to significantly affect the performance and score of the typical test taker.
Task Manipulation	It appears that the most significant parameter is that of planning time. If we add it, performance improves; remove it or reduce it, and performance worsens.
Rating Scale	The rating scale should be explicitly linked to what we are trying to say about the test taker – it should link our definition of the construct and the test task. So, if we are trying to make claims about how well our test taker will perform in a business meeting, then we need to know exactly what kind of language he / she will use in such a meeting, and how linguistic success might be measured in this meeting.
Rater Performance	The rater will (we hope) be mostly influenced by the test taker's performance when awarding a score – however, he / she may also be influenced by his / her affective reaction to the task, to the rating scale, and to the test taker.

Table 27.1 Summary of research findings

Before you can even begin to understand how and why all this is relevant, it is first necessary to think about the validation process. This is important because it can tell us how all the various parts of the assessment jigsaw fit together. Figure 27.1 overleaf gives us an idea of what the important elements of a speaking test are and how they fit into the testing system.

Tables 27.2 to 27.5 on pages 237–240 briefly explain what each of these elements mean. If you are interested in reading more about this, try Weir (2005) or O'Sullivan and Weir (2011).

PRACTICAL APPLICATION

In practice, we look at tests from the perspectives of possible format, task type, and rating scale. In the following subsections, I will briefly outline the most important aspects of these three.

TEST DESIGN

When we make our initial design decisions, we decide first on the people who will be involved in each test event (though, of course, choice of setup will obviously depend on the task types you decide to use; see the next section).

1. The most obvious setup in this regard is the *one-to-one interview*. This is the most traditional and the easiest to use in a classroom test, since you only need the teacher and

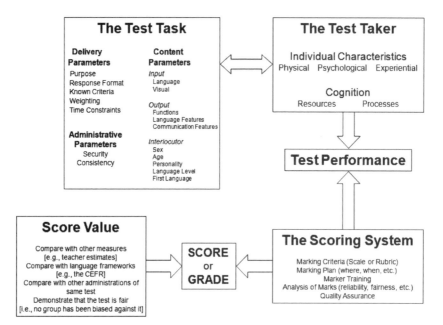

Figure 27.1   The speaking test

a student. The drawbacks are that the teacher may be influenced by factors other than the performance on the day (past performance, the relationship between the two, etc.).

2. The next most commonly used design is the student *monologue*. In this setup, the student is typically given some time to prepare a short talk on a given topic (often one to two minutes planning time for two minutes speaking time). Whereas this setup is only likely to result in one type of language being produced (informational functions), the fact that the test giver / teacher has control over the input and over the length of output means that it is likely to result in a similar experience for all test takers.

3. The other setup is the pair or *small group interaction*. Here, the test takers are asked to discuss one or more issues, often coming to a conclusion or decision. This setup has the advantage of allowing us to examine more than one student at a time, though it can be difficult for the less outgoing student to shine.

4. In the *recorded stimuli* setup, the test takers are asked to record their responses to a series of questions or short tasks that are played to them aurally. The questions or tasks used here can be the same or very similar to those used in the above three setups. This type of test is usually taken in a language laboratory, with the recording done either on tape or more recently directly on to computer.

5. Finally, we can always consider using *self-, peer, or teacher assessment* on an individual's performance in general (remember that if we ask for marks based on performance on the specific task, we are not really changing the setup but just the scoring system).

We then need to decide whether our test will be *live* or *recorded*. We are likely to base this decision on whichever of these five setups we would like to use. The advantages to recording are that there is a permanent record of the event, and that this can be later marked by more than one rater. However, some teachers point out that their students are often reluctant to perform at their best when they know they are being recorded. One solution to this is to regularly record classroom task performance or to include recorded warm-up materials at the beginning of any speaking test.

Physical / Physiological	
Short-term ailments	Toothache, cold, etc.
Longer-term disabilities	Speaking, hearing, vision (e.g., dyslexia)
Age	Suitability of materials, topics, etc. Demands of tasks (time, cognitive load, etc.)
Sex	Suitability of materials, topics, etc.
Psychological	
Memory	Related to task design, also to physical characteristics
Personality	Related in speaking primarily to task format (e.g., number of participants in an event – solo, pair, group, etc.; can impact on how shy learners will perform)
Cognitive Style	This refers to the way individuals think, perceive and remember information, or their preferred approach to using such information to solve problems (if a task is primarily based on one aspect of input such as a table of information, this may negatively affect some candidates)
Affective Schemata	How the candidate reacts to a task. Can be addressed by the developer through carefully controlled task purpose (even a sensitive topic can be addressed if the candidate is given a reasonable purpose – e.g., allowing a candidate to personalize a topic can help them negate many adverse affects) and / or topic (all examination boards have taboo lists – i.e., list of topics to avoid, such as death, smoking, etc.)
Concentration	Related to age and also to length and amount of input
Motivation	Among other things this can be related to task topic or to task / test purpose
Emotional State	An example of an unpredictable variable. Difficult to deal with, though may be approached from the same perspective as Motivation or Affective Schemata.
Experiential	
Education	This can be formal or informal and may have taken place in a context where the target language was either the principal or secondary language.
Examination Preparedness	Can relate either to a course of study designed for this specific examination, examinations of similar design or importance, or to examinations in general.
Examination Experience	Again can relate to this specific examination, examinations of similar design or importance, or to examinations in general.
Communication Experience	Can relate to any of the above, e.g., where communication experience is based only in classroom interactions or where the candidate has lived for some time in the target language community and engaged in "real" communication in that language.
TL-Country Residence	Can relate to Education (i.e., place of education) or to Communication Experience (e.g., as a foreign or second language)

Table 27.2a   The test taker (personal characteristics)

COGNITIVE PROCESSES

This refers to the mental process we go through to produce spoken language. This is too complex to discuss in detail here, but if you are interested you can read about the theory in Levelt (1989) or the practical application in Weir (2005).

COGNITIVE RESOURCES

Content knowledge

Internal	The test-takers' prior knowledge of topical or cultural content (background knowledge)
External	Knowledge provided in the task

Language knowledge – all references to Buck (2001)

Grammatical	Literal semantic level: includes phonemes, stress, intonation, spoken vocabulary, spoken syntax
Discoursal	Related to longer utterances or interactive discourse between two or more speakers: includes knowledge of discourse features (cohesion foregrounding, rhetorical schemata, and story grammars) and knowledge of the structure of unplanned discourse
Functional	Function or illocutionary force of an utterance or longer text + interpreting the intended meaning: includes understanding whether utterances are intended to convey ideas, manipulate, learn, or are for creative expression, as well as understanding indirect speech acts and pragmatic implications
Sociolinguistic	The language of particular socio-cultural settings + interpreting utterances in terms of the context of situation: includes knowledge of appropriate linguistic forms and conventions characteristic of particular sociolinguistic groups, and the implications of their use, or non-use, such as slang, idiomatic expressions, dialects, cultural references, figures of speech, levels of formality, and registers

Table 27.2b   The test taker (cognitive processes and resources)

TASK TYPE

Just what type of task we decide to use in our test depends on what we are trying to say about the students. In this section I will briefly present some options, and discuss their advantages and disadvantages.

1. One very commonly used task, particularly at the lower levels, is *reading aloud*. We usually give the person time to read the text silently before reading aloud to the teacher. This task is quite useful for assessing pronunciation and stress, though it should not be seen as an indication of a student's ability to actually speak. It is, however, quite difficult to assess as even native speakers vary in their ability to read aloud.

2. In a *mimicry* task, students are asked to repeat a series of sentences after the examiner. The results are then recorded and analyzed. Whereas we can test a large number of students at one time, and have control over the input (and output), the task is usually only of use at the beginner level and using it at any higher level can lead to student dissatisfaction.

DELIVERY PARAMETERS

Purpose	The requirements of the task. Allow candidates to choose the most appropriate strategies and determine what information they are to target in the text in comprehension activities and to activate in productive tasks. Facilitates **goal setting** and **monitoring.**
Response format	How candidates are expected to respond to the task (e.g., interview, interaction, monologue). Different formats can impact on performance.
Known criteria	Letting candidates know how their performance will be assessed. Means informing them about rating criteria beforehand (e.g., rating scale available on Web page).
Weighting	Goal setting can be affected if candidates are informed of differential weighting of tasks before test performance begins.
Time constraints	This can relate either to pre-performance (e.g., planning time), or during performance (e.g., response time)

CONTENT PARAMETERS

Input

Language	In terms of input this can be written or aural (input from examiner, recorded medium, etc.). Usually expected to be set at a level below that of the expected output.
Visuals	Visual input can include photos, artwork, etc. or graphics (charts, tables, etc.).

Output

Lexical, Structural, and Functional Range	Described in terms of a curriculum document or a language framework such as the CEFR.

Interlocutor

Sex & Age	Evidence that candidates tend to perform better when interviewed by a woman (again can be culturally based), and that the gender of one's interlocutor in general can impact on performance. Some evidence that age can have a similar effect in some cultures.
Acquaintanceship	There is evidence that performance improves when candidates interact with a friend (though this may be culturally based).
Personality	Related to candidate characteristics – evidence that candidates with different personality profiles will perform differently when interacting with different numbers of people.
Language Level	Where there is a significant difference between two or more test takers this can affect both in different ways (e.g., the better speaker may lower the level of their language to accommodate his / her interlocutor).
First Language	Can be dictated by the construct definition (e.g., where a range of accent types is described) and / or by the context (e.g., where a particular variety is dominant in a teaching situation).

Table 27.3 The test task

Criteria / Rating Scale	The criteria should be based on the theory of language upon which you base your test and reflected again in the contents parameters. They should also reflect "actual" language production for the task or tasks included in the examination.

Rating Procedures

Training	There is evidence that training improves harshness, consistency, and ability to stay on standard.
Standardization	Raters are expected to internalize the criterion level (e.g., pass / fail boundary) and this should be checked using a standardization procedure.
Conditions	All rating / examining should take place under optimal conditions. Where possible, these conditions should be set, so that all examiners have an equal opportunity to perform at their best.
Moderation	This involves monitoring the performance of raters to ensure that they stay on level.
Analysis	Statistical analysis of all rater performances will ensure that individual candidates will not lose out in situations where examiners are either too harsh / lenient or are not behaving in a consistent manner. This is the part of Scoring Validity that is traditionally seen as reliability (i.e., the reliability of the scoring or rating system).
Raters	When we discuss the candidate (in terms of physical, psychological, and experiential characteristics), we should also consider what we know of the examiners in terms of these same characteristics. Little research has been undertaken in which these have been systematically explored from the perspective of the rater.
Grading & Awarding	The systems that describe how the final grades are estimated and reported should be made as explicit as possible to ensure fairness. These are usually a combination of statistical analysis of results and qualitative analysis of the test itself.

Table 27.4   The scoring system

Other Measures	One way to find out if your test is doing what you intended it to do is to compare the outcomes with other criterion measures. These can be teacher estimates of learners' speaking ability, scores awarded on other tests of speaking, etc. However, we should be careful that we are making realistic comparisons. Just because two test scores are similar doesn't mean that the tests are similar, so choose your criterion measures carefully.
Language Frameworks	It has become more and more popular to compare a learner's language performance with established descriptors of language such as the CEFR. In terms of speaking, this can work quite well, as the speaking section of the CEFR is probably the best defined. However, the CEFR really only tells about the functional side of performance, as yet we know little about progression through the levels in terms of syntax or even vocabulary.
Multi-Administration	This refers to the stability of the test – if I administer it on a number of occasions, will test takers produce similar language and end up achieving the same (or very similar) score or grade?
Fairness	Is the test fair to all test takers? Topics or formats can be biased toward or against particular students. After large-scale tests, we often review the results (using statistics such as "differential item or test functioning") to check that groups were not affected. In speaking tests, we try to gather qualitative evidence of fairness from test takers and teachers.

Table 27.5   Score value

There is also a possibility that we are evaluating other skills such as short-term memory and listening.

3. In the *oral presentation* (or individual long turn) the student performs a monologue on a given topic (see Number 2). The advantage here is that the teacher has control over the input and the length of output. The teacher can also predict (at least in terms of language functions) the output, making it easier to score. However, to make a test fair we need different topics for the students to speak about. It can be difficult to ensure that these different topics are likely to elicit similar levels of performance. One issue of course is the time given to prepare. The optimum for a two-minute talk seems to be about one to two minutes – some teachers allow students to prepare prior to coming to class, making this a test of memory really.

4. When students work together in pairs or small groups, we often ask them to perform an *information transfer* task. This typically entails them sharing information (e.g., Student A has access to information X and Student B has access to information Y) provided by the teacher. This can be in the form of written text, photos, or charts, or even real objects (or a mixture of these). Although the task type is popular as it is likely to elicit a broad range of functions (informational, interactional, and discourse management), there are real issues with how to mark it. This is because the language outcome is the result of an interaction between the students, so exactly how to award scores to the different contributors is not always easy to decide.

5. The *role-play* task has been around for some time. Here students take on a specified role in an interaction and are marked on their ability to maintain the role. The role-play, which can be open or guided, has the advantage of resulting in realistic use of the language, though less outgoing students tend not to perform terribly well.

6. Within the *interview* task (see Number 1) we can have different formats. The interview can either be free, where the conversation unfolds in an unstructured fashion, or structured, where the test developer predetermines the series of questions or tasks. Whereas the former format appears to be truly authentic, it suffers from the likelihood that every test event will be different, making them impossible to compare. In either case, it is vital that the examiner is very well trained in how to deliver and score the test.

7. In a *discussion* task, the students are asked to interact among each other to talk about a given subject. Although there are issues for less outgoing students and for marking (how to award scores fairly as all participants can contribute in some way), the format is popular as it is seen by students as a truly authentic task. Occasionally, test developers try to broaden the discussion to include the examiner. In almost all cases this fails, as the power distance between the examiner and the students is too great to allow for a true interaction, so it typically degenerates into an interview with the examiner asking questions of each student in turn.

THE SCORING PERSPECTIVE

A major decision that needs to be made is how the test performance will be scored. By this we mean:

- What type of scale will be used?
- How will we decide on the score (e.g., what constitutes a pass)?
- Who will do the rating and how will these people be trained?
- Where and when will they do the scoring?

CRITERIA

Here, we have two broad choices, the holistic type or the analytic type. As with many other decisions that are made in language testing, the final decision as to which one to opt for is often down to practicality – for example, it may be unwise to ask an examiner who is also the interlocutor to award scores on a complex analytic scale since, as we will see, it involves awarding multiple scores (so the person just may not have the time to get involved in such a complex task).

The holistic scale offers a single global score or grade, based on a series of descriptors. Essentially, the examiner matches the performance to the closest descriptor. An example of this type of scale is shown in Table 27.6. The greatest advantage of the holistic scale is its simplicity and speed. In addition, it is relatively easy to train raters to agree to within a band of the observed performance (this is the typical level of agreement set in standardization procedures). However, the disadvantages of this scale include the danger of "trial by first impression," meaning that since the examiner is asked to give one score only, he or she may rely on his or her first impression of the candidate. The other danger is that the scale represents at best a crude measure of the ability we are attempting to examine.

	Band
9	Expert speaker. Speaks with authority on a variety of topics. Can initiate, expand and develop a theme.
8	Very good non-native speaker. Maintains effectively his own part of a discussion. Initiates, maintains and elaborates as necessary.
7	Good speaker. Presents case clearly and logically and can develop the dialogue coherently and constructively. Rather less flexible and fluent than band 8 performer but can respond to main changes of tone or topic. Some hesitation and repetition due to a measure of language restriction but interacts effectively.
6	Competent speaker. Is able to maintain theme of dialogue, to follow topic switches and to use and appreciate main attitude markers. Stumbles and hesitates at times but is reasonably fluent otherwise. Some errors and inappropriate language but these will not impede exchange of views. Shows some independence in discussion with ability to initiate.
5	Modest speaker. Although gist of dialogue is relevant and can be basically understood, there are noticeable deficiencies in mastery of language patterns and style. Needs to ask for repetition or clarification and similarly be asked for them. Lacks flexibility and initiative. The interviewer often has to speak rather deliberately. Copes but not with great style or interest.
4	Marginal speaker. Can maintain dialogue but in a rather passive manner, rarely taking the initiative or guiding the discussion. Has difficulty in following English at normal speed; lacks fluency and probably accuracy in speaking. The dialogue is therefore neither easy nor flowing. Nevertheless gives the impression that he is in touch with the gist of the dialogue even if not wholly master of it. Marked L2 accent.
3	Extremely limited speaker. Dialogue is a drawn out affair punctuated with hesitations and misunderstandings. Only catches part of normal speech and unable to produce continuous and accurate discourse. Basic merit is just hanging on to discussion gist, without making major contribution to it.
2	Intermittent speaker. No working facility; occasional, sporadic communication.
1	Non-speaker. Not able to understand and / or speak.

Table 27.6   Holistic rating scale (Carroll, 1980)

In an analytic type scale the developer first identifies the language operations involved in responding to the task(s) and then attempts to create a marking scheme specifically to reflect these operations. This results in a multi-faceted scale, each component of which adds to an overall score. The most famous of all analytic scales is the Foreign Services Institute (FSI) scale (Wilds, 1975), upon which most others have been based; see Figure 27.2. The analytic scale is composed of a set of components. To arrive at an overall score the rater awards an individual score for each of the criteria in the scale. Nowadays, these marks are either added together to find the total, or they are averaged. The original plan with the FSI scale was that the criteria should be weighted (i.e., each criterion contributing differently to the total) though the idea was dropped after it became clear that the weighting could not be justified empirically.

It is possible that these same criteria could be used to prepare a holistic version of the scale, by collapsing the different criteria into a single band. The analytic scale has been criticized for being simply a set of holistic scales – so that the distinction between the two is not at all as clear as we might first think. In this way, the analytic scale suffers from the same disadvantages as the holistic scale (magnified by the number of criteria included in the scale). The main advantage of this type of scale is that it can be more reliable than the holistic type – though with complex tasks it is more difficult to use accurately.

TEST LEVEL

What does it mean to pass? Some ways of doing this are:

1. Make a set of recordings over time and agree (with other teachers who teach at the level) which are fails, borderline fails, borderline passes, and clear passes. The mere process of doing this helps you to understand the critical boundary. The other advantage is that you have real examples to base your judgments on.

2. Use a well-trusted set of standards (such as the CEFR) and identify the level through the written descriptors contained there.

3. Combine the above two by first looking to the descriptors, and then identifying performances that match the descriptions you feel are relevant to your test.

THE EXAMINER

If you are the teacher, you may decide to swap with another teacher so that you are not examining your own students. This can help prevent any bias on your behalf (either toward or against students you know). You might also want to think about training – get yourself acquainted with the test tasks and with the rating scale. Ideally you should also try to fully understand the critical boundary between passing and failing so that you are consistent. Research shows that even a very basic level of training can improve reliability, at least in the short term.

THE RATING PLAN

It might seem obvious, but it is very important to make a plan for where, when, and how the marking will be done. If you have decided to use a "live" test design, then the decision is made for you (and maybe the decision as to which scale type to use as well). Otherwise

Accent

1   Pronunciation frequently unintelligible.

2   Frequent gross errors and a very heavy accent make understanding difficult, require frequent repetition.

3   "Foreign accent" requires concentrated listening and mispronunciations lead to occasional misunderstandings and apparent errors in grammar and vocabulary.

4   Marked "foreign accent" and occasional mispronunciations which do not interfere with understanding.

5   No conspicuous mispronunciations, but would not be taken for a native speaker.

6   Native pronunciation, with no trace of "foreign accent."

Grammar

1   Grammar almost entirely inaccurate except in stock phrases.

2   Constant errors showing control of very few major patterns and frequently preventing communication.

3   Frequent errors showing some major patterns uncontrolled and causing occasional irritation and misunderstanding.

4   Occasional errors showing imperfect control of some patterns but not weakness that causes misunderstanding.

5   Few errors, with no patterns of failure.

6   No more than a few minor errors during the interaction.

Vocabulary

1   Vocabulary inadequate for even the simplest conversation.

2   Vocabulary limited to basic personal and survival areas (time, food, transportation, family, etc.)

3   Choice of words sometimes inaccurate, limitations of vocabulary prevent discussion at some stages of the interaction.

4   Vocabulary adequate to participate in the interaction, with some circumlocutions.

5   Vocabulary broad and precise, adequate to cope with more complex problems.

6   Vocabulary apparently as accurate and extensive as that of a native speaker.

Fluency

1   Speech is so halting and fragmentary that conversation is virtually impossible.

2   Speech is very slow and uneven except for short or routine sentences.

3   Speech is frequently hesitant and jerky; sentences may be left uncompleted.

4   Speech is occasionally hesitant, with some unevenness caused by rephrasing and groping for words.

5   Speech is effortless and smooth, but perceptively non-native in speed and evenness.

6   Speech on all topics is as effortless and smooth as a native speaker.

Comprehension

1   Understands too little for the simplest type of conversation.

2   Understands only slow, very simple speech on the most basic topics. Requires constant repetition and rephrasing.

3   Understands careful, somewhat simplified speech directed to him / her with considerable repetition and rephrasing.

4   Understands quite well normal speech directed to him / her, but requires occasional repetition and rephrasing.

5   Understands everything in normal conversation except for very low colloquial or low frequency items, or exceptionally rapid or slurred speech.

6   Understands everything in both formal and colloquial speech to be expected of a native speaker.

Figure 27.2   The Foreign Services Institute (FSI) Analytic Rating Scale

it is important to set out a plan so that where possible all of the scoring is done under the same conditions – this will clearly help with the reliability of the system.

CONCLUSION

In this chapter I have presented a brief and, I hope, practical overview of how speaking is tested. I have also tried to present you with some idea of the theory behind my thinking, though I accept that this is really quite dense and not easy to assimilate. If you really feel the urge to know more, I'd suggest that you search out my book (O'Sullivan, 2008) or Cyril Weir's overview on validity (Weir, 2005).

While some people will argue that speaking is the most difficult skill to test, I disagree. As I hope this chapter tells you, it can be relatively straightforward if you are well prepared and are willing to accept that any test is a fine balance between all the competing requirements. Before this is possible you need to see the bigger picture, so having a working idea of the theory behind the test (Figure 27.1) will help you to begin to piece together the various pieces of the assessment jigsaw.

Suggested resources

Fulcher, G. (2003). *Testing second language speaking*. Harlow: Pearson Longman.

Luoma, S. (2004). *Assessing speaking*. Cambridge, UK: Cambridge University Press.

O'Sullivan, B. (2008). *Modelling performance in oral language tests*. Frankfurt: Peter Lang.

Discussion questions

1. What are key issues for you in assessing speaking in the classroom?

2. Are there any particular differences between what you are expected to do and what major examining boards currently do?

3. How do you take the test taker into account when you design your speaking tests?

4. How do you think training might affect examiner performance in classroom tests of speaking? What kind of training would be appropriate in your context?

5. These days, the paired-format speaking test is used widely. What are the main advantages and disadvantages with using this task type?

References

Berry, V. (2004). A study of the interaction between individual personality differences and oral performance test facets. Doctoral theses. London: The University of London.

Carroll, B. 1980. *Testing communicative performance*. Oxford: Pergamon.

Foster, P., & Skehan, P. (1996). The influence of planning and task type on second language performance. *Studies in Second Language Acquisition*, 18, 299–323.

Foster, P., & Skehan, P. (1999). The influence of source of planning and focus of planning on task-based performance. *Language Teaching Research*, 3(3), 215–247.

Fulcher, G. (1996). Does thick description lead to smart tests? A data-based approach to rating scale construction. *Language Testing*, 13(2), 208–238.

Kunnan, A. J. (1995). *Test taker characteristics and test performance: A structural modelling approach*. Cambridge: Cambridge ESOL & Cambridge University Press.

McNamara, T. F. (1996). *Measuring second language performance*. London: Longman.

McNamara, T. F., & Lumley, T. (1997). The effect of interlocutor and assessment mode variables in overseas assessments of speaking skills in occupational settings. *Language Testing*, 14(2), 140–156.

Norris, J. M., Brown, J. D., Hudson, T., & Yoshioka, J. (1998). Designing second language performance assessments. *Technical Report #18*. Hawai'i: University of Hawai'i Press.

North, B. (1995). The development of a common framework scale of descriptors of language proficiency based on a theory of measurement. *System*, 23(4), 445–465.

O'Loughlin, K. (2001). *The equivalence of direct and semi-direct speaking tests*. Cambridge: Cambridge University Press.

O'Sullivan, B. (1995). *Oral language testing: Does the age of the interlocutor make a difference?* MA thesis. Reading: University of Reading.

O'Sullivan, B. (2000). Exploring gender and oral proficiency interview performance. *System*, 28(3), 373–386.

O'Sullivan, B. (2002). Learner acquaintanceship and oral proficiency test pair-task performance. *Language Testing*, 19(3), 277–295.

O'Sullivan, B. (2008). *Modelling performance in oral language tests*. Frankfurt: Peter Lang.

O'Sullivan, B., & Rignall, M. (2007). Assessing the value of bias analysis feedback to raters for the IELTS Writing Module. In M. Milanovic & C. J. Weir (Eds.), *IELTS research in writing and speaking* (pp. 446–476). Cambridge: Cambridge University Press / Cambridge ESOL.

O'Sullivan, B., & Weir, C. (2011). Language testing and validity. In B. O'Sullivan (Ed.), *Language testing: Theories and practices* (pp. 13–32). Oxford: Palgrave.

O'Sullivan, B., Weir, C., & Horai, T. (2006). Exploring difficulty in speaking tasks: an intra-task perspective. *IELTS Research Reports* 7 (pp. 117–160). London: The British Council.

Ortega, L. (1999). Planning and focus on form in L2 oral performance. *Studies in Second Language Acquisition*, 20, 109–148.

Purpura, J. (1999). *Learner strategy use and performance on language tests: A structural equation modeling approach*. Cambridge: Cambridge University Press / Cambridge ESOL.

Weir, C. (2005). *Language testing and validation: An evidence-based approach*. Oxford: Palgrave MacMillan.

Wigglesworth, G. (1993). Exploring bias analysis as a tool for improving rater consistency in assessing oral interaction. *Language Testing*, 10(3): 305–336.

Wigglesworth, G. (1997). An investigation of planning time and proficiency level on oral test discourse. *Language Testing*, 14(1): 85–106.

Wilds, C. P. (1975). The oral interview test. In R. L. Jones and B. Spolsky (Eds.), *Testing language proficiency* (pp. 29–44). Arlington, VA: Center for Applied Linguistics.

CHAPTER 28

Assessing Students' Grammatical Ability

Wayne Jones

INTRODUCTION

If you ask a foreign language student what is one of the most important aspects of learning a language, he / she will invariably and instinctively reply: "grammar." Similarly, in terms of language teaching, the centrality of grammar went largely unchallenged for many years and the robust grammatical syllabus formed the backbone of many language textbooks and pedagogy.

Understandably, the assessment of our students' *grammatical knowledge* also changed little for many years; characterized by the use of discrete-point testing where grammatical structures were presented in sequences, traditional tests tended to utilize a very narrow range of test methods such as multiple-choice questions.

However, our understanding of the concept of grammatical knowledge and the role it plays in defining general *language ability* started to significantly change in the 1980s and 1990s. Although these changes did not diminish the underlying importance of grammatical knowledge, they did substantially alter our conceptualization of the construct of grammar and the way in which it should be taught and, more importantly here, how it should be assessed.

BACKGROUND

Although there is a certain amount of agreement today as regards the important role of grammar within *language ability*, Purpura (2004) has highlighted "the surprising lack of consensus when it comes to defining *grammatical knowledge* and developing tasks to elicit that knowledge for testing purposes" (p. 4).

The fact that grammar is important does answer the question: "Why should we assess grammar?" However, these two key issues – defining the construct of grammar and designing tasks to elicit performance from students that can be used to make inferences about their language ability – constitute the "what" and the "how" of the assessment of grammar.

WHAT ASPECTS OF GRAMMAR SHOULD WE ASSESS?

For language-testing purposes *construct definition* is vital in order for us to have a sound understanding of the particular skill or construct that we want to measure. Batstone (1995) refers to the "two fundamental ingredients" of *syntax* and *morphology* which together "help us to identify grammatical forms which serve to enhance and sharpen the expression of meaning" (p. 4). Without syntax, utterances would consist of a meaningless collection of unrelated words or lexical items; without morphology, we would be unable to modify verbs and nouns to indicate concepts such as time, number, and gender. These two aspects of grammar can also be jointly referred to as *morphosyntax*.

Bachman and Palmer's (1996) conceptualization of *language ability* also includes the knowledge of *vocabulary*, *phonology*, and *graphology* under the general heading of grammatical knowledge. Both *grammatical knowledge* (grammar at the sentential and sub-sentential levels) and *textual knowledge* (language at the discourse level) are subsumed under *organizational knowledge* (how language and structures are produced to form grammatically correct utterances and sentences).

Bachman and Palmer's work also built on earlier notions of *communicative competence* (cf. Hymes, 1974; Canale and Swain, 1980), which refers to a language user's ability to use his / her *grammatical knowledge* (e.g., syntax, morphology) to communicate through spoken utterances and writing. In this way, grammar is not only a set of abstract rules, but is fundamental to the creation of meaning. Thus, for Purpura (2004), *grammatical knowledge* embodies two closely related components: *grammatical form* at the subsentential, sentence, and discourse levels, and *grammatical meaning*, which includes both the literal and intended meaning of utterances and sentences as a way of accounting for "meaning in both content-impoverished (e.g., multiple-choice tasks) and context-rich (e.g., problem-solving tasks) test situations" (p. 63).

Finally, for testing purposes, an important distinction needs to be made between *knowledge* and *ability*. As they relate to grammar, a person's *grammatical knowledge* is represented by the structures that he / she has accumulated over a period of time and are stored in the person's long-term memory; *grammatical ability*, on the other hand, refers to "an individual's capacity to utilize mental representations of language knowledge built up through practice or experience in order to convey meaning" (ibid. p. 86).

HOW SHOULD WE ASSESS GRAMMATICAL ABILITY?

The notion of *communicative competence* raises a critical question: Why is it necessary to assess discrete grammatical items explicitly in a separate test when they could be tested implicitly through speaking and writing test tasks? Surely Speaking and Writing are more important than the individual abilities that constitute these skills.

Large-scale, internationally known and respected proficiency examinations, such as the Educational Testing Service's *Test of English as a Foreign Language* (TOEFL) and Cambridge University's suite of ESOL examinations, are revised and updated in light of research and developments in the fields of Second Language Acquisition and Language Testing and may therefore provide us with some insights into current thinking regarding this issue.

At the lower end of Cambridge University's range of ESOL exams, both the Key English Test (KET) and the Preliminary English Test (PET) assess the four main skill areas and do not incorporate a separate grammar component. On the other hand, the higher-level exams do contain a separate "Use of English" paper that, according to the First Certificate in English (FCE) Handbook (2007), "focuses on the language knowledge structures or system(s) that underpin a user's communicative language ability in the written medium" (p. 4).

Similarly, in the Internet-based TOEFL (iBT), there is no separate grammar test; candidates are awarded a composite score based on their performances in the four main skill areas. However, a substantial part of the Paper-based TOEFL (PBT) is devoted to grammar in the "Structure and Language" section of the exam.

Finally, the design of appropriate *test tasks* or *test methods* to elicit samples of performance that represent students' *grammatical knowledge* cannot be over-emphasized. In addition to the large number of factors that might negatively affect a student's performance on a test (e.g., personal attributes, language background, and motivation), "some of the most important factors that affect grammar-test scores, aside from *grammatical ability*, are the characteristics of the test itself" (Purpura, 2004: 100). For instance, it would be remiss of a test designer to create a test solely of traditional three- or four-option multiple-choice questions if the aim was to assess the extent to which test takers could actually use grammatical structures in given contexts rather than simply recognize them.

In terms of *test method effect*, Weir (2005) also points out that "the choice you make about format will critically affect the cognitive processing that the task will illicit" and that "you have to be certain that the technique you choose does not adversely affect the cognitive processing you would want to occur to answer the tasks you set" (p. 62).

Using a multiple-choice question as an example once again, although the test takers may actively attempt to identify the correct answers from the three or four choices available to them, this format may also allow test takers to answer the question through the process of guessing or eliminating unacceptable distractors.

LITERATURE REVIEW

The most comprehensive version of a multi-componential view of *language ability* for testing purposes is Bachman and Palmer's (1996) framework. Their explanation of *grammatical knowledge* has been criticized for being limited inasmuch as it focuses far more on grammatical form than on meaning. However, their multi-componential view of *language ability* does account for this aspect to a certain extent as *functional knowledge* and *sociolinguistic knowledge* incorporate the actual use of language in communicative contexts.

One of the issues raised earlier by such models and frameworks was whether or not a communicative approach to grammar necessitates the explicit assessment of *grammatical ability*. Weir (1990) specifically deals with language testing from a communicative standpoint.

As regards *construct definition*, Batstone (1995) provides a detailed description of many aspects of the construct of grammar but deals with it more from a teaching perspective. For assessment purposes, Purpura's (2004) insightful discussions focus solely on assessing *grammatical ability*. A detailed account of the development of the construct of grammar is provided.

In terms of designing test tasks to assess *grammatical ability*, Purpura (2004) devotes considerable time to task design and development. More practical information on designing tasks and the negative and positive aspects of individual task types can be found in Hughes (2007). Although not directly related to the testing of grammar, Weir (2005) examines the potential effects of test method on *theory-based validity* and discusses techniques for assessing the main skills.

Finally, it is worth mentioning that the handbooks that accompany language tests within the Cambridge ESOL suite of examinations are available in print and online (www. cambridgeesol.org). These are extremely useful inasmuch as they offer us a clear idea of the theories underpinning the assessment of constructs such as grammar in examinations, such as the previously mentioned PET and KET.

PRACTICAL APPLICATION

Let us now return to a number of grammar-related issues raised earlier as regards the importance of grammar; *construct definition* and the need to consider both *grammatical form* and *grammatical meaning*; whether or not we need to explicitly test grammar; and the desire to minimize *test method effect*.

Modern commercial textbooks usually adopt a multi-layered approach to syllabus design focusing on grammatical and lexical components as well as the main skills in an attempt to reflect the complex nature of language learning. On the surface, the four main skills of reading, writing, listening, and speaking may appear to be far more high profile than the underlying "enabling" or subskills; nevertheless, if we actually look closely at the textbook and the accompanying teacher's book, we may be surprised by the extent of their focus on grammar. Furthermore, it is also worthwhile remembering that "it has to be accepted that grammatical ability, or rather the lack of it, sets limits to what can be achieved in the way of skills performance (Hughes, 2007: 173).

For many teachers *construct definition* is tantamount to the course syllabus or outcomes. Most achievement tests used in language institutions, for instance, are based directly on these outcomes and curricular objectives, and it is common to find a well-developed grammatical syllabus in textbooks that forms the basis of grammar tests. These *syllabus-based construct definitions* enable teachers to directly assess students' mastery of a clearly defined set of grammatical structures. In contrast, *theory-based construct definitions* rely on theoretical models of language ability, such as the aforementioned models posited by Canale and Swain (1980) and Bachman and Palmer (1996). In addition, communicative language-teaching methodology has been with us for a long time and modern textbooks place great emphasis not only on correct grammatical form, but also on the effective and appropriate use of structures to convey meaning.

Whether or not we use a test to independently assess grammatical ability depends on the purpose of the assessment. There are occasions when the knowledge gained from detailed information is beneficial for teachers and students. For instance, diagnostic and placement tests often have a grammar element since detailed information may be required regarding a student's grammatical ability; a separate test is conducive to the assessment of a wider range of grammatical structures than can be tested when assessing a student's writing and speaking abilities. Furthermore, it is possible to test and score a considerably large number of items in a relatively short period of time. Similarly, in achievement and proficiency tests, the inclusion of a grammar component, such as the "Use of English" paper in the higher-level Cambridge ESOL examinations, might be deemed necessary simply as it can give us more information regarding students' grammatical ability.

Finally, the choice of appropriate *test methods* or *test tasks* is paramount due to the potential negative effects they might have on test performance. Weaknesses of testing formats like multiple choice, however, may often result from the way that they have been used rather than because of some inherent defect. For instance, employing only multiple-choice questions to assess a students' grammatical knowledge is severely limiting and may prove detrimental to a test taker's performance, so teachers should be encouraged to use a number of different question types depending on the structures they want to test.

This is certainly reflective of the current trend in large-scale proficiency tests, such as the International English Language Testing System (IELTS), where there is a desire to reduce the possible negative effects of specific test formats by using a variety of question types in the same test (Weir, 1990).

A helpful way to categorize test tasks is according to the types of responses they require from students: selected-response tasks, limited-production tasks, and extended-production tasks (Purpura, 2004). Here follow some examples of these types.

SELECTED-RESPONSE TASK TYPES

As the name suggests, in this task students are presented with an item and are required to select one appropriate response. These task types only assess students' ability to *recognize* correct or incorrect grammatical structures in their written form. Consequently, actual test performance will provide us with limited information about the extent to which a particular student is capable of using these grammatical structures in order to express himself / herself in writing or speaking.

Type A

Circle the correct answer:

I _____ hard last week, and now I'm tired.

A. studied

B. study

C. have studied

D. have been studying

Focus: knowledge of grammatical form (*-ed* affix denoting past tense) and meaning (past time reference)

Figure 28.1a   Multiple-choice tasks Type A

Type B

Circle the correct answer:

A: Is that a new dress? You look great in it.

B: Thanks but _____

A: That's not true. It really suits you!

a. I love it, too.

b. it makes me look fat.

c. you look great.

d. I like your dress.

Focus: knowledge of grammatical form and meaning (a compliment followed by disagreement signaled using "but")

Figure 28.1b   Multiple-choice tasks Type B

Type C

Match each question with the appropriate response:

Question	Response
1. Going to see a film tonight?	A. No, I didn't.
2. How was the film?	B. Yes, I probably will.
3. I can't stand war films, can you?	C. Actually, I quite like them.
4. So you went to the cinema.	D. All right, nothing special.

Focus: knowledge of grammatical forms (interrogative, affirmative, and negative verb forms and question tags) and meaning (present, past, and future time references and question / response adjacency pairs)

Figure 28.2   Matching task

Type D

Select the underlined word or phrase that is incorrect or inappropriate:

1. I am <u>worried</u> that you <u>will</u> be <u>angry</u> <u>to</u> me
      A   B   C D

2. There <u>are</u> many <u>reason</u> for the <u>increase</u> <u>in</u> crime.
      A   B   C   D

Focus: knowledge of lexical forms (adjective + preposition and plural noun)

Figure 28.3   Error identification

LIMITED-PRODUCTION TASKS

The task types included in this section require test takers to produce grammatical forms in different ways within a highly controlled manner.

Type E

1. *Make a sentence out of these words:*

is   today   very   it   warm   indeed

_____.

Focus: knowledge of syntactic form

Figure 28.4   Rearrangement items

Type F

Fill the gaps in the following sentences:

1. A: Quiet! We _____ (study) for the test!

   B: Oh, sorry. What kind of test?

   A: Grammar. We _____ (have + always) a grammar test at the end of term.

Focus: knowledge of morphosyntactic forms (verb *to be* + *-ing* and the position of adverbs of frequency in relation to verbs) and meaning (tense and aspect – present progressive)

Figure 28.5a   Completion / Gap-fill tasks

Type G

Fill in each gap with an appropriate word:

Mr. Francis: Good morning, Mr. Paul. Please come in and take a seat. Now let me see. Which college _____?

Mr. Paul: The Aviation College.

Mr. Francis: And when _____?

Mr. Paul: At the end of the summer last year.

Focus: knowledge of grammatical form (interrogative form of the past tense) and meaning (past time reference signaled by the final sentence)

Figure 28.5b   Completion / Gap-fill tasks

Type H

Complete the sentences:

a. Fatema has been very successful at school. She always listens to her teachers and always does the assignments. *(because)*

_____.

b. You will be able to buy a brand new car. You save a little money every month. *(if)*

_____.

Focus: knowledge of grammatical forms (subordinating conjunctions and dependent clauses) and meanings (causal and conditional relationships between two facts)

Figure 28.5c   Completion / Gap-fill tasks

> **Type I**
>
> *Rewrite these sentences:*
>
> 1. It's been six years since I last saw him.
>
> I _____ .
>
> 2. She is good at tennis.
>
> She plays _____ .
>
> **Focus**: knowledge of lexical form and meaning (adjective + preposition) and morphosyntactic form and meaning (present perfect tense and aspect and changing the adjective *good* to its adverbial form *well*

Figure 28.6   Paraphrase / Transformation tasks

EXTENDED-PRODUCTION TASKS

These tasks measure an examinee's ability to use grammatical forms and structures to convey meaning at discourse level through writing and speaking. Input is provided in the form of a prompt that elicits performance from which we can assess the extent of a student's *grammatical ability*. The assessment of *grammatical ability* is usually carried out with reference to holistic or analytic scales where grammar is only one aspect of the *communicative language ability* being assessed. An assessment of a test taker's *grammatical ability* in this context can be made in terms of the accuracy and range of grammatical structures that are deployed, as well as sentence level complexity.

Tasks in this category were referred to earlier as being "context-rich" and could include essays and report writing and speaking tasks involving information and problem solving, simulation, and role-play activities.

CONCLUSION: FUTURE DIRECTIONS

Although limited in scope, this discussion has attempted to demonstrate the advances made in the assessment of grammar over recent years in response to a shift in focus away from linguistic form and accuracy to the more communicative aspects of language use.

As regards construct definition, Purpura (2004) has extended Bachman and Palmer's (1996) conceptualization of grammatical knowledge by formulating a definition of this concept that incorporates both grammatical form and grammatical meaning. However, this distinction does raise some theoretical challenges since "making finer distinctions between form and meaning will require adjustments in how we approach grammar assessment and may require innovation" (p. 257).

From a communicative perspective, it is interesting to consider what an examinee's performance on a test actually indicates about his / her ability to perform in real life or target language use (Bachman and Palmer, 1996) situations. If the aim of teaching is to prepare students to do this, then multiple-choice test questions, for example, are not appropriate and *extended-production tasks* would probably be more suitable. However, in the case of such tasks, it has to be remembered that detailed assessment criteria also need to be generated and piloted, which can be a very time-consuming process.

Finally, when constructing a valid test of grammar, the notion of *test method effect* is paramount. Research in this area has tended to focus on a small number of task types such as multiple choice; more research on other test types using techniques such as think aloud is sorely needed. When creating grammar tests, teachers and test designers have to ensure they select the appropriate task types to elicit the kind of performance from test takers which will allow them to make valid and complete assessments of their *grammatical ability*.

Suggested resources

The development of theoretical models and frameworks of *communicative language ability* and *grammatical ability*:

Bachman, L. F. (1990). *Fundamental considerations in language testing*. Oxford: Oxford University Press.

Bachman, L. F., & Palmer, A. S. (2010). *Language assessment in practice*. Oxford: Oxford University Press.

Fulcher, G., & Davidson, F. (2007). *Language testing & assessment: An advanced resource book*. New York: Routledge.

Linguistic systems and English grammar:

Celce-Murcia, M., & Larsen-Freeman, D. (1999). *The grammar book: An ESL/EFL teacher's course* (2nd ed.). Boston, MA: Heinle & Heinle.

The designing of test tasks and examples of test formats for *assessing grammatical knowledge*:

Coombe, C., Folse, K., & Hubley, N. (2007). *A practical guide to assessing English language learners*. Ann Arbor, MI: University of Michigan Press.

Folse, K. S., Ivone, J., & Pollgreen, S. (2005). *101 grammar tests: Reproducible grammar tests for ESL/EFL classes*. Ann Arbor, MI: University of Michigan Press.

Heaton, J. B. (1995). *Writing English language tests*. New York: Longman.

The *role of grammar* at the discourse or suprasentential level:

Luoma, S. (2004). *Assessing speaking*. Cambridge: Cambridge University Press.

Cushing Weigle, S. (2002). *Assessing writing*. Cambridge: Cambridge University Press.

The *relationship* between second language acquisition and the testing of grammar:

Ellis, R. (2001). Some thoughts on testing grammar: An SLA perspective. In Elder, C., Brown, A., Grove, E., Hill, K., Iwashita, N., Lumley, T., McNamara, T., & O'Loughlin, K. (Eds.), *Experimenting with uncertainty: Essays in honour of Alan Davies* (pp. 251–263). Cambridge: Cambridge University Press.

Discussion questions

1. Given that assessment systems usually weight skills and subskills according to their perceived importance, is grammar adequately assessed and represented within your assessment system?

2. Do the grammar tests you use elicit a representative sample of students' grammatical knowledge? Do these grammar tests focus mainly on form, meaning, or both?

3. How important is grammatical accuracy in relation to the communication effect of grammatical utterances and sentences?

4. What task types are appropriate for the different grammar tests that are administered in your institution?

References

Bachman, L. F., & Palmer, A. S. (1996). *Language testing in practice*. Oxford: Oxford University Press.

Batstone, R. (1995). *Grammar*. Oxford: Oxford University Press.

Cambridge ESOL (2007). *First Certificate in English: Handbook for teachers*. Cambridge: University of Cambridge Local Examinations Syndicate.

Canale, M., & Swain, M. (1980). Theoretical bases of communicative approaches to second language teaching and testing. *Applied Linguistics*, 1(1), 1–47.

Hughes, A. (2007). *Testing for language teachers*. Cambridge: Cambridge University Press.

Hymes, D. (1974). *Foundations in sociolinguistics*. Philadelphia, PA: University of Pennsylvania Press.

Purpura, J. E. (2004). *Assessing grammar*. Cambridge: Cambridge University Press.

University of Cambridge ESOL Examinations. (2007). *First Certificate in English. Handbook for teachers for examinations from December 2008*. Cambridge: Cambridge University Press.

Weir, C. J. (1990). *Communicative language testing*. Hemel Hempstead: Prentice Hall.

Weir, C. J. (2005). *Language testing and validation. An evidence-based approach*. New York: Palgrave MacMillan.

CHAPTER 29

Assessing Vocabulary

John Read

INTRODUCTION

The first question in defining this area is: What is vocabulary? Our everyday concept of vocabulary is very much influenced by our experience with dictionaries, which present words as independent semantic units, each with its own entry. The fact is that content words can be treated as meaningful units by themselves to a much greater extent than other linguistic elements like sounds, letters, morphemes, or function words. Thus, conventional vocabulary tests assess knowledge of the meaning of particular content words (nouns, verbs, adjectives, and adverbs) selected from a list, which may in fact have been previously given to the learners to study, either as a stand-alone list or as a component of a unit in their textbook.

Even if we restrict our attention to content words, there is still the issue of what constitutes a word. Headwords in a dictionary are technically known as *lemmas*, which represent several different word forms. For instance, the verb lemma *write* covers *write*, *writes*, *writing*, and *wrote*, whereas the noun lemma *minister* includes *ministers*, *minister's* and *ministers'*. We normally regard these as different grammatical forms of the same word. On the other hand, another way of grouping word forms is as members of the same word family. If we take the word *attract*, we can recognize that it is closely connected in meaning and form not only to *attracts*, *attracting*, and *attracted* (the lemma forms) but also *attractive*, *attraction(s)*, *attractively*, *attractiveness*, and indeed *unattractive*. The words share a core meaning but are differentiated by part of speech and particular contexts of use. The question here is whether we take just the headword of the family (say, *attract*) as the item to be assessed, or do we need to test knowledge of individual members of the family as well? This has obvious implications for one basic purpose of vocabulary assessment, which is to estimate how many words a learner knows overall.

A further complication in considering the nature of vocabulary is that lexical units do not consist of just a single word. One category is compound nouns, like *bank account*, *speed limit*, and *pocket money*. Another familiar challenge for learners is represented by phrasal verbs such as *set out*, *put up with*, and *take over*. Then there are common set phrases like *in addition*, *on time*, *on the other hand*, and *as well as*. One more traditional focus of attention in vocabulary learning are idioms of the *kick the bucket* and *barking up the wrong tree* variety, where the meaning is not transparent even if the individual words are known. It is important to keep in mind this wider perspective on vocabulary as comprising multiword units as well as individual word forms. Thus, although the term "word" has been used as a matter of convenience in the discussion that follows, it should be understood as referring to larger lexical units as well.

BACKGROUND

It is a commonsense notion that vocabulary knowledge is a core component of competence in a second language but that does not necessarily mean that tests of word knowledge have always been an accepted component of language teaching. In the heyday of the communicative approach in the 1980s, it was argued that a test of learners' knowledge of individual words was not very informative because what really counted was the ability to process words rapidly as an integral part of carrying out authentic comprehension or production activities. An associated idea was that learners would naturally acquire knowledge of vocabulary through interaction and meaningful engagement with the target language, particularly if they were living in an environment where the language was widely used around them.

However, fashions change and formal vocabulary study has made a decisive comeback in the literature from the 1990s on – which is not to say that it ever went out of fashion for most ordinary teachers and learners. From the learner perspective, words are salient in the sense that, even at an advanced level, learners are very conscious of lacking vocabulary for concepts and ideas that they can readily express in their mother tongue. Thus, the development of an adequate vocabulary knowledge is one of the key challenges for learners and, especially for those in foreign language environments, conscious study and memorizing of words is an indispensable means of building the vocabulary knowledge they need, in the first instance, to pass their exams but more importantly to meet whatever communicative needs they have in the second language.

A fundamental concept in vocabulary studies – and therefore in assessment – is word frequency. In English, as in any language, a small number of words occur very often in any kind of written or spoken text, whereas most of the vocabulary is low in frequency. The most frequent words in English are function words – *the*, *of*, *and* – but content words, like *say*, *make*, *man*, *time*, and *go*, are also very common. It is generally accepted that priority should be given in vocabulary learning to high-frequency vocabulary, which for English is conventionally defined as the 2,000 most commonly occurring word families, accounting for at least 80 percent of the running words in any text. As learners advance in their proficiency, the lower-frequency words they need to learn become more diverse, depending on their communicative needs, their interests, their subjects of study, their job requirements, and so on – but still the general principle applies, that more frequent words should have priority in learning and assessment. Conversely, the assumption underlying a great deal of work in vocabulary assessment is that the more frequently a word occurs, the more likely it is to be known. Research shows that this applies broadly to most learners. In the case of English vocabulary, though, speakers of French, Spanish, and other Romance languages constitute an exception to this pattern, because historically English has borrowed a large number of lower-frequency words from Latin and French, and thus Romance language speakers are likely to be more familiar with these words than with high-frequency English vocabulary of Germanic origin.

In vocabulary assessment the most obvious application of word frequency data is in tests of vocabulary size, which sample across frequency levels to produce an overall estimate of how many words a learner knows. Computer corpus analysis has enormously increased our capacity to obtain frequency data for English as a whole (as in the lists from the British National Corpus: http://ucrel.lancs.ac.uk/bncfreq and the American National Corpus: www.anc.org), as well as for more specific domains of language use (such as the Academic Word List: www.victoria.ac.nz/lals/resources/academicwordlist). Most major learner dictionaries now use such corpus data to draw readers' attention to more frequent words by various forms of highlighting and coding.

Whatever the source of the frequency information, vocabulary size tests normally take a large sample of target words from a range of frequency levels and use a simple item format to test whether each word is known. This usually involves matching each word with a synonym, a short definition, or an L1 translation. Here is an example of a matching format. In this particular case, the test takers write the number of the word next to the corresponding definition.

1. authority

2. culture
          _____ beliefs and customs of a group
3. injury
          _____ something that can be used when needed
4. range
          _____ checking the quality of something
5. evaluation

6. resource

Corpus analysis also provides much better quality information about the contemporary usage of words in both spoken and written form. This leads us to a consideration of another concept which has become influential: depth of vocabulary knowledge. The argument is that learners need to be able to do more than just match the form of an L2 word with its meaning if they are to use their vocabulary knowledge effectively for communicative purposes. Depth of knowledge has been conceived in a number of ways, which have varying implications for the design of vocabulary assessments (Read, 2004). If we take the *attract* word family used as an example above, one aspect of depth is knowing the main members of the family and their grammatical functions, as verb, noun, adjective, or adverb. In terms of frequency, *attract* is a very common word (in the second thousand frequency band) but not as frequent as *draw*, which has a similar meaning in certain contexts. On the other hand, *attract* is broader in meaning than the less frequent words *entice* and *lure*. Synonyms of *attractive* include *pleasant*, *desirable*, *good-looking*, and *appealing*. The collocations *physical attraction* and *tourist attraction* are both very frequent, but *attraction* has a somewhat different meaning in each case, and so on.

Clearly, there are numerous aspects involved in a "full" knowledge of this word family, but it is impractical to test individual words so comprehensively. There is no agreement on what the key components of depth of vocabulary knowledge are and no standard test of depth. Meara (2009) argues that depth should not be seen as associated with individual words but with the overall state of learners' vocabulary knowledge, as reflected in the density of connections among the words they know. For example, in a Web-based test called V_Six (co-developed by Meara with Clarissa Wilks and Brent Wolter), the learners select from sets of six words a pair of words that are related in meaning. However, the measures devised for this purpose remain research instruments rather than practical assessment tools.

RESEARCH

The most thorough review of research on this topic can be found in Read's (2000) book, which as part of a series on language assessment also considers how vocabulary testing relates to the field as a whole. A recent volume by Milton (2009) covers more up-to-date research, especially studies undertaken by staff and doctoral students at Swansea University, a noted center for vocabulary studies in the UK. A major focus of Milton's book is on tracking the growth of vocabulary size among various groups of learners and exploring the variables that might influence that growth. Nation's (2001) comprehensive volume on L2 vocabulary research and practice has one chapter devoted specifically to testing but much of the rest of the book's content also has relevance for vocabulary assessment.

Probably the single most influential and widely used L2 vocabulary test has been Nation's Vocabulary Levels Test (VLT), which was originally developed in the early 1980s to provide classroom teachers with a profile of their learners' word knowledge at five different frequency levels. Subsequently, revised and expanded versions of the test were validated on a large scale by Schmitt, Schmitt, and Clapham (2001). Although it is often treated as such, the VLT is not strictly a measure of overall vocabulary size. For that purpose, Nation has now developed the Vocabulary Size Test (VST), which samples from the 14,000 most frequent word families in English, using a multiple-choice format, with options that require learners to have more than just a general understanding of what the target word means, as in this example:

restore: It has been restored.

a.   said again

b.   given to a different person

c.   given a different price

d.   made like new again

Beglar (2010) investigated the validity of the VST with Japanese learners of English at various proficiency levels, obtaining very positive results.

PRACTICAL APPLICATION

As already noted, the VLT and VST are examples of vocabulary size tests, which can be used to estimate the total number of words a learner knows. Tests of this kind are useful for placement purposes, providing one efficient basis for assigning students to classes in a multi-level language-teaching program. They also have diagnostic value, in indicating whether the learner has adequate vocabulary knowledge to undertake particular reading tasks, such as reading a simplified novel, a newspaper, or a university textbook. Another kind of screening role for vocabulary tests is illustrated by DIALANG (www.lancs.ac.uk/researchenterprise/dialang/about.htm), the Web-based diagnostic system that allows learners of 14 major European languages to assess their proficiency in the target language and get advice on how they can further enhance their skills. DIALANG includes a 50-item vocabulary test which, along with a self-assessment instrument, has the function of determining whether the learner is at an elementary, intermediate, or more advanced level, so that when the learner moves on to take one or more of the specific skills tests, they can be presented with items at the appropriate level of difficulty.

This highlights the point that vocabulary tests are useful not only for assessing vocabulary knowledge but also as a broad measure of the level of a learner's language competence.

It is well established in reading research that, for both native speakers and L2 learners, vocabulary knowledge is the single best predictor of reading comprehension ability. And in his research on DIALANG, Alderson (2005) found substantial correlations (.61 to .70) between the vocabulary-screening measure and the tests of reading, listening, writing, and grammar. However, the use of vocabulary tests in this way should be confined to low-stakes purposes such as placement, diagnosis, and research. For high-stakes proficiency and achievement testing, it is necessary to assess the learners' ability through a range of tasks that more closely simulate actual communicative uses of the language.

In the classroom context, vocabulary tests normally have a narrower focus than the learners' total word knowledge. The nature and scope of vocabulary assessment will depend on how much specific attention is paid to vocabulary learning in the textbook and in the teaching syllabus that the teacher follows. In the early stages of language learning, encouraging learners to build their knowledge of high-frequency words and phrases is important, and regular vocabulary tests have a role in providing the necessary motivation. A useful distinction can be made between *recognition* and *recall* tests. In recognition, learners are presented with L2 words plus possible definitions and are required to link each word to its meaning, by means of test formats such as multiple choice, matching, and picture identification, as in the examples previously given. Recall tests are more demanding, since they present the learners with a meaning and prompt them to supply the appropriate L2 word, using formats like filling a gap in a sentence, translating an L1 word into its L2 equivalent, and labeling a picture or diagram. An example of a gap-filling item is the following, designed to test the word *audience*:

> After the talk, the speaker invited the _____ to ask questions.

Recognition and recall tests may assess not just the link between meaning and form but also various aspects of depth of knowledge, as discussed in the paragraph above. For instance, the learners may be required to show that they can identify various members of a word family and their respective parts of speech; they may be asked to supply words that can collocate with the target word; or they may need to compose a sentence which correctly includes the word. Here is a format to test knowledge of verb–noun collocations:

> *Which of these verbs* – do, make *or* take – *goes together with each of the following nouns?*
>
> _____ a holiday
>
> _____ a mistake
>
> _____ some homework

To complement recognition and recall tests, particularly as the learners' proficiency advances, it is important to assess vocabulary ability through communicative tasks. This means that vocabulary is just one component of the assessment rather than the main focus. In the assessment of reading and listening comprehension ability, it is common practice to include a number of test items that test learners' ability to understand certain keywords and key phrases in context and even in the absence of explicit vocabulary items, limited vocabulary knowledge is likely to be reflected in poor performance in such tests overall. In speaking and writing assessment, it is not possible to specify in advance which particular words will be tested, unless the task is a very controlled one; rather, learners are judged on their ability to use vocabulary correctly and appropriately in relation to the task. A number of lexical statistics have been devised to measure aspects such as the range of different words used, the percentage of content words, and the percentage of low-frequency words, but this is another case where research tools are not suitable for practical assessment. The alternative is to specify vocabulary use as one of the assessment criteria for a speaking or writing task, to be allocated a certain number of marks or rated on a scale.

CONCLUSION

There are certain limitations in contemporary vocabulary assessment, which will be mentioned here by way of a conclusion. The first is that vocabulary studies have always been strongly associated with the written language, and with reading in particular. Corpus analysts are starting to redress the balance at one level by undertaking the still laborious task of transcribing spoken texts and looking at the frequency and usage of vocabulary items in speech. However, vocabulary assessment is still overwhelmingly conducted through the written medium. Milton (2009) reports on his research with a spoken vocabulary size test called AuralLex but it has not yet been released for general use. A related point is that speed of access to vocabulary is rarely measured in tests, even though automatic recognition of high-frequency words is a prerequisite for fluency in both spoken and written uses of language.

One final limitation was mentioned at the outset: the focus on individual words. One current trend in vocabulary studies – again under the strong influence of corpus analysis – is a greater recognition of the role of multiword lexical units in normal language use. These formulaic sequences include idioms but also a much wider range of common expressions that contribute to the fluency of proficient users. A new Academic Formulas List (Simpson-Vlach and Ellis, 2010) provides one basis for selecting relevant lexical items, but it remains to be seen whether they should be assessed through conventional test formats or through some new approach to assessment.

Suggested resources

Cobb, T. (n.d.) The Compleat Lexical Tutor. Available online at: www.lextutor.ca/tests.

Milton, J. (2009). *Measuring second language vocabulary acquisition*. Bristol, UK: Multilingual Matters.

Nation, I. S. P. (2001). *Learning vocabulary in another language*. Cambridge: Cambridge University Press.

Read, J. (2000). *Assessing vocabulary*. Cambridge: Cambridge University Press.

Schmitt, N. (2010). *Researching vocabulary: A vocabulary research manual*. Basingstoke, UK: Palgrave Macmillan.

Discussion questions

1. Look at each of the following words and outline what you know about each one: *take, lovely, organ, parabola, undersell, mouse,* and *phlebitis.* Think about different meanings, spelling and pronunciation, grammatical aspects, contexts of use, and so on.

2. As a language teacher, how do you monitor your learners' vocabulary development in the classroom? Is it appropriate to give regular vocabulary tests in your situation?

3. What are the advantages and disadvantages of the multiple-choice format as a method of testing whether learners know words or not?

4. How can we get learners to show that they can use words effectively in their own speech or writing, rather than just performing well on vocabulary tests?

References

Alderson, J. C. (2005). *Diagnosing foreign language proficiency*. London: Continuum.

Beglar, D. (2010). A Rasch-based validation of the Vocabulary Size Test. *Language Testing*, 27, 101–118.

Meara, P. (2009). *Connected words: Word associations and second language vocabulary acquisition*. Amsterdam: Benjamins.

Milton, J. (2009). *Measuring second language vocabulary acquisition*. Bristol: Multilingual Matters.

Nation, I. S. P. (2001). *Learning vocabulary in a second language*. Cambridge: Cambridge University Press.

Read, J. (2000). *Assessing vocabulary*. Cambridge: Cambridge University Press.

Read, J. (2004). Plumbing the depths: How should the construct of vocabulary knowledge be defined? In P. Bogaards & B. Laufer (Eds.), *Vocabulary in a second language: Selection, acquisition and testing* (pp. 209–227). Amsterdam: Benjamins.

Schmitt, N., Schmitt, D., & Clapham, C. (2001). Developing and exploring the behaviour of two new versions of the Vocabulary Levels Test. *Language Testing*, 18, 55–88.

Simpson-Vlach, R., & Ellis, N. C. (2010). An academic formulas list: New methods in phraseology research. *Applied Linguistics*, 31, 487–512.

SECTION 4

TECHNOLOGY IN ASSESSMENT

The three chapters in this section examine the increasingly important role of technology in assessment. Just as computers are becoming more ubiquitous in our everyday lives, so too are they in education. Technology has the potential to greatly enhance the development of language tests, how they are administered, how they are rated, and how they are used to improve teaching and learning. The chapters in this section focus on computerized testing, Web-based language testing, and the application of software to improve test development and rating.

Davidson and Coombe, in Chapter 30, begin by outlining the many benefits of computerized testing, specifically the production of more valid and reliable tests, numerous administrative benefits, and the positive impact that this can have on teaching and learning. Despite these benefits, the authors contend that although some of the larger testing bodies have invested a great deal, computerized testing has not been widely adopted by teachers and teaching organizations. This could in part be explained by the numerous shortcomings of computerized testing, which the authors also expand upon. They conclude by providing a research agenda that they argue must be fully addressed before teachers can embrace computerized testing to its fullest potential.

In Chapter 31, Shin complements the previous chapter by focusing more specifically on Web-based language testing (WBLT). She argues that one of the advantages that WBLT has over computer-based testing is logistical flexibility, enabling for example testing on demand, and that it can enhance both situational and interactional authenticity. WBLT also allows teachers to develop their own online classrooms tests using institutional course management tools or other online authoring tools. However, the author cautions that, as with computerized testing, there are a number of shortcomings associated with WBLT and a number of key issues need to be addressed before it is likely to be more widely adopted.

Lee, in Chapter 32, delves into the technical detail by introducing the main features and applications of three software programs: Quest, Facets, and Turnitin. Firstly, she demonstrates how Quest can be used to analyze test data from objectively scored items (e.g., multiple-choice questions, short-answer questions) to improve the effectiveness of individual test items. The author then explains how Facets can be used to improve subjectively scored performance data (e.g., speaking and writing) by taking into account the harshness or leniency of the rater, and the difficulty of the task. Finally, she shows how Turnitin can be used to detect student plagiarism as well as for peer review.

CHAPTER 30

Computerized Language Assessment

Peter Davidson and Christine Coombe

INTRODUCTION

These days the use of computers in education is reasonably widespread in developed countries, and is increasingly being adopted in many developing countries as well. However, it is surprising to note that the use of computers in English language testing has been rather minimal. While some of the larger testing bodies such as the Educational Testing Service (ETS) and Cambridge ESOL have invested heavily in computerized testing, only a limited number of educational institutions have embraced computerized testing, and few individual teachers use computer-based tests with their students, which explains why paper-based tests still dominate. As noted by Frase (1997) over 15 years ago, most of the problems associated with computerized testing are more theoretical and conceptual than technical. This chapter examines the reasons why institutions, educationalists, and testers have been slow to adopt computerized testing. After examining the benefits of computerized testing, an analysis of some of the disadvantages of computerized testing is provided, which in part helps to explain why it has not been widely adopted. Finally, a research agenda is proposed that needs to be addressed before the benefits of computerized testing can be fully realized in education.

BACKGROUND

There are essentially two types of computerized tests – computer-based tests (CBTs) and computer adaptive tests (CATs). A CBT is simply a paper-based test that has been put onto a computer in the same linear fashion as the paper-based version of the test. A CBT may look slightly different to its paper-based version if it has been embellished with a different layout, fonts, colors, and other visuals, but essentially it is the same as the paper-based version of the test. With a CAT, however, all candidates answer a different set of questions as they are each presented with a question, and their response to that question affects the next item that the computer selects for them to attempt. If the candidate gets the answer to a question correct, the computer selects a slightly more difficult item for them to attempt on the next question. Conversely, if they get a question wrong, the computer selects a slightly easier question for them to answer. In other words, the computer adapts the test to the estimated ability of the test taker, hence the name, computer adaptive. This process continues until the computer has sufficient data on which to make a precise judgment about the test taker's ability, or until a predetermined number of questions have been answered – usually around 20–25 items.

RESEARCH

THE BENEFITS OF COMPUTERIZED TESTING

The numerous benefits that computerized testing has over paper-based tests have been well documented (Chalhoub-Deville, 2001; Chapelle and Douglas, 2006). Because candidates taking computerized tests enter their responses directly onto the computer, test writers can easily utilize item and statistical analysis to help them identify effective and ineffective questions and write better tests. To utilize the same item and statistical analysis with a paper-based test, someone has to enter all the candidate's responses onto the computer. Item analysis can determine the facility value (level of difficulty) and the discrimination index (the extent to which strong students get an item correct and weaker students get it incorrect) of individual test items, as well as the performance of distractors used in multiple-choice tests. In addition, test path data, which provides information on the order in which test takers answered questions, the time it took them to answer questions (item latency), which items they skipped and went back to, and which answers they changed, can easily be collated and used to improve the validity and reliability of a test.

Computerized testing also has the potential to increase content validity as more content can actually be tested through the use of more test formats, including the use of interactive question types that can assess complex problem-solving skills, which may not be possible with paper-based tests (Huff and Sireci, 2001). The reliability of marking tests can also be increased significantly as computerized testing allows for automated scoring. Recent advances in technology have resulted in automated scoring programs, such as e-rater (www.ets.org/research/topics/as_nlp), which automatically rates written work, and Pearson's Versant speaking test (www.versanttest.com). These automated scoring programs have been shown to produce high correlations between computer-rated and human-rated tests.

The consequential validity of computerized tests can also be higher than paper-and-pencil tests as research has found that many test takers prefer it to traditional non-computerized tests. Test takers have responded favorably to the fact that CATs are usually shorter than paper-based tests (Meijer and Nering, 1999), which invariably reduces the impact that test fatigue can have on the performance of the test taker. One study (Powers, 2001) found that test takers experienced less test anxiety when taking tests on computer than when taking a paper-based version of the same test. Test takers have also commented positively on the fact that they receive their test results quickly, and that there are more test administrations than with paper-based tests. Another positive aspect of CATs that test takers have identified is that they do not have to answer questions that are too easy or too difficult as the computer selects test items that approximate their ability.

Computerized testing has many administrative benefits. Test administration can be simplified and can be more standardized across different implementations. Computerized testing also allows for more flexible testing administration schedules, or "testing-on-demand," as it is referred to, because not all test takers need to be in the same place at the same time (Roever, 2001). Automated marking means that teachers are relieved from the time-consuming task of rating tests so that large numbers of tests can be rated accurately and quickly (Meijer and Nering, 1999; Pomplun et al., 2002). As a consequence, test takers can receive their test results immediately. Another obvious administrative advantage is that CATs result in shorter tests. Test security can be increased when using CATs as copying answers from another candidate is virtually impossible because all the test takers are exposed to different items and no two students ever take the same test (Huff and Sireci, 2001). A final administrative benefit of computerized testing is that it allows for item banking whereby items are securely stored electronically for easy retrieval and use at a later date. This in part explains why computerized testing has the potential to be cheaper than paper-based tests in the long term (Pomplun et al., 2002).

One of the benefits of computerized testing that is often overlooked is the positive impact that it can have upon curriculum. Computerized testing has the potential to provide test takers with immediate and comprehensive feedback (Pomplun et al., 2002). Individual test items that are related to a particular skill or content knowledge domain can be "tagged" to provide test takers with feedback on particular areas of strength or weakness. Test path data, mentioned earlier, can provide significantly more information to teachers about their students' ability than if the only information they received was whether a student got an answer right or wrong (Roever, 2001). The diagnostic feedback and test path data of individual students can be used by teachers to individualize students' learning, and can be collated and analyzed by curriculum developers to create more relevant and targeted curriculum in order to enhance students' learning. The potential of computerized testing to impact on curriculum development should not be underestimated.

THE DRAWBACKS OF COMPUTERIZED TESTING

As noted by Bachman (2000: 4), "The challenge in applying [such] technologies to language assessment will be to recognize not only the potential benefits, but also the limitations of these technologies." One of the major limitations of computerized testing is construct-irrelevant variance, or the testing of irrelevant constructs such as computer literacy. For example, the ability to use a mouse, or the ability to use the scroll bar when reading longer texts, may unintentionally be tested on a computerized test. Research has indicated that reading on a computer screen involves fundamentally different processes, and hence different constructs, than reading from a hard copy. Construct irrelevance can result in decreased test validity, and can also contribute to another disadvantage of computerized testing, namely the lack of equivalence between computer-based and paper-based versions of the same test.

When examining the equivalence of the computer-based and paper-based versions of the Test of English as a Foreign Language (TOEFL), a number of studies (Eignor et al., 1998; Taylor et al., 1999) revealed that 16 percent of test takers were not familiar with computers and that their scores were negatively affected when they took the test on a computer. However, more recent research by Cambridge ESOL (Blackhurst, 2005; Green and Maycock, 2004) comparing the paper-based and computer-based International English Language Testing System (IELTS) indicates that both versions of the test are equivalent. Allowing candidates to choose which format of the test they want to take employs what Jones (2003: 4) refers to as a "bias for best" approach whereby the candidates choose the test format that they feel will benefit them the most.

Other variables which may contribute to the lack of equivalence between a computer-based and a paper-based test, identified by Davidson (2009), include: an overdependence on keyboarding skills; different layout between the two tests; different graphics (font style, font size, color, clarity); the use of sound on a computerized test; a different number of questions on the screen and on the paper copy; pop-up error messages; highlighting the question the test taker is answering; information on the number of unanswered questions; the fixed pace of some computerized tests; and the inability of the test taker taking a computerized test to review the test, to highlight words or phrases in a text, to see all of the text and all of the questions, to answer selectively, to back track, to delete distractors, and to change answers.

The validity of computerized testing, especially CATs, can also be undermined by construct underrepresentation and a lack of content validity, due to the limited number of item formats or test task types that are currently utilized. The development of computer-based tests that measure test takers' higher-order knowledge, skills, and competencies is at this time still in its infancy. Face validity can also be threatened by computerized tests, especially CATs. The developers of some CATs, for example, claim that a test taker's level of language proficiency can be determined after she or he has answered as few as eight test items. Understandably, test takers often question the validity of making inferences about their ability based on such a short test, especially when they are used to taking paper-based tests that have many more items than a typical CAT. The reliability of automated scoring has also been called into question (Chapelle and Douglas, 2006), and research by Powers et al. (2001) found that it is possible to trick automated essay-scoring programs; hence the need for human raters remains.

Test security has become one of the major challenges associated with computerized testing (Chapelle and Douglas, 2006; Meijer and Nering, 1999). Claims that computerized testing increases test security need to be considered in light of recent breaches to tests delivered on computer. Educational Testing Service (2002) suspended the computer-based Graduate Record Exam (GRE) and reintroduced the paper-based version in China, Hong Kong, Taiwan, and Korea after an investigation "uncovered a number of Asian language Web Sites offering questions from live versions of the computer based GRE General Test [which] included both questions and answers illegally obtained by test takers who memorize and reconstruct questions and share them with other test takers."

Another problem with computerized testing is that in some locations there is not sufficient access to computers to provide for large-scale implementation of computerized tests. After switching to computerized testing in a number of countries in 1998, ETS reinstated paper-and-pencil tests in more than 20 countries after acknowledging that access to the computer-based tests was being denied to a number of test takers. In 2002, ETS phased out 84 computer testing centers around the world due to a lack of test takers. It is likely that this drop in candidate numbers is partly due to the increased expense of computerized tests over paper-and-pencil tests. Computerized tests, especially CATs, are very expensive to create because large item pools are needed due to the adaptive nature of the tests (Meijer and Nering, 1999). Now test developers talk of item lakes, and even item oceans, consisting of thousands of items that are needed for CATs to determine test takers' proficiency, particularly at the higher and lower ends of the scale. Furthermore, test items need to be replaced regularly as they become obsolete or overexposed, especially those items with a high level of discrimination. As a consequence, considerable financial and human resources are needed to set up and maintain a CAT program. Another obvious disadvantage of computerized testing is that the technology may fail. At the present time, for contingency purposes, a paper-based version of a CBT needs to be on hand for when there are technical problems. As a consequence, the need to ensure equivalence between paper-based and computer-based versions of a test (Davidson, 2009).

Finally, computerized testing can also have a negative impact on the curriculum. Shorter tests may have a harmful effect on test takers' study and test preparation. Test takers may also engage in misguided test-taking strategies, especially with CATs, where they spend too much time on the first few questions, and therefore have less time to spend on the latter questions. Test takers taking CATs have also been known to use "gaining strategies" whereby they purposefully answer the first few questions incorrectly based on the false assumption that they will get an easier question. Another potentially negative impact on curriculum with regard to computerized testing is that there can be an overreliance by teachers on the computer to analyze, interpret, and make inferences about test results. Given the validity issues regarding computerized testing outlined in this chapter, the computer may be making incorrect inferences about what students can and cannot do, and as a consequence may also be giving them the wrong diagnostic feedback to the detriment of their learning.

PRACTICAL APPLICATION

As the use of computers in education becomes more prevalent, so too will the use of computers in English language testing. However, given the numerous limitations and problems associated with computerized testing, it is not difficult to see why it has not been widely adopted in education. In order for computerized testing to become more widely implemented, a number of issues related to the key testing concepts of validity, reliability, and practicality need to be addressed. Specifically, more research needs to be conducted to ensure that computerized tests are in fact measuring what they claim to be measuring. We need to know, for example, the impact that construct-irrelevant variance has upon test taker performance, and which variables put candidates that are not familiar with computers at a disadvantage. We also need to know how the process of reading on screen differs from reading a printed page, if the process of writing on a computer is different from writing by hand, and if the process of listening is different when the test taker can see the person talking on a computer screen as opposed to only hearing him or her on a CD.

More research also needs to be conducted to determine if construct underrepresentation, a lack of content validity, and a lack of face validity affect the validity of computerized tests. Test writers need to determine the equivalence of computerized and paper-based tests, and identify more succinctly which factors can result in a lack of equivalence. Test developers need to ensure that all candidates can easily navigate and use the computerized test, and that computer interfaces do not interfere with the overall assessment. Innovative question types need to be developed to exploit the interactive nature of computers. Automated scoring methods need to be investigated to determine if they are a reliable means of marking test takers' writing. Finally, the technical problems and lack of security also need to be addressed if computerized testing is to become more widely adopted.

CONCLUSION

The potential for computerized assessment to have a major positive impact on teaching, learning, and testing is indisputable. Computerized testing can help us produce more valid and reliable tests that are more accurate measures of candidates' ability, that also take less time to administer and rate than paper-and-pencil tests. Computerized testing can also have a significant positive impact on curriculum, providing test takers and teachers with immediate diagnostic feedback that can result in individual learning plans. However, computerized testing is not used to any significant degree in education for reasons that are more theoretical than technical. The possibilities of computerized testing have led to a major re-examination of the key principles of testing, namely validity, reliability, and practicality. Key issues, such as the impact of construct-irrelevant variance on test taker performance, the equivalence of computer-based and paper-based tests, and test takers' attitudes toward computerized testing and how this impacts on their performance, all need to be examined further before teachers and testers embrace computerized testing and before its numerous benefits can have a positive impact on teaching and learning.

Suggested resources

Bugbee, A. C., & Bernt, F. M. (1990). Testing by computer: Findings in six years of use 1982–1988. *Journal of Research on Computing in Education*, 23(1), 87–100.

Chalhoub-Deville, M. (2001). Language testing and technology: Past and future. *Language Learning and Technology*, 5(2), 95–98.

Chapelle, C. A., & Douglas, D. (2006). *Assessing language through computer technology*. Cambridge: Cambridge University Press.

Davidson, P. (2009). Computerized testing. In C. Coombe, P. Davidson, and D. Lloyd (Eds.), *Fundamentals of language assessment: A practical guide for teachers* (pp. 236–248) (2nd ed.). Dubai, UAE: TESOL Arabia Press.

Fulcher, G. (2000). Computers in language testing. In P. Brett and G. Motteram (Eds). *A special interest in computers*. Whitstable: IATEFL.

Huff, K. L., & Sireci, S. G. (2001). Validity issues in computer-based testing. *Educational Measurement: Issues and Practices*, 20(3), 16–25.

Discussion questions

1. How can computerized tests help test writers write better tests?

2. Can computers really rate students' essays?

3. How can computers be utilized to assess speaking?

4. Which variables might contribute to a lack of equivalence between a CBT and a paper-based version of the same test?

5. How can we ensure test security when implementing computerized tests?

6. How can computerized testing be used to facilitate learning?

References

Bachman, L. F. (2000). Modern language testing at the turn of the century: Assuring that what we count counts. *Language Testing*, 17(1), 1–42.

Blackhurst, A. (2005). Listening, reading and writing on computer-based and paper-based versions of the IELTS. *Research Notes*, 21, 14–17.

Chalhoub-Deville, M. (2001). Language testing and technology: Past and future. *Language Learning and Technology*, 5(2), 95–98.

Chapelle, C. A., & Douglas, D. (2006). *Assessing language through computer technology*. Cambridge: Cambridge University Press.

Davidson, P. (2009). Computerized testing. In C. Coombe, P. Davidson, and D. Lloyd (Eds.), *Fundamentals of language assessment: A practical guide for teachers* (2nd ed.) (pp. 236–248). Dubai, UAE: TESOL Arabia Press.

Educational Testing Service (2002). Paper-based GRE General Test returning to parts of Asia. Retrieved August 6, 2003, from: www.ets.org/news/02072301.html

Eignor, D., Taylor, C., Kirsch, I., & Jamieson, J. (1998). Development of a scale for assessing the level of computer familiarity of TOEFL examinees. *Educational Testing Service: Research Reports, Report 60*. (RR-98-7).

Frase, L. T. (1997). Technology for language assessment and learning: Introduction and comments on the state of the art. In A. Huhta, V. Kohonen, L. Lurki-Suonio, and S. Luoma (Eds). *Current developments and alternatives in language assessment*. Jyväskylä: Jyväskylä University.

Green, A. & Maycock, L. (2004). Computer-based IELTS and paper-based versions of IELTS. *Research Notes*, 18, 3–6.

Huff, K. L., & Sireci, S. G. (2001). Validity issues in computer-based testing. *Educational Measurement: Issues and Practices*, 20(3), 16–25.

Jones, N. (2003). The role of technology in language testing. *Research Notes*, 12, 3–4.

Meijer, R. R., & Nering, M. L. (1999). Computerized adaptive testing: Overview and introduction. *Applied Psychological Measurement*, 23(3): 187–194.

Pomplun, M., Frey, S., & Becker, D. F. (2002). The score equivalence of paper-and-pencil and computerized versions of a speeded test of reading comprehension. *Educational and Psychological Measurement*, 62(2), 337–354.

Powers, D. E. (2001). Test anxiety and test performance: Comparing paper-based and computer-adaptive versions of the Graduate Record Examinations (GRE) General Test. *Journal of Educational Computing Research*, 24(3), 249–273.

Powers, D. E., Burstein, J. C., Chodorow, M., Fowles, M. E., & Kukich, K. (2001). *Stumping e-rater: Challenging the validity of automated essay scoring*. Educational Testing Service: GRE Board Professional Report No. 98-08bP. (RR-01-03).

Roever, C. (2001). Web-based language testing. *Language Learning and Technology*, 5(2), 84–94.

Taylor, C., Kirsch, I., & Eignor, D. (1999). Examining the relationship between computer familiarity and performance on computer-based language tasks. *Language Learning*, 49(2), 219–274.

Web-Based Language Testing

Sun-Young Shin

INTRODUCTION

Web-based language testing (WBLT), as its name suggests, utilizes the Internet as a medium of test delivery. It is written in the Hypertext Markup Language (HTML) located on the server and test takers can download HTML data and respond to the test items using Web-browser software. The test takers' responses might be scored on their computers in low-stakes tests which do not seriously impact the test takers' lives, such as a diagnostic test. Alternatively, their responses might be sent back to the server for scoring in medium-stakes tests, such as a placement test, or high-stakes tests, such as an admissions test which may significantly affect the test takers' future. Typically, because of test security problems, WBLT has been recommended for low-stakes tests (Roever, 2001). Nonetheless, since the capacity for automatic scoring by computer has increased in recent years, with sophisticated server side programming and sufficient storage, WBLT has also started to be employed for making medium- or high-stakes decisions.

Recently, interest in WBLT has been growing in the language-testing area because it has started to be widely used as a major delivery format for most of the standardized English proficiency exams such as IELTS, TOEIC, and the TOEFL Internet-based test (iBT). WBLT has also been extensively used for various testing projects, such as the UCLA WebLAS project (2003) for online college ESL placement test development and the DIALANG project (Alderson and Huhta, 2005) for developing self-assessment tools to help L2 learners to determine their proficiency level, based on the Common European Framework of Reference (CEFR).

BACKGROUND

Compared to computer-based testing, which is done offline, the use of the Web as a testing medium has brought about various beneficial outcomes to language-testing practices and qualities. Perhaps foremost among these is logistical flexibility. For example, test takers can register for the test online and take it anytime and anywhere that is convenient to them as long as they have access to the Internet. Another logistical advantage of WBLT is that test takers can be provided with immediate feedback and scoring results on their responses. For practice and learning purposes, it can allow test takers to proceed at their own pace in the tasks and to utilize online dictionaries or other online support materials during the test, if needed.

WBLT may also improve important aspects of test qualities. For example, it can enhance two different aspects of authenticity: situational and interactional authenticity (Chapelle and Douglas, 2006). The former is related to the extent to which the test tasks mirror the features of a specific language use situation, and the latter is associated with the amount of language ability involved in successfully completing the test task (Bachman, 1991). WBLT may enhance situational authenticity by incorporating various mass media into the test contents so that the features of real-life language use are more closely replicated in the test items. In addition, it can increase interactional authenticity as well, by allowing the constructed response items to elicit more language knowledge than dichotomously scored items normally do (Chapelle and Douglas, 2006).

Reliability can be improved in WBLT because of consistent scoring by computer with regard to common construct features. Interrater and intrarater reliability issues pertaining to scoring test takers' productive skills will not be an issue in WBLT. Once a reliable scoring algorithm is developed and applied to test takers' responses, complete consistency in scores will be applied to all test takers.

However, the use of technology for test delivery does not always guarantee a positive outcome on the language test qualities. There are several drawbacks in the use of WBLT. Firstly, the fact that a test is delivered via the Internet may introduce some construct-irrelevant variance, which is often related to varying degrees of computer or Web familiarity among test takers. Secondly, the advantage of administrative efficiency and flexibility can introduce security problems in a medium- or high-stakes test. Unless test takers are all supervised, WBLT is always subject to fake identification and problems with cheating. In addition, despite the fact that automated scoring enables test takers to produce the constructed responses in large-scale tests, the automatic scoring system itself can be another source of measurement error when it fails to take into account misspellings, synonyms, and paraphrases as alternative answers. Lastly, technical glitches can pose serious threats to the use of WBLT for making medium-to-high-stakes decisions when test takers' responses may not be stored correctly, for example, or wiped out completely from the server in the worst-case scenario.

RESEARCH

Although WBLT seems to provide great efficiency in terms of test administration and scoring, its capacity to improve validity and reliability is still questionable. A few studies have been done as to whether validity and reliability can be established for WBLT, for low- to high-stakes tests. With regard to validity issues, Chapelle et al. (2003) addressed the validation process pertaining to the design of their low-stakes Web-based ESL testing. They justified the use of the diagnostic test by providing evidence regarding how texts and items were aligned with different levels of difficulty, based on theoretical rationales, such as theories of text and item difficulty and theories of lexical and grammatical development. They also emphasized that the intended use should guide the entire validation process. Roever (2006) showed that his Web-based pragmatic test was a valid tool for measuring different aspects of pragmatic knowledge: implicatures, routines, and speech acts, by documenting correlational analyses and comparisons between groups. With regard to the use of WBLT for placement decisions in the medium-stakes listening testing context, Shin (2008) investigated the construct validity of Web-based listening tests, including three different constructed response formats – an incomplete outline, open-ended questions, and a summarization task. This study suggested that the three different response formats can all provide valid measures of academic listening in terms of test takers' understanding of the hierarchical organization of academic lectures, but with varying degrees of sensitivity to different aspects of academic listening comprehension across different tasks. In a high-stakes testing context, Sawaki et al. (2009) established the construct validity of TOEFL iBT by demonstrating that a total score, together with four scores corresponding to the modalities measured in the TOEFL iBT, manifest two different constructs claimed for the test: (1) a single general English proficiency factor (ESL/EFL ability); and (2) four separate language skill factors (reading, listening, speaking, and writing).

Reliability issues have been related particularly to the use of automatic scoring for constructed-response items. Automated scoring makes constructed-response item formats possible in large-scale tests by reducing the high cost of scoring and the reporting time needed for manual scoring of such items. However, it may not accurately represent the underlying language ability of the test takers' performance on WBLT, by ignoring the important aspects of the construct. For instance, WBLT may not be able to handle spelling errors and paraphrased responses, and thus fail to score the acceptable answers correctly.

According to the length of possible responses that the automated scoring system can capture, Carr (2008) introduced an approach to automatic scoring processes called Natural Language Processing (NLP), in which test takers' lengthy responses are analyzed and scored by algorithms constructed on the basis of pattern recognition, keyword scoring, and exact scoring.

With the help of NLP technology, extended responses, such as essays and speech samples, can be automatically scored. In the WBLT context, essays have been scored by automated essay evaluation systems such as e-rater (Attali and Burstein, 2005) and speech samples by SpeechRater deployed for the TOEFL iBT Speaking Practice test (Xi, 2008), both developed by Educational Testing Service (ETS). E-rater has been used to accomplish low-stakes purposes such as providing diagnostic feedback to help learners and teachers evaluate their essay-writing skills and identify areas that need improvement. Although the ultimate goal of SpeechRater v1.0 is to provide diagnostic feedback, to date it can only provide learners with immediate score feedback (Xi, 2008). Another example using NLP in spoken language testing would be Pearson's Versant (Pearson, 2009) in which the test taker responds orally to a series of recorded spoken prompts on various item types including sentence repeating and building, short-answer questions, and story retelling. In the Versant test, test takers' responses are scored automatically on the categories of sentence mastery, vocabulary, fluency and pronunciation, and listening comprehension.

On the other hand, short open-ended questions with one- or more-word responses can be scored using keyword matching, which looks for the particular keywords in test takers' responses. The UCLA online placement test employed this keyword-matching system for scoring test takers' responses on short open-ended reading and listening comprehension questions. Lastly, for scoring responses of a single word or phrase in a very limited productive-response format, exact match scoring can be utilized. Most licensed online course management programs (i.e., WebCT) have adopted this scoring approach in their Web-based testing section. Language test developers can choose one of these automated scoring methods, depending on the response formats used in the test and the developer's budget and programming expertise.

PRACTICAL APPLICATION

WBLT provides great efficiency for all stakeholders involved in language tests. First, it enables test takers to take the test at their convenience. They can schedule their tests at a time and place that suits them. Once test takers log into the system with appropriate user names and passwords, they are given screen pages of general instructions and a brief practice test, and then they begin the real test. During the test-taking process, an online clock manages timing and lets test takers know how much time remains. Once test takers have answered all the questions and submit their responses for scoring, they are automatically informed if they have answered all the questions and then the whole test process is terminated. After that, their answers are immediately scored and the results can be automatically transmitted to all the stakeholders involved.

WBLT also provides a relatively simple and easy tool for language teachers who want to develop their own classroom tests. Language teachers with some knowledge of HTML and Java Scripts can easily create an online language test if they have access to a standard Web browser. Even without knowledge of these languages, they can still develop their own classroom tests using an institutional online course management tool, such as WebCT, in which course instructors are allowed to add such tools as discussion boards, mail systems, and live chat. Other types of freeware such as Hot Potatoes (Half-baked, 2009) are also available. Hot Potatoes allows language teachers to develop various response formats for the test including interactive multiple-choice, short-answer, jumbled-sentence, crossword, matching / ordering, and gap-fill exercises. If teachers want more sophisticated commercial WBLT development tools to incorporate sound, video, Java, and Macromedia Flash to their tests, authoring tools such as Blackboard (2009) and Questionmark (2009) are available. However, if they want to be in control of the administrative and scoring process, the best way would be to develop their own in-house WBLT authoring tool. This will give them more flexibility to create different response formats and a scoring report system, although it will require greater financial resources and expertise on program development. The caveat at the beginning stage of WBLT development is that test writers should be aware that technical problems may occur which would make test takers' responses completely unreliable. In order to minimize such potential problems, an appropriate interface design should be well incorporated into WBLT so that online help or feedback can be provided to test takers when they choose inappropriate functions. In case of server / computer breakdown, it would also be wise to have backup files on alternative servers for the secure storage of test data or to make all the items retrievable on the test takers' computers by having them downloaded at the beginning as part of a script (Roever, 2001).

CONCLUSION

With the help of advanced computer and network technology, WBLT has become a major medium of test delivery for both low-stakes and high-stakes tests. Online testing can improve the way we measure language ability in various ways. Particularly, WBLT may enhance test authenticity and reliability by making possible a rich contextualized input, various response formats, and automated scoring. However, to date there is little evidence to suggest whether online testing can actually help us to make more valid interpretations and uses of test scores. In addition, more research should be conducted to see if reliable scoring can be obtained through automated scoring systems for constructed responses.

In the future, advances in technology might be able to improve various language-testing practices. One emerging trend would allow the use of performance testing to become a practical option through the use of simulations. Another trend would be toward a more sophisticated and powerful automated scoring system that allows us to use a variety of constructed-response test items.

Suggested resources

Bachman, L. F. (2000). Modern language testing at the turn of the century: Assuring that what we count counts. *Language Testing*, 19(1), 1–42.

Brown, J. D. (1997). Computers in language testing: Present research and some future directions. *Language Learning & Technology*, 1(1), 44–59.

Chapelle, C. A. (2001). *Computer applications in second language acquisition: Foundations for teaching, testing, and research.* Cambridge: Cambridge University Press.

Chapelle, C. A. (2003). *English language learning and technology: Lectures on applied linguistics in the age of information and communication technology.* Amsterdam: John Benjamins.

Chapelle, C. A., & Douglas, D. (2006). *Assessing language through computer technology.* Cambridge: Cambridge University Press.

Discussion questions

1. Past research has found no meaningful differences of test scores obtained between the WBLT and the paper-based language test. If this is the case, what would be the rationale behind the use of WBLT? Would it be worthwhile to develop the Web-based test platform?

2. Do you think the potential advantages of WBLT outweigh the potential risks of compromised test security?

3. Are there ways that you could incorporate WBLT into the classes you teach? Where do you think it would be useful?

4. What potential enhancements or threats to the validity of WBLT score interpretations and uses would an automated scoring system introduce?

References

Alderson, J. C., & Huhta, A. (2005). The development of a suite of computer-based diagnostic tests based on the Common European Framework. *Language Testing*, 22(3), 301–320.

Attali, Y., & Burstein, J. (2005). *Automated essay scoring with e-rater v.2.0.* (Educational Testing Service Research Report No. 04-45). Princeton, NJ: Educational Testing Service.

Bachman, L. F. (1991). What does language testing have to offer? *TESOL Quarterly*, 25(4), 671–704.

Blackboard. (2009). Blackboard Learning System. Blackboard, Inc. Retrieved April 30, 2009, from www.blackboard.com.

Carr, N. (2008). Decisions about automated scoring: What they mean for our constructs. In C. A. Chapelle, Y. R. Chung & J. Xu (Eds.), *Towards adaptive CALL: Natural language processing for diagnostic language assessment* (pp. 82–101). Ames, IA: Iowa State University.

Chapelle, C. A., & Douglas, D. (2006). *Assessing language through computer technology.* Cambridge: Cambridge University Press.

Chapelle, C. A., Jamieson, J., & Hegelheimer, V. (2003). Validation of a web-based ESL test. *Language Testing*. 20(4), 409–439.

Half-baked. (2009). *Hot Potatoes. Version 6.2*. Half-baked Software, Inc. Retrieved April 30, 2009, from http://web.uvic.ca/hrd/halfbaked.

Pearson (2009). *Versant Pro-Speaking*. Pearson Knowledge Technologies, Palo Alto, CA. Retrieved April 30, 2009, from http://ordinate.com/products/proSpeakingDetails.jsp.

Questionmark. (2009). *Questionmark Perception*. Questionmark Corporation. Retrieved April 30, 2009, from www.questionmark.com/us/perception/index.htm.

Roever, C. (2001). Web-based language testing. *Language Learning & Technology*, 5(2), 84–94.

Roever, C. (2006). Roever, C. (2006). Validation of a Web-based test of ESL pragmalinguistics. *Language Testing*, 23(2), 229–256.

Sawaki, Y., Stricker, L. J., & Oranje, A. H. (2009). Factor structure of the TOEFL Internet-based test. *Language Testing*, 26(1), 5–30.

Shin, S. Y. (2008). Examining the construct validity of a web-based academic listening test: An investigation of the effects of constructed response formats in a listening test. *The Spaan Fellowship Working Papers in Second or Foreign Language*, 6, 95–129. English Language Institute, University of Michigan.

UCLA Department of Applied Linguistics and TESL & Center for Digital Humanities. (2003). Retrieved April 30, 2009, from WebLAS. www.weblas.ucla.edu.

Xi, X. (2008). What and how much evidence do we need? Critical considerations in validating an automated scoring system. In C. A. Chapelle, Y. R. Chung, & J. Xu (Eds.), *Towards adaptive CALL: Natural language processing for diagnostic language assessment* (pp. 82–101). Ames, IA: Iowa State University.

CHAPTER 32

Software to Facilitate Language Assessment: Focus on Quest, Facets, and Turnitin

Young-Ju Lee

INTRODUCTION

The purpose of this chapter is to introduce teachers to three computer programs: Quest, Facets, and Turnitin. Although Microsoft Excel is also very useful for entering, manipulating, and analyzing data, Quest and Facets are test-oriented and we can gain much from using them for specific test-related purposes. For classroom teachers who are keen on dealing with plagiarism and are interested in gaining peer feedback about their students' work, Turnitin should be very helpful.

Quest and Facets are what we call Rasch-based software programs but each handles different data types. By Rasch-based we mean they are based on a type of statistical analysis developed by the Danish statistician George Rasch in 1960, which is based on probability. We use Quest to deal with objectively scored items (where there is a right or wrong answer and an answer key is used by the teacher, so the teacher does not have to make any decisions), while we use Facets for subjectively scored performance data in speaking and writing (where the teachers must decide on the quality of the performance and award a score). To run Quest and Facets effectively, we need a sound background knowledge of Rasch measurement, though even some basic understanding of test and item analysis can help any teacher to use these tools in their school-based examinations.

The innovative nature of Rasch measurement is that item difficulties and candidates' abilities are measured on a *single* scale. That is, through a mathematical model, we are able to create a ruler to measure item difficulties and candidates' abilities on the same scale. This scale is called a *logit* (pronounced *low jit*) scale. For an extensive discussion of Rasch measurement, see Bond and Fox (2001) or for a more reader-friendly description, see McNamara (1996).

In this chapter, I will outline some practical aspects of each software program, focusing principally on the following three questions: What are the main features of each software program? How can you purchase it? How can you benefit from using each one in your teaching context?

BACKGROUND

QUEST

QUEST (developed by Adams and Khoo in 1996) allows us to analyze multiple-choice items, Likert-type rating scales, short-answer items, and partial credit items, using Rasch measurement theory. Please visit the following Web site for general inquiries about purchasing Quest software: http://assess.com/xcart/home.php.

In order to run the program, we need two separate files: a data file and a control file. Data files and control files should be saved as text files. The data file, unsurprisingly, contains the score data. The control file contains all of the commands for the program to follow. Each line in the control file tells the program to perform specific analyses. It is crucial to follow the control file formats (see Chapter 3 of the Quest manual, Command Structure) and write them correctly. Failure to do so will result in either incorrect analysis or no analysis at all. Quest creates four output files: (1) item estimates / difficulty file (with a file extension name of *.diff*); (2) overall summary file (*.sum*); (3) case / test taker ability file (*.p*); and (4) item analysis file (*.itns*).

FACETS

Facets is a Rasch measurement program which is suitable for essay grading, portfolio assessment, and other kinds of judged performance (Linacre, 2008). The current version (Facets 3.68) was released in July 2011. The free evaluation / student version called Minifac is also available and can be downloaded from http://winsteps.com/minifac.htm. You can download a free Facets manual at www.winsteps.com/aftp/facets.pdf. You can purchase a Facets single-user license, a circle-site license, or a multi-user site license. For general inquiries about the software purchase, please visit http://winsteps.com/facets.htm. You can also take online courses on Rasch Measurement at www.statistics.com/ourcourses.

In order to run Facets, you need a specification file, which might be considered a combination of the control file and data file you prepare for Quest. As you did for control files in Quest, you should save specification files as text files in Microsoft Word, or simply write the file in text format. The Facets program became more user friendly after version 3.5 since it can now import Excel (.xls) files directly; and so we do not have to reformat data files (saved as text files). The current Facets 3.68 version can even import Excel 2007 .xlsx files.

In the Facets program, the most essential element is the identification of facets. To better understand what the facets are, please consider the following example. A hundred students take essay tests and each student is presented with two tasks: one on personal experience and the other on graph interpretation. Each student's essay is independently rated by two teachers randomly chosen from a rater pool of ten. Raters will be asked to provide holistic scores (i.e., a single overall score) for each task. In this situation, there are at least three factors that will affect students' final scores: (1) the ability of the student (high or low); (2) the severity of the teacher (harsh or lenient); and (3) the difficulty of the task (difficult or easy). Each aspect of the rating situation is called a facet – so, in the current example, we have three facets: students, teachers / raters, and tasks. Specific individuals, raters, or tasks within each facet are called elements – so, in this example, we have 100 elements for the first facet (students), ten elements for the second facet (raters), and two elements for the third facet (tasks).

Facets create one output file with various tables, though the most important ones for the regular user are the candidate report (listing the scores achieved by each candidate), the rater report (showing the leniency and internal consistency of the raters), the task report (showing how well the tasks worked and how easy or difficult each task was), and the scale report (showing how well the rating scale – or rubric – worked).

The really interesting thing about Facets is the fact that the final score for each candidate is presented in two ways. First there is a mathematical average score of the marks awarded by each rater. Then there is what is called the "fair average" score. This score takes into account the ability of the candidate and (in our example of three facets) the harshness / leniency of the raters, and the difficulty of the task; so, the fair average score may be slightly higher or lower than the mathematical average.

TURNITIN

If your main interest is writing assessment itself, you will greatly benefit from Turnitin, a widely used plagiarism detection software. Turnitin has expanded beyond just plagiarism detection and has recently been renamed Turnitin WriteCycle, a Web-based solution to support writing instruction (Turnitin Manual, 2008). The core components of Turnitin WriteCycle are Turnitin originality checking, Peer Review Tools, and GradeMark digital grading tools. The technology to provide a plagiarism detection service was developed and finally completed in its current form by Barrie, a co-founder of Turnitin. For an interesting story on the development of Turnitin, see Barrie (2008).

Turnitin originality checking allows teachers to check students' submitted papers for improper citation or potential plagiarism by comparing them against documents stored in the Turnitin database. The Turnitin database consists of various types of repositories such as (1) billions of Web pages from the Internet; (2) papers from journals, periodicals, and publications; (3) institution repository of student papers; and (4) a repository of papers previously submitted by Turnitin users (Turnitin Manual, 2008). Teachers have a choice of including or excluding one of these repositories. Either ESL students' linguistic deficiency or unfamiliarity with what comprises plagiarism in academia might cause them to plagiarize unintentionally in writing. Turnitin can be ideally used as a deterrent rather than identification of plagiarizing students in that students who are well aware that their papers will be scrutinized are more likely to produce original works and acquire citation skills (Turnitin Manual, 2008).

The second component of Turnitin WriteCycle is the Peer Review system. This is a valuable tool for teachers which reduces their administrative load by allowing for peer review of students' work. There are no problems with photocopying, carrying, and distributing students' papers. The peer review system has benefits such as automatic paper distribution, anonymous reviews (the default setting), and contextual review marks. Grade-Mark is Turnitin WriteCycle's grading tool which allows instructors to grade papers with greater flexibility; instructors do not have to worry about carrying students' papers home or writing comments on insufficient margins of papers.

The discussion of Turnitin in this section will be limited to originality checking. You can purchase a Turnitin individual license, department license, or campus license. For general inquires about Turnitin software purchase, please visit www.turnitin.com/static/index.html. Free manuals for students as well as instructors are available from the following Web site: www.turnitin.com/static/training.html. You can have free introductory online training sessions from the Web site, which are very helpful.

PRACTICAL APPLICATION

QUEST

Multiple-choice (MC) items, whether you like them or not, are the most popular item format due to perceived ease of construction, administration, and cost. In this section, the discussion of practical application of Quest will be limited to MC items. You can use Quest to analyze students' multiple-choice responses to see which items worked well and which did not.

Suppose a grammar test consisting of 22 items was given to 72 students. Each item has three options. In this situation, data are dichotomous, that is, students will get 1 point for a correct response and 0 points for an incorrect response.

While scoring students' answer sheets, you realize that strong students in your class did not perform well on item 19. By running Quest, you can easily detect what went wrong with item 19.

Among the four Quest outputs, the item analysis results (with a file extension name of *.itns*) are particularly useful for MC item analysis. As you can see from Figure 32.1, the output for the item analysis includes detailed information about the item, such as facility values (the percentage of candidates who answered the item correctly), discrimination index (represented by point-biserial – an estimation of how well high-level candidates performed on the item compared to low-level candidates), item difficulty in logits (the point on the logit scale where the item will appear – represents an estimate of the true difficulty of the item), and Infit MNSQ (an estimate of item stability – less than .7, it may be telling you information you already have from other items so the item may be redundant; over 1.3, it is "misfitting" and not stable so is likely to be a poor item). Please recall that you can calculate item statistics such as item facility and item discrimination manually using the Excel program (for details of test data analysis, please see Chapter 12 of this book). By using Quest, you can get not only these item statistics easily but also detailed item information like options analysis (i.e., how well the different options are working).

```
Item Analysis Results for Observed Responses
all on all (N = 72 L = 22 Probability Level= .50)


Item 19: item 19                          Infit MNSQ = 1.22
                                          Disc = .15


Categories      a*          b           c        missing

Count           42          20          7           3
Percent (%)     60.9        29.0        10.1
Pt-Biserial     .15         .01        -.25
p-value         .116         .479        .021
Mean Ability    1.87        1.68        1.09        2.03


Step Labels                  1
Thresholds                 1.17
Error                       .27
```

Figure 32.1   Partial output for the item analysis

Although item 19 is not technically misfitting and hence acceptable, as indicated by the Infit MNSQ of less than 1.3, this item has a low item discrimination index of 0.15 (at the upper right corner of the output). Please note that the correct response to items is marked with an asterisk. For item 19, the key is *a*. While 60 percent of candidates chose option *a*, 39 percent of candidates were attracted by options *b* and *c*, as can be seen from Figure 32.1.

Also note that the low item discrimination index suggests some high-performing students got the item wrong, while some poor students got the item right. Therefore, it is worth examining options *b* and *c* to see if there are any irrelevant elements to distract students from choosing option *a*.

Suppose further that you need to reduce testing time by eliminating five items. Based on the same output, you can identify redundant items that give us no new information about students' performance. Items with Infit MNSQ indices less than 0.7, for instance, can be good candidates because they are redundant and do not contribute at all. We do not want redundant items in the same test because they have the effect of lowering standard errors and increasing reliability. This can mislead us into thinking that the test is measuring better than it really is.

The extreme example of redundant items are as follows: Item 1 asks, "What is the name of the current president of the United States?" and Item 2 asks, "How do you spell the name of the current president of the United States?" Items 1 and 2 are dependent; so, if you do not know the name, you cannot spell it. In this example, they are redundant and either Item 1 or Item 2 can be deleted. In a real testing system, you are unlikely to be able to spot redundancy as easily as in this example. However, the same logic applies. If the answer to one item is a clue to the answer to another item, these two items are dependent and any redundant items can be detected by item analysis outputs from Quest.

FACETS

The most prevalent use of the Facets program in language testing is the analysis of judged performance. Facets can analyze scores awarded by teachers / raters to students on their performance on a number of rating criteria for each of several tasks.

Suppose 61 students took computerized writing assessments after they read articles and listened to lectures. Each student's essay was scored by two independent raters, based on the analytic rating criteria consisting of the following six criteria: organization, content, grammar, use of sources, avoidance of plagiarism, and mechanics. It is worth noting that rating criteria in Facets are treated as items. We have six items, that is, six elements under the facet of items. Each analytic rating criterion was rated on a scale of 1 to 4. Suppose further that the average of six analytic scores in whole numbers, for instance, 1, 2, 3, and 4, is used for placing students into one of four writing courses.

Total Score	Total Count	Obsvd Average	Fair-M Average	Model Measure	S.E.	Infit MnSq	ZStd	Outfit MnSq	ZStd	Estim. Discrm	Candidates
37	12	3.1	3.43	3.51	.54	.90	−.1	.84	.2	1.25	46
33	12	2.8	3.06	2.34	.55	.77	−.5	.70	−.6	1.36	47
35	12	2.9	3.25	2.93	.54	.50	−1.5	.48	−1.5	1.66	48

Figure 32.2 Partial output of candidate measurement

Please refer to Figure 32.2, a partial output from the candidate measurement report which lists the performance of three students out of 61 in ascending order according to their ID numbers. Taking student ID 47, for example, the observed average for six analytic scores was 2.8. When the rater severity and item difficulty are taken into account, the fair average is 3.06. The score calibrated in logits is 2.34. Please recall that each analytic rating criterion was rated from 1 to 4. The fact that student ID 47 had the observed average of 2.8 but a fair average of 3.06 illustrates that this student could get two different scores (i.e., 2 or 3 in the current example) depending on who rated the essay, which might result in different placement decisions.

TURNITIN

Turnitin creates originality reports that show submitted papers and source materials side by side on a single page. The left column of the originality report shows a copy of the submitted paper and highlights any unoriginal text that is compared with documents in the Turnitin database. The right column shows sources of the matching text. The biggest advantage of Turnitin is these easy-to-read originality reports. The color of the report icon indicates the amount of matching with the percentage range from 0 to 100 percent; blue (0% of text matching), green (1% to 24%), yellow (25% to 49%), orange (50% to 74%), and finally red (75% to 100% of text matching). The color-coded report icons are very similar to traffic signals. As a red traffic signal tells us that we should stop walking, the red report icon warns of possible trouble with the script. As soon as instructors encounter red report icons, they need to make a judgment call whether or not detected unoriginal works result in plagiarism.

Please take a look at the following screenshot in Figure 32.3 of an originality report. The top of the report page shows information about the submitted paper, including the paper title, user identification number, the word count, and how many submissions have been made to the assignment. The student with ID 38980536 submitted a paper with 614 words entitled "Tabitha Testing." Please note that this example from the Turnitin manual is not in English. As the report icon top left indicates, this student's paper shows 83 percent matching to the Turnitin database. The color (not visible here) and number in the submitted paper (i.e., left column) correspond with the source document (i.e., right column). For instance, 13 percent of matching (as indicated in number 2) was found from Internet material that can be downloaded from http://ezenlaweb.com. You can view the text from its Internet site by clicking on the Web page link.

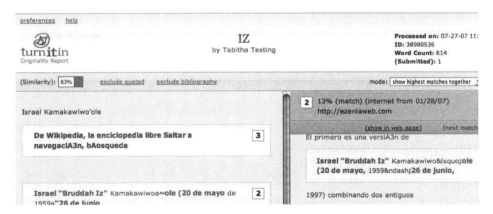

Figure 32.3   Example of originality report (reproduced from Manual, 2008: 45)

The percentage of matching text should be interpreted with great caution. The originality report index of 20 percent does not necessarily mean that a student plagiarized; instead, about 20 percent of the submitted paper contains similar text to that contained in the

Turnitin database. The decision as to whether or not a student plagiarized should be made after a close examination of both the submitted paper and any detected sources (Turnitin Manual, 2008).

CONCLUSION

In this chapter, I introduced three computer programs, Quest, Facets, and Turnitin, and discussed the applications and main features of each program. These three programs can be very useful tools for school-based examinations. The discussion of each software program in this chapter was not intended to be exhaustive (actually impossible due to limited space); instead, I aimed to introduce key components of each program as a starting point for you to explore it.

Although Turnitin is very straightforward to use, you might find it very challenging to run the two Rasch-based software programs (Quest and Facets) and interpret various tables in output files. Once you become familiar with the concept of Rasch measurement, as well as the writing of control and specification files, you will eventually get used to running Quest and Facets. I hope that the introduction of these three computer programs will be very useful for readers so that they can understand their main features and apply what they have learned in their teaching situations.

Suggested resources

Linacre, J. M. (2008). *A user's guide to Facets: Rasch model computer program*. Chicago: Mesa Press.

McNamara, T. F. (1996). *Measuring second language performance*. New York: Longman.

Turnitin Instructor User Manual. (2008). Retrieved January 19, 2008, from www.submit. ac.uk/static_jisc/documentation/Instructor_Manual.pdf.

The Institute for Objective Measurement (www.rasch.org) is a really valuable starting point for all things Rasch. Find links here to freeware and paid programs, as well as links to research and publications.

Plagiarism.org (www.plagiarism.org) contains links to Turnitin and other detection programs (such as WriteCheck and iThenticate). It also offers some discussion of issues around plagiarism.

For a free alternative to Turnitin (the plagiarism scan is free but there are charges for other Turnitin-type procedures), see Viper (www.scanmyessay.com).

Discussion questions

1. Which of the three programs is most likely to be of use to you in your daily work? Why?

2. Have you ever used any of these programs? Did you encounter any problems? If so, what kind of problems? On the other hand, have the programs helped you deal with any kind of problems?

3. Please discuss some advantages and disadvantages of using Turnitin. Which component of Turnitin have you used in your teaching? Are there any additional features, if any, that you would like to see?

References

Adams, R. J., & Khoo, S. T. (1996). *Quest: The interaction test analysis system [computer program]*. Australian Council for Educational Research.

Barrie, J. (2008). Catching the cheats: How original. *The Biochemical Society*, 16–19.

Bond, T. G., & Fox, C. M. (2001). *Applying the Rasch model: Fundamental measurement in the human sciences*. Mahwah, NJ: Lawrence Erlbaum.

Linacre, J. M. (2008). *A user's guide to Facets: Rasch model computer program*. Chicago: Mesa Press.

McNamara, T. F. (1996). *Measuring second language performance*. New York: Longman.

Turnitin Instructor User Manual. (2008). Retrieved January 19, 2008, from www.submit.ac.uk/static_jisc/documentation/Instructor_Manual.pdf.

SECTION 5

ADMINISTRATIVE ISSUES

The final section of the Guide looks to an often-neglected aspect of assessment, test administration. Whereas the publication of Weir's (2005) validation frameworks have had the positive effect of highlighting the importance to test validation of systematic and standardized administration, there is very little empirical evidence from the language-testing literature on the topic. The three chapters in this section take very different perspectives and offer the reader an insight into this neglected area.

In Chapter 33, Brady suggests that teachers of large classes (which he defines as holding between 30 and 50 learners) need to move away from the relatively informal techniques typical of the small classroom and adopt a more systematic approach to assessment. Advocating a group-based strategy for this type of assessment context, in which the teacher and the learners contribute to the process, Brady outlines and exemplifies a number of key approaches upon which the language teacher can build a working assessment system.

Green and Hawkey discuss the rating scales used in performance-based assessment (for writing and speaking) in Chapter 34. Beginning with a critical description of the different types of scale, the authors move on to briefly outline how a scale was produced by a major examination board in the UK. They conclude the chapter by stressing the need for rater training and for a greater understanding of the necessity to consider not only the scale to be used in a performance test but also the broader rating context – suggesting that the entire process (from the raters to the rating process to the scales used) should be considered as a key aspect of validity.

In Chapter 35, the final chapter of the section, Taylor broaches the subject of accommodation (or special measures) in language assessment. Linking her work to the ethical dimensions of testing (see Chapter 13 by Brown), Taylor discusses the background to the area and highlights the lack of empirical evidence in the research literature. Taking the accommodations offered by the University of Cambridge ESOL examinations board as a case study, she presents a broad picture of the types of measures typically available to the test taker. Taylor finishes the chapter by highlighting the key areas she feels should concern future researchers and practitioners in the area.

CHAPTER 33

Managing Assessment in Large EFL Classes

Brock Brady

INTRODUCTION

In a survey related to this study, one teacher wrote, "I can't stand large classes." For another, large classes were "exhausting." A third's advice on large classes was "pray."

The debate about when classes become large will continue. Few would dispute that language classes become large at a point between 30 and 50 students. Still, context matters, and small classes become large when:

- ambitious course goals surpass time available
- student diversity increases
- societal expectations about good teaching, learning, and class size are not met

Teachers know large courses when they are assigned to them. Typically, such assignments do not bring joy. Teachers commonly feel that large courses mean:

- physically challenging conditions (little space to move, stuffiness, or having to speak loudly)
- an overwhelming amount of grading and feedback
- a loss of classroom control
- difficulty "reading" class attitudes
- problems determining who is participating and progressing and who is not
- difficulties reaching struggling students
- abandoning good teaching practices

With the exception of physical conditions, all these consequences are related to assessment capacities. In "small" classes, assessment can be informal because participation and progress can be evaluated spontaneously. When difficulties arise, they can be immediately addressed. In fact, one "problem" with large classes is that they require ongoing, managed assessment. Large-class grading and feedback may be overwhelming because teachers apply the same assessment techniques to large classes that they use in small ones.

Large EFL classes exist because of resource limitations. This will not change. We must dramatically rethink how we manage large-class assessment to address teacher frustration. Recent research in EFL settings, in large university content courses, and in U.S. K-12 classrooms (where high-stakes testing makes effective classroom assessment critical), suggests a cost / benefit approach to large-class assessment, one that will obtain enough information with less overall effort.

BACKGROUND

Too often, mentioning large classes to EFL teachers results in a wave of eye-rolling and hand-wringing, followed by competition regarding who has the largest class. Whereas teachers desire to manage large classes more effectively, there is also an engrained belief that really not much can be done to make large classes more manageable. Teachers may resist change because change implies additional effort, and they believe classes require too much effort already. Therefore, improving large-class assessment involves a risk. Teachers must risk:

- giving up relatively detailed student comparisons (for grades) to start using assessment as a tool to evaluate teaching, determine progress, and know when to reteach
- making students partners in the learning / assessment process, taking responsibility for their learning and assessing their needs and progress
- having faith that the classroom experiences provided will lead all students to reach course goals without regular, time-consuming formal assessments designed to compare students.

For those ready to accept such risks, we propose one principle and three approaches to effectively manage assessment in large EFL classes.

PRINCIPLE

Groups are Good: Whether for learning or assessment, groups are the most effective way for students in large classes to have sufficient language practice time. Groups cause students to "norm themselves" against other members, compensate for individual weaknesses, and social coercion keeps activities on track. Even when space limitations are great, students in the odd rows of the class can still turn to face students in even rows to form groups.

APPROACH I

Pay As You Go: using formative assessment (ongoing, low-stakes assessment of overall student progress) to supplement judicious summative assessment (end-of-unit / course, higher-stakes assessment). Formative assessment becomes a series of quick snapshots that gauge overall student control of requisite knowledge and skills, and the effectiveness of teaching.

APPROACH 2

Divide and Conquer: using various techniques to gauge progress through representative sampling rather than whole-class assessment.

APPROACH 3

Know Thyself: using various techniques to help individual students develop awareness of how they learn, so that they can take responsibility for their learning (and slightly reduce their teacher's).

These recommendations will provoke skepticism. However, research on large EFL classes supports expanded small-group work as a way to better manage and assess large classes (see, for example, Purgason, 2007); the "pay as you go" approach of informal, on-the-fly assessment has become an established practice in many U.S. K-12 classrooms (e.g., dip-sticking; Saphier et al., 2008), as well as in large university classes (e.g., Bonwell and Eison, 2005). Assessment schema based on sampling are supported by research in EFL: increasing learner responsibility to reduce teacher workload and build student metacognition is well recognized across a variety of instructional contexts (Allwright, 1989; Shamim et al., 2007; Kinsella, 2006).

LITERATURE REVIEW

ASSESSING LARGE CLASSES IN EFL SETTINGS

While research on large EFL class assessment is limited, research on *teaching* large EFL classes is not. The breadth of these efforts was captured by Lancaster-Leeds Language Learning Research Project (Coleman, 1989) of the late 1980s to early 1990s which led to several metastudies (see Allwright, 1989, for one example) and a comprehensive bibliography of large class research (Coleman and Bishop, 2002). Some key findings from the Lancaster-Leeds Project are:

- Large classes show little negative impact on learning.
- Large classes are a source of teacher anxiety and dissatisfaction.
- Increasing student responsibility can reduce the teacher anxiety about keeping learners on track.

Hess's *Teaching Large Multilevel Classes* (2001) is another resource on large EFL class assessment, summarizing the benefits and challenges of large classes, suggesting eleven principles for managing large multilevel classes, and offering a compendium of activities for teaching and assessing large language classrooms.

ASSESSING LARGE UNIVERSITY CONTENT COURSES

Much recent research on assessing large lecture hall settings comes from the "active learning movement" which holds that "students must do more than just listen. They must read, write, discuss, or be engaged in solving problems" (Bonwell and Eison, 2005: 1). Active Learning advocates using "stop and do" assessments such as "minute papers," "student active breaks," and "student response note cards," to provide interactive assessment and encourage student reflection on how they could learn more effectively. Learning and Teaching in Large Classes is a Web site managed by the University of Queensland (2002–2006), providing numerous studies on innovative large-class teaching techniques across disciplines, and devoting one entire section to large-class assessment.

ASSESSMENT IN ACCOUNTABILITY-DRIVEN K-12 CLASSES

In this era of mandated teacher accountability where all students must achieve high standards according to external standardized assessments, feasible, ongoing assessment of student progress is crucial. While U.S. K-12 classes may not be considered large relative to other countries, the high-stakes atmosphere where no child can be left behind results in even relatively small classes sharing challenges comparable to large classes: time-consuming assessment, maintaining order, reaching out to struggling students, and meeting diverse standards for diverse students in a limited amount of time.

Saphier et al. (2008) provide a number of "on-the-fly" activities that are used in many U.S. K-12 classrooms to ensure that students are mastering subskills before moving on to the next activity. To keep pace with challenging curricula, such assessments, called "dipsticking," take little time from teaching and allow teachers to quickly sample learning to decide whether to move ahead or reteach.

Popham (2008) has developed an approach to K-12 formative assessment that he calls *transformative assessment*, which focuses on first unpacking lesson standards and goals to determine essential content and subskills. Then, corresponding course units are constructed, sequenced, and formatively assessed to ensure that students are mastering subskills as they go, as well as improving awareness about these skills.

As a whole, the literature suggests that large-class EFL assessment is most effectively managed if:

- relatively low-stakes formative assessments are used during teaching to quickly gauge progress (with support from limited higher-stakes summative assessment);
- student progress is assessed through sampling, rather than assessing all students always; and
- assessments are designed so students can discover how they learn and develop strategies to take responsibility for their learning.

PRACTICAL APPLICATIONS

PAY AS YOU GO

Using short, informal, low-stakes assessments that confirm knowledge and skills at each step sacrifices less instruction to assessment and reduces instructor time for scoring and feedback. Such formative assessment must start early. The first step is to unpack course goals to discover skills and knowledge learners need to master. Students also have to have time to practice skills they need to engage in. Follow-up reassessment is crucial to determine if students have internalized what they were taught. Such reassessment may seem to cut into instructional time, but students must internalize subskills to meet course goals.

Informal assessment of this kind is a two-way dialogue: The instructor asks students what they understand and need to know, and students ask the instructor about their progress and adjust their participation based on that feedback. This kind of interaction creates significant payoffs: Learners build confidence by checking their skills as they go and they develop learning strategies they can trust. Teachers can pass on some responsibility to students, worry less about anonymous students slipping through cracks, and have less concern about cheating or plagiarism because assignments are course-specific, often based on group consensus.

TECHNIQUES

Breaks to consolidate: Instructors stop periodically to allow students to write out and restructure their notes, or they stop periodically throughout classes to ask for oral recaps (i.e., students restate what they learned to create a conceptual framework to retain learning).

Dipsticking: Activities that allow teachers to have quick global assessments of student progress without stopping for formal assessments. For example, teachers can ask questions and have all students signal thumbs up for "true," thumbs down for "false," and thumbs sideways for "not sure." Similarly, students can be provided with four cards, A, B, C, and D, and respond to whole-class multiple-choice items. For higher-order learning, providing students with personal whiteboards or slates can show individual answers to the instructor's whole-class questions. With dipsticking, teachers face an important decision: How many students need to be off-track to justify reteaching – 10 percent, 20 percent? However, once a threshold is established, and once it is met, teaching moves on.

DIVIDE AND CONQUER

Again teachers must surrender some control to reap management returns. As Popham suggests, "don't let the pursuit of the instructionally perfect prevent you from reaping the rewards of the instructionally possible" (2008, ix). Some elements of this approach are familiar good teaching practices, such as providing clear assessment criteria before assignments and providing model assignments. In large classes these techniques are more than good practices; they are crucial to student success and often ensure that the instructor receives a better product to evaluate. Such front-loading entails additional course preparation time, but produces fewer off-track assignments and better assignments overall.

Self- and peer assessment: The instructor benefit of these practices is clear: If students self-evaluate and revise, and revise again after peer evaluation, assignments that reach the instructor will be better edited. Self- and peer assessment build meta-awareness and reinforce understanding of processes involved in the assignment. Peer assessment also introduces students to the benefits of "a second pair of eyes" on work (whether those eyes belong to an expert or to a peer). Obviously self- and peer assessment require clear criteria that students can easily apply, their benefits must be discussed, and peers need to see themselves as partners, not mutual critics.

Writing assessment techniques: Managing writing feedback means picking one's battles carefully. For example, instructors select only a few writing features to focus on, and comment only on those features. Or teachers may provide extensive feedback on only the first few pages of a writing assignment, then ask students to edit the remainder using the feedback provided.

Group projects: Group projects permit low-stakes formative assessment of initial project elements and group revision of those elements, so that when final projects are submitted for a high-stakes assessment, they will be better designed. Traditionally, the key challenges with group work include difficulties scheduling meetings and perceived unfairness of members receiving a single grade for varying individual contributions. However, if group work is done in class, scheduling is less of an issue. Concerning fairness, if early low-stakes project assessments carry sufficient weight, and the final project evaluation is determined through a variety of instruments (e.g., individual reflections, consensus analyses of member participation, and instructor evaluation of student performance in group roles), then concerns about fairness will recede.

Sampling techniques: Instead of giving the entire class a twenty-item quiz, divide the class in quarters and give each quarter five items. Since the quiz focus is on student mastery, not comparing students, the instructor only needs a sampling of student performance to decide whether to move on or review. Another approach for language classes having regular quizzes or short compositions is to score only a percentage of the assessments (chosen at random) at each sitting, while giving all other students a pass grade for having had the experience of completing the assessment. Then for each subsequent assessment, another random sample of students is scored while others pass simply for completing the assessment until all students have taken an equal number of scored and pass / fail assessments. This limits scoring time considerably, yet gives instructors data for comparing students.

KNOW THYSELF

This involves the calculated risk that devoting class time to building students' strategic awareness will result in learners who can take charge of their learning, self-assess progress, and report it honestly to the instructor. In this way, instructors structure and facilitate learning experiences, and learners in groups have the necessary cognitive strategies and collaborative skills to teach and assess themselves. This approach requires transparency. Instructors must discuss the challenges of learning languages in large classes – especially the need for sufficient practice, and the need for students to discover how they learn well and how to work in groups, so they can have this essential language practice.

TECHNIQUES

KWL activities, where students discuss what they already **KNOW** about the topic (to activate background knowledge), what they **WANT** to know about the topic (to spark motivation), then, after the lesson, what they **LEARNED** (to consolidate knowledge and create conceptual frameworks for retention), are the essence of metacognitive awareness building, helping learners establish learning goals and later assess / review what they actually learned.

Another type of "Know Thyself" activities includes self-surveys or inventories that help learners understand how they tackle certain skills and processes (see Table 33.1), then suggest other strategies that they can try.

READING	WRITING	VOCABULARY
• I think about what I already know about the reading. • I make a prediction, then read ahead to see if I'm right. • I stop and summarize.	• I plan before I write. • My writing has a beginning, middle, and end. • I ask other people to look over my writing.	If I don't know a word: • I read before and after it to try to understand. • I try to find its part of speech. • I look to roots and affixes for clues to meaning.

Table 33.1   Know thyself activities (adapted from O'Malley and Valdez Pierce, 1993)

"Do now" activities are self-assessment activities that help develop learning strategies and make good use of available class time (Kinsella, 2006). Students start the activity when they enter the classroom. For example, students may receive a list of vocabulary for the day's lesson and be asked to rate each item:

1. I don't know this word.
2. I've seen it before but I'm not sure what it means.
3. I could use this word in a sentence.
4. I could teach this word to somebody else.

In this way, students not only learn what it means to know a word, they determine their familiarity with particular words and they are introduced to concepts from the day's lesson.

Learning Contracts help learners develop learning strategies and assess their personal effectiveness by allowing them to decide which practices they want to use to improve their learning and participation during a specified period. For example, "During October I will speak at least once in every class, review our lessons every evening, and keep a list of new words, using them in sentences."

CONCLUSION

Although no hard evidence indicates that larger classes negatively impact learning, EFL teachers clearly find larger classes challenging because of difficulty determining whether all students are engaged and learning. While such assessment happens more holistically and intuitively in smaller classes, larger classes require more systematic ways to gauge student achievement. Keeping to the principle that "groups are good," and using assessment approaches such as "pay as you go," "divide and conquer," and "know thyself," teachers can sample class progress quickly and regularly in ways that structure learning and retention, encouraging students to take responsibility for their own learning. Such approaches to large EFL class assessment require faith, planning, and commitment. Faith that it is acceptable to assess *some* of the students in *some* ways *almost all* of the time; planning, in that course goals must be analyzed to determine requisite knowledge and skills; and commitment to developing systematic assessment. The benefit is that if learners do more of the work, assessment effort is better distributed, and students develop strategies and skills that will serve them for years.

Suggested resources

Fauzia, S., & Smith, R. (2010). *Teaching English in Large Classes (TELC) Project / Network*. Retrieved January 15, 2011, from www2.warwick.ac.uk/fac/soc/al/research/projects/telc.
A useful collection of quite recent research on large EFL classes.

Hess, N. (2001). *Teaching large multilevel classes*. New York: Cambridge University Press.
A standard reference on large EFL classes, focusing primarily on large class activities.

Larson, M. J. (1992). *Teaching English as a Foreign Language to large, multilevel classes*, ICE ref. M0046. Washington, DC: Peace Corps.
A standard work for large classes in EFL settings that emphasizes responding to learner diversity and learning styles.

Popham, W. J. (2008). *Transformative assessment*. Alexandria, VA: ASCD.
An excellent overview of assessment techniques and strategies in U.S. K-12 classes.

Teaching and Educational Development Institute (2002–2006). *Teaching large classes*. Brisbane, AU: University of Queensland. Retrieved January 15, 2011, from www.tedi.uq.edu.au/LargeClasses.
An extensive, well-managed, and up-to-date site for research and advice on teaching large classes.

Discussion questions

1. Why do many EFL teachers resist alternative approaches to large-class assessment?

2. What are some challenges to teaching large classes and some concrete ways to respond?

3. Many "know thyself" and "pay as you go" techniques are formative assessments. Why does the author distinguish between the two?

4. Can you think of some "divide and conquer" activities to use with your students?

5. The author suggests that more frequent systematic assessment can reduce assessment time and effort for teaching in large EFL classes. Does this seem counterintuitive to you? If so, why? How could a doubtful EFL teacher be convinced to try these approaches?

References

Allwright, D. (1989). *Is class size a problem? Project Report* 3. ERIC Documentation Reproduction Service No. ED322754.

Bonwell, C., & Eison, J. (2005). *Active learning: Creating excitement in the classroom.* ERIC Documentation Reproduction Service No. ED340272.

Coleman, H. (1989). Lancaster-Leeds Language Learning in Large Classes Research Project. Leeds, UK: University of Leeds.

Coleman, H., & Bishop, C. (2002). *Learning and teaching in large classes.* Retrieved October 5, 2008, from www.hywelcoleman.com/learning.htm.

Hess, N. (2001). *Teaching large multilevel classes.* New York: Cambridge University.

Kinsella, K. (2006). *Scholarship and strategies to bolster academic English language use and learner engagement in linguistically diverse classrooms.* Healdburg, CA: Educational Consulting and Training.

O'Malley, J. M. & Valdez Pierce, L. (1996). *Authentic assessment for English language learners: Practical approaches for teachers.* Upper Saddle River, NJ: Pearson.

Popham, W. J. (2008). *Transformative assessment.* Alexandria, VA: ASCD.

Purgason, K. (2007). Managing communicative classes of 50 or more with student teams. TESOL Resource Center. Alexandria, VA: TESOL. Retrieved January 15, 2010, from www.tesol.org/s_tesol/trc/trc_submission_detail_new.asp?id=586.

Saphier, J., Haley-Speca, M. A., & Gower, J. (2008). *The skillful teacher.* Acton, MA: Research for Better Teaching.

Shamim, F., Negash, N., Chuku, C., & Demewoz, N. (2007). *Maximising learning in large classes: Issues and options.* Addis Abbaba: The British Council. Retrieved January 15, 2011, from www.teachingenglish.org.uk/sites/teacheng/files/ELT-16-screen.pdf.

Teaching and Educational Development Institute (2002–2006). *Teaching large classes.* Brisbane, AU: University of Queensland. Retrieved January 15, 2011, from www.tedi.uq.edu.au/LargeClasses.

CHAPTER 34

Marking Assessments: Rating Scales and Rubrics

Anthony Green and Roger Hawkey

INTRODUCTION: SCORING SHORT-ANSWER TASKS

At first sight, marking a test, or awarding points for performance, may appear a relatively straightforward matter, but anyone who has been involved in test development soon comes to appreciate that it can be extremely involved. Even where test takers simply tick a box or write a letter to indicate which answer they have chosen, where scoring may seem to be simply a mechanical exercise, decisions need to be taken and mistakes are made. Test takers can make mistakes with their answer papers – perhaps writing their answers in the wrong box or selecting more than one answer where only one is required. Markers – those who read or listen to the test takers' responses to score the test – may make errors, such as misreading answer keys or incorrectly adding up scores.

All such mistakes serve to distort the picture that a test or assessment can give of the test taker's true level of ability. It is therefore important to provide instructions both to test takers and markers that are as foolproof as possible, to provide answer papers and answer keys that are clearly laid out, to have rules about the treatment of ambiguous responses (such as the selection of two options) and to have at least a proportion of the scripts marked by two people so that it can be established whether, or rather how often, mistakes have been made and corrective action can be taken. Even computer marking does not eradicate errors; scanners may fail to recognize the test taker's selections or may misinterpret dirt on an answer sheet as the intended response. All scoring systems require careful management to minimize mistakes.

The more open-ended the questions, the more decisions are required on the part of the marker and the more challenging it becomes to score the test fairly. If a test taker is required to write (or speak) even a single word, this immediately raises a number of questions. By way of an example, consider this simple one-word gap-fill item: *The teacher asked her students to sit quietly in the classroom and do their work without _____.* Here the intended answer was *supervision*, but you can probably think of a number of other possibilities: *oversight, help, talking, her*, etc. The test developer will need to anticipate the range of possible answers and decide which are acceptable. If the task instructions call for a single-word answer, how should multi-word answers like *leaving the room* be treated? What if the multi-word answer includes a word that is on the list of acceptable responses: e.g., *any supervision*? The treatment of spelling errors is another consideration: Should correct spelling be required? Is *supervizion* acceptable? Or *soopavijun*? Such issues must be considered and dealt with consistently in a manner that is in line with the theory informing the test design. Often when such items are piloted, a list is made of the range of answers given and decisions about their acceptability are taken by the test developers so that an appropriate answer key can be drawn up. If individual markers are allowed to award points based on their own intuitions, the reliability and validity of the test will inevitably suffer.

IMPRESSION SCORING

As we have seen, the use of selected response formats, such as multiple choice or matching, greatly simplifies the task of the marker and readily allows for machine scoring. However, by restricting the range of responses, such formats give the test taker little opportunity to demonstrate the ability to use language *to communicate*. As language in use has come to play a greater part in the constructs underlying testing programs, the trend in language testing over the past three decades has been to make increasing use of more open-ended tasks rather than such objectively scored right / wrong items. These tasks include traditional essays and interviews, but also tasks such as written or spoken summaries used to test reading and listening comprehension or tests of integrated skills involving, for example, listening to a lecture, reading related texts, and then writing an essay on the basis of these inputs.

As answer keys cannot be used in these circumstances, traditionally essays and inter-views have often been scored using impression scoring. In impression scoring, the rater (one of several terms used in the language testing literature to describe a marker who makes judgments about a performance to generate a score – others include judge and assessor) considers the quality of the work and awards a score out of some predetermined total to reflect the quality of the performance: 63 out of 100 (63%), or 15 out of 20, or ten out of ten. A problem with this approach is that different raters may have quite different ideas about the standard represented by different scores. For one rater an "outstanding" essay should score 15 out of 20, for another it is 20 out of 20; one marker's idea of "outstanding" may be the same as another marker's idea of "good." Another threat to test fairness and consistency with general impression marking is that different raters are free to attend to different features of a performance – one rater is looking for correct grammar, another awards points for the quality of the test taker's ideas, while a third pays attention to the handwriting and neatness of presentation.

Because of such issues, the results of impression scoring are notoriously unreliable. Not only do raters fail to agree with each other (so there is poor *interrater reliability*), they also tend to award different scores to the same performance if they are presented with it a second time (there is poor *intrarater reliability*). Researchers have repeatedly found that results obtained by individual test takers might depend as much on their luck in encountering a generous rater, and at the right time of day, as on the qualities of their performance.

ERROR COUNTING

What is required in scoring performance on more open-ended tasks is a means of making the judgments as consistent as possible so that all raters will assign the same score to each sample of performance. One response to this requirement that was popular in the 1970s and is still occasionally used today is to replace subjective judgments with the supposedly more objective procedure of error counting. In this approach, marks are deducted from the total for each error that is identified. Unfortunately, this has turned out to be far less straightforward than was first assumed as raters will inevitably disagree about what should or should not be counted as one error. Because such decisions are in fact highly subjective, levels of reliability are not improved. The approach is also likely to have unfortunate educational consequences as it encourages test takers to be very conservative in their use of language. In an attempt to avoid mistakes, they may restrict themselves to simple language and try to avoid taking risks. This is not a situation that is likely to promote learning.

RATING SCALES

Rating scales (also known by various other names such as scoring rubrics and marking schemes) are the established means of guiding raters to improve their level of agreement with their colleagues. Rating scales consist of graded descriptions intended to characterize different levels of ability. The rating scale guides the rater in making a decision about which level best matches the sample of language being assessed.

Weigle reviews rating scales used to score tests of writing (although her observations apply equally to tests of speaking) and identifies two distinctive features that can be used to characterize different types of scale:

> (1) whether the scale is intended to be specific to a single writing task or generalised to class of tasks (broadly or narrowly defined), and (2) whether a single score or multiple scores are given to each script. (Weigle, 2002: 109)

Some scales, known as *analytic scales*, require the rater to award a number of different scores across a range of categories or *criteria*. For example, the First Certificate in English (FCE) Speaking exam (extract in Table 34.1) includes the following criteria: grammar and vocabulary, discourse management, pronunciation, and interactive communication.

Score	Grammar and Vocabulary	Discourse Management	Pronunciation	Interactive Communication
3.0	Grammar is sufficiently accurate. Uses appropriate vocabulary in dealing with tasks.	Uses adequate range of linguistic resources to deal sufficiently well with the tasks. Contributions may occasionally be limited or lack coherence.	Produces individual sounds and prosodic features sufficiently well to be understood. L1 accent may cause occasional difficulty.	Has sufficient interactive ability to carry out the tasks. Maintains flow of language when carrying out the tasks although may occasionally lack sensitivity to turn taking and hesitation may occur while searching for language. Does not require major assistance or prompting to carry out the tasks.

Table 34.1   Extract from an analytic scale – FCE (Level B2) Speaking (in use until December 2008)

Analytic scales require decisions on whether it is appropriate to apply *weighting* across categories. If a test specification emphasizes one communicative construct, this can be more heavily weighted and so carry more marks than another (for example, if a five-point scale is used, the score for a key category – e.g., interactive communication – might be doubled to give ten marks while other less central categories such as grammar and vocabulary might each carry only five marks).

Other rating scales that, in common with analytic scales, use descriptions intended to characterize different levels of ability, but describe a single, global continuum are known as *holistic scales*. The research we will describe by Hawkey and Barker (2004) on a common scale for writing (CSW – see Table 34.2), helped to develop a holistic scale aiming to cover the entire range of levels of the Main Suite of Cambridge ESOL examinations (see www.cambridgeesol.org). Note that this scale identifies categories (such as: range of topics, stylistic devices, variety and appropriacy of vocabulary, accuracy of grammar or vocabulary, organizing ideas), but these are not presented as discrete scales as they would be for analytic rating.

LEVEL	MASTERY
C2	CERTIFICATE OF PROFICIENCY IN ENGLISH: Fully operational command of the written language. Can write on a very wide range of topics. Is able to engage the reader by effectively exploiting stylistic devices such as sentence length, variety and appropriacy of vocabulary, word order, idiom and humour. Can write with only very rare inaccuracies of grammar or vocabulary. Is able to write at length organising ideas effectively.
LEVEL	EFFECTIVE OPERATIONAL PROFICIENCY
C1	CERTIFICATE IN ADVANCED ENGLISH: Good operational command of the written language. Can write on most topics. Is able to engage the reader by using stylistic devices such as sentence length, variety and appropriacy of vocabulary, word order, idiom and humour though not always appropriately. Can communicate effectively with only occasional inaccuracies of grammar and vocabulary. Is able to construct extended stretches of discourse using accurate and mainly appropriate complex language which is organisationally sound.
LEVEL	VANTAGE
B2	FIRST CERTIFICATE IN ENGLISH: Generally effective command of the written language. Can write on familiar topics. Shows some ability to use stylistic devices such as variety and appropriacy of vocabulary and idiom though not always appropriately. Can communicate clearly using extended stretches of discourse and some complex language despite some inaccuracies of grammar and vocabulary. Can organise extended writing which is generally coherent.
LEVEL	THRESHOLD
B1	PRELIMINARY ENGLISH TEST: Limited but effective command of the written language. Can write on most familiar and predictable topics. Can communicate clearly using longer stretches of discourse and simple language despite relatively frequent inaccuracies of grammar or vocabulary. Can organise writing to a limited extent.
LEVEL	WAYSTAGE
A2	KEY ENGLISH TEST: Basic command of the written language. Can write short basic messages on very familiar or highly predictable topics possibly using rehearsed or fixed expressions. May find it difficult to communicate the message because of frequent inaccuracies of grammar or vocabulary.

Table 34.2 A holistic scale: Cambridge ESOL Common Scale for Writing

A validated *common* scale for writing or for speaking would enable test users to relate the written performances of candidates from different test levels, or to identify the typical ranges of performance across all five CEFR (Common European Framework of Reference) levels, each exam with its own benchmark pass level.

When we develop a holistic rating scale, one decision to be made will be how many points are appropriate for the scale. In the case of the CSW (Common Scale for Writing), there are five levels, aligned with the six levels of the CEFR for Languages (Council of Europe, 2001), but with the A1 (Breakthrough, basic user) level excluded as at this level foreign language learners would not be expected to cope with continuous writing in the target language.

Such is the influence now of the CEFR that language rating scales for many languages in many countries are aligned with its six levels, A1 to C2, defining usefully the upper and lower ends of foreign language proficiency, as well as levels in between. Of course, the process of aligning writing, speaking, or other tests with the CEFR is complicated, involving both qualitative and quantitative validation methods (see "How are rating scales developed?"). But the existence of the CEFR, with its many example scales, both global (covering all the language skills) and skill or activity specific, is a significant support for rating scale developers and users.

ADVANTAGES OF HOLISTIC AND ANALYTIC SCALES

Analytic criteria provide for a more detailed description of a performance and so can give useful feedback to the learner. Using holistic scales, raters assign a single overall level or score to the performance. Holistic scales are generally more straightforward to use as the rater has only to select one level for each test taker's performance, for example Level C2, Mastery. The research evidence suggests that analytic scales tend to give more reliable results, perhaps because they encourage the rater to focus on the variety of features intended by the scale developer, while the holistic scale allows the rater to give differential weighting to the elements included.

Scales can be designed for more and less specific purposes. Weigle (2002) terms *primary trait* scales those which are designed to be used with a particular task, but scales can also be designed for use within a specific test that includes several tasks (as is the case for the example in Table 34.1), for a range of tasks that might be undertaken in a language program (Table 34.2), or for application to a wide range of contexts including across languages (as is the case for the CEFR). An advantage of the task-specific approach is that the scales can communicate the features of a successful response very clearly and in some detail to the rater and to learners, perhaps helping the learners to improve their performance. However, primary trait scales have two serious shortcomings. Firstly, every time a new task is devised, a new scale is also required, making such scales expensive and impractical for most purposes. Secondly, the results from such a scale may not be readily generalizable. When the scale allows us to report that a test taker is able to carry out one very clearly described task, it may not provide enough information about how well the test taker might be expected to perform on other kinds of tasks. For these reasons, most operational scales are more generic in nature.

Alderson (1990) refers helpfully to "constructor-oriented," "assessor-oriented," and "user-oriented" scales; band descriptions may be used in developing language tests, to rate test taker performance, or to interpret performance for test takers or those using the test results to make decisions about them, for example receiving organizations or potential employers. Of course the uses of many scales include all of these categories and more. The CEFR, discussed further in the next section, is intended to inform test constructors, assessors, test users, and test takers and as well as providing learning objectives for language programs. However, it has been questioned whether any one scheme can fulfill such a variety of functions.

HOW ARE RATING SCALES DEVELOPED?

As the impact or stakes of English language tests become ever higher with trends such as globalization and international mobility, the requirement for fair, reliable, and valid rating scales grows. Itself among the most ambitious of scale development projects, the Common European Framework of Reference provides a useful overview of the important task of developing valid rating scales. According to the CEFR (Council of Europe, 2001) this involves three approaches: *intuitive methods, qualitative methods*, and *quantitative methods*. The best scales, the CEFR (2001: 207) suggests, combine all three approaches in a "complementary and cumulative process."

The CEFR, followed by later rating scale researchers (e.g., Green, 2005; Hawkey and Barker, 2004), sees *intuitive* methods of developing rating scales as involving "the principled interpretation of experience." This process may include using informants, for example teachers, testers, and raters, to suggest revisions and redraftings of existing scales and other relevant source materials, such as syllabus specifications and tests, resulting in a "house consensus" scale for further development and validation.

The CEFR approach to scale development then (p. 209) describes *qualitative* methods of scale development as a follow-up to the intuitive stage. These methods may include the use of expert or participant-informant reactions to the draft scales and / or the analysis of typical writing (or speaking) performances using "key features" or "traits" to refine provisional criteria and scales and relate them to proficiency levels. Hawkey and Barker (2004: 122–159) obtained a corpus of 288 writing performances from candidates at three different Cambridge exam levels (B2, C1, and C2), all responding to the same writing task. Each script was graded by more than one marker, using a single trial rating scale. The scripts were then read and graded by the main researcher, who added comments on salient features of each script. Subcorpora of scripts of four similar proficiency levels according to the band scores assigned by their raters were next identified for closer analysis, with the aim of identifying, then checking through expert consultation, typical features of the writing samples for each level.

In the Hawkey and Barker Common Scale for Writing project, the next *quantitative* step was a computer analysis of the subcorpora to corroborate or refute, where feasible, the characteristics identified as typical of each of four proficiency levels specified in the four draft level descriptors. Features of the selected scripts investigated using WordSmith Tools software included: whole script, sentence, and paragraph lengths; title use; vocabulary: range, type-to-token ratio, single occurrence words, and word lengths; behavior of individual words in concordances and collocations; and candidate errors. Most of the script analysts' findings were supported by the computer corpus analysis; additional features were also indicated as significant, namely titling, word length, and vocabulary range across levels. This approach clearly reflected the CEFR proposal for the *discriminant analysis* of sets of performances rated and "subjected to a detailed discourse analysis to identify key features," after which multiple regression could be used "to determine which of the identified features are significant in determining the rating which the raters gave." These features can then be incorporated in the required level descriptors, as in Fulcher's (1996) *multi-dimensional scaling*, "a descriptive technique to identify key features and the relationships between them" (p. 210). The *Rasch model* used in the development of the CEFR to "scale descriptors of communicative proficiency," associates descriptors of communicative performance with proficiency levels.

Green (2005) set out the requirements for a Common Scale for Speaking to cover the five levels of the Cambridge Main Suite tests (see cambridgeesol.org), aligning them more closely with the CEFR and replacing the independent scales that had previously been used at each level. As with the CSW, this project included intuitive, qualitative, and quantitative phases. In the quantitative phase, 48 video-recorded test performances were rated by stratified groups of raters. Multi-faceted Rasch Measurement (MFRM) was used as the method of analysis for its capacity to estimate the relative harshness of raters and the consistency of marking. The new scales resulted in improved levels of agreement between raters and fuller use of the range of marks available. This was taken as validity evidence for the Common Scale for Speaking, to be used in assessing performance on Cambridge ESOL tests of Speaking for the ESOL Main Suite and BEC exams from December 2008.

RATER TRAINING

Marking schemes and rating scales are central to the validity of a test. Carefully developed answer keys and marking guidelines can help to eliminate ambiguity and ensure consistent scoring. A well-written scale helps to define the test construct for the raters so that they are guided to features they should attend to in a performance, enhancing levels of agreement. However, rating scales alone are not sufficient. Raters must be trained to use a rating scale effectively and consistently, and quality control procedures are needed to ensure that this happens. In large-scale testing programs, before a rating session raters are usually required to rate a set of previously scored performances to ensure that their judgments are consistent with the consensus interpretation of the scales. As the effect of training can be transient, raters are monitored over time to ensure that they remain consistent, perhaps by requiring them periodically to score additional performances that have already been assigned scores or by comparing their judgments with those of other raters. Scores are obtained from two or more raters and compared. Where disagreements occur, a third rating may be obtained to resolve them.

As computer technology advances, automated scoring of more open-ended performances is becoming a practical alternative to human ratings for large-scale test providers. Automated essay scoring has already been in use for many years and with advances in speech recognition, automatic scoring of tests of speaking is also becoming increasingly popular. Training these scoring systems usually involves obtaining large numbers of human ratings and developing a statistical model that will allow a machine to reproduce the human scores accurately. The model is then applied to performances that have not previously been rated. The levels of investment required to train automated scorers means that rating scales will probably remain the most suitable means of obtaining consistent scores on performance tests for all but the largest test providers for many years to come.

CONCLUSION

It is not possible to develop a valid language test without also deciding how the test will be marked. Both mark schemes and rating scales must, through their selection of appropriate categories of language use, reflect the constructs of the test. Combined with efficient answer keys covering all response possibilities unambiguously, and effective rater training, *scoring validity* may be added to the other forms of language test validity covered in this volume.

Discussion questions

1. What kind of short-answer tests would suit your students' needs? Why?

2. What kind of marking seems to suit the teaching or testing situation *you* are in?

3. Would you ever use error counts or impression marking? Under what circumstances?

4. Consider a group of language learners that you know; suggest some language proficiency categories that would be suitable to include in rating scales to assess their writing or speaking. Draft a rating scale using these.

5. What would be your five or six main points of advice to someone who needs to make a rating scale?

References and further reading

Alderson C. (1990). Bands and scores. In C. Alderson and B. North (Eds.), *Language testing in the 1990s* (pp. 71–86). London: Modern English Publications and British Council.

Council of Europe (2001). *Common European Framework of Reference for Languages: Learning, teaching, assessment*. Cambridge: Cambridge University Press.

Fulcher, G. (1996). Does thick description lead to smart tests? A data-based approach to rating-scale construction. *Language Testing* 13(2), 208–238.

Green, A. (2005). The ESOL Common Scale Project: Working towards a common scale for speaking. Paper presented to the Second International ALTE Conference, Berlin 19–21 May 2005.

Hawkey, R. & Barker, F. (2004). Developing a common scale for the assessment of writing. *Assessing Writing*, 9(2), 122–159.

Weigle, S. C. (2002). *Assessing writing*. Cambridge: Cambridge University Press.

CHAPTER 35

Accommodation in Language Testing

Lynda Taylor

INTRODUCTION

This chapter addresses an increasingly important area in language testing usually referred to as "accommodation" or "accommodations" (Abedi, 2008; AERA/APA/NCME, 1999; Fulcher and Davidson, 2007). These terms are used to describe the principle and process of modifying test content, format, or administration in order to meet the specific needs of an individual test taker, or group of test takers, in the interests of fairness and equity. Special arrangements are made in advance so that, as far as possible, the test taker can take the test on an equal footing with other candidates. Accommodations are commonly used in tests of content knowledge where the test takers are not native speakers of the language of assessment (Abedi, 2008; Rea-Dickins et al., 2009). In the specific context of second language testing, however, test accommodations are normally made to meet specific test taker needs resulting from a temporary or permanent disability, and this constitutes the primary focus of this chapter. The terms "test modifications" and "test adaptations" are also commonly used to describe such special arrangements (AERA/APA/NCME, 1999: 101).

Here we explore why accommodation has attracted increasing attention from language testers in recent years, what the current state of research and practice is in the field, and how things might develop in future.

BACKGROUND

Since the early 1990s there has been considerable debate about the ethical dimensions of testing and assessment (see, for example, Davies, 2008; Kunnan, 2000, 2004, 2008; McNamara, 2000; McNamara and Roever, 2006; Shohamy, 2008). The debate has contributed to the development of various language-testing-specific codes and guidelines for good practice (ALTE, 1994; ILTA, 2000, 2007; EALTA, 2006) that can be used to guide the process of test development and use in a socially and ethically responsible way. Such codes and guidelines seek to ensure that test washback onto the learning curriculum and classroom practice, combined with the impact of test use in education and society more widely, are as positive and beneficial as they can be. (For more on washback and impact see Alderson and Wall, 1996; Cheng, 2008; Cheng et al., 2004; Green, 2007; Hawkey, 2006; Wall, 2005.)

An important measure of the social responsibility or ethical standing of any test provider is the extent to which they acknowledge the particular needs of candidates in certain minority groups or with special requirements. This applies whether the test provider is an individual classroom teacher devising a local test for her or his own students or an examination board offering high-stakes international tests on a large scale. Test takers with disabilities, which may be temporary or permanent, constitute one such group in education and civic life – though we must also remember that this constituency is still a highly diverse one.

Educational, employment, and social opportunities for people with disabilities have increased steadily over recent years. This growth, combined with a greater awareness of individual human rights and associated legislation, has in turn led to increased demand for access to testing and assessment provision. Language test providers routinely need to be able to offer special arrangements not only for test takers with visual, hearing, or physical impairments but also those with learning difficulties. Providing such special arrangements typically involves departing from the established testing protocol and modifying test content, format, or administration so as to minimize the impact of those test taker attributes that are irrelevant to the ability construct being measured. In the case of a language test, for example, a test taker who broke her wrist in a cycling accident the day before the test is likely to need the assistance of a scribe to record her listening test answers or to complete the writing part of the test. Similarly, a visually impaired candidate may need a specially prepared Braille or enlarged print version of a reading test for him to demonstrate his reading ability.

RESEARCH

There exists relatively little research in the educational measurement field, either theoretical or empirical, that can be drawn on to inform language testers' policy and practice with regard to language test accommodations in the English as a Foreign Language (EFL) context. Two major reviews of the literature into special arrangements by Thompson et al. (2002) and Sireci et al. (2003) contain no studies directly relevant to language testing and assessment (O'Sullivan and Green, 2011). Most of the published research relating to accommodations in language assessment has been conducted in the United States with English language learners (ELLs) who are typically immigrants and indigenous groups in school-based learning and assessment contexts (see Abedi, 2008). This research tends to focus on the language of instruction, though some studies have investigated the effectiveness and validity of accommodations for language learners with disabilities. Thurlow et al. (2006) summarize the most common types of accommodation policies in the United States according to five categories (presentation, response, timing and scheduling, setting, linguistic), while Sireci et al. (2005) seem to conclude that the accommodation of giving extra time to test takers with disabilities in reading tests offers the most significant benefit when compared with nonaccommodated test takers (see Khalifa and Weir, 2009, for further discussion of extended time and Braille accommodations). It is still the case that relatively little is known or understood about how different accommodations benefit (or fail to benefit) particular students, or about how they affect the nature of the test itself and the meaning of the scores generated. Not surprisingly, practical constraints of research in this field, for example small sample size or nonrandom selection of subjects, mean that empirical studies in this area are often difficult to design, carry out, and interpret (AERA/APA/ NCME, 1999).

This means that decisions about the nature and extent of modification to test content and delivery tend to be based largely upon professional judgment, rather than shaped by measurement-oriented research findings. What constitutes a reasonable and appropriate accommodation is likely to be determined by logical, ethical, and practical considerations, sometimes informed by research findings. However, given the obvious difficulty of conducting experimental research in this area, especially studies that are large-scale, and quantitatively or statistically focused, the role of smaller-scale qualitative or mixed-method studies, including individual case studies, should not be underestimated. There is considerable scope in the future for this sort of research agenda, and it is encouraging to see signs of developments in this direction (see for example, the multifaceted case study investigating provision for candidates with dyslexia in writing assessment, reported in Shaw and Weir, 2007: 20–27).

PRACTICAL APPLICATION

In this section we review the practical application of test accommodations, drawing upon selected practices and examples commonly found in the field of large-scale language testing. Although each test taker requiring accommodation is likely to present a specific and unique set of needs, there are some frequently occurring categories of special need for which large-scale test providers – examination boards, such as University of Cambridge ESOL Examinations (Cambridge ESOL) or Educational Testing Service (ETS), for example – can make routine provision in terms of specially modified test materials and administrative procedures. This allows a test provider to respond quickly and positively to applications from test takers requiring accommodations. A hallmark of a commercial test provider's commitment to quality and fairness will be the extent to which it publicizes its provision for candidates requiring accommodation, for example through its Web site and through other information channels, such as documentation for candidates and other test users.

Most of the specific examples that follow come from the range of accommodations offered by Cambridge ESOL for its suite of English language proficiency tests (see www. CambridgeESOL.org; see also Gutteridge, 2008; Khalifa and Weir, 2009; O'Sullivan and Green, 2011; Shaw and Weir, 2007; Shuter, 2003; Taylor and Gutteridge, 2003). A similar range of provision will be offered by most other large-scale quality test providers. The following list of provisions presented is designed to be informative and illustrative of the wide variety of accommodations that can be provided for test takers with special needs; it is not intended to be either exhaustive or prescriptive, or indeed to determine what should constitute good policy or practice. Readers are encouraged to consult the public Web sites of other assessment providers to explore what individual provisions are offered by different testing organizations.

Typical categories of accommodation offered may include:

1. Provision for test takers with hearing / speaking difficulties
   - hearing aids, headphones, or specialist amplification equipment for a listening test, plus assistance from a supervisor to control the sound level appropriately
   - a lip-reading version of a listening test, in which the supervisor may read out the listening test material instead of playing it on a CD, including built-in pauses for the test taker to write the answers
   - taking a speaking test in a single rather than paired / group format

- extra time given in a listening or speaking test
- a separate room in which to take the listening or speaking test
- exemption from taking a listening and / or a speaking test

2. Provision for test takers with visual impairments

- Braille question papers, using either uncontracted (Grade 1) or contracted (Grade 2) Braille format[1]
- modified large-print question papers, for example enlarged versions using different print and / or paper sizes with standardized fonts and simplified layout
- use of specialist equipment for reading, for example magnifying glass, screen magnifier, screen-reading software, closed-circuit television, hand-held scanning apparatus
- assistance from a reader, that is, someone who will read and re-read the test questions
- use of specialist writing equipment, for example Braille keyboard (possibly linked to printer); typewriter, computer (usually with spellcheck, grammar check, and thesaurus functions disabled)
- an amanuensis, that is, someone who reads out the test questions, to whom the test taker speaks the answers and who then writes them down
- extra time to read the questions or write the answers (normally up to about 25 percent, although this figure needs to be balanced against the fatigue that a test taker may experience if a test is too long)
- taking supervised breaks during a test, often in addition to extra time
- a special version of a listening test, for example where the recording can be paused by the supervisor so that the candidate has time to read questions and write and check answers
- a special version of a speaking test, for example the use of verbal rather than visual material (that is, no photos), the use of enlarged pictures, or Brailled descriptions
- a separate room in which to take the test

3. Provision for test takers with specific learning difficulties, for example dyslexia, attention deficit disorder

- extra time to complete a test, normally up to about 25 percent
- supervised breaks, especially for those with diagnosed concentration difficulties
- use of a computer to write answers (normally with spellchecker, grammar check, and thesaurus function disabled)
- assistance of a copier or transcriber who will write out the test taker's answers
- assistance in completing an answer sheet that is sequentially numbered
- transparent colored overlays to aid reading and comprehension
- use of other relevant / necessary equipment, for example screen magnifier

4. Provision for test takers with other kinds of physical disability, for example motor difficulties, back trouble. This will vary considerably depending on the nature of the disability, for example broken arm / wrist / leg / ankle, bad back, wheelchair user, but it may require:

- specialist equipment, for example adapted computer keyboard
- specialist furniture, for example raised desk to accommodate wheelchair

- a separate room on the ground / first floor to enable wheelchair access
- frequent supervised breaks to avoid fatigue and to allow exercises
- some of the other accommodations mentioned in earlier sections

In many cases, it will be necessary to make several different test modifications and special arrangements. For example, a blind candidate may need *separate facilities* for taking a test (e.g., a dedicated room), a *specially modified question paper* (e.g., contracted or uncontracted Braille, depending on which system s/he is familiar with), extra *support personnel or equipment* (e.g., an individual invigilator, an amanuensis, or a Braille machine), and *extra time* to complete his or her papers. It is also important to note that individuals with similar disabilities will not necessarily all need or benefit from the same accommodations; for example, not all blind candidates will use Braille.

Clearly, the range of test accommodations that can be offered will vary across test providers, depending upon factors such as national legislation on disability discrimination, the nature of the tests involved, the level of demand for special arrangements, the availability of resources, expertise and specialist equipment, as well as what it is reasonable to expect in a given location or set of local circumstances. Nonetheless, by improving their awareness of what can be done to support test takers with special needs, language teachers should be better equipped to advise their students when taking a particular commercial test, to select an appropriate commercial test for their institution, or to make suitable accommodations to their own in-house tests.

CONCLUSION: FUTURE DIRECTIONS

Clearly the issue of accommodations raises important theoretical, practical, and ethical considerations for language testers, in particular:

- how to determine a disability that requires accommodation, especially in the case of specific learning difficulties which are often less evident, or less well diagnosed, than many physical disabilities;
- what type (or types) of accommodation to provide, and in what combination; and
- how to interpret test scores produced in circumstances where the test content or administration has been modified.

This last point relating to the interpretation of scores from accommodated tests is particularly important since adaptations to test content, format, and delivery risk changing the ability construct, and thus the meaning of the test scores. It is important that sufficient and relevant information about test score meaning is properly communicated to test users, such as university admissions officers or employers, who in turn will have to interpret and make decisions based on test outcomes. In some cases, for example, it may be appropriate to add an endorsement (sometimes referred to as a "flag") to a test taker's certificate which indicates that some objectives of the test could not be assessed due to the candidate's disability in some respect. However, this approach needs to be carefully handled to ensure that it does not unduly or unfairly label test takers as having taken a modified test and thus lead to them suffering subsequent discrimination. (See the AERA/APA/NCME 1999 *Standards*, for a helpful discussion on this point.)

The area of accommodations is complex and sensitive precisely because it requires a careful balancing act. On the one hand, test modifications and special arrangements should enable test takers with disabilities to be placed on an equal footing with all other test takers, giving them a level playing field; on the other hand, such adaptations should not advantage them to the extent that the assessment objectives of the test and the meaning of scores are compromised. The challenges involved in maintaining this equilibrium are likely to grow in the future as awareness of equity and fairness issues expands in society, and as demands for access to social and educational opportunities increase.

Technological advances over the coming years will no doubt resolve some of the issues but will also raise fresh challenges for language testers. Computer-based tests, for example, can offer a wider range of options for candidates with disabilities, opening up opportunities for them to take part in assessment programs. Increasing numbers of language learners with disabilities are using *access technology* (i.e., technological aids and specialist equipment) to assist and support their learning activities, and this has implications for approaches to assessing them as well as on their teaching / learning environment. The expansion of access technology will also raise some interesting policy and practice issues for language testers relating to technological support and test security, as well as equity. This highlights the urgent need for more empirical research and investigative case studies on the nature and impact of accommodations in language testing and assessment. Findings from future studies should help test providers design and construct modified tests that are better suited to the needs of test takers requiring accommodations, and which will enable them to participate ever more fully in mainstream academic, professional, and public life.

Suggested resources

Abedi, J. (2008). Utilizing accommodations in assessment. In E. Shohamy and N. Hornberger (Eds.), *Encyclopedia of language and education* (2nd ed.). *Language testing and assessment*, Vol. 7 (pp. 331–347). New York: Springer Science + Business Media LLC.
This chapter reviews the extensive research that has been conducted into accommodation in the past decade, examining effective accommodations for language learners, mostly in the context of English language learners (ELLs) in the United States. The author discusses both the accommodations needed by ELLs in relation to tests of content knowledge and those required by students with disabilities (SDs) where the L2 is the focus of assessment, as well as the relationship between the two.

AREA/APA/NCME. (1999). *Standards for educational and psychological testing*. Washington, DC: Author.
The AERA/APA/NCME *Standards* contain a complete section dedicated to the testing in general (not specifically language testing) of individuals with disabilities. It considers the issues involved and discusses strategies for test modification, use of modifications in different testing contexts, and score reporting on modified tests. It also lists 12 professional standards and helpfully comments on the complexities and challenges associated with each of these.

Kunnan, A. J. (2008). Towards a model of test evaluation: Using the Test Fairness and Test Context Frameworks. In L. Taylor & C. J. Weir (Eds.), *Multilingualism and assessment: Achieving transparency, assuring quality sustaining diversity*. Proceedings of the ALTE Berlin Conference May 2005 (pp. 229–251). Cambridge: UCLES / Cambridge University Press.
This paper presents and discusses two conceptual frameworks that offer an accessible and useful means of analyzing key features of language tests. The Test Fairness Framework considers microfeatures such as validity, absence of bias, access, administration, and social consequences. The complementary Test Context Framework enables analysis of the

wider macrocontext in which a test functions. Both have direct relevance to the issue of accommodations in language testing.

Thurlow, M. L., Thompson, S. J., & Lazarus, S. (2006). Considerations for the adminis-
tration of tests to special needs students: Accommodations, modifications, and more.
In S. Downing and T. Haladyna (Eds.), *Handbook of test development* (pp. 653–673).
Mahwah, NJ: Lawrence Erlbaum Associates.

This chapter provides a useful and up-to-date summary, together with specific examples, of test accommodation policies in the United States according to the five main categories of presentation, response, timing and scheduling, setting, and linguistic.

Discussion questions

1. What legislation exists in your country or state in relation to extending access to educa-
tional opportunities, including test taking, for people with various kinds of disability? How does this affect language testing and assessment?

2. Share any past experience you (or your friends / colleagues) have had of accommodations in language tests. Does your current institution provide tests with accommodations? What did / do you think of the accommodations? What did / do they achieve? Were / are they fair?

3. Think of some examples of test accommodations that risk distorting the ability construct a test is designed to measure. In what way do they do this? How big a problem is it? What could be done to minimize the risk?

4. Can you think of any ways you could contribute to the research agenda in this area that might broaden our knowledge and understanding of the benefits and risks associated with test accommodations?

References

Abedi, J. (2008). Utilizing accommodations in assessment. In E. Shohamy & N. Hornberger
(Eds.), *Encyclopedia of language and education* (2nd ed.). *Language testing and
assessment*, Vol. 7 (pp. 331–347). New York: Springer Science + Business Media
LLC.

AREA/APA/NCME. (1999). *Standards for educational and psychological testing*. Washington, DC: Author.

Alderson, J. C., & Wall, D. (Eds.). (1996). Special issue on washback. *Language Testing*,
13(3).

Association of Language Testers in Europe (ALTE). (1994). *Code of practice*. Retrieved
August 20, 2009, from www.alte.org/cop/index.php.

Cheng, L. (2008). Washback, impact and consequences. In E. Shohamy & N. Hornberger
(Eds.), *Encyclopedia of language and education* (2nd ed.). *Language testing
and assessment*, Vol. 7 (pp. 349–364). New York: Springer Science + Business
Media LLC.

Cheng, L., Watanabe, Y., & Curtis, A. (Eds.). (2004). *Washback in language testing:
Research contexts and methods*. London: Lawrence Erlbaum.

Davies, A. (2008). Ethics, professionalism, rights and codes. In E. Shohamy & N.
Hornberger (Eds.), *Encyclopedia of language and education* (2nd ed.). *Language
testing and assessment*, Vol. 7 (pp. 429–443). New York: Springer Science + Business
Media LLC.

European Association for Language Testing and Assessment (EALTA). (2006). *Guidelines
for good practice in language testing and assessment*. Retrieved August 20, 2009, from
www.ealta.eu.org/guidelines.htm.

Fulcher, G., & Davidson, F. (2007). *Language testing and assessment: An advanced resource book*. London: Routledge.

Green, A. (2007). *IELTS washback in context: Preparation for academic writing in higher education*. Cambridge: UCLES / Cambridge University Press.

Gutteridge, M. (2008). *ESOL Special Circumstances in 2007: A review*. Retrieved August 21, 2009, from: www.cambridgeesol.org/assets/pdf/speccirc_report_2007.pdf.

Hawkey, R. (2006). *Impact theory and practice: Studies of the IELTS test and Progetto Lingue 2000*. Cambridge: UCLES / Cambridge University Press.

International Language Testing Association (ILTA). (2001). *Code of ethics*. Retrieved August 20, 2009, from http://iltaonline.com/index.php?option=com_content&task=view&id=57&Itemid=47.

International Language Testing Association (ILTA). (2007). *Guidelines for Practice*. Retrieved August 20, 2009, from http://iltaonline.com/index.php?option=com_content&task=view&id=122&Itemid=133.

Khalifa, H., & Weir, C. J. (2009). *Examining reading: Research and practice in assessing second language reading*. Cambridge: UCLES / Cambridge University Press.

Kunnan, A. J. (2000). Fairness and justice for all. In A. J. Kunnan (Ed.), *Fairness and validation in language assessment*. Selected papers from the 19th LTRC, Orlando, Florida (pp. 1–14). Cambridge: UCLES / Cambridge University Press.

Kunnan, A. J. (2004). Test fairness. In M. Milanovic & C. J. Weir (Eds.), *European language testing in a global context* (pp. 27–48). Cambridge: UCLES / Cambridge University Press.

Kunnan, A. J. (2008). Towards a model of test evaluation: Using the Test Fairness and Test Context Frameworks. In L. Taylor & C. J. Weir (Eds.), *Multilingualism and assessment: Achieving transparency, assuring quality, sustaining diversity*. Proceedings of the ALTE Berlin Conference May 2005 (pp. 229–251). Cambridge: UCLES / Cambridge University Press.

McNamara, T. F. (2000). *Language testing*. Oxford: Oxford University Press.

McNamara, T. F. and Roever, C. (2006). *Language testing: The social dimension*. Malden, MA, and Oxford: Blackwell.

O'Sullivan, B., & Green, A. (2011). Test taker characteristics. In L. Taylor (Ed.), *Examining speaking: Research and practice in assessing second language speaking* (pp. 36–64). Cambridge: UCLES / Cambridge University Press.

Rea-Dickins, P., Yu, G., & Afitska, O. (2009). The consequences of examining through an unfamiliar language of instruction and its impact for school-age learners in Sub-Saharan African school systems. In L. Taylor & C. J. Weir (Eds.), *Language testing matters: Investigating the wider social and educational impact of language assessment* (pp. 190–213). Proceedings of the ALTE Cambridge Conference, April 2008. Cambridge: UCLES / Cambridge University Press.

Shaw, S. D., & Weir, C. J. (2007). *Examining writing: Research and practice in assessing second language writing*. Cambridge: UCLES / Cambridge University Press.

Shohamy, E. (2008). Introduction to Vol. 7: *Language Testing and Assessment*. In E. Shohamy & N. Hornberger (Eds.), *Encyclopedia of language and education* (2nd ed.). *Language testing and assessment*, Vol. 7 (pp. xiii–xxii). New York: Springer Science + Business Media LLC.

Shuter, R. (2003). Producing modified versions of Cambridge ESOL examinations. *Research Notes 11*, pp. 5–6. Retrieved August 21, 2009, from www.cambridgeesol.org/rs_notes/rs_nts11.pdf.

Sireci, S. G., Li, S., & Scarpati, S. (2003). *The effects of test accommodations on test performance: A review of the literature. Center for Educational Assessment Research Report, No 485.* Amherst, MA: School of Education, University of Massachussetts.

Sireci, S., Scarpati, S., & Li, S. (2005). Test accommodations for students with disabilities: An analysis of the interaction hypothesis. *Review of Educational Research* 75, (4), 457–490.

Taylor, L., & Gutteridge, M. (2003). Responding to diversity: Providing tests for language learners with disabilities. *Research Notes 11*, pp. 2–4. Retrieved August 21, 2009, from www.cambridgesol.org/rs_notes/rs_nts11.pdf.

Thompson, S. J., Blount, A., & Thurlow, M. L (2002). *A summary of the research on the effects of test accommodations: 1999 through 2001* (Technical Report 34). Minneapolis, MN: University of Minnesota, National Center on Educational Outcomes. Retrieved August 21, 2009, from http://education.umn.edu/NCEO/OnlinePubs/Technical34.htm.

Thurlow, M. L., Thompson, S. J., & Lazarus, S. (2006). Considerations for the administration of tests to special needs students: Accommodations, modifications, and more. In S. Downing and T. Haladyna (Eds.), *Handbook of test development* (pp. 653–673). Mahwah, NJ: Lawrence Erlbaum Associates.

Wall, D. (2005). *The impact of high-stakes examinations on classroom teaching: A case study using insights from testing and innovation theory.* Cambridge: UCLES / Cambridge University Press.

Note

[1] Grade 1 – or uncontracted Braille – consists of 63 symbols made up of all the possible variations of a series of six dots. Twenty-six of these represent the letters of the English alphabet and others represent punctuation marks. These symbols can be used to reproduce a letter-by-letter copy of print. Grade 2 – or contracted Braille – was developed to reduce the size of books and to make reading quicker. It uses combinations of symbols to represent common letter combinations or words. Some characters may change their meaning depending on how they are used.

Index

NOTES

NOTES

NOTES

NOTES